RÉPUBLIQUE FRANÇAISE

UNE INDIVISIBLE

VAINCRE OÙ MOURIR

FRENCH
REVOLUTION

FRENCH REVOLUTION

FRANÇOIS FURET AND DENIS RICHET

TRANSLATED BY STEPHEN HARDMAN

THE MACMILLAN COMPANY

PHOTOGRAPHIC ACKNOWLEDGEMENTS

Archives photographiques des monuments historiques de Paris; 145: Bibliothèque Nationale, collection Destailleurs; 394: Bibliothèque Nationale,
collection Hennin; 256, 283, 331, 380–1: Bibliothèque Nationale Estampes;
17, 20, 21, 27, 33/2, 34, 36, 62, 68, 101, 106, 111, 114, 117, 131, 136/2, 137/1,
139/1, 139/2, 142, 151/2, 152/2, 153/1, 182, 189, 201/1, 201/2, 204–5, 213, 237,
245, 257, 261, 263, 272/1, 272/2, 273/1, 273/2, 273/3, 277/1, 308, 317, 320–1,
329, 345, 346, 347, 349, 351, 357, 376, 379, 387/1, 397: Bibliothèque Nationale
Imprimés; 33/1, 375: Bulloz; 25/1, 57, 73, 79, 134–5/1, 136/1, 157, 158–9,
167/1, 179/2, 191, 197, 202, 203/1, 208, 212, 214, 229, 232, 233, 287, 301, 305,
354, 385, 387/2, 390: Collection of Prince Ludwig of Hesse; 39: Collection
of Prince Roland Bonaparte; 395: Flammarion; 239: Giraudon; 6, 25/2, 61,
106, 136/3, 193, 211, 349, 355: Hachette; 30, 297, 328, 392: Peter Heilman; 39:
Musée Carnavalet; 79, 86–7, 90, 95, 133, 135/2, 137/2, 144, 153/2, 157, 169,
179/1, 191, 197, 203/1, 203/2, 225, 234 (collection Liesville), 242, 253,
(collection Lesueur), 276, 277/2, 279/2, 332, 338, 339/1, 339/2, 339/3, 339/4,
343, 361: Musée Condé, Chantilly; 25/2, 61: Musée d'Aix en Provence; 73:
Musée d'Amiens; 74: Musée Dauphinois, Grenoble; 53: Musée de Bruxelles;
385: Musée de Cholet (B.R.A.C. Cholet); 173: Musée de Dijon; 354, 355:
Musée de la Malmaison; 303: Musée de Lille; 179/2: Musée du Louvre;
136/3, 145, 353: Musée de Quimper; 155: Musée de Versailles; 43, 152/2,
211, 251, 310–1: Musée Lambinet, Versailles; 93, 151/1, 195.

ⓒ Librairie Hachette et Société d'Études
et de Publications Économiques 1965
Copyright ⓒ by Weidenfeld and Nicolson 1970

Library of Congress Catalog Card Number: 70-81243

First American Edition 1970
Published in Great Britain in 1970 by Weidenfeld and Nicolson, London
First published in France in 1965 by Librairie Hachette under the title
La Révolution

The Macmillan Company
866 Third Avenue, New York, N.Y. 10022

Printed in Great Britain

CONTENTS

1

THE FRANCE OF
LOUIS XVI

The Bastille is still regarded as the symbol of France under the Old Regime, but the historian must concern himself first of all with the everyday economic realities of the period. In France at this time, man's struggle to obtain a livelihood, primarily his daily bread, presented all the familiar features: the overwhelming predominance of agriculture in the nation's economic wealth, the low productivity of labour and the precarious balance that existed between the size of the population and the quantity of food available. The economy was based on the principle of survival: the combined effects of backward technology, natural population-growth and the uncertainties of the harvests meant that, in the short term, men had to hope for the best and fear the worst. The convulsions of the short term were aggravated by the stagnation into which the country's economy had been allowed to sink over a long period – economic growth and material happiness were to be revolutionary aspirations.

In cultivating the land the peasants were hampered by having to depend on outdated techniques; moreover, crop-rotation was much more complex than the traditional distinction between three-course and two-course systems suggests, and consequently a large area of land was left uncultivated, which the peasants used as pasturage for their underfed herds. Harvesting was done with scythes, and corn was threshed with flails or under the hoofs of farm animals. The most common type of plough was the old wooden swing-plough, drawn by an ox, which scratched away at soil that produced a meagre crop (the average corn harvest in relation to seed sown was roughly in a ratio of five or six to one).

In an average year the grain harvest was on the whole sufficient for most of the population's needs; but in a particularly bad year of frost, hail or drought, or whenever war came bringing devastation to the fields, then the scarcity of cereals dominated the economic and social scene. At times like these, food was stocked up feverishly and prices soared (especially the price of bread). A crisis of this sort inevitably affected the poorer sections of society more than the rest:

7

in both town and country deaths from famine reduced the population to a level compatible with the nation's total food resources. This was what happened in 1709 – the gravest crisis of all – and again in 1741. Once a crisis was over and the necessary 'purge' had been effected society would begin to reorganise itself, returning to its normal precarious state.

However, in the France of the Old Regime agriculture not only lay at the mercy of archaic techniques and the uncertainties of the weather. It was also dominated almost entirely by the seigneurie. There was hardly any land in France that was not subject to the old seigneurial rights: nearly all proprietors and tenants were obliged to pay some kind of 'feudal' dues, which were scrupulously recorded in the manorial rolls, and every effort was made to see that the dues did not lapse as the result of prescriptive claims. This state of affairs represented a survival from the old days when the seigneur, in exchange for agricultural labour and the payment of dues, gave protection to those under him, lowering his drawbridge to give them asylum in the event of danger. Admittedly, since the economic boom of the sixteenth century some of the bourgeois of the towns – commoners who had made their fortunes in commerce or by usury – had succeeded in infiltrating into the ranks of the lords and had acquired seigneuries. In the course of the eighteenth century, however, the nobility absorbed these newcomers more and more slowly; and in any case, the bourgeois attained the rank of seigneur usually as the result of royal ennoblement or service in the upper reaches of the bureaucracy. Consequently, the nobles were able to remain the masters of their vast age-old domains, which comprised both those lands which they occupied themselves and those over which they exercised their old feudal rights. The ecclesiastical nobility had yet another source of revenue, the tithe, a tax equivalent to roughly one-twentieth of the harvests of the whole country. Finally, the financial position of the nobility, based as it was on the ownership of land, was secured even more firmly by a fiscal privilege: exemption from payment of the taille, *the nation's basic direct tax.*

These were the foundations which supported the two dominant social orders of the kingdom of France, the nobility and the clergy, who lived by cultivating their own estates and by exacting the old annual taxes over the whole sphere of rural activity. Small land-owning peasants were so common in France at this period (their numbers ran into millions) that they owned nearly half of the kingdom's cultivable land, and they had to pay their lords a multitude of dues, both in kind and in money. There were few acts of rural life that did not involve the payment of dues: the annual crop- and wine-harvests, the sale of properties, etc., were all subject to some such payment. And the seigneur enjoyed the right to hunt at will over any part of the land which was held from him in fief, even though this meant trampling over precious pastureland or across fields of ripe corn. He was only the master of his estate, and not particularly interested in making a profit: that was something for the bourgeoisie to worry about.

Although the supremacy of the clergy and nobility was founded in the first place on the possession of land, it was also something deeply embedded in the

8

minds of the people. To them, the social order was not just an historical fact —
it existed by divine right. In other words, it derived not from the concerted
efforts of men, but from a unanimous recognition of a hierarchy willed by God.
Thus impiety could be regarded as synonymous with anarchy; but impiety was
still rare and, because unvoiced and restricted to certain spheres of cultivated
society, not as yet very dangerous. The mass of the people, illiterate and im-
prisoned within the very narrowest kind of local life, had no opportunity to
question the old beliefs which bound the social pyramid so firmly.

Even if the common people had been given the opportunity to protest, the idea
would never have occurred to them, for religion was the very foundation of their
daily existence and mental habits. It gave a rhythm to the lives of individuals
and to the community as a whole, so that the clock on the tower of the village
church was for one and all the symbol of the transience of human life. From
birth until death, through times of rejoicing and times of misery, the Church
and the priest were the arbiters of the way of life of the common man.

In the temporal domain, above the power of the lords and the hierarchy of
rights and privileges, which conditioned the whole of society from God to the
kingdom's humblest subject, the crowning authority was the king of France, the
hereditary incarnation of the old monarchic principle. He was an absolute
monarch who was considered to hold his rights directly from God; 'father' of
all his subjects, supreme overlord of all the lands in the kingdom and himself
the proprietor of a vast area of France, the king wielded all the powers which
have since come to be distinguished as the executive, the legislature and the
judiciary. He had become the head of a centralised bureaucracy based at
Versailles, of which the immense and complex fiscal machinery undoubtedly
constituted the most important element.

The monarchy was, indeed, absolute since it derived its authority from God,
but it was also to some extent the product of time. From the time of Henry IV,
(1589–1610) the French kings had built their supreme authority on the ruins
of the old territorial power of the lords and had tamed the political activity of the
lords by reducing them to the service of the monarch and the frivolous existence
of the court. As this absolute authority was gradually built up, the king of
France acquired a kind of double nature: he remained true to his origins, the
supreme overlord, the most powerful feudal landowner in the kingdom; but, at
the same time, as absolute monarch he possessed an authority that extended far
beyond his feudal rights, making him a national symbol, the head of government
and ultimate director of economic policy, the arbiter of conflicting social interests.
The creation of absolute power had not involved the abolition of all the local
privileges of the past, but it did give the economically unstable society of old
France the rock-like authority of a state.

This, broadly, was the structure of the France of the Old Regime. Despite
the hazards of the harvest and the pressure of circumstance, the old system
did create the conditions in which wealth could be produced and in which human
life could continue. Although it was based on a social inequality that was not

simply the result of bad harvests, but something prescribed by law and tradition, it did give the kingdom a certain cohesion. Royal absolutism, founded as it was on the preservation of seigneurial privilege and strengthened both by the diminution of the political power of the nobility and by the religious convictions common to the majority of the population, provided society with a much-needed stability. This stability was not an unchanging, static thing; it was constantly being adjusted and reshaped by the bureaucracy, though the structure as a whole was never called in question.

Why, then, the events of 1789? When and where did cracks begin to appear in the apparently solid structure of old France?

Paradoxical though this may seem, the primary cause of disintegration lay in the very fact of the nation's prosperity, for prosperity was something quite new for France. The events of 1789 did not occur in the last stages of a century of poverty: on the contrary, they erupted in a country which had been steadily building up its wealth. True, this prosperity was relative, in that it depended on a comparison with France's own recent past and with the economic state of the majority of European countries in the eighteenth century; nevertheless, it was the product of an economic vitality that was one of the most important features of eighteenth-century French history.

Though the general features of France's prosperity in the eighteenth century are clear enough, it is not possible for the historian to measure them in full detail. The eighteenth century was slow to discover the value of statistics, and as a result there exists only a very small body of documentary evidence from which to draw sound conclusions. It simply is not possible to give reliable figures either for any increase in the total volume of production or for an increase in agricultural productivity. One can, however, draw the general conclusion that the nation's total wealth did grow during the century. A study of population-growth figures for the period between the calculations of Vauban and Lavoisier (i.e. the greater part of the century) shows that the population of France rose from twenty to twenty-six millions. The rise in population was due to a major change in mortality rates: the hitherto common cycles of mortality, which had been governed largely by famine, were gradually being modified, even though famine had not yet vanished altogether; there was another important factor influencing population growth – war had at last ceased to wreak its havoc on the territory of France.

It was not only the total volume of production that grew during the eighteenth century: the total value of production rose simultaneously, bringing in its wake increased prices. The rise in prices, following a long period of depression that extended over the entire reign of Louis XIV (1643–1715), began in the '30s and by the eve of the Revolution had reached fifty to sixty per cent. In the course of this long and gradual process the normal ten-year cycles did not cease to operate, nor did sudden seasonal price-rises, but both were absorbed in a flux of economic expansion which lessened their effect on the population. It was this general movement of economic expansion that made population growth possible.

It would obviously be wrong to conclude that all Frenchmen benefited equally from the economic trends of the eighteenth century. The rise in agricultural prices and the even greater rise in farm rents was chiefly of advantage to the landowners with seigneurial incomes. They were of little benefit to the mass of peasants who tried to make a living from their little plots of land and never had any surplus to take to market or to hoard for the following year. The only cultivators who did benefit were the proprietors of large farms in the few areas of France where a capitalist agrarian system was slowly evolving.

The great landowners, the lords both spiritual and temporal, who already enjoyed considerable fiscal and juridical privileges, were thus the only persons to derive any increase of wealth from economic expansion. During the eighteenth century land revenues doubled. The rise in land revenues was accentuated by the fact that, as the population increased and manpower with it, the real value of wages diminished (wage increases had lagged behind price rises), and so production costs were reduced and the real value of land rents further increased. The redistribution of land revenues operated very unequally, to the detriment of both the peasant-farmer, whether landowner or tenant-farmer, and the wage-earning class as a whole. It is not difficult to imagine how greatly such a trend must have intensified the hatred the country people felt for their privileged masters. In the event of a depression, or some other form of economic crisis, the peasants could point to the source of their misfortunes: privilege, and the seigneurial regime.

But the peasants were not alone: they were beginning to discover an unexpected and invaluable ally in the bourgeoisie, which was helping to create new wealth in the towns. The towns of France grew as the nobles invested their land revenues in building private houses and, at the same time, those peasants who could not find work in the country came into the towns to look for work and homes. The new prosperity which the towns were enjoying encouraged the growth of private enterprise in many different forms. This development of commercial activity was of greatest significance at the lower levels of society: vast numbers of small shopkeepers, tradesmen and artisans were beginning to devote themselves wholeheartedly to the principles of hard work and profit-making. Most of these men were employers controlling an urban population, many of whom belonged to one of the corporations or guilds. As commercial outlets multiplied, manpower increased and annual profits soared, the general trend of prosperity acted as a stimulus to individual success. Vast numbers of private contractors began to establish themselves in France's two leading industries of the period, building and textiles. Commerce also grew, despite the tariffs which divided the home market. Maritime trade flourished during the latter part of the century and gave merchants and trading companies extraordinary high profits: the handsome buildings of Nantes and Bordeaux were financed with money earned from the slave trade in the West Indies. All this new urban wealth represented a direct threat to the old financial privileges of the landowners.

And yet the towns of eighteenth-century France were not chiefly dominated by the new capitalists. In addition to the luxury-loving nobility who had their fine houses there, the towns were also the centres of more traditional and cautious financial activity: they swarmed with rentiers *and state officials who were investing the money they had acquired in the performance of their public duties — in fact, this great body of public investors was very closely bound up with the social structure of the Old Regime. It is true that, on the whole, the bourgeoisie of eighteenth-century France was a pre-capitalist bourgeoisie; but the way it acted suggests that it already felt to be in control of the economy and regarded such control as a means to a more important political end. Indeed, the bourgeoisie was much more mature in its political and social attitudes than in its economic views.*

The eighteenth century was discovering the force of public opinion. The towns were fast becoming breeding grounds for ideas, where public sentiments and even some kind of political conscience were being formed. This intellectual ferment was concentrated, naturally enough, among the educated élite *of the towns, particularly of Paris, who gathered round the publicists proclaiming their programmes of reform. The lawyers, government officials and other professional classes of the towns together formed a distinct social group in themselves, and were the forerunners of those men, who, in the nineteenth century, came to be known as the* capacités *('men of ability'); this body of professional men provided writers with a new reading public, and so freed them from dependence on the old system of royal patronage. Books about history, economics and travel now became marketable articles which could bring their authors great wealth. Even if some authors continued to benefit on occasion from the patronage of the king and aristocracy, this in no way interfered with their intellectual independence.*

One dominant theme ran through the whole of eighteenth-century thought — the spirit of reform. This ideal existed in a variety of different and often contradictory guises, and was the subject of much controversy: the enlightened despotism of the state expounded by the Physiocratic school was not the enlightened liberalism of Montesquieu, even less the egalitarian democracy of Rousseau. But the very diversity of conflicting opinions served to nourish the reforming zeal of the age and enabled the new priorities of reason, happiness and tolerance to find their expression. By 1750 the battle was largely won.

The accusations constantly hurled by the cultured bourgeoisie in an attempt to remove the sacred aura surrounding the Old Regime — accusations against the absurdity of the old social system, the irrationality of revealed religion and the parasitic existence of the seigneurs — were all the more formidable for not being based solely on arguments about what was reasonable or socially desirable. The arguments used by the accusers derived part of their strength from the more obscure forces of social repression and humiliation: it was aristocratic privilege which, fortified in all its aspects by the trends of the century, really roused the anger of the bourgeoisie.

Thus the stability of an entire social system began to weaken under the pressure of demographic, economic and intellectual change. The misery of the peasant and the wage-earner, and the frustrated strength of the bourgeoisie, caused these sections of society to join together in a common indictment of tradition. However, though the larger part of the population was at one in attacking the old system, its demands were not usually of a radical nature. The accusers were quite prepared to grant the aristocracy a reprieve – they were asking for reform, not revolution.

During the eighteenth century the traditional reforming activity of the monarchy had slowly declined. Not that there was any lack of bold planning or men of ability; and on occasion the king would decide to exercise his supreme beneficence in some way or other. But the forces of resistance had become more powerful than the monarchy's sporadic zeal for reform. The nobles were at last beginning to take their revenge for their political exile under Louis XIV. They began to gain control of the state administration by securing positions of high office, both lay and ecclesiastical; their wealth, political conservatism and sheer strength of numbers enabled them to stifle the king's occasional beneficent impulses and to suppress the plans for reform put forward by an often very capable administration. The nobles were attacking absolutism in the name of tradition and the past, while the enlightened opinion of the Third Estate was directed against the same target, but in the name of reform: these two converging forces weakened the royal power, reducing it to the state of inertia which was the nobility's primary object. The time was approaching when the personal intervention of the French monarch would no longer be effective, as Turgot was to learn to his disadvantage in 1776.

With the royal power now ineffectual, the most serious problem of internal politics facing France, her financial and economic condition, was to remain unsolved. The old tax structure, by which the nobility were exempted from the taille *and the Church was allowed to escape lightly by making an occasional 'free gift', was more than unjust. At a time when land-rents were soaring, these tax-exemptions meant that by far the greater part of the nation's wealth was being hoarded by the privileged classes, and an even heavier burden was being imposed on the already limited earning capacity of the common people. The eighteenth-century French reformers urged the introduction of a single land tax graded according to income. But the king refused to sacrifice 'his' nobles, and so the financial crisis was allowed to assume ever greater dimensions: the survival of an entire society was at stake.*

Because the crisis threatened the whole of society, it soon began to have international repercussions, as the disruptive trends of eighteenth-century France made themselves felt beyond her own frontiers. In the economic field, the rise in prices and the increase of total national wealth in France affected Catalonia, North Italy and the Rhineland. At the same time Great Britain discovered in industrial capitalism a revolutionary method of stimulating her own newly-found prosperity. In the intellectual field, the only monopoly France enjoyed was that of language: during the century the exchange of ideas enjoyed uninterrupted growth, and little by little the bonds of international enlightenment were forged.

13

In this movement of ideas Great Britain and France certainly played the major roles, but the whole of Europe – even as far afield as St Petersburg – and the colonies of North America also became involved. Never was a culture more spontaneously cosmopolitan than the culture of the intellectual élite of the eighteenth century.

Chronologically, France was by no means the leader of the ferment of ideas. In 1776 the British colonies of North America laid down the principles of independence in a great liberal and egalitarian document that was to inspire the whole of enlightened Europe. Furthermore, in the later years of the eighteenth century the new ideas were already undermining the authority of long-established ruling power in the old aristocratic societies of the West: in Geneva there occurred the clash between democracy and oligarchy, in Ireland the patriots were rebelling against British oppression, in the Netherlands a liberal coalition opposed the dictatorship of the House of Orange and in Belgium there was a revolt against Austria. However, buttressed by the principle of monarchy, the old European order had as yet begun to feel only the first warning tremors of catastrophe – the real convulsions were still to come.

The crisis threatening the leading kingdom of Europe also heralded dangers of a quite different order. Within the monarchic and aristocratic structure of Europe, where positions of power were occupied by persons related to one another by ties of consanguinity and affinity, France was soon to become the focal point of general alarm and unrest, just as it was also to become the source of hope. It remains now to observe how all these ingredients of revolution combined to bring the final cataclysm.

During the ten years preceding the Revolution tensions were steadily building up. The reign of Louis XVI had been marked by a long depression of corn prices. The depression was relative, no doubt, since prices were still high by comparison with the early years of the century, but contemporary commentators were comparing them with the heyday of the '60s. Even so, corn was less affected by the depression than wine, the second basic element in France's traditional agricultural activity; the wine industry had been boosted by the increase in urban demand, but now, after a period of high prices extending from 1766 to 1778, wine prices suddenly crashed both relatively and absolutely. The cause of the crisis was over-production, and its very sudden effects only aggravated the difficulties caused by the long depression of cereal prices.

It might be thought that France was suffering from general economic stagnation at this time, but this was not the case. Vine-growing has always been subject to wide annual variations in market conditions. During the very years when the French wine industry saw its urban market collapse, its external trade enjoyed a spectacular increase. In heavy industry, moreover, all the signs point to a sharp boost in urban construction during the eighteenth century. Even agricultural prices (livestock, produce and timber) rose in conformity with general trends. It therefore seems likely that, during the '80s, the depression of cereal and wine prices, which was in any case by no means uniform, mainly affected the peasantry and did not cause any real damage to the economy as a whole.

Nevertheless, land revenue of every kind also suffered the effects of the depression: the cultivator who sold his produce, the large-scale farmer of Picardy or the Cambresis region and, in particular, the great landowners were all affected. Although they were caught up in the general trend of rising prices, the nobles were able to some extent to make good their losses by selling timber from their forests; determined to preserve their extravagant way of life at all costs, they also tried to pass the burden of economic depression onto the peasants by increasing feudal dues and by claiming various seigneurial rights which had long been buried and forgotten. This was the economic aspect of the aristocratic reaction.

At the same time, for the same motive of self-preservation, the nobles were more anxious than ever before to monopolise all high positions for their posterity, and in particular the high offices of state. In 1781 the 'four quarterings' edict was promulgated: this edict made all direct commissions into the king's army (i.e. all commissions except those gained by rising from the ranks) subject to proof of pure noble blood – the 'four quarterings' in question were the heraldic emblems of a noble descended from four noble grandparents.

The doors were thus being closed more and more firmly against a bourgeoisie which had multiplied, enriched and educated itself in the course of the century. The 'aristocratic reaction' and bourgeois ambition were the conflicting forces which provided the dynamite for the explosion that was imminent. Aware of the dangers threatening it, the old society, with its clearly distinguished orders, insisted on reaffirming its right to exist for ever, and tried to strengthen its position as best it could. At the court the nobles kept an ever more watchful and jealous eye on the power they wielded; but, by launching their counter-offensive, they were to sting both town and country into revolt.

Was the Revolution inevitable? In theory, the king still retained his power of arbitration and his right to introduce reforms. But Louis XVI was losing control of his kingdom. Over the past one hundred and fifty years many opinions have been expressed concerning the king's notorious 'weakness' and his psychological characteristics; but it has not been sufficiently emphasised that the king's weakness was, above all, a reflection of the state's weakness. As the year 1789 drew near, royal absolutism was becoming no more than an idea. Repudiated by the whole of public opinion, it no longer possessed the authority necessary to solve effectively a problem that daily became more complex. The edifice of royal power was tottering: as in previous centuries, it had become the victim of aristocratic intrigues. However, though the members of the court were divided by personal rivalries, they were united in their essential purpose – the preservation of the old tax system and social privilege. Since the American War the treasury deficit had assumed such vast proportions that loans and other such expedients were quite useless. As the king could not get money from those who had it (i.e. by taxing the nobles), he resorted to a desperate remedy – the convening of the Estates-General. In doing this, he was yielding once more to the privileged classes, who expected to dominate the assembly as they had done in the past.

The summoning of the Estates-General marked the beginning of the great political upheaval of 1788–9. It so happened that this political crisis coincided with a grave economic crisis which was undermining the profits of the small peasant landowners, and had begun with the bad harvest in the second half of 1788: the rains and floods of '87, then drought and the hail-storms of 13 July '88 which ravaged the whole of western France, wrought havoc with the summer harvest of '88. The familiar pattern of short-term economic chaos was now established. After the decline that had set in at the end of the '70s, the prices of cereals soared, and by the end of June '89 had reached their highest level of the century. Once again bread was scarce and therefore expensive. The fact that the amount by which prices rose in the years '86–9 was less than the rise of '63–70 was of little significance: this time the increase hit peasants whose resources had been drained away by ten years of bad harvests, and who consequently had no more stocks to fall back on and no surpluses to sell. In the towns the rise in prices drastically reduced the food consumption of the common people and cut off industrial outlets. Trade was all the more vulnerable because the Franco-British trade agreement of 1786 had lowered import duties on British goods coming into France, which meant that the French now faced formidable competition. As textiles declined, jobs in that industry became fewer and prices went up.

The economic and revolutionary cycles of eighteenth-century France were bound up one with the other. Not that one can explain the Revolution simply in terms of economics. But the economic situation did act as a catalyst to explode the social and political tensions that had been building up throughout the century. Above all, it brought a new class, the common people, into the great debate that had been raging between the king, the privileged classes and the urban bourgeoisie. Both king and nobles were helpless against the great alliance of the Third Estate, which had come into being simply through the pressure of events, and was destined to sweep away the Old Regime.

THE PRIVILEGED ORDERS

Under the Old Regime the social order was not a political problem subject to the hazards of citizens' deliberations, but a product of the divine order of things. Instead of emerging from below, authority came from above, and its legitimacy was therefore intimately bound up with conformity to religious tradition: the king of France held his throne from God and bequeathed it to the eldest of his descendants.

But – and this is what distinguishes monarchy from despotism – the king's subjects did not form a single, uniformly unprivileged class: they did not share the kind of negative equality which despotic power imposes on a people. For the same divine necessity which endowed the monarchy with its authority, also bestowed a fixed, unchanging

The monarchy is a hierarchy: the king reigns supreme by divine right. The archbishop of Reims crowns Louis XVI.

form on French society, which comprised three 'orders', each with clearly defined prerogatives and duties.

Two of these three orders were privileged: the clergy and the nobility. The clergy consisted of all the servants of the Catholic Church, both secular and regular (around 150,000 persons), and enjoyed all the privileges of membership of the state religion – honours, wealth and independence. For instance, they were exempt from compulsory fiscal contributions: they merely made the king a 'free gift', deciding from time to time on the amount to be given and levying it themselves. However, the clergy contained within its ranks both commoners and nobles, and a cleric's position in the hierarchy of responsibility and influence depended largely on his social rank;

consequently, the only true aristocracy was the nobility, in which all privilege was concentrated.

There was indeed a very real social inequality in France at this time. The nobility preserved its own customs, and in particular the law of primogeniture. Among the legacies of the old feudal system which had been bequeathed to the nobles were a share in the dispensing of justice and the civil administration of the villages, various honorary prerogatives such as the reservation of pews in church, monopolies in activities such as hunting, the right of raising taxes, and so on. Moreover, the nobles left the imprint of their mode of life on the whole of French society: *vivre noblement* was the social ideal of the Old Regime.

The barrier of birth still retained all its old importance and prestige, separating and distinguishing several hundred thousand persons from the rest of society. This heritage was more and more jealously guarded until, by the end of the century, in a kind of neurotic obsession with self-preservation, the French nobility had succumbed to a genealogical fever which a contemporary dubbed *titromanie*.

The world of the aristocracy held a strange fascination for the rest of French society – in other words, the vast majority of the population, who formed the third 'order', the Third Estate. By far the greater part of the Third Estate continued to accept the old traditions, retaining a spontaneous respect for 'rank'; a minority, who formed the upper stratum of the Third Estate, the bourgeoisie, began to feel humiliated by their lack of birth and by the injustice of a situation for which there appeared to be no remedy, and came to the conclusion that society was in need of reform. The key to an understanding of the psychological and political reactions of eighteenth-century France must therefore be sought in the position of supremacy which the aristocracy enjoyed under the Old Regime.

Of the two privileged orders the clergy enjoyed pre-eminence: they owed their special position both to the sacred character of their office and to the part they played in the administration of the state. The clergy endowed the social, political and intellectual structures with the holy aura of eternity. The Catholic religion was, in fact, the state religion, by virtue of a statue incorporated in the Concordat of 1516. In law, therefore, all subjects of the French king were Catholics. Admittedly, there were two religious minorities: the six hundred thousand Protestants who clung to their own traditions (particularly in southern France) and who eventually, in 1787, obtained *de facto* recognition, and the Jewish communities of Alsace and the south-west, who were regarded as foreigners. But the existence of these two minorities in no way affected the monopoly of Catholicism. Moreover, the clergy were in charge of several public services: charity (especially hospitals), education (six hundred schools taking seventy-five thousand pupils) and the registration of births, marriages and deaths. In fact, the clergy, with their essentially Gallican concern to be independent of both the king and Rome, were the only one of the three Estates to be organised as an 'order': they held their own assemblies, convened every five years to discuss financial matters and to defend the faith, and they also had their own special courts. Furthermore, their economic strength was very great, not only because they were exempt from taxes and were able to make their annual 'free gift' to the king as small as possible, but also because they were landowners with vast estates. It seems they owned as much as one-tenth of the land of France, chiefly in the north, and their annual revenue has been estimated at ninety to one hundred million *livres*; to this should be added the eighty million *livres* they received in tithes from the peasantry.

To appreciate the extent to which the Catholic faith dominated the land of France at this time, one must imagine what the contemporary foreign traveller saw as he made his way across the country. He must surely have been struck at once by the sheer multitude of religious buildings. One might almost say that space itself was Catholic: in Paris there were some fifty parishes for a population of six hundred thousand, and a quarter of the city's area was occupied by monasteries and convents. The foreign visitor would find, placed at the junctions of country roads and carved in the stone of houses, representations of the Stations of the Cross, crucifixes and statuettes which everywhere bore witness to the people's respect for God. The national calendar, the cycles of work and the innumerable feast-days that were celebrated show that not only space, but time also was Catholic. No human act of any importance could be performed without the divine blessing, and positively to ignore a command of the Church was unthinkable: no one, for example, was allowed to marry during Advent or Lent.

Did the ascendancy of religion in society extend also to the in-individual soul? The answer is yes, to a very great extent. There is plenty of evidence to indicate how assiduous the people were in attending Mass and taking part in processions; the religious life of the time was a matter of great intensity, and in the country villages was often bound up with old superstitions. As the Old Regime drew to a close, unbelief was a numerically and socially limited phenomenon in a country steeped in the Catholic faith.

Although the clergy were all members of the same 'order', they did not form a homogeneous social group. The division amongst them was caused not by the differences between the secular and the regular clergy, between the seventy thousand priests serving the nation's one hundred and thirty-five dioceses and the sixty thousand monks and nuns, but simply by the fact that the privileges attached to

A ceremony typical of the time: a thanksgiving procession of former Christian slaves freed by two religious orders specialising in work of this kind. The procession (from the abbey of Saint-Antoine to Notre-Dame) took place on 17 October 1785.

the order were enjoyed almost exclusively by the higher clergy, who were numerically small.

The higher clergy comprised prelates, the canons of the wealthier chapters, abbots and the superiors of the larger monasteries and convents: three thousand persons in all, most of them from the nobility, and more often than not from the higher nobility. It was common for the youngest sons of the great noble families to enter the high offices of the Church in order to make careers for themselves, and not out of any sense of vocation. They could then proceed to enjoy the Church's vast wealth, though in varying proportions: the bishop-prince of Strasbourg received four hundred thousand *livres* in revenue, while the bishop of Venice received only seven thousand. And yet, though their respective shares of wealth and influence varied, they were all closely associated with the social system by which their supremacy had been built up and preserved.

This is not to suggest that the higher clergy neglected their spiritual

Illuminations for Louis xv's visit to Strasbourg in 1744. The episcopal palace of the Rohans in Strasbourg was owned by the family until 1789.

duties altogether. True, the laziness and moral laxity of the regular clergy were constantly denounced by the *philosophes*. There were also scandals, such as the affair of the 'queen's necklace', in which Cardinal de Rohan was involved, but these were the exception rather than the rule. The most striking feature of the prelates of the last years of the Old Regime was that they included a great many excellent diocesan administrators and very few men endowed with truly spiritual vocations – in fact, most of them lived at the king's court. This was the price that had to be paid for confining recruitment to the narrow field of the upper nobility.

The middle clergy, drawn from the Third Estate, served the towns and cities and in many cases shared in the relative prosperity of urban society. The lower clergy of the villages and remote hamlets of France were in their origins very close to the peasants they served; they were able to make themselves the peasants' allies socially without losing the respect due to their office. The emolument of seven hundred *livres* per year which these country priests received from the Church's total tithe revenue in no way isolated them from their flocks, no more than the Mass Latin they had to learn. Some of them came under the influence of the new ideas of reform at the same time as their parishioners. When the moment finally arrived, these priests were to become the natural spokesmen of the aspirations of the people.

As the eighteenth century advanced, the predominance of the aristocracy in French society became ever greater, as the result of two converging trends. The first of these trends occurred on the political plane. With the death of Louis XIV the aristocracy's counter-offensive began: while the nobles were not able to destroy royal absolutism, they did succeed in gradually gaining a controlling influence over the king by securing an almost exclusive monopoly of high offices. This they did both directly, by obtaining appointments to the ministeries, councils and intendancies, or indirectly, through the Paris parlement, which had regained its old authority. But the nobility's seizure of power extended even further afield: by the end of the century there remained not a single bishop in France who was not of noble origin; the edict promulgated in 1781 made it necessary to have four noble grandparents in order to obtain a direct commission into the royal army; and, at the same time, the monarchy was losing much of its power of arbitration, its stabilising influence and its reforming zeal.

The second trend which served to strengthen aristocratic power took place in the economic sector, where the dominant role was played by agriculture. As the total value of agricultural production (cereals, wine, timber) increased, revenues from land soared even more rapidly, doubling between the '30s and the '80s. This was naturally something of a windfall for the privileged orders of clergy and nobility, who were not only the owners of a large area of the French kingdom (the nobles alone owned a quarter of the land), but also exacted dues from the multitude of peasant landowners. The clergy's chief source of wealth, apart from their own properties, was the tithe: in theory the tithe was a tax in kind of one-tenth of a farmer's produce, though in practice it amounted to one-twentieth; this tax gave the clergy as much as the revenue from their own properties. The nobles, for their part, laid claim to the old seigneurial rights which their ancestors had exercised as feudal lords providing protection for the local peasants; by claiming these rights they were able to compel their own peasants to pay large taxes both in money and in kind: the *cens* (quit-rent), the *champart* (in many ways similar to the tithe), the *lods* and *ventes* (dues levied on the transfer of property), the *banalités* (the obligation to use the seigneur's mill, bakehouse or wine-press), and so on.

In difficult times the nobles sought to increase the dues levied on peasant farming. The 'aristocratic reaction' of the latter part of the eighteenth century was a concerted attempt by the privileged orders to preserve the economic and juridical *status quo*. Consequently, the one fact of eighteenth-century French history that stood out in the eyes of contemporary observers was not the inevitability of the decline of the aristocracy, as expounded after the event by historians determined to explain everything in terms of the 'inevitable'. It was, rather, the counter-offensive launched on a broad front by a nobility bent not merely on strengthening its old economic and social supremacy, but also on re-establishing the political power that had been lost in the reign of Louis xiv.

While the clergy comprised a number of very distinct social categories, united only by the common bond of the holy office of priesthood, the nobility formed a coherent body whose uniformity derived from the basic principles of birth and the inheritance of landed property, and from the cult of being 'different' – a cult that had become a whole way of life diametrically opposed to the middle-class virtues of moderation and thrift. Throughout the eighteenth century the nobles maintained this unity by defending the traditions and the way of life which were theirs and by fighting for the preservation of the privileges that had made them a distinct and wealthy class: some of these privileges were honorific, such as wearing a sword, having the family coat of arms on one's carriage and a pew reserved in church; others were of a more practical kind and included the multitude of seigneurial rights, special laws and jurisdictions, exemptions from the *taille* and the *corvée royale* (statute labour for the maintenance of roads).

The nobles did not have to think back far to imagine forms of government preferable to royal absolutism; in fact, they had never resigned themselves to the political impotency to which Louis xiv had reduced them. This was why the demands of the liberals for some kind of control of royal power by intermediary bodies contained nothing in principle which offended the nobles – on the contrary, it was the nobles who were responsible for launching eighteenth-century Anglomania and the cult of English institutions. But they were interested in political reform only as a means whereby to perpetuate the old social structure; for the nobility as a class there could be only one possible society, the aristocratic society founded on tradition and the hierarchies of birth.

Although the class as a whole was fundamentally united, there did exist more than one order of nobility. The different strata can be distinguished first of all according to origins: the *noblesse d'épée*, proud of its crusader ancestors, hated to be confused with the *noblesse de robe*, who had received their titles much more recently by purchasing some high office or by service in the royal bureaucracy. However, the most clear-cut division was that which depended on wealth and social influence and produced two broad categories, the upper nobility and lower nobility.

The upper nobility was made up of the several thousand members of those families which had been 'presented' to the king after submitting their titles of nobility for rigorous examination by the royal genealogists; it was the upper nobility that dominated the court at Versailles. These nobles occupied positions on all the councils and shared the king's favours and pensions among themselves, living mainly at Versailles and Paris; in the capital they were beginning to move away from the Marais district into the new houses they were building for themselves in the Faubourg Saint-Germain. The land rents and feudal dues from their estates, which were managed by intendants, were barely enough to support their extravagant tastes and habits.

A few members of the aristocracy ignored the social 'rules' and tradition and surrendered to the spirit of the times by engaging in commerce: the Duc d'Aiguillon had his ironworks, while the Noailles and Ségur families cultivated vast plantations in Santo Domingo. Nonetheless, the nobility's principal source of wealth remained land revenue and royal favour, the two pillars of the *douceur de vivre* of which Talleyrand was to speak in his nostalgic evocation of the latter years of the Old Regime.

The luxurious existence enjoyed by the upper nobility was something quite beyond the resources of the majority of minor provincial nobles who constituted by far the greater part of the aristocracy (i.e. several hundred thousand persons in all). The force of tradition, the fear of 'losing caste' and the narrowness of local and provincial horizons barred them from speculating in finance and from benefiting from royal favours. They depended for their livelihood on estates of moderate size which were leased for the greater part to tenant-farmers and *métayers*. The land was inefficiently cultivated, and provided only just about enough for everyone to live on. Consequently, the local seigneur was constantly trying to increase his share of land rents; he was understandably anxious to preserve all fiscal exemptions, and was always claiming feudal dues on the use of a bridge, mill or wine-press, wrangling with his peasant neighbour over some miserable patch of ground or searching through the old manorial rolls for ancient and obsolete taxes to reimpose on his farmers. In conditions such as these, it is hardly surprising that tensions should have gradually mounted in the rural areas.

If the son of one of the minor nobles wished to escape from his father's dilapidated manor and estate, he had no choice but to go into the army. It was for young men in this position that the edict of 1781 was passed, under the pressure of various groups of the nobility,

Eighteenth-century France:
(*right*) the elegance of a
morning tête à tête; (*below*)
the Duc d'Orléans arranges
a horse race.

restricting direct commissions to those nobles who could give proof of four noble grandparents. The Comte de Saint-Germain opened a dozen military colleges, including Brienne and La Flèche, where six hundred young aristocrats learned to become professional soldiers. Even then, the sons of the lower nobility had little hope of rising as high or as quickly as the sons of the Versailles aristocracy.

This was probably to the detriment of the Old Regime because the sons of the lower nobility very often had a more genuinely idealistic view of army service than did the great seigneurs. They had not been tainted by the refined masochism that was luring the entire court of Versailles to performances of 'The Marriage of Figaro'. But the upper nobility had at least retained its prestige in the eyes of its poorer brethren, even if it had lost all sense of being the nation's *élite*. In its struggle against royal absolutism it swept the minor nobility along with it in a common desire to recover the past and regain the power it had once wielded.

The equivocation inherent in the political attitudes of the nobles is best seen in their relationship with the Third Estate. Their only motive in subscribing to the general liberalism of the century and to demands for constitutional reform was a determination to contain the egalitarian ambitions of the Third Estate: despite a tactical alliance against absolutism, the aristocratic and bourgeois concepts of the ideal society remained quite contradictory. Only a small minority of the upper nobility, grouped around men like La Fayette who had been influenced by American liberalism, was prepared to accept the necessity for broad social reform: the overwhelming majority of the privileged orders resisted absolutism solely in the name of seigneurial tradition. This demonstrates how a provisional alliance can be founded on what are basically quite different aspirations. The liberal aristocracy was to be something of a sorcerer's apprentice in the history of the bourgeois revolution.

THE THIRD ESTATE

The Third Estate was simply the rest of the kingdom, the first two Estates being the clergy and nobility; it represented ninety-eight per cent of the total population, which rose from twenty to about twenty-six millions in the course of the century. Admittedly, it is not possible to give exact figures, because at this time there was no national census; but the science of statistics was rapidly becoming an important field of study, and in some of the provincial *généralités* (administrative divisions each under a royal intendant) complete counts were taken. For the kingdom as a whole there are the registers of births, marriages and deaths, which can be used as guides in making general estimates:

The provincial nobility were often poor, so their sons had to seek a career in the army. In this engraving, entitled *Le patriotisme français*, the eldest son of the family is being sent to military college by his father.

although detailed figures cannot be given, the overall trend was very definitely one of growth. The increase that occurred between the estimates of Vauban and Lavoisier, at the beginning and the end of the century was thirty to forty per cent.

What was the cause of the increase? The birth-rate remained stable – in other words very high. If there was in fact any fluctuation, it seems to have been downwards, if one is to believe certain eighteenth-century demographers who protested against the growing use of the 'coïtus interruptus' as a contraceptive method. One of the most concerned of them, Messance, spoke of the 'effects of moral depravity on the population'. Another wrote: 'These deadly secrets unknown to any animal but man have already penetrated into the country areas; even in the villages nature is being cheated.' However, the alarms sounded by these 'populationists' were rather premature in old Catholic and peasant France: the birth-rate of France was still very high by any standard. The reason for the general increase in population was a reduction in mortality, especially in those mortality crises which decimated the most vulnerable sections of society in times of food-shortage and famine. In short, as E. Labrousse has put it, what the French people gained from the economic expansion of the century was not an increase of income, even less an increase of happiness: what they did gain was life itself, survival pure and simple. The France of 1789 consequently had a large population, in fact the largest in the whole of Europe. It was also a young kingdom, in which thirty-six per cent of the population was under twenty years of age and only twenty-four per cent over forty years of age. These figures go a long way towards explaining what was soon to happen in France: both the mobs of the Revolution and the victories of Napoleon were to be heavily dependent on sheer strength of numbers.

TOWN AND COUNTRY

Within the Third Estate (which, as Sieyès observed, already *was* the French nation, and which was steadily increasing in numbers) the towns were leading the way, though they still formed only a minority sector.

It was from the towns and cities that the middle-class or *bourgeoisie* arose, as the etymology of the word indicates, and the bourgeoisie was the dominant stratum of the Third Estate. The bourgeoisie benefited from the slow progress of technology which at this time was calling forth the admiration of the editors of the *Encyclopédie*: the beginnings of coal-mining, for example, or the gradual introduction of English techniques into France's textile industry. It was the bourgeoisie, moreover, that benefited from the multiplication of methods of payment, the rise in prices and the increase in the quantities of articles produced and sold – the Farmers General, speculators or bankers who made their fortunes from the state's debts, merchants engaged in foreign trade whose total value had by this time increased five-fold, manufacturers of coal, silk and cotton cloth who were unable to keep pace with public demand. And yet, this is to oversimplify the real nature of a very elementary form of capitalism, in which all kinds of monetary and banking activity, commerce, the naval armament industry and manufacturing were often handled by one and the same person. The size of annual profits, coupled with the virtues of planning and hard work cultivated by the newly rich, made possible the amassing of huge fortunes which were attributed by their possessors not to good luck, and even less to birth, but to sheer merit: the very concept of merit was already a revolution in itself.

It was of little significance that, here and there, drawn by the spirit of the time or simply by the desire for money, some members of the nobility associated themselves with the new economic movement: their involvement was a negation of their own tradition and of the social order on which their very existence depended. It was the spirit of capitalism, the capitalist contractor, that gave the movement its impetus. The textile industry had its great patrons such as Dollfuss at Mulhouse and Oberkampf at Jouy-en-Josas. Metallurgy made progress in Creusot, which had been founded by de Wendel, and in Alsace in the six ironworks owned by Dietrich, the 'iron king' of the period. At Nantes and Bordeaux new buildings were erected, financed with the money of the 'slavers'. Indeed, the advantages of the profit system had been seen most clearly in the field of large-scale commerce, particularly the trade with the islands of the West Indies which had been growing rapidly since the end of the American War. Christian France – which was also the France of the Enlightenment – entertained no moral scruples about selling cargoes of negro slaves, snatched in raids along the coasts of Africa, to the planters of the Antilles in exchange for sugar and cotton. From Santo Domingo and Martinique, French merchants transported back to Europe sugar, tobacco, cotton and indigo.

However, beneath the new prosperity founded on big industry and commerce the bourgeoisie was composed of many different strata: in fact, there existed a number of distinct bourgeoisies. Private investment continued in its traditional forms – land, the purchase of posts (*offices*) in the public services and loans to the state (*rentes*). At the end of the Old Regime the bourgeois of Paris still sought the security of a quiet life based on modest financial resources. Most important of all were the small contractors who formed the very framework of urban society: the craftsmen and masters of the trade guilds or corporations.

Although the guilds constituted a single juridical entity they were nonetheless a highly diversified group socially: a master mason, for instance, might be either a genuine building contractor employing several dozen men, or a craftsman working on his own or with a few journeymen. All the different strata of the bourgeoisie had one thing in common, however, and this was to be involved in the general movement of social betterment and increasing wealth which was the fruit of economic expansion. The towns of eighteenth-century France were growing and enriching themselves, and in so doing they began to extend beyond the boundaries of the old city-wall.

The city-wall had been the symbol of a city's fear; it was no longer in keeping with the spirit of the age or with national ambitions. The city and town had now acquired a moral cohesion and a culture of their own. The middle class had become one vast public which was imposing its desires, tastes and demands on an intelligentsia that had emerged from its own ranks and had become independent of the king and the nobles. The demands of the middle class were both economic (the unification of the national market, free trade and the free movement of labour) and political (the redistribution of power). But ambition and self-interest were not the only motives inspiring the members of the middle class. There was also a great collective feeling of social frustration, the humiliation which the middle class suffered before the barrier of birth: Manon Phlipon, the future Mme Roland, never forgave her hosts for inviting her to dine in a château and then asking her to eat with the servants. Barnave became a revolutionary in childhood, on the day his mother was ejected from her theatre box by an aristocrat. The unity of the bourgeoisie, composed as it was of so many different social groups, derived primarily from the spontaneous and unanimous rejection of the time-honoured system of discrimination and privilege which had been based on birth.

The bourgeoisie was all the more bitterly opposed to the hierarchical society of the Old Regime because it did not feel that the urban working classes on its 'left' presented anything of a threat to its own position. The working classes, constantly growing in size, did not yet constitute a modern proletariat: between the simple wage-earner who was free to sell his labour as best he could – Marx's proletarian – and the small artisan there were innumerable intermediate categories. There was the journeyman, closely bound up in the corporative system and living under his master's roof; then there was the *chambrelan*, the man who worked in his own home and owned his own loom but not the raw material which he wove for the merchants on a piece-work basis; and there was also a multitude of small proprietors who added to their incomes by working for others. The forms of production were still too diversified for the working people to have

The economic boom was most spectacular in commerce. This engraving, entitled *La belle négociante*, emphasises the international aspect of trading.

as yet any real sense of being a class. This was why, when the urban masses protested as a body, they did so as consumers rather than as producers: it was anger at rising prices, and in particular bread prices, that induced the people to riot, and not so much the urge to strike and make wage claims. For this reason it mattered little that wages should have fallen behind prices in the course of the century; the wage-earners had not yet organised themselves into a united social force. But whenever seasonal crises occurred and grain became scarce, whenever the price of bread rose significantly above the 'normal' price of three *sous* per pound (the average daily wage was about one *livre*, i.e. twenty *sous*), it was then that the working people were made to feel their poverty and were stung into protest.

The rioting of the working classes gave the bourgeoisie no cause for alarm, since it was directed chiefly against the hoarding practices of the monarchy and aristocracy, the wealthy recipients of land revenue who were able to stock cereals and then wait for prices to go up. The bourgeoisie found it easy to divert popular resentment away from themselves and direct it instead against the common enemy, privilege, and towards a common objective, the reform of the monarchic state. And so, the diversity of social status within the working class, the multiplicity of individual relationships between employers and workers and even the acts of violence committed by the workers all conspired to draw them into the political camp of the bourgeoisie.

The country population of France under the Old Regime formed over three-quarters of the total population of the kingdom; in other words, the mode of life most characteristic of the time was that of the peasantry. This peasant society, idealised in the literature of the latter years of the century by writers like Restif de la Bretonne, who contrasted rustic purity with urban depravity, was not just a matter of simple family virtue as depicted in pastoral poems and novels. It was certainly a society traditionalist in nature, with strong family structure, deep religious beliefs often mingled with local superstitions, village folklore and community habits. But the essence of peasant tradition lay in illiteracy and isolation. At this period transport was slow and expensive, and the kingdom was still a conglomeration of local markets, so that the peasant was the prisoner of his mental and geographical horizons – in other words, the prisoner of routine.

He cultivated the land his parents and ancestors had cultivated before him: the 'bleds' where wheat, rye and buckwheat were grown (wheat bread was only for the prosperous; the poor had to make do with bread made from rye and buckwheat). Vineyards were common and were to be found both in the north and in the south, on good soil and poor soil. This subsistence type of agriculture was at the same time a communal activity; because of the lack of manure, crop-

Engraving of a glass factory under royal patronage (*manufacture royale*). The workers were subject to strict monastic discipline.

The workshop of a tinsmith. There were just over two million workers and artisans in France at this time.

This engraving, entitled *Ca n'durra pas toujours* ('It won't last forever'), stresses the contrast between the misery of the peasants and the prosperity of the privileged orders. Tithes and taxes accounted for three-quarters of some peasants' income.

rotation was based on the two-year and three-year systems, the latter being by far the most widespread method used in France at the time. The land belonging to each village was divided up into three groups of plots known as *soles*. One was planted with wheat in the autumn, another with oats or barley in the spring and the third was left fallow and used for grazing (though this was only true where the soil was rich – in the poorer areas an even greater proportion of land lay fallow and was thereby wasted). It is easy to see how the old rural habits of France only served to perpetuate the very low productivity of agrarian labour, the key to peasant poverty.

The economic developments of the eighteenth century had little effect on agricultural habits. As far as can be judged from contemporary sources, crop-yields made hardly any progress and, in the case of wheat, always hovered around the ratio of one to six. In the second half of the century there were indeed some agriculturalists who were all for abandoning the old communal system and replacing it with a system of individual cultivation, and who wanted to scrap the fallow method in favour of a revolutionary kind of rotation involving the planting of fodder-crops. These innovators were only partially successful, for a reason which the leading economists of the century, the Physiocrats, saw very clearly: new methods could succeed only if applied to large-scale farming. Agrarian capitalism, though it was beginning to spread among the large farms of the north and in the Paris basin, remained a rare phenomenon in France at this time.

On the whole agriculture was based on a system of small-holdings run by families of peasants; the farmer was either a tenant-farmer (*fermier*) or a share-cropper (*métayer*) who retained a half-share of his produce. The peasants often owned their small-holdings: even before 1789 they owned nearly half the land in France. But the peasantry as a whole gained little from the rise in agricultural prices which was the general trend of the century. The only farmers to benefit in any way were those who had an annual surplus to sell after providing for their families and paying their dues: peasants in this category were known as *laboureurs*, and were in fact quite well-off and able to share in the nation's growing prosperity. It was probably the *laboureur* who was the first to indulge in the fine oak chest that became such a popular article of furniture in farm living-rooms during the years 1750–80.

What about the rest of the peasants? Most of them simply had to get by as best they could from one year to another. It should be remembered that, on top of their families' upkeep, the annual replacement of equipment and, in the case of tenant-farmers, the renewal of leases, the peasants had to cope with the heavy threefold burden of the royal *taille* (the basic direct tax of the Old Regime), ecclesiastical tithes and seigneurial dues. Usually the annual harvest was just about enough to meet these obligations, but in the event of a poor harvest it simply was not possible for the peasants to look after their families (the size of the average peasant family grew continuously throughout the eighteenth century). This meant that the peasant, even if he owned his own land, had to look for some extra source of income: and so he spent his winter evenings working in one or other of the various rural industries and crafts, or was forced to resign himself to seasonal migration. But very often overpopulation in the rural areas simply resulted in unemployment, begging and vagrancy. By the end of the century criticism of this kind of social injustice had reached a climax.

It is not difficult to see in what direction peasant resentment was

After two years of bad
harvests, the misery of the
peasantry reached its
climax in 1789. The
peasants could rarely
afford meat; hence the
irony of this engraving
entitled *Quand ce ra la
Poule au Pot.*

directed. At this stage it was aimed not at agrarian capitalism, which
was developing slowly and unequally, but at royal taxation which
seemed all the heavier for not being applied uniformly throughout the
kingdom, and all the more unfair because aristocratic wealth was left
relatively untouched. In fact, the revolt against taxation in the latter
part of the century represented a revolt against the nobles rather than
the king. The nobles, both ecclesiastical and lay, provoked intense
hatred among the peasantry: even though the feudal system had long
since lost its *raison d'être* and serfdom had almost entirely disappeared, it

36

was in the name of feudalism and tradition that the peasant landowner had to give part of his harvest to the Church, pay dues to his lord, submit to statute labour, watch hunting parties trampling over his land and use his lord's bakehouse, mill and wine-press. The bitterness which the peasants felt at their degradation increased towards the end of the century because the seigneurs had been able to tighten their grip. Here again, the 'aristocratic reaction' found itself in conflict with an opposing force, as the country areas of France came under the influence of the propaganda which the towns were directing against privilege and the old order in general.

THE KING AND HIS COURT

To preserve an air of mystery and aloofness is part of the task of being a king. Louis XVI was no exception to this rule of personal power. He never said much, wrote even less and played a passive rather than an active role in affairs of state. His tragic end earned him a glory that he had never really deserved, for behind his secretiveness, his silence and the courage he showed at the guillotine there was probably little more than a simple attachment to tradition.

Born in 1754, the grandson of Louis XV (1715–74) and king at twenty years of age, Louis XVI was very much a Bourbon. He had inherited the Bourbon physique, the famous family nose and the Bourbon passion for hunting and other outdoor activities; his only mark of individuality was the rather unkingly pleasure he took in pottering about with his hands. His contemporaries noticed particularly in his general bearing an awkwardness and timidity that were probably the psychological symptoms of a physical deformity which appears to have required surgical treatment and kept him away from women and even from his own wife for a period of seven years. In a famous passage of the *Nouveaux Lundis* Sainte-Beuve stresses this psychosomatic characteristic: 'Louis XVI was not impotent, no more than one who stammers is dumb; but, as both husband and king, he was simply awkward, self-conscious and inhibited.'

This was why Louis could say with even more justification than his grandfather: 'I am an indescribable person.' Let us then accept the verdict of those close to him who summed him up as 'indefinable', and go on to consider the more certain aspects of his kingship, how this indecisive temperament responded to the functions of royalty. Louis XVI clung to the traditional view of monarchy. He never once questioned either the extent of his inherited power or the religious foundations on which it was built. He exercised this power conscientiously but rather gently, without any deep interest in politics or any real urge to dominate those under him. The personal satisfaction he derived from his position was of a mean kind, for Louis delighted in police methods, secret correspondence, the gossip of court and city and dubious anecdotes.

And yet, though the king sometimes fell asleep at Council sessions, he was not lacking in political intelligence, and during the first two years of his reign gave Turgot his personal backing. Later, in 1787 when crisis was threatening, he gave his approval to the fiscal reforms which Calonne was compelled to introduce. When the moment of decision came, however, and he was confronted with the counter-offensive launched by his entourage, 'his' nobles, he yielded just as he had always done to the extravagant whims of his queen. In the end he opted for tradition – 'his' tradition – and against reform; the weakness of the monarchy derived not only from the personal psychology of the king, but from the solidarity of the aristocracy and the firm hold it kept on political power during the last years of the Old Regime.

The queen had character but no political sense. When the crisis of the Old Regime reached exploding-point she was at the height of her unpopularity. After having first been nicknamed 'l'Autrichienne' she had now come to be known as 'Madame Déficit'. Since the 'queen's necklace affair' of 1786, which had left the public convinced of her complicity, she had not dared to go to Paris any more and had stopped giving great banquets at Versailles; instead she shut herself up with her friends and her children, to whom she now became a more and more loving and vigilant mother.

Marie-Antoinette's character and tragic destiny can be explained to a large extent by psychology. Sensual but virtuous, she had had an unhappy and even positively humiliating married life for seven whole years, and so she completely threw herself into the whirl of courtly pleasure in an attempt to forget her sorrow; her reaction was all the more violent for stemming from an essentially melancholy nature: 'What do you expect me to do, I'm frightened of being bored!' Because she had a husband who was not able to counterbalance her mother's influence, she remained obsessed with her childhood, the simple and loving atmosphere of Schönbrunn. Hence her fondness for small family gatherings in the rustic setting of the Trianon, gatherings from which were excluded all those likely to be either bored or boring – in other words, the large majority of courtiers, whom she now regarded as her enemies. Hence, also, the ardour with which she defended the interests of Austria, even when they were opposed to the interests of France. In the service of her mother and then of her brother Joseph II, Marie-Antoinette had played the role of a loyal and invaluable intelligence agent. Frustrated on the conjugal level, her femininity was diverted into an undiscriminating obsession with politics, which she always managed to turn into a matter of personal antagonisms. Hypersensitive in her opinion of herself, she adopted an attitude of

Portrait of Marie-Antoinette at le Petit Trianon.

hostile aggression in her personal relationships, because courage and pride became confused in her mind and never permitted her to give way to anyone. This unhappy woman and ill-fated queen was aware of her tragic destiny: 'I only hope he succeeds. . . . I always seem to bring bad luck,' she said, weeping, when she decided to recall Necker in 1788.

The king and his family were the central figures in a never-ending pageant of worldly pleasure which was the focal point of the kingdom – the court of Versailles. There were in all fifteen thousand persons in the service of the king, queen, princes and princesses of the royal blood, divided into two households, the civil and the military. The upper nobility had for a century been concentrated round Versailles, where they had devoted their lives to serving, watching over and entertaining the royal family; but, though the setting was still the same, everything else had changed in those hundred years. Louis xiv had used Versailles to domesticate the aristocracy; by the end of the eighteenth century the aristocracy had been able to use Versailles to establish its supremacy over the king. The building was the same, but its significance quite different.

By its very splendour the exquisite worldly civilisation of Versailles aroused a steadily mounting tide of public opinion against itself: the towns were at last rising up against the royal court. Jealous of a world from which it was excluded and hostile to the life of luxury that was a negation of its own principles of thrift, the bourgeoisie was ready to use any weapon that came to hand to fight the court, the symbol of social privilege: and so bourgeois propaganda accused Versailles of being ruinous to the national economy, reactionary and debauched, and proclaimed its own ideals of reason, progress and morality.

In charging the royal court with being reactionary and debauched the bourgeoisie was by no means unjustified. The court lived a politically and morally dissipated existence centred on the pleasures of the moment. How much truth was there, however, in the accusation that the court was bringing ruin upon the nation's economy? Versailles was consuming a mere six per cent of public revenue. The accusation was made at a time when France's public finances were in chaos, but public opinion confused two quite different forms of court spending: the money lavished on royal pomp and ceremony and on banqueting, and the payments made to the vast number of courtiers and other persons occupying various posts in the royal household. In a book of memoirs written around the time when Turgot was active the following comment is found: 'The extravagant ceremonial of court life is probably the least of the vices of Versailles. Infinitely more reprehensible is the way in which a crowd of valets is eternally preoccupied with inventing every possible sort of financial business. . . .' Public money certainly was being squandered by the monarchy's indiscriminate granting of royal favours, and not only to the 'valets': there was a permanent confusion at Versailles of distinctions between pensions, gifts, remuneration for public service, resale of offices and other financial gambits.

If he had made all these fine people squeal a little by cutting court expenditure, Louis would not have done much to restore stability to the nation's finances; quite a large part of the six per cent of treasury revenue granted to the court was consumed in necessary expenses that could not possibly be curtailed. But, if he had been prepared to make a few cuts, even if only to the extent of three or four million *livres*, the king would have sweetened the psychological and political atmosphere of France: the Revolution was the result not only of economic and social trends, but of scandal, scurrilous anecdotes and, to a certain extent, pure accident. By effecting spectacular economies at the court Louis would not have wiped out the national deficit, but he might have been able to repair the damage done by the scandalous affair of the 'queen's necklace'. He never did manage to make a decision of this kind, however, and this is why the Third Estate's indictment of the court, though not wholly justifiable, was founded on reality: the king's refusal to reform the court was regarded as proof of the monarchy's solidarity with the privileged orders.

THE MACHINERY OF THE ROYAL GOVERNMENT

The real power wielded by the king of France at the end of the eighteenth century can only be estimated by studying the workings of the political system of which he was the centre.

Royal absolutism still retained its traditional appearances and prerogatives. The king, answerable only to God, continued to be the supreme power of the realm, in theory at least, and the *lettre de cachet* (an order for the arrest and imprisonment of a person without trial), though used but rarely, was regarded as the ultimate symbol of that power. Master of the judiciary and the legislature, the king was at the same time the head of the executive, a centralised bureaucracy of jurists whom he appointed and dismissed as he wished. There had been no 'prime minister' leading the bureaucracy since the death of Cardinal Fleury in 1743; there were six officials of importance whose respective functions were not quite as clear-cut as their titles suggest: the Keeper of the Seals or Chancellor of France, the Controller-General of Finances and the four Secretaries of State for War, the Navy, Foreign Affairs and the *Maison du Roi* (whose many responsibilities included internal security of the city of Paris). These six ministers worked together with a number of high dignitaries (princes of the royal blood or members of the high nobility) in the royal councils, which were of a purely deliberative nature: the supreme council, known simply as 'the Council', concerned itself with general political problems. The king himself presided over the Council, but during the eighteenth century, as a result of Louis xv's neglect of the Council and the growing complexity of its business, it had become customary to hold preparatory meetings in the king's absence; these meetings were attended by the principal officials from each department. Under Louis xiv monarchy had meant government by the king; under Louis xvi it had come to mean something rather different – in certain respects it was now government by ministers and their departments.

Since the time of Louis xiv, administrative power in the provinces had been wielded largely by the intendants, who were appointed by the king and could be dismissed by him, and who had gradually built up a monopoly of power in the districts (*généralités*) under their control. In the eighteenth century the nobles, who already occupied all the highest positions at Versailles, also succeeded in dominating the intendancies, and were thereby able to serve their king with greater independence than they had enjoyed in the past – indeed, they often revealed great administrative ability. Eighteenth-century France, which was discovering the social sciences (in particular economics, demography and statistics), was beginning to appreciate the virtues of calculation and planning. The bureaucracy of Versailles became the centre of a wholesale modernisation of administrative methods; as the century advanced the French monarchy was more 'enlightened' intellectually than it had ever been.

And yet it was a long time since the authority of the monarchy had been less heeded. The royal power, real as it undoubtedly was, was confronted with two major obstacles, one of them deriving simply from the traditional structure of old France, the other a quite new and purely political obstacle.

The traditional obstacle confronting absolutism derived from the imprescriptible nature of privileges once acquired, and from the inequality of status of individuals and social groups. That privilege and inequality should have survived was a sign that the process of administrative centralisation was not yet complete: power was still exercised individually and locally in a variety of ways. Under the Old Regime France had no single system of law: the regions to the south of the Loire had inherited a code of written law from the old Roman law, while other parts of France were subject to a mass of unwritten common law which comprised hundreds of different customs. The kingdom was divided vertically into four basic administrative categories: military, judicial, ecclesiastical and economic; these categories were represented by the twelve military 'governments', the presidials,

Painting of Louis XVI by Duplessis.

the dioceses of the Church and the *généralités*, respectively. Moreover, depending on the circumstances and date of their annexation to the French kingdom, some provinces had preserved a broad measure of autonomy and were administered by their own Provincial Estates, which were controlled by the privileged orders: in Languedoc the royal intendant had less power than the local bishops, and in Brittany less than the nobility. It should be remembered, finally, that there was another factor contributing to the independence of officers of the realm, and this was the venality of offices: posts were bought and could be handed down to heirs, and the monarchy deliberately increased the number of office-holders in order to fill the coffers of the treasury. An army officer bought his regiment, a magistrate his bailiwick or seneschalsy and a *parlementaire* his position in one of the thirteen parlements.

In the seventeenth century the independence which officials enjoyed in the exercise of their duties had been partially offset by the political submission which Louis xiv had imposed on them. In the eighteenth century, however, the independence which these administrators derived from the very nature of their office was strengthened by the political freedom they had regained. The high officers of the realm, especially the nobles of the parlements, gave voice to the people's hostility to absolutism. Immediately after the death of Louis xiv the parlements, led by the Paris parlement with its vast area of jurisdiction, had restored a tradition that had been broken by the great king, and once again became the mouthpieces of anti-absolutism. At a time when public opinion was seeking spokesmen for its grievances the higher nobility gave continuous expression to the anti-absolutist feeling that was binding the aristocracy and bourgeoisie together. The nobles were trying to raise the legislative authority of the parlements into a 'fundamental law of the realm', above the will of the king himself.

Louis xvi found himself more and more isolated and his powers less and less real. Everything acted against him: the progress of knowledge generally and of administrative methods in particular, the preservation of an archaic system of government, the political ambitions of the bourgeoisie and the aristocratic reaction. The French nation was still undoubtedly monarchist, but nevertheless it had rejected the principle of absolution. Even before 1789 absolute monarchy had ceased to exist, except in name. The financial crisis was to sweep it away once and for all.

2

THE REVOLT OF
THE NOBLES

The financial crisis was not merely the catalyst of Revolution: it bound together the social tensions inherent in the structure of the Old Regime and brought social problems into the arena of politics and revolutionary ferment. The state had ceased to be the remote and lofty abstraction of more peaceful times; it was losing its autonomy as it became enmeshed with the frustrations and ambitions of society.

Thus, absolutism was having to resign itself in advance to the public will. Calonne, at the end of his tether, sketched out afresh the great reforms which, it was hoped, would rationalise the nation's tax structure. He suggested to Louis XVI that his reforms should be submitted for the approval of an Assembly of Notables, counting on that ancient body's docility when confronted with his programme of fiscal equality. In this way, Calonne thought, the path would be made smooth for the registration of the reforms by the Paris parlement. The king and his minister imagined they had hit upon a solution, little realising that what they planned to do would set the machinery of public opinion in motion.

The Assembly of Notables convened in 1787 was composed almost entirely of members of the privileged orders; this meant that the French nobility was now presented with an excellent opportunity to give public voice to the hostility of absolutism that had united them throughout the century. How could the king and his minister have possibly expected them to accept timidly the proposed reforms? Having removed Calonne from office, the Notables proceeded to oppose his successor (one of their own number) in any attempt to encroach on their fiscal privileges. When the king dismissed the Assembly the nobles had not only succeeded in mobilising public opinion against Versailles, but had discovered a ready-made platform, the parlements, from which to defend their position. The great magistrates of the parlements were now to have their moment of popularity.

In 1787 and 1788 the bourgeoisie of the towns and cities gave its wholehearted support to the privileged orders, who had provided the revolutionary

45

movement with its initial impetus. The bourgeoisie gave its support in the name of liberty, and soon it was to go much further than the nobles were prepared to go, adding the slogan of equality to that of liberty. As soon as the nobles took up their unambiguous stand against the dynamics of 'enlightenment' at the end of 1788, the break was complete. The Revolution was finally set in motion in two distinct stages: the first stage was the combined assault launched by enlightened France against the Old Regime; the second was the convening of the Estates-General at the instigation of the parlementaires, who were quite unaware of the new role about to be assumed by that body.

The first blow struck against the old order was, then, the deliberate political initiative taken by the parlements. It might seem strange that the thirteen parlements of old France, which were simply judicial courts, should have managed to find themselves an active role in the politics of the nation. They were able to exercise political influence because, traditionally, all royal decrees had to receive formal 'registration' from the parlements. Although the parlements could not actually refuse to register a royal decree, they were entitled to declare their opposition in the form of 'remonstrances'; in fact, they were even able to compel the king to order registration of a decree himself in a special session known as the lit de justice; *whenever the king took such a step the magistrates were obliged to give way. Or, at least, they were obliged to do so according to the traditional doctrine of absolutism; but French jurisprudence had evolved considerably since the time of Louis XIV.*

In studying the evolution of jurisprudence in France it must be borne in mind that the office of magistrate in a parlement was bought, and therefore owned, by the holder. Since they owned their offices the magistrates enjoyed a certain independence from the royal power and also possessed a great esprit de corps, *a consciousness of being a caste apart. The office of magistrate in one of the parlements had to be bought at a high price; at the same time it brought with it a title which, on payment of a tax, could be handed down from father to son. In a society permeated with snobbery these high offices had become the goal of many an ambitious commoner who had made his fortune in commerce or finance. As membership of a parlement did not in itself give much of a return on the capital invested in its purchase, the holder of the office had to be someone with other sources of income who did not have to depend on the 'gifts' (épices) extorted from litigants. For the noblesse de robe the real advantage of belonging to a parlement lay in the political power that went with the office of magistrate.*

As the power of the monarchy weakened, so the activity of the parlements increased. They found their first great opportunity in the Jansenist controversy, in which the Paris parlement took advantage of the religious sensibilities of the people of the city to defend the autonomy of the Church of France against both Rome and Versailles. In the second half of the eighteenth century the anti-absolutism of the parlements shed its veneer of religion and revealed its political ambition: in 1755, and again in 1759, the Paris parlement, excercising its right to protest by 'remonstrance', reminded the king that the parlements held

46

their rights from the very origins of French monarchic history – from the Frankish assemblies and, later, from the curia regis *of the Middle Ages – and that they were therefore not simply courts of justice but the depositaries of all the fundamental laws of the kingdom, with the right to legislate; in refusing to register a decree, the Paris parlement argued, it was exercising its right to reject that decree. The prerogatives claimed by the parlements pinpoint one of the basic distinctions of the century, the distinction between monarchy and despotism.*

In spite of the fact that they had given the public constant proof of their essential conservatism and had even had Rousseau's treatise Emile *burnt and Calas condemned to death, this noble oligarchy succeeded in retaining the confidence of the urban population. Even when it opposed the* centième denier, *the re-imposition of the* vingtième, *the suppression of the* corvée *and later the introduction of a new stamp-duty, the bourgeoisie did not regard this reaction as implying resistance to fiscal equality, but rather as evidence of opposition to absolutism, and a reassertion of the old principle of 'no taxation without consent'. 'The people,' says Voltaire, who had no sympathy for the parlements, 'looks on a parlement simply as the enemy of taxation. The rich are deliberately encouraging the grumblings of the populace.'*

For the time being the people of France were blind to the real motives of the magistrates: for them the parlement was a temporary substitute for the elected assembly of which they dreamed. Indeed, every time that the monarchy had tried to resist the parlements in the eighteenth century it had eventually been compelled to give way. The power of the magistrates in the parlements, which had been broken by the Chancellor Maupeou in 1771, had been restored in 1774 largely through the efforts of Turgot, who was anxious to gain public approval for his experiments in reform. From this moment onwards, the influence of the parlements became ever greater, reaching a peak in the year 1788. One of the incongruities of eighteenth-century French politics was the fact that the assault on the absolutist system was launched through one of the Old Regime's most traditional institutions.

However, the ambiguity of the political attitude of the parlements, which had been sustained by all the trends of the century, was at last resolved when the old order was faced with its final crisis. It was then that the second great blow was struck against royal absolutism, and soon the tide of hostility had gathered such momentum that the parlements were no longer able or willing to follow it.

Ironically, it was the parlements that took the first step which precipitated the Revolution – the demand for the reconvening of the Estates-General. But the magistrates were expecting that assembly to take the form it had taken in the past, with representation biased in favour of the privileged orders so as to give them a built-in majority. In October 1788 the parlement of Paris, in demanding the convening of the Estates-General, referred explicitly to the terms of representation of 1614. What was the reason for the aristocracy's reactionary nostalgia, its determination to monopolise control of royal power? The privileged orders, and in particular the magistrates of the parlements, had throughout the century been in the forefront of the movement of Enlightenment.

47

The key to the attitude of the aristocracy is to be found in their obsession with the past. The hatred which their ancestors had felt for Louis XIV and his centralising bureaucracy, coupled with the effects of the liberalising explosion of 1715 and the Regency, are more essential to an understanding of the political sensibilities of the aristocracy than the speculations of Montesquieu or Malesherbes. The deep-lying motivations of particular social groups had been blurred by the modish literature of the philosophes *and the equivocations of liberalism. When the time came to put into practice the ideals of a society of equal opportunity and general betterment which had been outlined in eighteenth-century thought, the force of aristocratic prejudice reappeared in all its brutality. In the absence of the moderating influence of the monarchy, the whole of cultivated society, the world of Enlightenment, was torn asunder by conflicting passions and interests: the privileges of birth were at war with the frustrations of the bourgeoisie.*

France had reached one of the most critical moments in her history. Already the difficulties of any form of political or social compromise in the France of the Old Regime had become quite clear. By refusing to abandon any part of their fundamental privileges, and indulging in the nostalgic sentiments of the parlements, the aristocracy was jeopardising the creation of that society of property-owning equality which was the basic ambition of enlightened opinion; at the same time, it risked being caught up in the fate of royal absolutism, a concept it had always found abhorrent.

In the opposing camp things now began to happen very quickly. In July 1788 the Vizille Assembly showed that the predominance of an enlightened Third Estate need not be unacceptable to those members of the privileged orders who remained loyal to the development of eighteenth-century thought: what mattered now was not to defend aristocratic particularism, but to strive towards the creation of a 'nation', a new political and social structure.

The current of unrest was all the more powerful for having been swelled by an unforeseen and very important factor: the economic crisis of 1788–9, which added its own effects to the existing political crisis. The poor harvest unleashed the inevitable consequences of peasant misery, under-production in the towns, unemployment and rioting. Although such economic crises had been a habitual feature of French history, this particular crisis occurred at a time when revolution was already in the air. It obviously did nothing to moderate egalitarian aspirations: on the contrary, it gave them their momentum and their strength – especially the strength of numbers provided by the rural population. In defiance of the parlements and the majority of his nobles, the king yielded to the people's demands in the last months of 1788. He recalled Necker in August and agreed to the doubling of the Third Estate's representation in December. The scene was now set.

CALONNE AND THE NOTABLES

In the summer of 1786 Calonne, the Controller-General of Finances, whose early years of office had been marked by the failure of his financial management of the state, put forward a detailed plan for reforming the royal finances. The central item of this plan was a fiscal reform, the replacement of the two existing *vingtième* taxes by a single tax to be imposed on all land without exception and graded according to the proprietor's income; this land tax was to be paid in kind. In Calonne the great fiscal principle of the Physiocratic school had found a new champion.

Further measures were then proposed by Calonne with a view to increasing national production: the most important were free trade in grain and the total abolition of internal tariffs. Finally, Calonne proposed to set up a hierarchy of consultative assemblies through which the king's subjects were to play their part in the administration of the realm. He intended these assemblies to be elected by all property-owners throughout the land, which meant that there was to be no bias in favour of the upper classes.

Calonne realised that the parlements would not agree to register his edicts of reform, and so he decided to submit his programme to an Assembly of Notables who were to be appointed by the king and would therefore be likely to co-operate. The Notables gathered at Versailles on 22 February 1787. There were one hundred and forty-seven of them: in theory the nobility had only thirty-nine representatives, but in fact there were many more than this, if one takes into account all the bishops, magistrates and *anoblis* who were included in the ranks of the Third Estate. Calonne had been counting on their submissiveness, but the pressure of opinion in Paris was to prove much greater than his influence.

In his opening address Calonne spoke in revolutionary language denouncing the privileges of the clergy, the unpopular salt tax (*gabelle*) and all the 'abuses' which 'weigh so heavily on the working class, the producers.' He found himself admitting to a deficit of eighty million *livres*. Disturbed by what they had heard, the Notables demanded a detailed statement of the nation's finances. Calonne refused, but then confessed to an even higher deficit of one hundred and thirteen millions, putting the blame on his predecessor, Necker. He immediately found himself confronted with a solid phalanx of resistance composed both of the defenders of privilege and of those reformers who supported Necker. Ostracised by the royal court, which was uneasy about his plans, Calonne was dismissed by the king under pressure from Marie-Antoinette.

Among the Notables opposing Calonne was the archbishop of

Toulouse, Loménie de Brienne, who had expressed himself with particular vehemence. On 1 May 1787, after a brief interval, he was appointed by the king to take over the office of Controller-General of Finances. In order to win the confidence of the Notables, Brienne gave them full details of the nation's financial position and at the same time persuaded the king to announce cuts in expenditure of fifteen million *livres*. The archbishop, who was a *philosophe* wanted to divide the anti-absolutist camp, and thus introduced a number of liberal measures, among them the recognition of the civil rights of Protestants (Protestant marriages were now made legitimate, which angered the clergy).

Nonetheless, to obtain money, Brienne was forced to revert to Calonne's programme of reforms, and this meant clashing with the nobility and clergy. The assembly rejected his programme on the grounds that it did not possess the authority to approve tax measures: this was tantamount to saying that the Estates-General should be convened, a step that the entire aristocracy was now demanding. If the king had agreed to summon the Estates-General, he might have made the royal administration more popular and also have strengthened the monarchy by going over the heads of the hostile parlements and Notables; but he refused. All he could do now was to dismiss the Assembly of Notables. The parlements lost no time in leading the opposition to Brienne's reforms, and on 16 July the parlement of Paris demanded the convening of the Estates-General, the only body authorised to pass new taxes.

When the parlement of Paris refused to register Brienne's reforms, Louis xvi had to preside over a 'royal session' (*lit de justice*), held on 6 August 1787: the special purpose of this session was the registration of a new stamp tax which the parlement had repudiated on the grounds that only the Estates-General were competent to approve new taxation. On the following day the parlement declared the previous day's registration illegal. The people of Paris cheered the magistrates, shouting 'Long live the fathers of the people! No taxes!' Louis at once exiled the parlement to Troyes, but the *Chambre des Comptes*, the *Cour des Aides* and the provincial parlements immediately decided to give their united support to the Paris parlement. When the Comte d'Artois came to the Palais de Justice on 17 August to have the decrees registered he was booed by ten thousand rioters. The city was backing its parlement against the king, as it had always done. Eventually, Loménie de Brienne decided to negotiate for the termination of the Paris parlement's exile; he renounced the proposed land tax and new stamp duty and the magistrates returned in triumph to Paris. The treasury was still short of money, however, and Brienne resolved to launch a series of loans to bring in four hundred and twenty millions; he also promised to convoke the Estates-General in 1792 or thereabouts.

The loans had, of course, to be registered. Choosing the authoritarian method, and on the advice of Lamoignon, Keeper of the Seals, Louis XVI decided to register them without first putting them before the Paris parlement for final approval and a vote. The special session took place on 19 November. Louis and Lamoignon spoke in menacing tones, declaring that only the king was competent to judge whether or not to convoke the Estates-General. As the loans were being formally registered the Duc d'Orleans rose up and asserted that the king was acting illegally. 'No,' retorted Louis, 'this is legal because I will it.' The next day the duke was exiled to Villers-Cotterêts.

The Paris parlement continued to oppose the king – on 4 January 1788 it declared *lettres de cachet* to be contrary to 'public and natural law.' Then, on 13 April, the parlement made 'remonstrances' to the king against the 'illegal' registration of 19 November. Lamoignon thereupon resolved to smash the opposition, asking Louis to agree to a number of royal orders that would take away the power of the parlements. The most important of these orders were those which deprived the parlements of the right to register decrees and entrusted that function instead to a plenary court appointed for life by the king. On 3 May the Paris parlement struck back by proclaiming 'the fundamental laws of the kingdom': all subsidies, the parlement insisted, should be voted by regular convocations of the Estates-General; the parlements must retain their right to control legislation, and *lettres de cachet* should be abolished. Immediately, Louis XVI quashed the proclamation of 3 May and had two of the ringleaders, Duval d'Éprémesnil and Goislard de Montsabert, arrested. Then he dismissed the Paris parlement and imposed the registration of Lamoignon's special orders depriving the parlements in general of their powers. It was now the turn of the provincial parlements to revolt.

This revolt spread, through the parlements, to all the towns and cities of France. It focused the entire movement of anti-absolutist opinion which had been the product of eighteenth-century intellectual evolution. Its momentum was all the greater because there existed in France a vast network of legal offices which provided a close link between the bourgeoisie and the magistrates of the parlements: justices of the peace, advocates, attorneys and even court ushers – in fact, every level of the 'legal fraternity' played its part. Moreover, the spirit of reform had found one of its keenest champions in the legal profession under the Old Regime, and a little later the lawyers were to exercise a dominant influence in the revolutionary assemblies.

Public opinion was beginning to be obsessed with one thing – the convening of the Estates-General – though, as yet, nobody seemed to have any clear notion of the form the assembly should take.

It was the provincial towns and cities, even more than the capital, that led the way in the summer of 1788. The magistrates of the parlements, France's sovereign courts, came to the aid of their colleagues in Paris, giving the initial impetus to a mighty movement of unrest. From this moment onwards it was not just a matter of resistance, but of revolution. This was primarily the revolution of the magistrature and nobility, proclaimed in the name of traditional 'liberties': the privileged orders were the leaders of the struggle. The clergy added their own 'remonstrances' to those of the Paris parlement. The regions of France where the two leading social orders still occupied strong political positions were the most relentless in opposing the king and the decrees of Lamoignon, because it was in these regions that revolt could be organised most effectively. Some of these provinces had their own Provincial Estates, while the others could remember having them in earlier years, and now wanted them back in place of the powerless 'provincial assemblies' convened at the end of 1787, the futile remnants of Calonne's disastrous period of office.

Rioting broke out in all the towns which boasted a parlement – in Grenoble, Pau, Dijon and Toulouse – and was particularly violent in the provinces of Béarn and Brittany. In Pau, where it was feared that the Estates of Béarn might be suppressed, a mob reopened the Palais de Justice on 19 June, imprisoned the intendant, and reinstalled the parlement: that body, supported by the local nobility, at once issued a protest against 'any government that seeks to apply uniformity to the different provinces.'

In Brittany, demonstrations were all the more violent because resentment had its roots further back in French history, and had been slowly building up during the century; here the nobles immediately declared their support for their parlement. In Rennes, nobles, lawyers and students started demonstrating on 9 May. On the 10th the king's intendant, Molleville, and the military commander, the Comte de Thiard, were stoned by the crowds and had to take refuge in the governor's palace. The nobles sent a deputation to the king.

The most startling events occurred in the province of Dauphiné. When the parlement protested against Lamoignon's decrees it was dissolved, but continued to meet nonetheless. The Duc de Clermont-Tonnerre, who was the commander of the province, served the magistrates with letters of exile. On 7 June, the day fixed for their departure, revolution broke out in Grenoble. Men rushed from their work as the tocsin sounded. It was market-day in a very busy town and, as happened at Pau, the peasants came down from the mountains to swell the numbers of rioters. Clermont-Tonnerre's troops were bombarded with tiles hurled from roof-tops; the fighting was so fierce that the duke gave way and allowed the parlement to reassemble. This was not the end of agitation in Dauphiné, however; a 'central

A riot occurred at Grenoble in June 1788 when the Dauphinois heard that their magistrates had been exiled for protesting against the royal edicts.

committee' was formed under the leadership of lawyers like Mounier and Barnave, and its chief ambition was to restore effective power to the province's Estates. On 21 July, despite the opposition of Clermont-Tonnerre's successor in Grenoble, the Estates of Dauphiné were reconvened at Vizille in the château of the merchant Périer, commonly known as 'Milord Périer' because of his great wealth. There were present 165 nobles, 60 clergy (but no bishops) and 500 deputies from the municipalities, mostly from the communes near Grenoble.

There was one very important difference between events in Dauphiné and those in Béarn and Brittany, a difference that was a sign of things to come: the Third Estate dominated the Vizille assembly both in sheer numbers and in the authority it wielded. The assembly demanded regular meetings of Dauphiné's own provincial Estates, with double representation of the Third Estate; and, for the kingdom as a whole, Estates-General empowered to pass taxation measures. The assembly added that it was prepared to renounce the province's local privileges, if necessary, in order to play its part in a National Assembly. There was therefore no longer any question of aristocratic particularism: the Third Estate had laid its cards on the table, and a truly national revolution was now taking place, the construction of a new society; behind the united front of anti-absolutism which showed itself at Vizille, a powerful force could be detected – the ambition of the bourgeoisie.

In the face of this upsurge of militancy, which united the whole kingdom, Louis XVI made no attempt to take advantage of the divisions that existed below the surface of the movement. He chose – if 'chose' is really the right word – to give way: on 8 August he announced the convening of the Estates-General for 1 May 1789. It was high time, for on 16 August government payments had to be suspended. On the 24th Brienne was dismissed and Louis turned to Necker once more, as if to the saviour of France.

THE RECALL OF NECKER

The man recalled by Louis XVI in 1788 suffered from two great disadvantages: he was both a commoner and a foreigner. The son of a Genevan schoolmaster, Necker arrived in Paris in 1747, became head clerk and then a partner of the Banque Thelusson, and in the process displayed a flair for financial operations. He was very much the child of the Protestant middle class of Geneva, which occupied positions in all the stock exchanges of Europe. Having learned in advance of the signing of the peace treaty of 1763, he had amassed a huge fortune by speculating in the shares of the French East India Company (he made eight million *livres* in eight years). He set up his own bank in Paris in 1765 and became a powerful figure in the city. Not satisfied with this, Necker was consumed by political ambition, for he realised that a political career was the only thing that could bring him social status. He started with serious handicaps: he was, after all, a commoner, a foreigner and a Protestant. His success had been restricted to the world of private banking, and he occupied no official position in the royal administration or the public finances. Luckily for him his wife, the daughter of a Swiss pastor, ran a salon in Paris. At her Friday dinner-parties held in a private house on Rue Michel-le-Comte, in the Marais district, famous writers and scholars gathered in large numbers, and Necker very quickly won himself a reputation that went far beyond finance. He was awarded a prize by the Academy for his *Éloge de Colbert* (1772), a success which brought him double honour by making him a national celebrity and placing him in the monarchic tradition, hostile to the fanatical liberalism of the Physiocrats. He learned to humour the clergy and the nobility, and gratified the spirit of the age with his outspoken philanthropy.

He was appointed assistant to the Controller-General of Finances, and then in June 1777 was made Director-General: the traditional title of Controller-General could not possibly be given to a Protestant, a private banker who had never been in the king's service. For this same reason he was refused admission to the Council. This upstart, who was anxious for people to forget his lowly birth, his religion and his country of origin, was in no position to reorganise the tax structure of France or to 'soak the rich'. The prisoner of his own desire to please, he financed the American War by a series of loans on which he was continually raising interest-rates.

This banking expert made no attempt to attack the political problem, but he did succeed in retaining popularity. In 1781, in a counter-attack against the intrigues of the royal court, which was trying to have him replaced, he published what he claimed was a statement of the royal finances, a faked affair which made no mention of war expenditure and showed a 'surplus' of some ten million *livres*. When he was replaced by Calonne, in 1783, Necker continued to enjoy the confidence of the *rentiers* and the financial world in general, and also managed to keep friends at Versailles. As soon as he returned to power in August 1788 he obtained an advance of eighty-five millions from the treasury. He even loaned two millions from his personal fortune. But, beyond this, he had no more idea how to reform the administration than in 1778. He decided to swim with the tide, abolished the plenary court set up in May 1788, restored the right of registration of royal decrees to the parlements and had Lamoignon dismissed. All that remained now was to wait for the forthcoming assembly of the Estates-General.

But the weather seemed to have its own grudge against the king: the rains and floods of 1787, then drought and, finally, the hailstorms that ravaged the whole of western France on 13 July 1788 combined to produce a catastrophic harvest in the summer of '88. Rural under-production resulted in industrial under-production and unemployment. Private enterprise had already been made vulnerable by the Franco-British trade agreement of 1786, which lowered import tariffs for British goods coming into France; the worst-hit sector was textiles, Britain's industrial prodigy. At the beginning of 1789 there were 12,000 unemployed at Abbeville and nearly 20,000 at Lyons. Intendants all over France were reporting a rapid increase in the number of beggars and vagrants roaming the countryside.

The chief symptom of the economic crisis was, however, the very sudden rise in prices. After the stagnation that seemed to have affected prices since the end of the '70s (cereal prices, at least) they now shot up wildly, and the real earnings of peasants and urban workers, already reduced by unemployment, were depressed even further. Never in the course of the century had prices reached such a peak: in Paris the price of bread doubled, and in some provinces it trebled. Generally, the cost of living doubled, while employment became intermittent, or even ceased altogether. Quite naturally, discontent mounted everywhere. At the end of the winter of 1788–9, which had been severe, trouble broke out all over France.

Not every aspect of this great movement of unrest was new to French history: hit by the food crisis, the people directed their accusations at the king personally, as they had done in earlier times, because they had a naïve trust in the powers of the monarchy (as if the king could even control the weather) and also because they felt that the control of food supplies was the responsibility of whoever ruled the nation. The novel feature of the spring of 1789 was that people were making the economic crisis a political issue. For the time being it mattered little that the demands for economic control from the urban masses were not altogether those of bourgeois liberalism: this was a problem for the future, not the present. The fact of immediate importance was that the whole of the Third Estate appeared to present a united front in opposing seigneurial privilege and the nation's tax system, and in demanding reforms in the structure of the Old Regime. These ideas had been gradually developed by the bourgeois conscience and the downtrodden now had a leader, for the employer was marching with his workers and sharing in their protests. The towns banded together in a common assault on privilege, seeking support from the peasantry and organising the peasant's hatred of the seigneurs into an effective weapon. The economic crisis was channelling all the frustrations of the Third Estate into one mighty torrent.

University students fighting with nobles in the streets of Rennes. Class warfare broke out in many provincial towns during the winter of 1788–9.

Lamoignon had foreseen this when the aristocracy had risen up in protest against his policies: 'The privileged orders,' he said, 'have dared to resist the king; within two months there will be neither parlements, nobility nor clergy.' In fact, two months later there were still parlements, a nobility and a clergy, but they had been left behind by the gathering momentum of the Third Estate's ambitions. What had appeared to be a united front of opposition to absolutism had now broken down. When he convened the Estates-General on 8 August 1788, for May 1789, Louis XVI reverted to a tradition dating from before the development of the principle of absolute monarchy, for the last assembly of the three Estates of the realm had taken place in 1614, during the minority of Louis XIII. In taking this step, he yielded to the converging currents of aristocratic and bourgeois liberalism: the clergy, nobility and the Third Estate were all expecting great things from the forthcoming assembly, but they were not expecting the same things.

In convening the Estates-General Louis XVI had not stated whether the assembly would be conducted according to the traditional forms of the past, with the three social orders represented by exactly the same number of deputies, one vote for each order and separate discussions. The clergy and nobility were alarmed at the king's silence on this matter and at the possibility of some kind of reform that would jeopardise their automatic voting advantage. On 25 September the parlement of Paris demanded that the Estates-General should be 'regularly convoked and composed, according to the forms observed in 1614.'

In October the Notables of 1787, assembled by Necker, refused to countenance any changes in the traditional forms of the Estates-General, and the princes of the blood, with the exception of 'Monsieur' (the eldest of the king's younger brothers), gave the Notables their support in a memorandum to the king.

The break between the privileged orders and the Third Estate was now complete. After its declaration of 25 September the parlement of Paris lost all its former popularity. Now that the Estates-General had at last been convoked, the Third Estate insisted that the example of the Vizille Assembly should be followed, with double representation for itself and voting by heads instead of by orders. In other words, they wanted to be able to dominate the assembly, counting on the help of a number of nobles and some of the lower clergy who were forced to live on miserable incomes.

And so the summer of 1788 can be seen to mark a critical stage in the revolutionary movement: in addition to liberty, the Third Estate was also demanding equality, and hoped to end the structure of society based on the hierarchy of orders. It had won the battle against royal absolutism, and now it turned to oppose the privileged classes. As always, the Third Estate was strong in numbers, but as the eighteenth century drew to a close, it also possessed cohesion, foresight and ideas. It had found its leaders, its slogans and its strategy, and was to form the nucleus of the 'National' party.

THE NATIONAL PARTY: ITS PROGRAMME AND INFLUENCE

The formation of the 'National' or 'Patriot' party was to carry people's imaginations and aspirations far beyond the social boundaries of the old orders, towards the new horizons of a 'nation' of twenty-five million inhabitants for whom reform would bring happiness. The National party, soon to be represented in every town and province of France, consisted largely of the Third Estate and was co-ordinated by a committee of thirty members, known as the Society of Thirty. It also included in its ranks a great many members of the two higher orders: there were priests and nobles who welcomed the concept of 'nation' as implying the end of aristocratic particularism, and who were now eager to look at the future in terms of collective happiness. To this extent the pamphlets printed in thousands by the National party did express a single, coherent body of public opinion.

The commoners who formed the bulk of the party were of various origins. Brissot, the typical gifted provincial, was poor but ambitious and had spent his youth filling in the gaps in his education and trying to overcome the barriers of birth; he was one of a multitude of young men who had had the good luck to belong to the right generation. But there were also men who had been born into well-established middle-class families, men who nevertheless resented aristocratic privilege: Barnave, for instance, the son of an advocate who had his own house in Grenoble, and who was himself a brilliant young lawyer. In spite of his comfortable circumstances, Barnave had a deep sense of frustration, and tried to pinpoint the social causes of his unhappiness: 'Can great men still exist? . . . As soon as a man begins to look around him in the dawning light of his maturing intelligence, he sees nothing but desert. The roads are blocked in all directions. . . .'

The swell of opinion was by now so great that many nobles were already sacrificing some of their traditional privileges: La Fayette, known as the 'American', the Duc de La Rochefoucauld, who had an intense dislike for the royal court, his cousin Liancourt, the liberal philanthropist and agriculturalist admired so much by Arthur Young, and the Duc d'Aiguillon, one of the richest landowners in the kingdom. And yet all these great liberal seigneurs kept their distance, no doubt feeling that their own part in the new movement of ideas was simply a matter of adapting the aristocracy's ruling prerogative to meet the needs of the time. The bourgeois revolution was to find closer allies in two other 'deserters' from the upper orders: Sieyès, the son of a notary of Fréjus and a canon at Chartres Cathedral, and the author of *What is the Third Estate?*; and Mirabeau, the volatile son of a provincial noble, famous for his ugliness, scandalous habits and great talent, who put his name to numerous financial and political publications, though exactly how much he wrote himself and how much was written by his friends in Geneva cannot be known for certain.

It can never be too often repeated that all these men who devoted themselves to the National party, whether nobles or commoners, newly rich or already long-established in their businesses and professions, were above all the children of their century, nourished on the philosophy of Enlightenment, the *philosophie des lumières*. For never had an intellectual programme of such proportions and influence paved the way for social and political upheavals to the extent that the Enlightenment did in eighteenth-century France, even though the final launching of the Revolution and its subsequent ups and downs owed much to sheer circumstance or accident.

The society of the Enlightenment was far from being solely bourgeois. It also embraced sections of the privileged orders, both the idle aristocracy and the royal bureaucracy. As ever increasing importance came to be attached both to the pleasures of art and to things utilitarian, a new culture had begun to blur the old distinctions of order, a culture that was to result in the formation of a new *élite*.

Thus, the politicians of 1789 found themselves embarking on their careers with the backing of a whole intellectual movement. The final crisis of the Old Regime did not take them unawares. They had been preparing for this moment for years, and their remedies had been carefully thought out: 'We have no shortage of ideas,' said Mirabeau to the Constituent Assembly.

AWAITING THE ESTATES-GENERAL

The National or Patriot party was not a centralised political 'party' in the modern sense of the word; it was, in fact, public opinion itself, as represented by the towns and by the many clubs in the towns. Towards the end of 1788 these clubs, which had been closed down several years earlier by the minister Breteuil, began opening their doors once more, and at the same time new clubs sprang into existence. In Paris they were to be found everywhere: the Valois Club, which met in the Palais-Royal under the chairmanship of the Duc d'Orléans and included among its members Condorcet, La Rochefoucauld, Sieyès and Montmorency; nearby, the 'Sieur Massé's Club' where magistrates and military men gathered and which was known at Versailles as the 'Club des Enragés'; the Society of Thirty, to name yet another, was founded in November 1788 by Adrien Duport, a magistrate of the parlement of Paris, and was dominated by the liberal nobility. Some of the clubs had their contacts with the provinces, where agitation was growing as the old municipal spirit, bullied as it had been by the royal bureaucracy, began now to add its own demands to those of the unemployed and the poverty-stricken. Links were gradually forged between one town and another, irrespective of private interests and rivalries: it was fear, and the spirit of rebellion springing from fear, which brought unity to the kingdom of France at this hour.

But Paris was still the centre of the great debate, which now began to spread far beyond the walls of the clubs and their closed membership. Deprived of its power by Louis xiv, the capital was now quick to seize back all its old rights and assume the role that had been prepared for it by the whole evolution of eighteenth-century thought – the role of first city of France. In the six or seven hundred cafés of Paris, the traditional pastimes of gaming and witty conversation made way for political debate. The bohemian parasite who was the hero of Diderot's *Neveu de Rameau* had become a militant.

The new political activity of the cafés was most intense in the very heart of the city, in the enclosure of the Palais-Royal where, from 1781 to 1786, the Duc d'Orléans had been putting up new buildings all round his gardens, with arcades for trading. The only persons not

The Duc d'Orléans was the leading personality in the French masonic movement; he had been Grand Master of the Grand Orient of France since 1773.

allowed into the gardens were soldiers, servants in livery and women in a bonnet or apron. In the evenings the gardens began to look like a public forum with great lords and paid newsmongers mingling freely; in the shade of tall lime-trees the murmurings of intrigue and ambition could be heard, stimulated in particular by the duke's agents, who moved among the throng taking the opportunity to say the right word here and there, upholding the liberalism of their master and denouncing the retrograde attitudes of the royal court.

It is difficult for the historian to ascertain the true significance of the Orleanist conspiracy, and to define the role played by freemasonry in the Revolution: indeed, the two were linked, as the Duc d'Orléans had been Grand Master of the Grand Orient of France since 1773. A whole school of history has even seen in freemasonry the real but secret force behind the Revolution; as far as the major political events of the time are concerned, it simply is not possible to prove such a theory – and there is plenty of evidence to show that the opposite was true. Nonetheless, it can be stated with certainty that masonic lodges, which had been multiplying rapidly in the latter part of the century, did make an important contribution to the forming of public opinion and the National party. The really significant feature of the masonic move-

The secret rites of initiation for membership of a masonic lodge. To the right, a future member lies on the floor covered with a cloth, waiting to be initiated.

ment in France at this time was that it had no ideological unity and no revolutionary fervour. In some parts of the country it was a rationalist, vaguely deist (but not anti-clerical) phenomenon, and this was also true, on the whole, in Paris; in other parts it was a more mystical movement, imbued with the old millenarian ideals, as in Lyons and Strasbourg. But all over France its religious ritual, which had a profound appeal for a Christian country, gave an aura of sanctity to the moral values of the Enlightenment – tolerance, philanthropy and human brotherhood. Freemasonry paved the way for the reformist notions of the privileged orders, rather than a revolution of the masses, and it was one of the sources of strength of the National party.

It should be remembered that, by the end of 1788, the French nation was looking forward to peaceful and progressive evolution rather than revolution. The recall of Necker was regarded as a guarantee of the royal goodwill, and therefore the Swiss financier was anxious to make concessions to the National party: on 27 December, with the consent of the king and Marie-Antoinette, who were not at all reluctant to strike a blow at the privileged orders, he agreed to the doubling of the Third Estate's representation at the forthcoming assembly of the Estates-General. He said nothing, however, about abolishing the old procedure of voting by orders rather than by heads; if the old procedure were retained, then the concession of double representation would be meaningless. As always, Louis XVI's intervention was too late and too hesitant to be effective; he simply hardened the Third Estate in its attitude and at the same time upset the nobility, thereby aggravating the conflict between the National party and the privileged orders. The political temperature was rising. Civil war broke out in Brittany. In the meantime, the Third Estate elaborated more radical programmes of reform: in February 1789, in his celebrated pamphlet *What is the Third Estate?*, Sieyès ruthlessly excluded the nobility from membership of the nation: 'This class has surely alienated itself from the nation by its idleness.'

It remained for the Estates-General to speak.

3

THE THREE REVOLUTIONS
OF SUMMER '89

As the moment approached for the gathering of the Estates-General, the aspirations of the French nation were less ambiguous than at any other stage of the Old Regime: those aspirations were set down in detail in the lists of grievances (cahiers de doléances) which the various electoral districts submitted to their deputies for discussion by the Estates-General. The procedure was this: in each bailiwick (bailliage) or seneschalsy (sénéchaussée) the assemblies of each of the three orders drew up their own lists of grievances which were to be taken by the deputies to the Estates-General; throughout the kingdom, except for Dauphiné and the clergy and nobility of Brittany, every sector of society, down to the smallest rural community and trade corporation, compiled its own list of particular grievances to add to the more general demands of the bailiwick or seneschalsy. Obviously the poverty-stricken peasant and unemployed journeyman were not able to express their grievances personally in the cahiers because they could not write, and the local priest, lawyer or merchant who undertook to put their grievances in writing for them probably toned down the violence of their real feelings. In fact, certain similarities of language can be found in these documents which indicate that 'model' specimens were being set out from Paris to the provincial town and country areas. Yet, there can be no doubt about the genuine character of the cahiers as a whole; each one of them was discussed in detail before being accepted by the local deputy. There is nothing in history to compare with the cahiers as documentary evidence of the wishes of an entire nation: they are, indeed, a unique monument of social literature.

The sheer abundance of this evidence makes it difficult to explain in detail the aspirations of the French nation in the year 1789. From the mass of local and individual grievances aired in the cahiers, the historian must attempt to define the great collective yearnings common to the whole nation. The one overriding desire of all Frenchmen was to have some form of controlled monarchy at the *apex of power: on this everyone was agreed, both traditionally-minded aristocrats and ambitious bourgeoisie. In its hatred of the royal intendants and the 'ministerial despotism' and the Versailles bureaucracy, the Third Estate was at one with the privileged classes: it saw nothing contradictory in the sudden outburst of provincial particularism among the nobility and its own demands for equal rights for the entire nation. On the contrary, the nation, represented by the Estates-General, would provide the kingdom with a liberal, decentralised Constitution that would permanently guarantee the natural rights of individuals as proclaimed by the philosophy of the Enlightenment: liberty, the rights of property, intellectual and religious tolerance, equality in law and control of taxation by assemblies meeting regularly.*

In making such demands the Third Estate was not attacking either the king personally or the monarchy as an institution, for Louis XVI continued to enjoy a popular respect based on religious and filial piety. In fact, in the idealised Constitution proposed by a number of cahiers, *everything depended on a harmonious relationship between king and country. This ideal was most forcibly expressed in the document drawn up by the Third Estate of Paris, whose greatest concern was 'the rights and interests of the nation': legislative power was to belong to the nation conjointly with the king, executive power to the king alone. The bourgeoisie of Paris also anticipated the inevitable ritual that would go with the new Constitution: 'Every year on the anniversary of its receiving royal assent the Constitution will be read out in all churches, courts of justice and schools, to all members of the armed services and on board ship; and this day will be observed as an official holiday in every country ruled by France.'*

Violence played no part in this secular vision of the new society. 'Revolution' was not regarded as a means to an end – the word was simply the expression of the ideal society for which people longed. In the France of 1789, torn apart by hunger riots, the privileged classes and the peasantry together indulged in a great myth of reconciliation: they did not feel that violence was necessary to attain their common purpose. The philosophes *had outlined the features of the new society without troubling to explain just how that society was to be brought into existence. As far as they were concerned, all that was necessary was a general consensus of opinion: this would lead naturally to the creation of a society of human happiness founded on the principles of natural morality and practical usefulness, stripped of all supernatural elements. In the* cahier *drawn up by a little parish in the seneschalsy of Saintes is the following description of this earthly paradise in which man was to become his own end:*

> *People will no longer need to say 'If only the king knew!' Our king, the best of kings and father of a great and wise family, will soon know of everything. All vices will be destroyed. All the great virtues of industriousness, honesty, modesty, honour, patriotism, meekness, friendliness, equality, concord, pity and thrift will prevail and wisdom will rule supreme. The mutual love of princes and subjects will build this happy throne which alone is worthy of the king of France.*

The nation was, then, unanimous in its political thinking, and this was already a revolution in itself. But beneath the surface of unity all the old social tensions of the Old Regime were still apparent, causing divisions where a superficial analysis might suggest there was none: for example, rich peasants and poor peasants were divided over the enclosure of the commons, merchants and masters of corporations over the free movement of labour, bishops and priests over the need to make the Church more democratic, and nobles and clergy over the freedom of the press.

The greatest dividing factor, however, was the age-old barrier of privilege which set the clergy and nobility apart from the rest of the kingdom. The Third Estate not only demanded voting by heads instead of by orders, a reform that would establish its own political supremacy, and fiscal equality, which the majority of the nobility's cahiers *had already accepted in principle: it also sought full equality of rights, including admission to all public offices and military grades and the abolition of seigneurial rights and dues, with or without compensation – in other words, the Third Estate wanted to see the end of privilege in all its forms. The peasants of a village in the bailiwick of Sézanne expressed their hatred of privilege in these terms:*

It is we, the poor, who either freely or by compulsion, serve our king and country, it is we who pay for the cannons, mortars, shells, guns and all the other apparatus of war; it is we who have to bear the burden of accommodating our soldiers without ever being able to hope that our children will one day reach high positions in the army; the door is shut firmly in their faces and they are then told that they are incapable of commanding others; on top of all these burdens we are forced to provide the money for the noble officer's salary and pay for his crosses, ribbons, pensions, governorships and all the other favours heaped upon him.

When the privileged classes were confronted with the Third Estate's demands for a whole new social system based on equality, and not just a new method of government, they were naturally less than sympathetic, as can be seen from the vast majority of their lists of grievances.

The great mass of documentary evidence contained in the cahiers *presents a three-cornered political situation in which the king still held a number of trump cards: though he stood alone against the political liberal revolution demanded by his entire kingdom, he was still the arbiter in the clash of social interests between the nobles and the commoners, with each side anxious to win his support. He had not intervened in the preparation of the elections or in the drawing up of the* cahiers, *but had allowed the kingdom to speak out; he now possessed all the information necessary for a programme of reform.*

But time was running short. Although the cahiers *expressed the wishes of the nation in fairly calm language, it must be remembered that the grave economic and political crisis had sharpened their grievances. The king had very little time left in which to resolve this crisis in accordance with the people's will. Speed was essential for success, and hesitation likely to be fatal.*

66

THE REVOLUTION OF THE DEPUTIES

The royal ruling of 24 January had laid down a complex procedure for the election of deputies to the Estates-General comprising one, two, three or even four stages. The number of stages depended on the size of the particular electorate, and therefore varied from one order to another, and from one part of the country to another; but all male tax-payers over the age of twenty-five had the right to vote. It is impossible to say just how many Frenchmen used their vote, but eventually 1,165 deputies were elected (about 600 representing the Third Estate, and less than 300 each for the nobility and clergy).

Among the clergy, which had been divided by fierce internal conflict, there were only forty-six bishops and these included a number of liberals such as Champion de Cicé of Bordeaux and Talleyrand, who had been appointed to Autun the year before. The rest were of modest status, most of them simple parish priests. Among the nobility the advantages of enthusiasm, popularity and ability weighed heavily in favour of the ninety liberal deputies, who formed a third of the nobility's total representation, and who were dominated by the immensely competent Duport and the illustrious La Fayette. The Third Estate's solid deputation was, in contrast, strikingly uniform in its social and political character: there were no peasants, craftsmen or urban workers, but instead a broad selection of educated and serious-minded middle-class citizens who were at one in hoping to establish the state on a new basis. The deputies from the legal profession, who formed the largest single entity, felt quite at home with the merchants and tradesmen, and the provincials, whose moment of glory had come at last, were on an equal footing with the Parisians: full of the confidence of the times and their recent local successes, men like Mounier and Barnave from Dauphiné, Le Chapelier and Lanjuinais from Brittany, Thouret and Buzot from Normandy, Rabaut Saint-Étienne from Nîmes and Robespierre from Artois had no reason to feel inferior in the presence of their fellow deputy from Paris, Bailly, a member of the French Academy. Yet, as a sign of the influence still retained by the aristocracy the limelight was left for two deserters from the privileged classes: the Abbé Sieyès, elected as the Third Estate's deputy for Paris after his stunning pamphlet published in February – a man with a narrow, doctrinaire mind but strong in his convictions; and the Comte de Mirabeau, who had been rejected by his own order and elected by the Third Estate of Aix-en-Provence, his reputation in shreds but his political ability unlimited.

The Estates-General finally assembled at Versailles on 5 May in the great hall of the Hôtel des Menus-Plaisirs, on the Avenue de Paris. The main problem, which had not been solved in the Council meeting

The king presides at the opening of the Estates-General on 5 May 1789, as Necker delivers his speech on the financial situation.

of 27 December, was voting procedure, which was traditionally by orders and not, as the Third Estate was now demanding, by heads. Louis XVI opened the session with a short speech, mild and conventional in tone, which had obviously been carefully prepared. The Keeper of the Seals, Barentin, followed him and spoke so quietly that nobody could hear him; only the end of his speech was really audible, when Barentin exhorted the Estates to 'reject outright the dangerous innovations which the enemies of the public good would like to combine with the fitting and necessary changes that will lead to regeneration, His Majesty's prime concern.' Next came Necker, only recently the idol of the towns. His speech, which had first been submitted to the king, was so long that most of it had to be read by an assistant (it took three hours to deliver). The speech was a technical analysis of the financial situation, in which a deficit of fifty-six millions was admitted and a loan of eighty millions proposed. Necker might as well have told the deputies that, contrary to the expectations of the entire nation, the king was limiting their mandate to formal approval of a financial expedient. Nothing was said about a Constitution; nothing, or almost nothing, was said about voting by heads (Necker merely hinted that such a procedure might be envisaged in the future, and even then only for certain matters). The king's policy seemed to be to adopt half-measures, by accepting fiscal equality but refusing to go any further.

But it was already too late for financial expedients: the economic crisis had long ceased to be a purely technical problem, and had become the spark which was to ignite a political and national crisis. By refusing to adopt one of two obvious courses the king weakened his own authority: if he had ordered the assembly to divide up for separate discussions he would have had the clergy and nobility on his side, and if he had instructed the three orders to meet in common assembly he would have had the Third Estate on his side. Had he chosen either of these courses he would have stood all the more chance of being obeyed, because no-one as yet had contested the royal exercise of the executive power. But Louis succeeded in depriving himself of this power by his indecision. On 6 May the clergy and nobility undertook to verify the credentials of their members in order that their respective Estates should be formally constituted. The Third Estate refused to follow their example. The Estates-General were now paralysed.

By the beginning of June the Estates-General had still not made any real progress. Time was running short and excitement mounting. The galleries of the great hall of the Hôtel des Menus-Plaisirs were invaded daily by the public, and on 2 June Barentin had written to the king saying: 'The spectators are adding to the heated atmosphere of the Assembly.' The moment had come for bold words and the deputies of the Third Estate were well prepared. The long month of May had enabled them to get to know one another and had welded them into a single political unit; since the end of April the deputies from Brittany had been in the habit of gathering together after sessions and inviting their colleagues from other provinces to their deliberations; in this way a true collective spirit had been born, different talents had been discerned and the leaders of the future had been able to establish their authority: not only Sieyès and Mirabeau, but also men like Bailly, Target, Barnave, Mounier, Rabaut Saint-Étienne, Camus, Malouet and Le Chapelier.

On 10 June, at the initiative of Sieyès, the Third Estate resolved to 'have done with inaction' and invited the deputies of the other two orders to assemble for a joint verification of the credentials of 'all the representatives of the nation': any deputy who did not appear at this assembly would be regarded as an absentee from the Estates-General. The roll-call began on the evening of the 12th, but the Third Estate found itself alone. On the 13th three priests from Poitou made their appearance, and on the 14th and the 16th more came until there were nineteen clerics (including the Abbé Grégoire) sitting with the Commons. When the formalities for verifying credentials had been completed the assembly had to face up to the great problem: what new title was it to confer on itself? Before a suitable name could be chosen the assembly had to decide upon its nature and aims. Despite the cautious disapproval of Mounier and Mirabeau, Sieyès borrowed the term 'National Assembly' from one of his colleagues, and this title was adopted on 17 June after a debate lasting two days. The great act of revolution was accomplished: the Third Estate had destroyed the old political structure of France and created a new authority, independent of the king.

Immediately afterwards, Bailly, who was presiding over the Assembly, called on the deputies to swear a solemn oath of loyalty to the responsibilities which they had just taken upon themselves. On the following day the deputies voted themselves the powers of legislating on taxation, and at the same time promised all creditors of the state 'the protection of the nation's guarantee to honour all debts': this was their way of telling the crowd of *rentiers* who were close at hand that, if bankruptcy was a royal habit, the defence of the investing public was a revolutionary innovation.

France now had a new sovereign authority, an authority which the supporters of the old society could not possibly recognise without taking away the ground from under their own feet: resistance was their only course of action. The revolutionary initiative taken by the Third Estate had naturally deepened the divisions within both the clergy and the nobility. On 19 June the majority of the clergy declared itself to be in favour of reuniting in a common assembly with the Third Estate; eighty liberal nobles also voted in favour. But most of the bishops and by far the greater part of the nobility were more determined than ever to resist; relinquishing their own authority in favour of the royal power, they now turned to the king whom they had for so long despised and discredited. They looked on Louis XVI as their natural protector once again and made haste to Marly, where the king had retired since the death of his eldest son on 4 June and where, in the absence of the liberal-minded ministers who had remained at Versailles, the queen and the royal princes spent their time urging him to take action.

Louis had now to choose between the recommendations of most of his ministers, who were standing out for the rights of the Estates-General, and those of his immediate entourage, who favoured the use of force. Louis inclined towards the views of his queen and the princes, but would do no more than state what form his intervention would take: he announced a special royal session to be held at the Estates-General, originally for 22 June but subsequently postponed until the next day. In the meantime, the great hall of the Hôtel des Menus-Plaisirs was to be closed on the pretext that this was necessary to prepare for the royal session.

On 20 June the deputies of the National Assembly, who had not been told of the closing of the Hôtel des Menus-Plaisirs, found the doors shut when they arrived. Gathering together in the rain on the Avenue de Paris, the deputies decided to seek refuge in the indoor tennis court nearby. This vast, bare room lit by high windows, without seats and with its wooden galleries filled with members of the public, was now the solemn setting for the celebrated oath – the Tennis-Court Oath – drawn up by Target and read out by Bailly:

> The National Assembly, summoned to lay down the Constitution of this realm, to bring about the regeneration of public order and to maintain the true principles of monarchy, considers that nothing must prevent it from continuing its deliberations in whatever place it is compelled to assemble, and that, wherever its members are gathered, there the National Assembly is; this Assembly decrees that all its members will here and now take a solemn oath never to disperse and to continue meeting wherever circumstances allow until the Constitution of this realm has been established on solid foundations; and that, when the aforesaid oath has been sworn, all members will put their individual signatures to this unshakable resolution.

All the deputies present, save one, swore the oath. The revolutionary ideal now bore the seal of a solemn pledge.

The following day, 21 June, was a Sunday. On the 22nd the National Assembly, gathering in the nave of the church of Saint-Louis, welcomed one hundred and fifty members of the clergy who were ready to support the majority decision of 10 June. Everything now depended on the royal session.

One cannot but wonder what was in the king's mind on the morning of 23 June, what secret desires lay behind that silent, apathetic countenance. The historian can only keep to the known facts – and they are few. Three meetings of the royal Council were held, one at Marly on the 19th and the other two at Versailles (the court had returned) on the 21st and 22nd. The meetings were called to make preparations for for the royal session, and on the 19th Necker put forward his plan of reform: with the support of his liberal colleagues Montmorin, Saint-Priest and Bishop La Luzerne, he advocated fiscal equality and the admission of all to public office; he also accepted voting by heads in the constitution of future Estates-General, but not for the time being in any matter concerning seigneurial rights and the privileges of the clergy and nobility. As for the decisions taken by the revolutionary National Assembly, Necker's advice to the king was not to quash them openly, but to announce his programme at the royal session 'without mentioning the deliberations of 17 June'. In the course of a long debate (the meeting of 19 June lasted until nightfall) Barentin, the Keeper of the Seals, criticised Necker's concessions; he objected, not to the equality of taxation, but to the proposals to allow voting by heads at future Estates-General, the admission of commoners to commissions in the army and the refusal to stamp out the revolt of the Third Estate immediately and openly. On Sunday 21 June the king admitted his brothers to the Council and forbade Necker to be present.

Necker refused to attend the royal session on 23 June. The absence of the most popular of the king's ministers disturbed the Third Estate, which had already been upset by the placing of troops around the Hôtel des Menus-Plaisirs and by a humiliating wait at the doors of the great hall. But their bitterest disappointment was caused by the two declarations which Louis had ordered to be read out to the assembly; these two documents are of the greatest historical importance, the final testament of the old monarchical system: for the first and last time in his reign the king laid down clearly the limits within which the French monarchy was prepared to accept reform. Never had the doctrine of Louis xvi and his advisers been so unambiguously expressed. On the day of the royal session this weak-willed king knew what he wanted and what he did not want.

In the two documents the king accepted the right of the Estates-General to authorise taxation and loans, upheld the freedom of the individual and of the press and agreed to the decentralisation of the governmental system; he also assured the assembly that the privileged orders would accept equality of taxation. He said nothing, however, about unrestricted admission to public office, and reserved voting by head for a limited number of problems, explicitly rejecting this procedure for anything which might concern future Estates-General. Most important of all, he refused to consider any modification of the traditional hierarchy of aristocratic society. In other words, the monarchy was prepared to go some of the way to meet the demands of liberalism, but repudiated outright the principle of equality of rights. The only reforms it was willing to accept were those which the aristocracy would accept, and this in itself was enough to discredit the king's role of arbiter in the eyes of the Third Estate.

The Third Estate was all the more resentful because the royal declarations annulled its own resolutions of 17 June, and the final insult came when Louis closed the session with a haughty speech containing veiled threats to dissolve the Estates-General. The order to split up into separate Estates for discussions was given in categorical terms. As soon as the king had left the hall, followed by the nobles and prelates, the young Marquis de Dreux-Brézé, who was master of ceremonies, approached the silent and motionless deputies of the Third Estate and said: 'Gentlemen, you know what the king's intentions are.' In the next few minutes the bourgeois revolution found three stunning formulae for the new era that was dawning. Bailly: 'The nation in assembly cannot receive orders.' Sieyès: 'You are today what you were yesterday.' And Mirabeau: 'We will not move from our seats unless forced by bayonets.' The assembly was in fact insisting on the legitimacy of its own recent resolutions and proceeded to declare the inviolability of its members. Louis took no action against the rebels: it is difficult to say whether at this stage he could have imposed the policy laid down by the Council on 21 June, even had he wanted to do so; however, he made no such attempt. On the 24th the majority of the clergy returned to the National Assembly, over which the

The Comte de Mirabeau, painted by Boze. Though a champion of the bourgeois revolution, Mirabeau advocated a constitutional monarchy in the English tradition.

archbishop of Vienne presided conjointly with Bailly. On the 25th even the nobility's resistance began to break down, and forty-seven of its deputies joined the Assembly, led by Clermont-Tonnerre, La Rochefoucauld, Duport and the Duc d'Orléans. On the 27th Louis himself accepted the *fait accompli* by inviting his 'loyal clergy and nobility' to reassemble with the Third Estate. That evening, Paris was illuminated.

And so the revolution led by deputies of the Third Estate had succeeded. On 7 July the Assembly appointed a Constitutional Committee; ever since those critical days in June the Assembly had been, to all intents and purposes, the Constituent Assembly which it now formally became.

THE URBAN REVOLUTION

Since the end of June 1789 there had been two supposedly 'sovereign' authorities in France: the monarchy, on the one hand, and the National or Constituent Assembly, on the other. The two were by no means

The Comte d'Artois, brother of Louis XVI and a passionate believer in royal absolutism.

incompatible: for, since 27 June, the monarchy had implicitly recognised the existence of the National Assembly; and, even more significant, the Assembly was not intent on substituting its own authority for that of the king, for the bourgeois revolution was not a matter of all or nothing – the bourgeoisie was quite prepared to share power with the king and to govern the nation in harness with the liberal aristocracy.

Much depended therefore on Louis himself. Unfortunately, the manner in which the king made his decisions and put them into effect has always been an enigma. There can be no doubt that the royal court was keen on revenge; the queen, the Comte d'Artois, the Prince de Condé and Prince de Conti, the Prince de Polignac and the Maréchal de Broglie all did what they could to stir the king into action. If indeed there was any kind of serious counter-revolutionary plan being prepared by the court, it was never brought into the open. Necker's explanation seems the most plausible: 'There were all sorts of secret intrigues, and even the king was not aware of all that was going on.' It might have been that the Court was waiting for the right moment to push the king into taking measures which no one had yet dared to suggest to him.

Meanwhile, troops were being concentrated in and around Paris in ever increasing numbers: on 26 June the king issued marching orders to six regiments, and on 1 July to another ten regiments, mostly Swiss and German, after a series of acts of indiscipline by the French Guards. The pretext for these military measures was the maintenance of order in the capital, where people were hungry and frightened; but the National Assembly was worried by the build-up of troops, and on 8 July Mirabeau denounced what appeared to be an attempted counter-revolution; on the following day the Assembly voted in favour of making a formal protest to the king.

The Versailles conspiracy succeeded in forestalling the Assembly: on 11 July, even before all the summoned regiments had arrived in Paris, the king exiled Necker and dismissed his other liberal ministers. The new administration, which had been formed behind the scenes several weeks earlier, was very clearly a counter-revolutionary body. Barentin remained as Keeper of the Seals, Breteuil, a declared aristocrat, was the guiding force behind the movement, and the Maréchal de Broglie became Minister of War. The kingdom of France was on the brink of civil war.

The dismissal of Necker was a very dangerous move, for, since the end of June, Paris had been the scene of constant public meetings and general turbulence. Tempers in the poorer quarters of the centre and the east of the city were being frayed by the rise in the price of bread, and by unemployment, which was aggravated by the flow of poverty-stricken peasants from the rural areas into the capital. On 14 July – a symbolic coincidence – bread cost more than at any other time in the eighteenth century. Moreover, the fear of bankruptcy undermined the confidence of the *rentiers* and of all engaged in business and financial activities of any kind.

The convocation of the Estates-General and the revolution of the Third Estate at that assembly had reawakened in the popular imagination the old millenarian ideal of the vengeance of the poor and the happiness of the oppressed, an ideal that was to permeate revolutionary thinking. Paris was hungry, and the news from Versailles had done nothing to allay the people's deep-rooted suspicions of an 'aristocratic plot'. The city was on its feet, waiting.

There was no effective governing authority in control of Paris. The municipal administration, led by the provost of merchants and four magistrates, was more representative of the king than of the city it was supposed to be governing. As for the royal army, there were in Paris at this time, apart from troops on regular watch, two infantry regiments,

Swiss Guards and French Guards (some three or four thousand men in all). But the king could not rely upon the loyalty of the French Guards: these soldiers were resentful of the harsh treatment they received from their officers and were constantly approached by the citizens of Paris with offers of money and drink; furthermore, they had not escaped the influence of the great awakening of public spirit that had spread all over France – all in all, they seemed more likely to side with the Parisians than with the monarchy. On 30 June a vast mob had opened the gates of the Abbaye prison in Saint-Germain-des-Prés to release a number of French Guards who had been incarcerated for acts of indiscipline. Taking up their case, the National Assembly asked for the king's indulgence. Louis dared not refuse, whereupon the released soldiers returned solemnly to their cells so that they could be officially set free.

In this general crisis of authority, the bourgeoisie of Paris was organising itself. The electoral assemblies which had gathered in the spring of 1789 were still meeting, and a highly important role was now played by the four hundred electors of the second degree, who had themselves been elected by the sixty districts of the city. Since the end of June this body of men had formed a kind of semi-clandestine, semi-tolerated municipal administration at the Hôtel de Ville. They now suggested to the Assembly that a 'national militia' should be formed to keep order in Paris and, if necessary, to protect the Assembly's deputies, but the deputies dared not accept the proposal and adjourned the motion. In this atmosphere of mounting unrest, at about noon on Sunday 12 July, Paris learned of the dismissal of Necker.

For the people of Paris the treatment meted out to Necker was final proof of the existence of an aristocratic conspiracy; it was the sign both of counter-revolution and of national bankruptcy. As news of the events of the past few days filtered through to the capital, the people began to imagine themselves surrounded by the royal troops and expected the city to be bombarded and pillaged at any moment. The Parisians did not rise up in revolt simply to defend the National Assembly and its achievements; their main concern was to save their own lives. Once again the king was managing to rouse the hostility of the greatest possible number of people, as if driven on by some irresistible and destructive force inherent in the very nature of decadent power.

In the afternoon of 12 July public reaction was immediate: it was a fine day and the mob at the Palais-Royal flocked round orators before setting off on a triumphal march through Paris, carrying the busts of Necker and the Duc d'Orléans. At the Place Louis-xv there was a brief clash with the Royal German cavalry. Immediately, the French Guards came out of their barracks to join the fighting. During the night Besenval, who was commander of the royal troops in the capital, moved his men to the Champ-de-Mars and kept them there. The events of Sunday 12 July suggest that the administration that had taken over on 11 July had tried to seize the initiative without first reviewing the resources at its disposal.

In the meantime the mobs set about smashing toll-gates and driving the employees of the hated Farmers General from their offices. They really needed weapons, and therefore, throughout 13 July the Hôtel de Ville was thronged with men demanding to be armed. This was also the day on which the municipal revolution came into the open: the electors of the sixty districts of Paris set up a standing committee, in which they formed a majority, and decided at once to establish a bourgeois' militia, to be composed of eight hundred citizens and to be responsible for maintaining public order. These prosperous middle-class citizens were anxious to take the Parisian revolution in hand in order to prevent it from degenerating into anarchy and the destruction of property. On the night of 13–14 July the whole city was illuminated by order of the committee and the first patrols of the 'new society' could be seen and heard marching round the streets. The National Guard was now in existence.

During that night the people of Paris waited expectantly for the dawn to break; as daylight came large numbers of them went to the Hôtel des Invalides, with the member of the standing committee who had been instructed to claim the weapons promised the previous day by Besenval. Then, with the same purpose of collecting weapons, the mob made for the Bastille. The choice was no doubt made on the spur of the moment. But is it unreasonable to think that at this moment, deep in the hearts of the humiliated populace, there was also a vague feeling that the sombre fortress, with its eight huge gates facing onto the Faubourg Saint-Antoine, stood as a symbol of the enemy? The legendary prison, a monstrous anachronism of architecture, humanity and politics, must surely have played its part in rousing the fury.

The governor of the Bastille, Launay, who had only a small garrison at his command (80 Invalides and 30 Swiss Guards), had evacuated the outer courts and taken up his position behind the moat. He promised a delegation from the Hôtel de Ville that he would not give the order to fire unless he was attacked. But before long the mob had arrived and were swarming into the outer courts and across the first drawbridge into the inner court. Launay then ordered his men to open fire, and a hundred or so of the assailants were killed. The mob regarded this as treachery on the governor's part and screamed their hatred. When the news of Launay's opening fire reached the Hôtel de Ville that afternoon the crowds were provoked to fury, and though the electors tried to mediate, there was little they could do. A band of

On 14 July the French Guards, accompanied by an angry mob, fire on the main drawbridge of the Bastille and then attack the fortress.

citizens and three hundred French Guards, led by a non-commissioned officer called Hulin and a lieutenant of the Queen's Infantry by the name of Élie, then proceeded to drag four cannons, which they had taken from the Hôtel des Invalides that morning, to the Bastille, where they pointed them at the main drawbridge.

Around five o'clock Launay surrendered. Élie accepted his surrender and promised him safe conduct, but there was little hope of persuading the mob to respect this promise: the people felt they had been betrayed and wanted to avenge their dead. As soon as the main drawbridge had been lowered, the attackers poured into the fortress and perpetrated the first of the long series of atrociously bloodthirsty massacres that were to become a normal feature of the Revolution and the counter-revolutionary uprisings of the years ahead. Three officers and three soldiers were killed. Launay was dragged along the *quais* of Paris to the Hôtel de Ville, the mob striking and insulting him all the

A painting by Thévenin, showing the mob threatening to lynch Launay, the governor of the Bastille, in the main courtyard of the fortress. The French Guards decided to take Launay to the Hôtel de Ville, but he was stabbed and beheaded by the mob before reaching the building.

way, and was eventually beheaded on the Place de Grève. Flesselles, the provost of merchants, suffered the same fate. Their heads were stuck on pikes and carried to the Palais-Royal.

Confronted by the 'conquerors of the Bastille', most of whom were from the artisan population of the Faubourg Saint-Antoine, Besenval withdrew his troops to Saint-Cloud. Paris had defeated Versailles.

Louis XVI seemed to have surrendered already. One of the most striking features of 14 July was the absence of any positive reaction on the king's part. The queen and the Comte d'Artois were urging him to flee to Metz under the protection of the troops that remained loyal; his other brother, the Comte de Provence, known as 'Monsieur', and the Maréchal de Broglie were against the idea. Louis said he would stay – in other words, he was admitting defeat. On 15 July he went in person to the Assembly to announce the withdrawal of the royal troops from the city. The deputies applauded their king; now that they had been saved from counter-revolution by the Paris insurrection, they were glad to have obtained the royal co-operation which they considered indispensable for the new political system they hoped to build.

On 16 July Louis recalled Necker and the other ministers dismissed on the 11th. On that same day in Paris, Bailly and La Fayette, appointed respectively mayor and commander of the National Guard, took up their new duties. On the 17th, early in the afternoon, Louis went to Paris, escorted by the National Guard, and was met by a large crowd which gave him a rather cool reception. As he left the Hôtel de Ville, where he had put on the blue and red cockade, the crowd gave Louis an ovation. Paris was acclaiming its penitent king. The American, Thomas Jefferson, who was an eye-witness of the occasion, observed that Louis' act of public reparation was a gesture no monarch had ever before made to his people.

Jefferson was right. The Revolution had won its battle. Already, as the Paris Bourse was welcoming a restoration of financial confidence reflected in a recovery of share prices, the first emigration of aristocrats had taken place: the Comte d'Artois, the Prince de Condé and Prince de Conti, the Maréchal de Broglie, Barentin, Breteuil and the Polignacs had set the precedent on the night of 15–16 July. At Versailles the huge, semi-deserted palace was reduced to a melancholy shadow of its past glories. The north wing, which the Condé family had occupied, was almost empty. The south wing, which had been the scene of all the royal festivities and where the Comte d'Artois and the Polignacs had lived, was closed for ever.

The victory won in Paris was indeed a decisive moment in the Revolution, but it was by no means the only victory of its kind. Almost every town in France followed the example set by the capital, directing the torrent of popular agitation into the most effective channels. The time had now come for the *bourgeoisie* (in the strict etymological sense of 'people of the towns') to assume the role that had been prepared for it by the whole economic and intellectual evolution of the eighteenth century.

The towns had an old score to settle with the centralised royal bureaucracy. Under Louis xiv they had lost what independence they had possessed and since then had been 'governed' by oligarchies which were answerable to the king rather than to the local inhabitants, and which were themselves subject to the tutelage of the royal intendants. The sudden disappearance of the central power in 1789 gave the towns the opportunity to revert to the system of medieval 'communes' with their comparative freedom of administration. The dismissal of Necker, the general unrest and the dangers of civil war meant that the towns simply had to revert to some such system of local government. In a vast kingdom sliding rapidly into anarchy, where the intendants were powerless and the municipal authorities had no troops at their disposal, the bourgeoisie was the only social class capable of taking over the responsibilities of royal power. As news of the events in Paris reached the provinces, a whole new municipal democracy quietly established itself. In many towns the new municipal bodies did not immediately replace the old oligarchies, but were formed as additions to the existing administrative structure, which they gradually supplanted: such was the case at Dijon, Rouen, Nantes, Bordeaux and Lyons. Elsewhere, in towns like Vernon in Normandy, the old municipal authorities showed themselves incapable of dealing with bread and grain riots and had to make way for committees formed by the men of the 'new France'.

Wherever the new municipal councils established themselves, they managed to secure a monopoly of power, for the simple reason that they enjoyed the confidence of the overwhelming body of public opinion. They made themselves more powerful than the royal intendants had ever been by taking responsibility for the administration of justice and the maintenance of public order, in addition to the organisation of food supplies. Following the example of Paris, they set up their own National Guards; weapons had to be obtained at random from the royal depots and arsenals, and often were not available in large enough quantities to arm the hordes of volunteers. In Bordeaux, on 29 July, the local citizens' guard quietly set about arming itself at the garrison of the local military commander, who dared not put up any resistance.

The great liberal programme of decentralisation which had been proclaimed so relentlessly throughout the eighteenth century had now won the day. The victors were not the nobles and their Provincial

Estates, but the bourgeoisie and its 'communes'. In August the towns of France, with authority concentrated in the municipal committees and the National Guards, began to forge links with each other by drawing up mutual-aid pacts and instituting 'federations' of communes. Indeed, as the old system of administrative centralisation broke up, the towns maintained a keen devotion to the ideal of political unity based on the principles laid down by the Revolution. Now that they had thrown off the yoke of bureaucratic and fiscal oppression, they were anxious to make their regained freedom the foundation of a broader national solidarity.

THE PEASANT REVOLUTION

The revolution of the deputies of the Third Estate, consolidated by the revolution in Paris, was now further strengthened by the peaceful municipal revolution achieved by the provincial towns. In a kingdom such as France, where the existence of a multitude of regional markets, the slowness of communications and the survival of old feudal habits already exerted a powerful divisive influence, both the weakness of the central power and the weight of public opinion had had a shattering effect on national unity; the intellectual and political cohesion of the bourgeoisies of Paris and the provinces naturally acted as a strong unifying force in such circumstances. But there was another revolution taking place in France at this time, the revolution of the peasantry, which was of a quite different order: in these new times when people were no longer merely the king's subjects but citizens in their own right, and when the effectiveness of a social force tended to be in direct proportion to its size, the peasants were able to offer the Revolution the invaluable asset of huge numbers: however, they also wanted their share of benefits, a fact which the bourgeois of the towns were inclined to forget.

The peasant revolution had been smouldering since the spring of '89, when the electoral situation and, in particular, the food shortage, had caused the peasants to react violently against payment of seigneurial dues: the *cahiers de doléances* or lists of grievances drawn up on their behalf were almost certainly a much watered-down version of their real feelings. In March the seigneurs of Provence found themselves being attacked in their manors by bands of peasants, and in May similar events occurred in Picardy and Cambrésis. In the environs of Paris and Versailles, where most of the royal hunts took place, game was exterminated and forests devastated. Moreover, the economic crisis was driving hundreds of beggars and vagabonds onto the roads, which meant that new dangers were being added to the traditional insecurity of rural life. In the following year, 1790, when matters had somewhat

improved, the National Assembly's committee for mendicancy calculated the number of destitute inhabitants in the newly-formed departments to be about one-ninth to one-fifth of the total population. If the
situation was as bad as this in 1790, it must have been infinitely worse
in July 1789. The fear of 'brigands', already inborn in the minds of
the peasantry as a heritage from the past, was now intensified by the
very real dangers surrounding the villages of rural France.

The uprisings in the rural areas began in earnest in the second half
of July 1789, at the same time as the more peaceful revolution of the
provincial towns. In some parts the rural revolution took the form of
open peasant revolt – social warfare at its simplest. In the wooded
districts of Normandy, in Hainault, Alsace, Franche-Comté and the
valley of the Saône, armed peasants attacked the local manor or abbey
and gleefully set fire to the seigneurial archives, the title-deeds of their
ancient bondage, as if by destroying them they were ridding themselves
forever of the hated tithe and *champart*. Even the bourgeoisie was not
spared. In Alsace the Jewish minority had to pay dearly for having
been the creditors of the peasants.

The peasant revolution was not everywhere as open as this. In most
regions of France it took a more complex form, which Georges Lefebvre
and other historians have rather curiously dubbed the 'Great Fear'.
News of events in Paris took some time to reach the country areas,
where outmoded methods of communication were made even slower
by the great distances to be travelled. Moreover, the peasant mentality
was deeply anchored in the irrational, and all kinds of fears and terrors
were roused by the precarious economic and social situation. Some
minor local incident was enough to spread panic over the countryside.
Everywhere the peasants imagined they were about to be attacked by
mercenaries hired by a scheming aristocracy or by invading armies
from abroad. As false reports passed from village to village they became
inflated with local fantasies and myths, spreading over valley and
plain; and so the peasants armed themselves and waited for the
imagined onslaught.

The ways in which the 'Great Fear' manifested itself varied greatly
from district to district, and even from one day to another in the same
district. Only in one province, Dauphiné, was the general mood of fear
and panic a direct prelude to open revolt: at the end of July '89, the
peasants in the region stretching between Grenoble and Lyons
gathered together and armed themselves when warned of an imminent
attack by troops from Savoy; when they discovered this to be a false
alarm, the peasants decided that, since they had found no enemy to
fight, they would 'pay a visit to the nobles and the priests who are
supporting them'. The following day local manor-houses were attacked
and pillaged. In most other parts of France, however, peasant revolt

was not directly related to the 'Great Fear' that had spread across the country: it was, on the contrary, a phenomenon quite unrelated to false rumours of an 'aristocratic plot', military aggression by the nobles and foreign invasion. But distinctions of this sort are of interest only to the historian. At the time it mattered little what were the immediate causes of the peasant revolution: by the beginning of August 1789 the peasants were on the alert, armed with guns, scythes and sticks, and angrily demanding their share of the bourgeoisie's victories – something that the bourgeoisie was reluctant to grant them.

THE COLLAPSE OF THE OLD REGIME AND THE DECLARATION OF RIGHTS

The revolution of which the eighteenth century had dreamed was never conceived as a bloody and violent thing, even less as a revolution of the poor: nevertheless, the poor had risen up in arms and were now reducing the old seigneurial system to anarchy. This explosion of violence was a threat not only to the interests of the nobility. The rebellious peasantry made little distinction between the true seigneurs of old France and those members of the bourgeoisie who had purchased seigneuries. In any case, the dividing line between feudal and bourgeois property was not always easily traced: the abolition of seigneurial land-rents or of quit-rents which a commoner had acquired would jeopardise the principle of contract, the very foundation of property-ownership. In fact, the aristocracy was able to protect itself to some extent by establishing a foothold in the world of bourgeois property.

The bourgeois revolutionaries were faced with a difficult choice. They could restore order by force, but this would mean disrupting the Third Estate's united front of 14 July by allowing the new citizens' militias to join up with the royal troops against the peasantry – the bourgeoisie would be putting itself at the mercy of the king. Or they could stop the conflagration by acceding to the peasantry's demands, though this would mean setting about the expropriation of ecclesiastical and aristocratic wealth much sooner and on a much larger scale than they had originally envisaged. By this stage, neither fiscal equality, nor the abolition of the old personal servitude of feudal times was enough to satisfy the peasants.

At first the use of force seemed to be the solution favoured by the deputies of the Third Estate. On 3 August one of the committees of the National Assembly made this report: 'From letters received from the provinces it appears that property of every kind is now exposed to acts of the most appalling vandalism. Taxes and seigneurial dues are simply not being paid any more.' In the evening of 4 August, at the opening session, Target, one of the Third Estate's deputies for Paris, put to the Assembly a motion phrased in uncompromising terms: 'The National Assembly, considering that the violent disturbances breaking out in various provinces are spreading alarm in people's hearts and constitute a most grave threat to the sacred rights of property and personal safety . . . declares that all traditional rents and dues must continue to be paid as in the past until this Assembly orders otherwise.'

During the day of 4 August, however, the majority of deputies had been won over to the alternative course of giving in to the peasantry's demands. On the night of 3–4 August a hundred or so deputies summoned together by the 'Breton Club' decided to seize the initiative at the Assembly by urging the need for concessions. The man appointed to be their spokesman was the Duc d'Aiguillon, one of the richest lords in the kingdom; the choice of d'Aiguillon represented an attempt to maintain the alliance of the Third Estate, the liberal nobility and the lower clergy which had made the decisive events of June possible. But at the Assembly on the 4th, after Target's motion had been read out, the Vicomte de Noailles managed to forestall d'Aiguillon; this younger son of a poor noble family brought to the attention of the Assembly the great swell of popular protest represented by the parish *cahiers*:

The parishes have put forward their demands. What is it that they are demanding? That excises be abolished; that taxes of every kind no longer be farmed out; and that seigneurial rights be either reduced or subject to redemption. For over three months now these parishes have watched their representatives devoting themselves to what we call the common good, to what is indeed the common good; but in their eyes the 'common good' means, above all, what is good for them, all the things they long for so ardently.

When the Vicomte de Noailles had finished, the Duc d'Aiguillon began his speech by attempting to justify the violent acts committed by the peasantry: 'The people are trying to shake off a yoke that has weighed on their shoulders for many centuries; it must be admitted, gentlemen, that this insurrection, though culpable in so far as any form of violence is culpable, can be excused by the sheer misery to which the people have been subjected.' But immediately he added: 'The seigneurs cannot be asked simply to renounce their feudal rights. These rights are their property and the principle of equity requires that no one should have to give up their property without just compensation.' The duke then repeated the suggestions made by the Vicomte de Noailles and proposed a very detailed motion for the Assembly's consideration: fiscal equality, outright abolition of statute labour and personal servitude, and redemption of other feudal rights at a rate of 3.3 per cent. The low rate of interest suggested by d'Aiguillon shows clearly enough that he intended to put the highest possible valuation on the 'capital' to be redeemed.

The all-night session of the Constituent Assembly on 4 August 1789 brought a total repudiation of everything the Old Regime stood for.

The two speeches were given an ovation which set the tone for the mood of general exaltation of that famous night of 4 August. Obviously, the enthusiasm of the deputies was not entirely unselfish: the idea was to convert the old feudal rights into hard bourgeois cash and to maintain interest-rates until the capital had been redeemed. The nobles would retain something of their traditional wealth, while the landowners of the Third Estate had everything to gain from equality of land rights. But what really seized the imaginations of deputies that night was the outright rejection of feudalism, and the Assembly was soon caught up in a frenzy of 'self-renewal'; there was a rush to surrender the privileges of the old social order, as nobles renounced their hunting rights and priests their tithes, as the deputies of Brittany, Burgundy, Dauphiné and Provence gave up their provincial privileges and their Estates, and as the great cities abandoned their old rights of economic and fiscal exemption. At three o'clock in the morning of 5 August the Assembly proclaimed Louis XVI 'the restorer of France's liberties' so that the monarchy could be associated formally with the birth of the new society.

However, the unanimity of the night of 4 August began to crumble in the days that followed, when the Assembly attempted to translate the noble ideals of that great occasion into the practical form of decrees. The debate started on the 5th and continued until the 11th. It was particularly lively when the deputies came to define those seigneurial rights that were not to be subject to redemption and to

86

discuss the abolition of tithes. In reply to Sieyès, who insisted that the tithe was a form of property and therefore must be made subject to redemption, Mirabeau submitted that it was merely a token of the public service with which the Church was entrusted, and could therefore be abolished without indemnification; when Mirabeau won his case, the clergy became the first to lose by the dissolution of the Old Regime.

The final decree of the Assembly, approved on the 11th, began with these words: 'The National Assembly abolishes the feudal regime in its entirety'; in fact, the decree put an end to most, but not quite all, of the features of the old social system: personal privileges were to exist no more, public offices were to be open to all, justice was to be both free and equal for everyone, all surviving forms of personal servitude were to be abolished without indemnity and, finally, ecclesiastical tithes were to be suppressed. Clearly, by advocating that the majority of seigneurial rights and all judicial offices be subject to redemption, the bourgeoisie of the National Assembly was simply substituting its own interests for the old privileges of the seigneurs. But, for the time being at any rate, it mattered little that the peasantry had no means of redeeming its age-old financial burdens: the one achievement of the night of 4 August which remained firmly in the memories of Frenchmen was the death-blow delivered to feudalism.

Having settled the problem of feudalism, the Assembly now resumed the debate begun in July on a Declaration of the Rights of Man and

87

the Citizen. The American Declaration of Rights of 1776 was in everyone's mind. Yet some of the more moderate deputies of the Third Estate had misgivings about the possible social consequences of such a Declaration in France. Malouet expressed their misgivings with lucidity on 1 August:

American society, newly-formed as it is, consists wholly of property-owners already accustomed to the idea of equality who have encountered none of the problems of feudalism on the soil which they are now cultivating. Such men were obviously prepared for the responsibilities of total freedom, since their social background made them perfectly suited for democracy. But we, gentlemen, have as our fellow-citizens a vast multitude of men with no property who depend for their living on security in their work, the maintenance of civil order and constant protection by the state ... It is my belief, gentlemen, that it is essential in a great empire such as ours for men placed by fate in a position of dependence to understand the just limits of natural liberty rather than to hope for an extension of those limits.

Mirabeau shared these bourgeois misgivings, and a group of deputies proposed an alternative declaration of the 'rights and duties of man'. However, at the request of Barnave, the Assembly ignored the doubters and on 4 August, a few hours before the great debate in the evening, resolved to draw up a great charter of liberty. Barnave had dubbed it in advance a 'national catechism': clothing the concept of authority in religious language was a custom which the new order had inherited from the old.

The debate was continued on 12 August. After considering a number of alternative drafts, the Assembly opted for that put forward by the committee presided over by Champion de Cicé, archbishop of Bordeaux. This draft, condensed and given a more radical form in a long discussion during which numerous amendments were made, was to become the celebrated Declaration of the Rights of Man and the Citizen, finally approved by the Assembly on 26 August. Its seventeen short articles, as admirable for the language in which they were expressed as for their intellectual content, did not appear to have been influenced in any way by those who had timidly advocated a cautious approach to the question of civil rights: by defining its objectives and achievements in uncompromising terms the French Revolution had acquired an international stature.

The central theme of the document was the rights of the citizen, and not his 'duties'; in other words, the deputies of the right and right-centre had been defeated. The Declaration was to be a manifesto of freedom; it began by declaring the rights of man to be 'natural and imprescriptible', and these rights were recognised by the Assembly 'in the presence and under the auspices of the Supreme Being': this was a double tribute to eighteenth-century thought – the deism of the *philosophes*, on the one hand, and the naturalism of the Physiocrats, on the other. But what exactly were these rights? Precisely those which the Old Regime, founded on inequality of birth and arbitrary methods of government, had so carefully ignored: the ghost of the old privileged order seemed almost to be hovering behind the abstractions of the Declaration as a permanent memento of the humiliation and insecurity of earlier days.

The first two articles contain the gist of the document. First of all appears the affirmation of the principle of equality, the great achievement of that night of 4 August: 'Men are born and remain free and equal in rights.' Then these rights are defined: liberty, property, personal safety and resistance to oppression. The third article deals with the control of executive power, which the Assembly knew by experience was essential to safeguard the rights it was proclaiming; the king was to be deprived of his ancient sovereignty, which was to pass to the nation: 'No body of men, no individual can exercise authority which does not issue expressly from the will of the nation.' Once again, the left wing of the Assembly had made no concessions: as far as basic principles were concerned the Assembly clearly had no intention of sharing authority with the king. The rest of the text develops the application of these principles: civil and fiscal equality, the freedom of the individual, admission of all to public office, *habeas corpus*, the non-retrospective character of new laws, freedom of opinion, speech and the press, the separation of the powers of the executive, the legislature and the judicature and the guarantee of the rights of private property. Bourgeois individualism now had its charter.

Indeed, France had become the home *par excellence* of civil rights. Not that the new principles belonged peculiarly to her. Like those of modern revolutions, they were the offspring of a great Internationale, the common achievement of the whole of Europe. They had already inspired the American insurgents, and, more recently, the Dutch patriots in their struggle against their *stathouder* and the Belgians in their conflict with Austria. But during the past fifty years the French *philosophes* had taken the lead and now, in its Declaration of Rights, the National Assembly proved it could rise to the level of their thought and style, producing a rare example of collective authorship which did full justice to the individual genius of the writers of the Enlightenment. This great document went far beyond its American model and gave expectant Europe its bible of the new times.

The Assembly had now approved the two fundamental texts of the bourgeois revolution – the decrees of 4–11 August and the Declaration of Rights. But were they immediately enforceable, or did they need the king's signature? The majority of the Assembly considered both the decrees and the Declaration to have issued directly from its own constituent power, and to be therefore in no need of royal sanction. Louis XVI thought otherwise and on 5 August had written to the archbishop of Arles: 'I will never consent to deprive my clergy, my nobility. . . . I will not give my sanction to decrees which would deprive them.'

In the second half of August, as the debate on the Declaration of Rights was drawing to a close, the problem of sovereignty of power caused the first schism within the National or Patriot party. This was an event of the greatest importance since it marked the first of a number of such schisms in the revolutionary camp. After only a few months of experience of revolution, men who in June had led the Estates-General to open revolt, and who had welcomed the events of 14 July, began concentrating their energies on stopping the mechanism they had set in motion. Events were occurring too fast for many of the liberal nobles, priests and moderate men of the Third Estate. As the Assembly set about its task of drawing up a Constitution, these men put forward proposals designed to bring stability to the political

Clermont-Tonnerre, one of the leaders of the Monarchiens. He was later to be killed in the revolt of 10 August 1792.

situation: the king should be granted an absolute veto on decisions made by the legislature, and a hereditary upper house should be created on the model of the British House of Lords. The 'Monarchiens', as they came to be called, broke away from the main body of the National party and regrouped themselves around Mounier, Malouet, Clermont-Tonnerre and Lally-Tollendal; they also gained the support of Necker. Duport, Barnave and Alexandre de Lameth then took control of the Patriot party, which used the Breton Club as its private headquarters; they rejected any form of royal veto and refused, with Sieyès, to consider any modification of the Assembly's sovereignty: if it was the royal sanction that was at issue, they argued, then let the king begin by signing the decree of 11 August and the Declaration of Rights. La Fayette tried in vain to mediate between the two factions: by the end of August the break between Monarchiens and Patriots was beyond repair.

Meanwhile, the liberals of the Palais-Royal were beginning to agitate against 'Monsieur and Madame Veto' and their supporters. The threat of another Parisian revolt brought the various elements of the right wing closer together, and former moderates became extremists. Clermont-Tonnerre and Mounier advised the aristocratic faction and the royal court to consider having the National Assembly moved out of Paris to Soissons or Compiègne, some twenty leagues away. But the king ignored their advice, unable to forget that they had only recently been his enemies. This general attitude of intransigence was paralysing the forces of reaction.

Then, on 2 September, Barnave suggested a compromise: the Patriots were to accept the king's exercise of a suspensive veto effective for a period of four years, in return for the promise of royal sanction for the decrees of 4–11 August. Necker gave his own personal guarantee to the bargain and on 11 September the Assembly approved the suspensive veto, after a motion proposing the institution of a hereditary upper house had been rejected the previous day by eight hundred and forty-nine votes to eighty-nine with over one hundred abstentions. The Monarchien had been crushed. It remained for the king to keep his side of the bargain, by giving the royal sanction to the August decrees so that they could be formally promulgated. The Assembly, its position all the stronger for having conceded the veto, demanded that he do so at once. Louis replied on the 18th; his hostility was concealed in a detailed criticism of the legality of the decrees. On the 21st, when the Assembly repeated their demand, the king indulged in another legal quibble: he agreed to 'publish' the decrees, which he pretended were in need of interpretative legislation, but refused to give them the formal 'promulgation' which alone would make them enforceable. At the same time he ordered the Flanders regiment to come to Versailles from Douai, where it was garrisoned; the regiment arrived on the 25th.

And so, after the first two crises of June and July, Louis now engaged in a third clash with the Constituent Assembly. In his September counter-offensive the king possessed a trump-card he had not held in July: his potential supporters in the Assembly had been swelled by the split within the Patriot party, as the more conservative bourgeois deputies joined the aristocrat party. However, the two groups remained quite distinct, and the king trusted only the latter. Once again, it is not easy to say exactly what Louis wanted and what decisions he made himself at the end of this summer of 1789; one can only be certain of what he did not want – he was refusing to sanction the end of the old aristocratic society, and in order to gain time was resorting to subter-fuge in his dealings with the Assembly. He was issuing a challenge, but did not seem to have any idea how to make it effective. Passive resist-ance of this sort was too feeble to succeed, and at the same time too strong not to need countering; Louis was simply disarming his sup-porters and mobilising his adversaries, just as he had done in July.

This time, however, there could be no illusions about the kind of reaction to be expected from Paris, as agitation had been growing in the capital for several weeks, stimulated by the municipal elections. On 25 July and 1 August, at the request of Bailly, the sixty districts of Paris elected an assembly of one hundred and eighty members repre-senting the Commune and replacing the assembly of electors. On 18 September the new assembly was replaced in its turn by a body of three hundred members charged with the task of drawing up a defini-tive municipal constitution. Elected on a property-qualification suffrage, these Parisian bourgeois included many men of great ability such as Lavoisier and Jussieu and others, like Brissot and Condorcet, who were to play an active part in the various revolutionary assemblies. For the moment, however, these men played only a secondary role: the most significant feature of the municipal elections was the stimulus they gave to local politics, especially in the sixty electoral districts of Paris. Each of the districts tended to establish itself as an autonomous commune with its own local administration, committees and general assemblies. Some of the more revolutionary districts, such as the Premontrés and the Cordeliers, on the hill of Sainte-Geneviève, chal-lenged the authority of the Hôtel de Ville and demanded a referendum, democracy in its most direct form. Many ambitious young Patriots, like Danton at the Cordeliers, served their political apprenticeship in the district assemblies. With their sights fixed on the Constituent Assembly, they passionately denounced the slightest hint of bourgeois moderatism: the 'new men' of the Revolution were already beginning to show themselves.

News travelled quickly from Versailles to the Palais-Royal, not only by being passed around by the members of the public who crammed the galleries of the Assembly and hurled insults at reactionary speakers: since July, many new journals and newspapers had sprung up in the new climate of freedom. Men like Camille Desmoulins, Loustalot and Gorsas never tired of warning the public against the royal court, and the queen in particular, revelling in a kind of libertarian euphoria. Marat, who founded *l'Ami du peuple* in September made himself the champion of the poor and of revolutionary extrem-ism, bitterly attacking Necker, Bailly and La Fayette as accomplices of the aristocrats.

As in July, the political crisis was aggravated by the economic and

Portrait of Jean-Paul Marat by
Garnesay.

social crisis, but now to a much greater extent. The harvest of summer
'89 had been good, but the corn had not been threshed, and the recent
troubles had made the transport of grain even less efficient than before.
The price of bread had not gone down since the spring. Unemployment
was made worse by the emigration of many aristocratic families, who
had dismissed their servants and had at the same time deprived the
makers of luxury articles of their traditional clientele. The unemployed
congregated in the streets, demanding work and better wages. In the
minds of the unhappy populace politics and economics became merged
once again in a common indictment of the 'aristocratic conspiracy'
which was being held responsible for the present misery. To add
further to the suspicions of the Parisians, the Flanders regiment arrived
at Versailles on 23 September.

Until late September, while the angry populace was roused to ever
greater fury by the slightest incident, which it interpreted as the work
of its persecutors at Versailles, the municipal government at the Hôtel
de Ville and the National Guard remained the bastions of law and
order amid the anarchy that had seized Paris. Bailly and, in particular,
La Fayette insisted on maintaining the new principles of legality, and
with the thirty thousand volunteers who had joined the National
Guard since July they were able to keep the situation under control.
But when the Flanders regiment reached Versailles on the 23rd the
National Guard was naturally suspicious: memories of the events of
July were still quite fresh. Why had the king sent for this thousand-
strong regiment, unless he was mistrustful of the new bourgeois
militia? When the municipal authorities put this question, the royal
ministers replied in the vaguest terms. The whole of Paris felt it was in
danger once again and began to talk of plans being made for a royal
counter-revolution – there was even a rumour that the king had fled

93

to Metz. Loustalot described the general mood of Paris at the end of September in *les Révolutions de Paris:* 'The coalition government needs troops at Versailles. It is afraid of citizens armed to fight for freedom. What dire plot is being hatched? We must be on our guard . . . Patriotism no longer has a home; we need a second revolution, and all the preparations are being made.'

It is by no means clear what were these 'preparations' to which Loustalot referred, but it is certainly true that, by the end of September, the Patriot Party, the Versailles deputies, the National Guard and Parisian democracy in general were beginning to think in terms of a second armed revolt to force the king to draw back. La Fayette and Bailly cannot have been unaware of what was in the minds of the Patriots, and did nothing to stop them. Mirabeau had always believed firmly in a strong royal power, but on the other hand was not in the habit of swimming against the tide; even he must by now have taken the measure of the king's character and was probably giving his support to the Orleanist faction which, if it were to succeed, might be the means of reconciling popular opinion to the monarchy.

In this tense situation only a spark was needed to produce the explosion, and this was provided by the royal family, and in particular by the queen. Marie-Antoinette behaved with such imprudence during these last few stormy days that Louis XVI seemed almost wise by comparison, spending his time as usual in hunting. On 1 October the officers of the royal bodyguard gave a dinner for the officers of the Flanders regiment in the handsome opera-hall at Versailles. At the end of the banquet, during which many toasts had been drunk to the royal family, the king and queen, with the dauphin in his mother's arms, appeared in their box. They were given a tremendous acclamation which continued as they returned to their apartments, where the tricolour cockade was then trampled underfoot. In the eyes of the common people, who attached such great importance to symbolism, this outrage was positive proof of an aristocratic conspiracy. Young nations are always the proudest.

THE OCTOBER DAYS

News of the banquet given by the royal bodyguard at Versailles appeared in Gorsas' *Courrier* on 3 October. It had the same effect as the dismissal of Necker in July: unrest turned once more into open revolution. The district assemblies were in permanent session and their delegates swarmed to the Hôtel de Ville. The Cordeliers, seizing on the insult that had been flung at the nation, wanted to make it obligatory to wear the tricolour cockade. All the districts demanded the

A procession of 6,000 angry women, armed with pikes and two cannons, marches to the palace at Versailles.

removal of the Flanders regiment and the granting of royal sanction for the decrees of the Assembly. On Sunday the 4th, the crowds at the Palais-Royal insisted on a march to Versailles. Paris was desperate both for revenge and for food, and the idea of bringing the king back to the capital now began to have immense practical and symbolic appeal as a guarantee against the court and against starvation.

On the following day the revolt gathered momentum. Although the course of events is not altogether clear, the whole affair was far too well organised to have been merely the product of chance. A procession of people from the Faubourg Saint-Antoine and the Halles, formed at the Hôtel de Ville. The procession consisted mainly of women not simply because they were more directly affected by poverty and hunger, but surely also because they must have hoped that they would touch the king's heart by letting him see poverty at its most vulnerable. At the same time, they possibly hoped· to humiliate the queen with a display of feminine solidarity. The procession was led by Maillard, one of the 'conquerors' of the Bastille, and was soon on its way to Versailles, followed at four o'clock in the afternoon by the National Guard led by La Fayette.

At about this time the procession of six thousand women had reached Versailles. Louis, returning hurriedly from a hunt, received them with gentle words and promised to have food supplies sent to Paris. Later that evening, at eight o'clock, he notified Mounier of his acceptance of the August decrees. But when the second troop arrived from Paris

tension mounted again: at eleven o'clock La Fayette presented himself to the king together with two commissaries sent by the Commune, who asked the royal family to come back with them to Paris.
This was the first time such a proposal had been put to the king of
France, but the ensuing drama was much briefer than anybody could
have imagined. La Fayette had positioned his troops around the
palace after coming to an understanding with the officers of the royal
bodyguard. Louis, reassured by the presence of his own soldiers, who
were allowed to remain inside the palace, decided to postpone his
decision until the next day.

While royalty and bourgeoisie slept peacefully inside the palace the
people waited in the streets. Lighting great fires to keep themselves
warm, they sang revolutionary songs as a substitute for sleep and drank
to the health of the Patriot deputies, never forgetting that they had
come to take the king back to Paris. At six o'clock that morning the
inevitable occurred: groups of demonstrators made their way into the
palace courtyard. One of them was killed by the royal guards, who
were compelled to retreat, leaving a number of their fellow-soldiers
dead in the courtyard. The mob chased them up the great staircase
to the queen's apartments. Marie-Antoinette, who had hardly time to
dress, fled to the king's room. Then some National Guards arrived on
the scene, helped the royal guards to defend the entrance to the
queen's rooms, and succeeded in regaining control of the palace.

Roused from his slumber, La Fayette now made his appearance and
managed to save a group of royal guards who had been surrounded by
the mob. But, once again, he was merely the symbol of the people's
victory: from the gilded balcony of the marble courtyard, where he
appeared with a silent and shattered Louis, and Marie-Antoinette,
who held the dauphin in her arms, he soothed the crowd with promises. Shouts of 'To Paris! To Paris!' were heard from below. A
moment later Louis came back onto the balcony: 'My friends,' he
said, 'I shall come to Paris with my wife and children; I entrust my
most precious possessions to the love of my good and faithful subjects.'
And, showing that, though weak and incapable as a king, he nevertheless possessed a keen sense of honour, he added: 'My guards have been
slandered. Their loyalty to the nation and to myself deserves my
people's esteem.' The reaction of the mob was enthusiastic: as had
happened in July, the defeat of the authority of the monarchy had,
paradoxically, restored Louis xvi's personal popularity. The Assembly,
which had regathered at eleven o'clock, decided to follow Louis to
Paris. The vast procession of thirty thousand set off early in the afternoon, and at nightfall, after being received at the Hôtel de Ville, the
king arrived at the Tuileries, a prisoner in his own capital.

4

A YEAR OF PEACE

After the dramatic events of early October, tension slackened a little. Though not much had yet been achieved in the way of reconstruction the most important objectives had been secured: the Revolution had won its battle against the Old Regime. Nobody quite knew what form the new society would take, but there was a general feeling that something irreversible had happened to France. With the decrees of August and the Declaration of Rights, the deputies of what had been the Third Estate had fulfilled their most cherished ambitions, and now that the king had been brought to Paris they felt even more confident.

Everything had happened so quickly. Only five months had elapsed between the meeting of the Estates-General and the imprisonment of Louis XVI in the Tuileries. Those five months were the most fateful in the history of the Revolution and possibly in the whole history of France. The political and social life of the nation had been turned upside down as one decisive event followed another. Time itself seemed to have suffered a violent change of rhythm, and the Old Regime had not prepared men for this change. Certainly, the eighteenth century had been obsessed with the necessity of reforming the old society and had criticised and resisted freely and openly; but the political writers of the period, however brilliant they may have been, were more concerned with ends than with means. Originating as they did from the aristocracy and the bourgeoisie, they devoted their intellectual energies to the strategy of reform rather than to the tactics of revolution. Of course it was their aim to uproot the old order, but they either looked to the king to initiate reforms, or put their trust in the spirit of the age and enlightened opinion: never did they contemplate violence as an instrument with which to achieve their purpose.

In this respect 1789 can be regarded as an inversion of the 1917 revolution in Russia. Lenin and the Bolsheviks planned the practical detail of the Russian Revolution with remarkable skill and foresight, but their vision of the society of the future was full of Utopian illusion: it was Stalin who brought Russia back to reality. In contrast, the French bourgeoisie of 1789 had a much clearer idea of its objectives than the Marxists of 1917. But the bourgeoisie refused to take into account the role which accident and circumstance play in the making of history; it never imagined how painful and bloody the road to revolution was to be.

The bourgeoisie underestimated the Old Regime's powers of resistance. This is not to say that the deputies of the Third Estate, who came to Versailles at the beginning of May, were lacking in boldness: these men, whose ideals had been formed by Montesquieu, Voltaire and the Physiocrats, and who had gathered for the Estates-General at the summons of the king, willingly put aside the purely financial problems which had been the original object of convening the assembly. They had come from their provinces to reform the state and to give it a constitution. Their first debates on the question of joint-discussions by all three orders, and the way in which they arrogated to themselves constituent power and sovereignty, show clearly enough that they knew just what they wanted. They were hoping to attain their ends with the king's co-operation, but Louis XVI immediately adopted the attitude which he was to maintain right up to the guillotine: resistance to any fundamental modification of the society of the Old Regime. On 23 June he indicated how far he was prepared to go: a measure of political liberty and equality of taxation (the latter had already been either requested or accepted by the majority of cahiers *drawn up by the clergy and nobility), but no tampering with the three orders of the social hierarchy. When Louis gave in to 'his' intransigent Third Estate on 27 June, he was in fact yielding to the pressure of events and the weakness of his own character. His dismissal of Necker a few days later was to bring France to the brink of chaos.*

The peaceful revolution led by the lawyers, liberal nobles and priests at the Estates-General had failed – the revolution of Enlightenment, of which the century had dreamed, was being blocked by the king. Some other outlet was bound to present itself. It is tempting for the historian to interpret the upheavals of summer 1789 as a chain of independent events inspired by a common political objective: the Paris uprising and the municipal revolution following the example of the deputies, and the peasant revolt delivering the final blow to the Old Regime. However, to view these events as a conspiracy of evil as the aristocracy did, or as ineluctable necessity as the Patriots did, would be to oversimplify.

There was no single 'Revolution' in the summer of 1789, nor was there simply a succession of interrelated revolutions. In fact there occurred a telescoping of three separate and nearly simultaneous revolutions which completely upset the timetable of the enlightened reformers: the revolution of the deputies at the Estates-General, the urban revolution, and the peasant revolution. Only the first was the result of responsible political thinking applied to the construction of a new society. The other revolutions were a mixture of nostalgia for the past and apocalyptic visions of the future. They owed as much to the old millenarian dreams of the poor as to the ideas of the philosophes. *Above all, they revealed a new aspect of the crisis undermining the Old Regime: the impatience of the populace and the violence to which it was prepared to resort.*

A Year of Peace

The reaction of the National Assembly to the uprisings in Paris and in the countryside was not one of satisfaction with the workings of some preconceived plan, but simply surprise. Nobody had consulted the deputies; Paris had certainly not risen up on their behalf, and the peasants were actually forcing their hand quite openly. In the eyes of the liberals the tax reforms demanded by the urban working classes were not sound economic doctrine and pointed to trouble ahead. Most of these deputies were lawyers, imbued with sophisticated notions of legality and procedure, and to them the bloodthirsty violence of an illiterate and poverty-stricken mob was a painful revelation. But their only hope of success in the face of hostility from both the king and the aristocracy was to embrace wholeheartedly the flood of revolution, so that they could direct its various currents and counter-currents to their own special purpose. They were not really prepared to go much further than they had originally intended in their demands for reform: the August decrees and the Declaration of Rights were straight from the heart of eighteenth-century French thought; but they were quite willing to speed events up a little – the revolts of the urban populace and the peasantry had increased the pace of revolution without as yet affecting its objectives.

Nevertheless, the unforeseen revolution of the masses was of great significance for the future. It had crystallised a popular revolutionary mentality which was not to be deceived or thwarted, and which existed side by side with the enlightened reformist opinion of the bourgeoisie. The Assembly had the power to legislate: but it also had to be obeyed. The peasants, in particular, brought this home to the deputies by insisting on outright abolition of seigneurial rights without indemnity. In both the towns and the country areas these new forces of revolution proved very difficult to control. The National Assembly had no longer to reckon only with the king; it also had to watch popular ambitions. To both right and left it had to resist any attempt to deviate from the course it had set itself, but steering this middle course in the summer of 1789 was no easy thing!

In fact, this course was impracticable. The economic situation was too unstable and anarchy too widespread for the Assembly to be able to restore order without the support of the common people. As early as September the Patriot party was divided over the necessity of popular support, and this was a dilemma that was to continue to confront French politicians in the years to come. The left wing of the Assembly, having learned by the experience of the past few months, deliberately and almost openly sought the backing of Paris, while the 'Monarchiens' (Mounier and his friends) joined the royal camp, though they were not to survive for long as a political force. The triumphant Patriots had at last succeeded in welding together the different revolutionary movements of the summer, but their victory had cost them their unity. Most of them were still anxious to consolidate their achievements by peaceful means, but there were now two unknown quantities involved in the situation: firstly, was Louis XVI likely to be the right kind of king for a constitutional monarchy?; secondly, would the summer revolution and the good harvest be enough to pacify the poorer classes? The Assembly was all-powerful – but it could not control the king's mind, nor public opinion.

99

THE NEW REGIME ESTABLISHES ITSELF IN PARIS

On 6 October 1789 the king and his court had been forced to leave Versailles and take up residence in Paris. In the old palace of the Tuileries, deserted by the monarchy since the time of Louis XIV, Louis XVI undertook his new role of constitutional monarch.

Though the royal household continued to exist, certain changes were made necessary by political and budgetary considerations. On 7 August 1790 the secretariat known officially as the *Maison du Roi* was replaced by the Ministry of the Interior, in which the court administration became a sub-department. From October 1790 the royal expenses came onto the Civil List, approved by the Assembly and administered by an intendant; therefore Louis had to abolish a number of official court positions in April 1791. Since the old royal bodyguard had tried to defend Versailles during the October Days, the king's personal protection was now entrusted to the National Guard. The old royal bodyguard and Swiss Guards were allowed to remain as part of the royal household, but the king had to be careful not to show them too often.

In memoirs written at this period, it is obvious that members of the court made little attempt to conceal their contempt for the men of the new institutions. Louis XVI himself complained of the lack of tact shown by his courtiers, for he feared that their careless talk might be his undoing.

The Constitution, based in theory on the separation of powers, had left the king with control of the executive and, therefore, with the choice of ministers. Until the latter months of 1790, the ministers who had been recalled immediately after the events of 14 July remained in office: Necker as Controller-General of Finances, Saint-Priest at the *Maison du Roi* and then the Ministry of the Interior, Champion de Cicé at the Ministry of Justice, La Tour du Pin at the Ministry of War, La Luzerne at the Navy and Montmorin, whose appointment dated back to 1787, at the Ministry of Foreign Affairs. All of them, except Necker, were nobles with liberal sympathies; nevertheless they all gradually became suspect in the eyes of the Assembly. The failure of the financial measures taken by Necker, who was fiercely opposed by Mirabeau and a whole band of rival bankers, led to his resignation at the beginning of September 1790; his departure aroused no protest, which showed how rapidly hc had lost popularity. The persistent attacks of the Assembly, between October and November, led to the resignation of all the other ministers except Montmorin, who was a member of the Jacobin Club, an ally of Mirabeau and was thought to be a sincere devotee of the Revolution. None of the new ministers enjoyed the complete confidence of the king; they did not even have

The Tuileries from a contemporary map of Paris. The greater part of the palace was destroyed in 1871.

the confidence of the Assembly. Respecting the king too much to impose ministers on him, and fearing him enough not to be suspicious of the men he selected, the Assembly ended by substituting its own supremacy for the theoretical duality of power on which the Constitution was initially based.

The Assembly had followed the king to Paris several days later, on 19 October. It was set up temporarily in the Archbishop's Palace and then on 9 November moved to the Manège, where all France's National Assemblies were to sit until May 1793. The Manège was an old riding-school built at the beginning of the eighteenth century along the Tuileries gardens on Rue Saint-Honoré. Tiers of seats had to be erected hastily. The public in the galleries caused constant chaos by interrupting the speeches of the Constituents with applause or angry shouts. But what could the Assembly do to prevent disorder of this sort? Since July '89 the deputies had realised that public opinion was their only strength.

It is difficult for the modern historian to judge the respective merits of the Assembly's orators. One can only go by the impressions formed by contemporaries, modifying these where possible by reading the speeches. First, Mirabeau – the noble who became the champion of democracy – of whom Chateaubriand wrote: 'When he looked at the people and shook his mane of hair he would hold them transfixed; when he lifted his paw and showed his claws the plebs would run off in a fury.' But neither Barnave, nor Robespierre, nor, on the right wing, speakers like Cazalès, could stir an audience as did the orators of the Gironde in later years. The Constituent Assembly earned its place in French parliamentary history, not by the speeches its deputies made, but by the realism with which it set about its task.

In the France of 1790 there were no political parties in the modern sense of the word. Not that the Constituents were unaware of the existence of the party system – they were indeed quite familiar with the structure of the British House of Commons. However, they had a deep contempt for the very idea of organised parties or factions, which to them were a contradiction of the principles of individualism and personal liberty that were so firmly rooted in the revolutionary and bourgeois mentality. Yet, when any of the major political issues came to be debated, there was inevitably a tendency for deputies to form groups. This tendency was aggravated by the seating arrangements at the Assembly: the terms 'right' and 'left', which were destined to become such a significant part of political vocabulary, derived simply from the positions occupied by the deputies in relation to the president's rostrum.

To the right sat all the opponents of the August decrees. They were known as the 'aristocrats', though the word soon acquired more of a political than a social meaning: side by side with the genuine nobles, whose most outspoken representative was the Vicomte de Mirabeau (Mirabeau-Tonneau), the brother of the more famous count, there were a great many commoners. One of them, the Abbé Maury, conducted all the parliamentary offensives of the right wing. Maury spoke in highly coloured and deliberately 'popular' language, never hesitating to denounce with the crude but effective vigour of the plebeian the evils, real or imaginary, which obsessed him. He belonged to that line of men of humble origins, so peculiar to France, who have devoted themselves heart and soul to the service of tradition because they have felt a profound nostalgia for the past.

Close to the 'aristocrats', but originating directly from the currents of revolution, were the 'Monarchiens'. The manner in which this group formed around Mounier in August and September 1789 has already been described. The 'Monarchiens' wanted the king to have an absolute veto and were opposed to the idea of a single assembly: they were in favour of creating an upper house on the model of the British House of Lords, and consequently became known as the *anglomanes* or 'Englishmen'. The events of the October Days had forced them into the royalist camp. Mounier had retired to his province, Dauphiné, but soon left to join the 'emigration'. Other 'Monarchiens' – Malouet, Lally-Tollendal and Clermont-Tonnerre, for instance – remained in the Assembly, where they continued to act as a small but influential core of resistance. The importance of this faction in the history of French political thought has not been sufficiently stressed: their principal tenet – the supremacy of the nobility controlling a 'liberal-conservative' regime – was to survive in other forms during the nineteenth century.

There were a good number of liberal nobles on the left wing of the Assembly. In fact, they often dominated debates and the Patriot party was proud to count among its ranks some of the greatest names in France: two La Rochefoucauld, Montmorency and Talleyrand-Périgord. The *noblesse d'épée*, which had distinguished itself on the battlefields of the eighteenth century, was represented by La Fayette, Beauharnais and the Lameth brothers. But the real source of strength of the Patriots was the bourgeoisie, which produced the deputies who formed the Assembly's committees and the experts who were to become such an indispensable feature of later regimes, men like Tronchet, Merlin de Douai and Lanjuinais.

There was fierce rivalry for the leadership of the left. Mirabeau's sheer eloquence had made him a natural leader ever since the meeting of the Estates-General in May 1789, but his venality was to be his downfall. By October 1789 he was already trying to oust Necker. The Assembly became suspicious of him and voted an amendment prohibiting deputies from becoming ministers. In May 1790 Mirabeau entered the pay of the royal court; his debts were settled for him and he received a pension of six thousand *livres* per month. This act of treachery, which he made no attempt to conceal, discredited him once and for all. In December 1790 he was overwhelmingly defeated by Robespierre at the Jacobin Club. When he died on 2 April 1791 pamphlets were being sold in the streets giving details of 'the great betrayal by the Comte de Mirabeau'. La Fayette, on the other hand, could have played a much more important role than in fact he did. Commander of the National Guard, surrounded by generals, bankers and journalists, he was a very popular figure in the early months of

1790. But he upset so many people; Mirabeau – whose services he had spurned and who avenged himself by poisoning the minds of the king and queen against him – and the left wing of the Assembly, which accused him of weakness in handling the aristocratic counter-revolution. This left wing, which was in fact the self-styled 'Patriot' party, was as mistrustful of popularity as of venality. It sought its leaders from amongst the finest minds of the eighteenth-century Enlightenment, or at any rate from amongst those who had rallied unreservedly and without self-interest to the regime formed during the summer of 1789. Gradually a 'Triumvirate' gained control of the party: Alexandre de Lameth, a member of the *noblesse d'épée*; Duport, one of the office-holding nobility or *noblesse de robe*, and Barnave, a lawyer. They were jealous of La Fayette, but reluctant to oppose him openly, and hostile towards Mirabeau, whom they considered a counter-revolutionary. They represented the brains behind the Patriot party until the end of 1790.

Political passions extended far beyond the walls of the Manège, and innumerable salons, societies and clubs now sprang up in Paris where deputies and journalists, great ladies of the nobility and little-known members of the liberal professions were able to meet. Chateaubriand described this new phenomenon in these words: 'If I am to depict French society in the years 1789 and 1790 I could not do better than to compare it with the architecture of the time of Louis XII (1498–1515) and François I (1515–47), when the Greek orders were mingled with the Gothic style. . . . In every corner of Paris there were literary gatherings, political societies and places of entertainment; men who were one day to be famous mingled anonymously with the crowds, like the souls waiting by Lethe who were soon to be shown the light.'

The 'aristocrats' or 'Blacks' had to be careful not to publicise their activities too much, and so little is known about their meeting-places. In April 1790 they founded the 'Salon Français' on the Rue Royale. Though it had to disband in May, the Salon Français continued to be a breeding-ground of royalist plots, and in July 1790 was responsible for preparing a plan for the king to escape to Lyons and for plotting an uprising in that city.

The 'Monarchiens' had established themselves in December 1789 at the *Club des Impartiaux* on the Rue de la Michodière. Later, in April 1790, they set up the Monarchien Club, which attracted the hostility of the populace. They also met at the salons of Mme de Tessé and the Princesse d'Hénin, where the Patriots were in the habit of gathering.

The Society of '89, which was founded by Sieyès and soon included all La Fayette's friends among its members, was a comparatively limited gathering: the annual subscription was high and therefore only the nobility or wealthy could meet there. Another important body was the Society of Friends of the Constitution, the origins of which are far from clear. On 30 April 1789 the Breton deputies of the Estates-General had founded a Breton Club at Versailles that was soon opened to Patriot deputies from other provinces, but it was not until December 1789 that the Society was actually formed. It established itself on the Rue Saint-Honoré in an old Dominican monastery and became known as the Jacobin Club ('Jacobin' was the popular name for the Dominican order). Initially the Jacobin Club was simply a 'brains trust' of left-wing deputies, but it soon opened its doors to the prominent revolutionaries of the bourgeoisie. The membership subscription of twenty-four *livres* meant that the poorer classes were excluded from the Club. Its organised debates and political aims – centred on state-control of all authority – made it the natural extension of the National Assembly. Similar societies had been formed in the provinces and became affiliated to the Jacobin Club of Paris. In June 1791 there were some four hundred and fifty such clubs which recognised the mother organisation in the capital. These provincial Jacobin Clubs were to be found in surprisingly dense clusters in some parts: there were ten in the Upper Rhineland, twenty in Vaucluse and fifteen in Puy-de-Dôme. The bourgeois revolution was weaving a spider's web around the Jacobins of Paris.

The new freedom enjoyed by the press led to a proliferation of newspapers and pamphlets: it has been estimated that there existed one hundred and fifty such publications in the year 1791, and even this figure is misleading since it refers largely to the Parisian press. Naturally, many of these newspapers and pamphlets enjoyed only a brief life, and others underwent so many changes that they were often hardly recognisable. However, some of them had a wide circulation, largely owing to the personalities of their respective editors. The majority of new pamphlets and journals came, quite naturally, from the popular press, greatly influenced by Brissot, Loustalot, Desmoulins and Marat.

When the Constituent Assembly had created eighty-three 'departments' to replace the old administrative divisions of France (the *généralités*), and made Paris one of these departments, it had not intended to reduce the capital's political influence. Even if the Assembly had wished to do so it would have failed, since the administration of the Department of Paris – which embraced the communes extending round the city from Le Bourget to Bourg-la-Reine and from Nanterre to Champigny – could never have been truly representative of Parisian opinion.

The political life of Paris was concentrated in three institutions: the Municipality (to be replaced by the revolutionary Paris Commune on 10 August) at the Hôtel de Ville, the sixty districts and the National

Pamphlets and newspapers exerted great political influence after the Declaration of the Rights of Man had proclaimed the freedom of the press.

Guard. The complex relationships between these institutions reflected two major characteristics of Parisian opinion: a preference for direct government (and consequently suspicion of any form of representative government) and a desire for some form of basic administrative unity (hence a reluctance to consider autonomous district government).

Sixty of the three hundred delegates of the municipal assembly formed the city council, which was divided into various sub-departments (police, food supplies, hygiene, etc.). The mayor, Bailly, presided over the council and was assisted by twenty-one administrative officers elected by the assembly who were responsible for settling inter-departmental disputes and appointing employees. The remaining two hundred and forty delegates of the municipal assembly formed a rather ineffective sort of parliament with ill-defined and much-resented powers – little more, in fact, than a glorified watch-committee.

The sixty districts formed the bulwark of Parisian local government. Although their electoral base had been broadened at the end of

August 1789, only citizens paying a direct personal tax (probably under twenty per cent of the city's population) were entitled to vote for delegates to the district assemblies. Yet, through their primary assemblies and through their committees, which had been granted police powers by the decree of 5 October, and by issuing their own decrees, addresses and petitions, the districts made it quite clear that they regarded themselves as the direct representatives of the sovereignty of the people. This explains their mistrustful attitude towards their own delegates in the Municipality; on 11 November the Cordeliers district (its centre was the Odéon quarter) made its delegates swear an oath of obedience to its own directives. The districts also found themselves clashing frequently with some of the old institutions like the Châtelet; the most famous case involved Marat, indicted for having made inflammatory speeches, and Danton, then president of the Cordeliers district, who had openly defended Marat. Unwilling to subordinate themselves wholly to the official Municipality of Paris, the districts were constantly organising joint-meetings of various kinds: one such meeting was the assembly, held in the Archbishop's Palace, which on 1 March 1790 began to work out a plan for municipal administration based on the principle of direct government. When the Constituent Assembly replaced the sixty districts with forty-eight 'Sections' in May 1790, it hoped to put an end to all this agitation, but it only succeeded in shifting the focal point of subversive activity.

The National Guard had been formed as a bourgeois militia in the spring and summer of 1789 to perform two functions: firstly, to protect the National Assembly and the Revolution against any attempt by the monarchy and aristocracy to use force; and secondly, to preserve the new order from the dangers of popular anarchy. It is tempting to think that the second of these objectives took precedence over the first, but in fact this was not so. It is certainly true that La Fayette regarded his National Guard as the bastion of a conservative revolution, but when the mob tried to prevent the king from leaving for Saint-Cloud on 18 April 1791 it was the grenadiers of the National Guard who seized the horses' bridles and stopped the royal carriage from moving on its way; La Fayette found it useless to talk of respect for legality and the freedom of movement to which the king was entitled as first magistrate of the realm – the crowd simply ignored him.

The municipal revolution of July 1789 was not simply a matter of individual towns independently setting up their own new administrations; in the face of the 'aristocratic conspiracy', which popular fears had exaggerated out of all proportion, the men who had undertaken to continue the work begun by the Constituent Assembly found themselves bound by new ties of brotherhood. In the vacuum created by the collapse of the Old Regime, the municipal councils and bourgeois

militias of the provincial towns were anxious to unite, not in submission to some central authority, but in the collective desire 'to be
free together, and no longer to suffer separately'. And so the 'Federation' was born, the first sign of an attempt to begin reconstructing the
foundations of that national unity which successive governments of
revolutionary France tried to achieve without ever being entirely
successful. Early in 1790 this movement began to spread and to change
character: ideology now took priority over national security. The
Federation, which had originally been conceived as a means to an end,
became an end in itself, proof that a nation had been born whose
citizens could not be separated one from another by any form of local
or provincial particularism. The *fédérés* representing Brittany and
Anjou declared in February 1790: 'We solemnly affirm that, being
neither Bretons nor Angevins but Frenchmen and citizens of the same
empire, we renounce all our local and personal privileges and for-
swear them as unconstitutional; we are happy and proud to be free.'
The *fédérés* naturally wished their movement to be crowned with the
approval of Paris, but neither the king nor the Assembly wanted to see
the movement grow: Louis XVI was suspicious of any form of spontaneous revolutionary activity, and the deputies, like all official representatives of the Revolution, were afraid that the movement might get out
of control and give the forces of counter-revolution an excuse for a
show of strength. It was therefore decided, at the suggestion of
Talleyrand, that only the National Guard would be allowed to send
delegates to Paris. A public ceremony was to be held in celebration of
the nation's new unity, and to make the occasion both a commemora-
tion of the past and a symbol for the future, the date chosen was the
anniversary of the fall of the Bastille. The Federation ceremony took
place on 14 July 1790. In the morning the *fédérés* joined up to the
north-east of Paris, between the Porte Saint-Martin and the Bastille,
and then made their way to the Champ-de-Mars. Mme de Staël has
left us a description of the preliminaries and of the ceremony itself:

The national militias were to assemble on the Champ-de-Mars, opposite
the military academy and not far from the Hôtel des Invalides; mounds of
turf for spectators to stand on were built up all round the perimeter of the
vast square. Women standing at the front of the crowd gave a helping hand
to the hordes of volunteers who had come to assist with the preparations for
the ceremony. In front of the military academy and opposite the river,
gardens had been laid out with a tent to accommodate the king, the queen
and the entire court. Eighty-three lances had been fixed into the ground
with the banners of the eighty-three departments fluttering from the top of
each, forming a great circle of which the amphitheatre where the royal
family were to sit formed part. At the other end of the square was an altar at
which M. de Talleyrand, then Bishop of Autun, celebrated Mass. After

Mass M. de La Fayette came up to the altar and swore loyalty to nation, law and king; his presence at the ceremony and the oath he had taken inspired an overwhelming feeling of confidence; the spectators were over-joyed because to them king and liberty seemed completely reconciled. A limited monarchy had always been France's most cherished desire: the Federation ceremony of 1790 was the climax of a great surge of national fervour.

The liberal nobility had an important part to play in the new era For anyone who kept a diary of the times the outstanding personality of 1790 must surely have been La Fayette, the 'Hero of Two Worlds', the noble who had fought in the American War of Independence and who in 1788 demanded that a national assembly be convened; the man who was commander-in-chief of the National Guard and the idol of the crowds. Albert Mathiez borrowed from Marat the title for one of the finest chapters of his *Révolution française*: 'La Fayette, Mayor of the Palace', though Mathiez was quite aware that La Fayette had nothing of Charles Martel about him and that Louis XVI was by no means a sluggard-king.

But La Fayette was an important figure in the Revolution, not only because of his own personal achievements, but also as a symbol: he set an example for all those liberal nobles who broke away from their social background and nearly succeeded in bringing about the pain-less birth of the new society for which the bourgeoisie yearned. A few simple statistics are most significant: of the fifty-four presidents of the Constituent Assembly, thirty-three were nobles. At the Jacobin Club, the presidency was occupied by both commoners and nobles, and among the latter were the Duc d'Aiguillon, Alexandre de Beauharnais and Victor de Broglie. The salons, where Patriot opinion evolved, were naturally frequented by the nobility, and in the departmental and district assemblies respect for the Second Estate of the realm was happily reconciled with commitment to the new society. Indeed, the year 1790 seemed to have avenged the nobility for the loss of its old powers under absolute monarchy and to have brought the promise of a redistribution of political influence as achieved in Great Britain. But this proved to be no more than a dream, and events were shortly to shatter the aspirations of this brilliant pleiad of aristocratic reformers.

THE ACHIEVEMENT OF THE CONSTITUENT ASSEMBLY: A NEW SOCIETY

LIBERTY AND EQUALITY – The events of 14 July 1790 seemed to have restored the brotherhood of all Frenchmen in a great collective expres-sion of 'patriotism'. But the word 'patriot', which had become a much-revered and highly significant part of revolutionary vocabulary, was not being used to refer to the France of old; it stood for a fanatical devotion to the new France of liberation.

The new France was summed up in a single sentence in the Declaration of Rights: 'Men are born and remain free and equal in rights.' Liberty, equality – those were the two words which caused the social repressions of the past to explode into violence. Far from being mere abstractions, they expressed all the frustrations of the old aristocratic society; the nobles were to pay dearly for the success of their liberal campaign, but as yet the egalitarian ambitions of the people were ill-defined and not yet to be greatly feared.

The new 'liberty' was, first and foremost, the negation of all forms of arbitrary power; in other words, it signified the personal liberty of individuals, the *habeas corpus* of English law. On the juridical plane it meant the abolition of the arbitrary authority of the king and his agents, and the end of inquisitorial procedures and the omnipotence of judges: as early as October 1789, the committee concerned with the reform of criminal law had done away with the old custom whereby a defendant was almost automatically assumed to be guilty, by specifying strict legal limits within which citizens could be arrested and ordered to appear before an examining magistrate, and by defining human rights in precise terms. In 1790 two more reforms were made, borrowed from English law: public trial, and the jury of twelve citizens drawn by lot from a list of two hundred names and responsible for deciding the guilt or innocence of the defendant. Henceforth judges simply had to apply the law, which was laid down in the penal code of September 1791; under the terms of this new code, punishments were to be made to fit the crime and all forms of torture, including the pillory and red-hot irons, were abolished.

Secondly, liberty meant freedom of opinion, the freedom of the press and of book-publishing, which were subject to hardly any form of censorship during the entire life of the Constituent Assembly, despite attempts by the Châtelet to prosecute Marat for his hysterical denunciations, and despite a law passed in August 1791 which was never put into effect: in fact, from the summer of 1789 all the organs of political propaganda – newspapers, books and clubs – were relatively free from control. Freedom of opinion also covered freedom of conscience, and in particular, religious conscience. The Protestants had been given religious freedom in 1787. The Declaration of Rights confirmed the principle of freedom of religious conscience, but the Assembly did not dare go further by introducing legislation permitting non-Catholic public worship.

However, the Assembly did tackle the question of human rights. Though the principle of religious toleration had already been given

Portrait of La Fayette, painted by Debucourt.

the force of law, this was not in itself a guarantee of equality of opportunity, the one reform demanded by the Third Estate which it could truly claim as its own special concern. On the night of 4–5 August 1789, decrees were passed abolishing personal privileges, collective tax-exemptions and inequality of land-ownership. On 19 June 1790 titles of nobility were abolished. France was at last becoming an egalitarian society in which men were no longer classified according to birth nor protected by the traditional social structure, but free to build their own futures.

It followed that minority groups should also enjoy equality of rights. Protestants were granted political rights at the end of 1789, and then Talleyrand, the Abbé Grégoire and Mirabeau posed the problem of the Jewish minorities. The Jews of southern France – in the south-west and the Rhone valley – received full citizenship in January 1790. The Jews of Alsace, many of whom had been the peasants' creditors and had suffered from strong local anti-semitism, were not admitted to full citizenship until September 1791, when the Constituent Assembly was going through its final sessions.

The kingdom of France had, in theory at least, become a society of individuals with equal rights. This was the significance of the term 'citizen' to which the revolutionaries attached such great importance, as if they were anxious to obliterate the world of title and rank once and for all; but the use of the term also suggested how fragile and abstract a notion equality was, for the new order that was beginning to take shape was not an idealised brotherly paradise, but a society dominated by the bourgeoisie – in other words, the 'citizens' of the towns. Nevertheless, the new society was genuinely founded on the principle of liberty and began by opening up a whole world of opportunity to men of talent.

INEQUALITY OF CITIZENSHIP – This new egalitarian society had released too many unpredictable forces not to feel the need for some form of safeguard for the future. Naturally enough, its primary concern was political power, the keystone of the social order.

The deputies of the Constituent Assembly had all learnt from the writers of the eighteenth century that an aptitude for governing was something developed by education and independence, and independence meant the possession of property. They knew by experience that intervention by the people in politics tended to lead to excess rather than compromise: the thought of mobs blindly led by demagogues was just as detestable in their eyes as the old hierarchy, in which the people had been subservient to the nobility. This was why the principle of equal political rights or universal suffrage, implicitly contained in the Declaration of Rights, was challenged by the Assembly.

All Frenchmen were equal in law, but not all were to enjoy the status of citizen. And not even all citizens were to have the same rights. 'Active' citizens (those with the right to vote) had to be either French-born or naturalised Frenchmen, domiciled in their canton for at least one year, not in domestic service, and paying taxes equivalent in value to at least three days' work, i.e. two to three *livres* per year. Despite a few isolated protests, the Assembly was generally agreed that all the poorest classes and all domestic servants – in other words, about one-third of the adult male population – should be excluded from 'active' citizenship (non-voting citizens were to be termed 'passive'). However, there were still over four million 'active' citizens, a startling figure compared with the mere two hundred thousand electors of the France of Louis-Philippe (1830–48) fifty years later. These four millions included all the poorer members of the rural population (peasants cultivating their own little plots, small tenant-farmers and day-labourers), with the sole exception of domestics, and the mass of artisans and journeymen in the towns.

But these poorer citizens were admitted only to the primary assemblies; a two-tier electoral system introduced in December 1789 had added further restrictions to those already imposed with regard to tax-paying status: the primary assemblies voted for candidates who then became the 'electors' of the secondary assemblies, electing deputies to the assembly. This meant that there existed two superior classes of citizens: the electors of the secondary assemblies and the candidates eligible for membership of the National Assembly. The electors of the second stage had to be persons paying taxes equivalent to the value of at least ten days' work (seven to ten *livres* per year). This was not a large sum, and so the voters at the primary assemblies had a wide choice of candidates. It was the tax qualification for eligibility for the office of deputy that aroused the most violent disagreement in the Assembly. The 'Monarchiens', who until September 1789 had dominated the Constitutional Committee, wanted to make membership of the Assembly the monopoly of the wealthy landed proprietors, since they considered wealth to be the sole guarantee of patriotism and independence. In September 1789 the new Thouret Committee proved to be less exclusive in its qualification requirements, making eligibility for the office of deputy subject to the possession of some landed property, however small, and the payment of taxes to the value of one silver mark (i.e. about fifty *livres*). When the 'silver mark' clause was finally made law it made allies of many former adversaries on the left and left-centre of the Assembly, bringing together men like Pétion and Mirabeau: many men of talent, but limited financial resources, felt their opportunities were being restricted by the substitution of a money barrier for the old barrier of social rank. The Paris

Jacques-Guillaume Thouret, several times president of the Constituent Assembly. The Revolutionary Tribunal later condemned him to death and he was guillotined on 22 April 1794.

press, the interpreter *par excellence* of political abilities and ambitions, shared Camille Desmoulins' sentiments: 'To show just how absurd this decree is, it is enough to point out that neither Jean-Jacques Rousseau, Corneille nor Mably would have been eligible.'

And so France's new political structure was beginning to take shape, with a very broadly-based electorate and a more limited choice of eligible candidates. The Constituent Assembly was to adjust the balance between electors and candidates towards the end of its mandate in the summer of 1791. After the king's flight to Varennes in June and the Champ-de-Mars massacre in July, the Assembly wanted stronger guarantees against revolutionary disorder and excess, and it also wanted the support of those men of ability who were barred from political office by the silver mark qualification. It therefore decided to impose the electoral 'brake' at the intermediate level, and not at the top: the tax qualification for electors entitled to vote deputies to the Assembly was raised, ranging from fifteen to twenty-five *livres* instead of ten; but henceforth all 'active' citizens were eligible for the office of deputy.

In its modified form the electoral system was broadly democratic. If it excluded from 'active' citizenship all the very poorest people in both town and country and barred them from the secondary assemblies, it did nevertheless open the doors of public life to the petty bourgeoisie. This was no longer government by the notables, but the beginnings of a 'meritocracy'. The system enabled men of greater revolutionary zeal than the deputies of the Constituent Assembly to prepare themselves for the power that was soon to be theirs.

THE NEW RULING CLASS – The two great cries of the Revolution had been local liberties, on the one hand, and national patriotism, on the other. The revolutionaries, anxious to rid France of ministerial despotism by decentralising the administration of the kingdom, had at the same time been determined to establish a new national unity and to strengthen their newly-acquired liberties by creating some form of federal system. The new 'citizens' of France, imbued with these same optimistic and contradictory ideals, were the men primarily responsible for trying to put the programme of decentralisation and unification into effect. It was to them, quite naturally, that the administration of France now fell: the confused pattern of local government under the Old Regime was replaced by a single hierarchy of administrative divisions – the departments, the districts and the municipal councils. At the lowest, strictly local level, the decree of 14 December constituted the municipal councils: like the towns, even the smallest village had its own council, which was elected by its 'active' citizens from those inhabitants whose tax status put them above the first qualification bar (payment of taxes equivalent to ten days' work). Every two years elections were held for the office of mayor, who was the head of the council, and for that of local attorney (*procureur*), who was responsible for the administration of the commune's properties and had a deputy in the larger towns. It was in the larger towns that municipal power really took root and flourished; councils acquired extensive prerogatives and in particular responsibility for maintaining civil order.

At the middle level were the districts, administered by a deliberative general council, a more restricted directory wielding executive power, and a district attorney (*procureur syndic*): persons were elected to all of these positions every four years, by the members of the municipal councils. The same pyramid of power was to be found at the department level: a general council, a directory and an attorney general (*procureur général syndic*). All of these elected bodies, which were invested with police powers and the right of requisition, were answerable to the executive (i.e. the king) only in so far as they were responsible for the application of the laws of the land. They were not hampered by the presence of local representatives of the royal power, for the Constituent Assembly had not wanted to perpetuate the old functions of the hated intendants. The deputies of the Assembly, loyal to the two great principles of revolutionary thought, were determined to unify administrative methods and divisions and at the same time to redistribute the old monolithic power of absolutism among elected bodies and individuals.

The same principles were applied to the reorganisation of the judiciary. Civil cases were handled by an elected justice of the peace in the cantons, and at the district level by a tribunal of five judges, also elected. Criminal cases were divided into three categories: minor offences were handled by the municipal council, more serious offences by the justice of the peace, and felonies by the departmental criminal court; in the criminal courts the guilt or innocence of the defendant was decided by a jury of twelve, drawn from a list of two hundred 'active' citizens. Even prosecution was not left entirely in the hands of the executive, but was divided between the king's commissioner and a public prosecutor elected by the 'active' citizens of each department. At the top of the judicial structure stood a supreme court of appeal composed of judges elected by each of the departmental electoral assemblies. The Constituent Assembly could hardly have demonstrated more clearly its mistrust of the executive and its insistence on the independence of the judiciary; but at the same time it had left all the more important judicial offices open to the men who had served under the Old Regime, for the legal profession had proved a most fruitful recruiting ground for the revolutionaries.

There remained the army, devoted to the principle of hierarchy of birth, which was strengthened further by the edict of 1781 (the 'four quarterings' edict had restricted direct commissions in the army to nobles boasting four noble grandparents). The Constituent Assembly did not dare tamper with the fundamental structure of the army by introducing conscription: the bourgeoisie of the towns abhorred the principle of compulsory military service just as much as the peasantry had detested the old militia. But the Assembly did tackle the problem of commissions and promotions. It had abolished aristocratic privilege in the army on 4 August 1789, and now it abolished venality of office in order to make commissions open to all men of ability. Henceforward commissions and promotion were to be based on seniority and competition, and the king's personal influence was strictly limited. In a Europe constantly threatened with the spectre of war, the Assembly dared not dismiss the aristocrat officers commissioned under the Old Regime in the way it had dismissed intendants and judges. But it was able to break aristocratic monopoly in the army, and all the more easily because the morale of the ordinary soldier was at last beginning to rise from the depths into which it had sunk.

The Assembly's most important military reform was its creation of a new army to stand side by side with the old. The National Guard, which had formed spontaneously in the fateful summer of 1789, was regularly organised in 1791 (only 'active' citizens could become Guards, and officers were elected). These soldiers in their blue uniforms, which were in such striking contrast with the white of the royal troops, were truly the army of the bourgeoisie, the defenders of the new regime. Henceforth army life was open to all, and men like Carnot were able to achieve success without coming up against the old barrier of birth.

Lazare Carnot, member of the Committee of Public Safety during the Terror of 1794–5 and elected to the Directory in 1795.

Indeed, the most significant feature of this part of the Constituent Assembly's work was what might be called a 'careers revolution': the highest offices in public life were now open to all – politics, administration, the law and the army. Young men lucky enough to have been born between 1750 and 1770 found they had almost too many possibilities from which to choose. These 'new men' of France may have been divided among themselves in their view of the future, but they were at one in turning their backs on the past.

THE INEQUALITY OF POWER – The new legislators of the Assembly, realising that the question of sovereignty of power was fundamental to the reorganisation of the administrative system and the liberation of society, were determined to give it priority. Undoubtedly, in the summer of 1789, popular uprisings had been just as responsible for broaching the problem of power as had the legislative activity of the Assembly; but in fact the deputies were already in sympathy with the views of the Parisian populace before they set about drawing up their Constitution. They had made this clear in August 1789 when giving their approval to the following article of the Declaration of Rights: 'The principle of all sovereignty resides essentially in the nation. No body of men, no individual can exercise authority which does not issue expressly from the will of the nation.' After proclaiming the Declaration of Rights, the Assembly had confirmed their support for the opinions of Parisians by rejecting the 'Monarchiens' proposal to set up a hereditary upper house. While repudiating those members of the Constitutional Committee who favoured the British parliamentary system with its House of Lords, the Assembly had decreed its own permanence and inviolability. It had taken on itself the right to initiate and approve legislation. In short, national sovereignty resided first and foremost in the Assembly – of this there could be no doubt.

How then was the Assembly to reconcile its own sovereignty with the legitimate royal power which the Old Regime had bequeathed to France? The existence of royal power and its necessity were not disputed; as yet there were no voices clamouring for its suppression. Yet the monarchy had lost its sacred aura, it had been stripped of its old authority and was now no longer supreme. Louis was simply 'king of the French, by the grace of God and the constitutional law of the state'. He must take an oath of loyalty to the nation and to the law. Despite the token of respect paid by the Assembly to the past and to the 'grace of God', the king who had wielded his authority by divine right was henceforth subject to the sovereignty of the nation. The 'conversion' to which the king had to submit must have been an affront not only to his pride, but to his whole system of religious faith.

The relationship between the two sovereignties of nation and king was clearly not based on any pretence of equality. Louis xvi did eventually secure the right to veto the decrees of the Assembly, but his veto was merely suspensive and in any case difficult to put into effect. He could appoint his own ministers, but they had to be men who were not members of the Assembly, and they were also liable to be summoned at any moment to appear before the legislature. The majority of public officials, who had to be elected, did not come under the executive, which meant that the king now had direct control only over his ambassadors and military leaders. In theory he still kept control of foreign policy, but in practice it was the Assembly that decided matters of war and peace and had the last word on treaties, after the king had put his signature to them.

Such was the fragile political compromise known as the Constitution of 1791, the first French Constitution of modern times. It attempted to disguise the Revolution as the heir of the Old Regime, but in fact its authors made little effort to conceal their mistrust of the king and the old traditions. Louis xvi was now simply the 'first public official' in France, paid and supervised by the nation. The administration of the kingdom, its legislative and judicial powers, were no longer his, but belonged to a bourgeois society which, while proclaiming the contrary, implicitly refused to share its sovereignty with him. Events had occurred too recently for confidence to have been restored between the king and his people; as yet the new regime could be certain only in its suspicions.

CONFLICTING INTERESTS AND COMPROMISE – In the economic field, the means of production had to be freed from old restrictions – monopoly and privilege had to be abolished. The Assembly had tackled the problem on the historic night of 4 August, and the decree published on the 5th declared that 'all the special privileges of provinces, principalities, towns, corporations and associations' no longer operated. Moreover, the Assembly was not slow to translate its words into actions, at least as far as the large organisations were concerned: the deputies had little compunction about demolishing what they regarded as the true strongholds of monopoly and 'unnatural' privilege. In the spring of 1790 they dismantled the huge French East India Company, which Calonne had revived in 1785 and which had opened up the Indian Ocean to ambitious merchants. In the following year French commercial interests in Senegal suffered a similar fate. The old laws governing the mining industry were also reformed: a royal decree of 1744 had given the big companies a monopoly of mining activity, supposedly in the national interest, but the Assembly now insisted on the prior rights of the peasant who happened to own the land where mineral deposits were found. The principles of individualism and private property were fundamental to the new democracy which the Assembly wished to create.

The problem of urban labour was much more complex. The decree of 11 August 1789 had made no mention of trade associations; the memories of the Paris uprising were still fresh in their minds and faced with total economic stagnation, the deputies had not dared to meddle with the small vested interests and traditions of the corporations and guilds. It was not until the spring of 1791 that they plucked up courage to act: a decree published on 2 March suppressed certain types of association, and this was followed by another decree on 14 June prohibiting all professional associations, both employers' and workers': the Le Chapelier law, as it was known, was a rigid application of the liberal principle of individualism, excluding all forms of 'combination' from social life and extending the primacy of the bourgeois principle of contract to the field of labour. It was a sign of the times that not a single voice was raised by the left wing of the Constituent Assembly in protest against the wage-earner's loss of his right to join a trade association.

Economic freedom had quite different implications for the small farmer. The old communal system of agriculture had given the poorest peasants a certain degree of protection; but the rich farmers had been demanding freedom of trade and of prices, the end of local restrictions, freedom of crop-rotation, enclosure of fields and meadowland and the abolition of communal pasturage. After all, the Physiocrats had insisted that these restrictions must be removed to enable agricultural productivity to increase. But this would pave the way for agrarian capitalism: the August decrees had freed the wealthy farmers from the grip of the seigneurs, and now they wanted to be rid of the burden imposed on them by the poverty-stricken mass of the peasantry. The Assembly hesitated, trapped between its own economic theories and the great alliance it had only recently formed with the rural population. In the end it compromised by agreeing to the abolition of price-fixing and to the free rotation of crops, while preserving communal pasturage and other communal rights for the benefit of the really poor peasants. The retention of the old communal rights and the rapid increase in the numbers of small peasant-landowners together enabled the pre-capitalist structure of French agriculture to survive the Assembly's radical reorganisation of the economy.

Reorganising the circulation of wealth did not pose any major social problems, at least not as far as internal trade was concerned. The Assembly managed to satisfy all sections of the nation by authorising the free passage of goods and the free movement of prices and profits. These reforms were obviously of particular advantage to the producers, but the lower orders also had reason to welcome the end of the old protectionist system of Colbert, for the Assembly had done away with all the consumer taxes so hated by the Physiocrats: the detested salt-tax, excises and town-tolls were soon no more than unpleasant memories. But in external trade the deputies of the Assembly, so often accused of being doctrinaire, dared not carry their theories to their logical conclusion – free trade. The Old Regime had showed them the way in 1786 with the Franco–British trade agreement, and again in 1787 when authorisation was given for the export of grain, but the deputies gave way to the old fear of famine which the food crisis of 1789 had just revived. Although the harvest of summer 1790 had been good, the Assembly prohibited the export of cereals; here, at least, the peasantry had been able to impose its will on the bourgeoisie.

How was the Treasury to fill its coffers? The release of the considerable funds provided by sale of Church lands was not enough. It was vital that the ordinary channels of revenue should be strengthened, especially now that responsibility for education and public assistance had passed from the Church to the state. The old fiscal system had been dismantled and was now replaced by a system based on equality, on the rejection of arbitrary methods and on the principle that the only true criteria of wealth were net agricultural income and the revenues of urban property-owners. Revenue was divided into three broad categories: firstly, the land, the most important source of wealth (the only one according to the Physiocrats), where taxes were expected to be of the order of two hundred and forty millions;

secondly, taxes on income and movable property, estimated at sixty millions; and thirdly, a tax on commercial and industrial profits.

Was this the kind of fiscal justice that had been so passionately sought in 1789? Owing to lack of information and a centralised administration, the new tax structure was inevitably, in its initial form, a remodelled version of the old; but, more important than the redistribution of taxes, the procedure for collecting them was radically changed: the authorities now elected for the purpose of tax-collection did not dare to bully free and responsible citizens – in other words, freedom from taxation came to be regarded as one of the rights inherent in the new liberty of the individual. The nation would have to cover its expenses without charging them to the wealth that was being produced, and so the assignat, originally a promissory note, became a bank-note.

Thus, there was much that was makeshift in the economic reforms of 1790. Bourgeois liberalism had to come to terms with small-scale private enterprise in both town and country. Everyone wanted a share of the benefits of the great revolutionary alliance and looked forward to a better life. It must also be remembered that the liberals still imagined aristocratic privilege to be their sole bugbear; confident in the virtues of democracy, they entertained no suspicions about left-wing opinion. In the economic field, as in the juridical and social fields, there had been a common enemy for the revolutionaries to defeat: privilege was now dead and free enterprise born.

5

THE REVOLUTION
BLOWN OFF COURSE

I n July 1790 the crisis seemed to be over and tensions were beginning to slacken. There was good reason to be satisfied with what had been achieved, for order had been restored and food supplies were back to normal; in fact, everything pointed to a period of stability and peace. The Constituent Assembly had now to go about its work of rebuilding France in the quiet atmosphere of its committees; on the ruins of the Old Regime, it was going to construct the France for which the Third Estate had been yearning, a country of opportunity in which talent, fortune and tradition would play their respective roles. To the citizens of France and their elected representatives the Revolution seemed complete.

The drama that took place in the Tuileries two years later, on 10 August 1792, involved much more than the personal destiny of Louis XVI and the fate of the Legislative Assembly. The achievements of the Constituent Assembly were undone at one blow: this time popular revolt opened the way to universal suffrage and the replacement of the monarchy by what was a republic de facto, if not de jure.

Were the events of 10 August 1792 the culmination of some inevitable historical process? According to the extremist right-wing view, as represented by the aristocrats who emigrated in July 1789 and their spiritual descendants, the storming of the Tuileries was simply the natural fruition of the seeds of social disintegration and destruction sown in the early sessions of the Estates-General, in the spring of 1789. In the opinion of the 'Monarchiens', the irreversible mechanism of revolution had been set in motion some three months later, during the 'October Days' when the authorities surrendered for the first time to the rioting mobs. At the other end of the scale there exists a whole tradition of left-wing opinion typified by the Soviet historian Manfred, who interpreted the events of 1792 as an 'irresistible movement of the masses'. Oddly enough, this supposedly materialist historian describes the very period when the bourgeoisie was unable to fulfil its ambitions as the 'ascendant phase of the bourgeois revolution'.

This kind of determinist history can be very misleading. To escape from its snares let us put the problem in very different terms and ask ourselves this question: under what conditions could the regime desired by the Constituent Assembly have survived? Or, better still: what exactly were the historical 'accidents' that led to the failure of the liberal revolution of the eighteenth century, the revolution which the French bourgeoisie was to bring to completion decades later?

The first 'accident' was financial. By undertaking to meet the debts incurred by the Old Regime, adding new commitments to the heavy burdens of the Treasury and abandoning the old detested taxes, the Assembly put itself in the same financially precarious position that had undermined absolutism. The solution it finally adopted, to convert the assignat into a bank-note, was inflationary, and in the long run created new divisions within French society. Inflation hit the middle-class investors in rentes *(government loans) who had always tried to 'live like lords' and now found themselves in even closer sympathy with the aristocratic opposition, and also wage-earners who were finding they could buy less and less with their money. Yet, in their financial policies, the deputies of the Constituent Assembly were quite 'orthodox': they had been able to observe the effects of the century's rising price-curve and thought that a slow, progressive rise in prices would stimulate economic activity. In the short term their thinking was fully justified, for 1790 and 1791 were prosperous years in all the key-sectors of the economy. In the long term they foresaw the advantages which the new state would derive from property and landowning wealth that would owe its very existence to the state. In other words, whereas in 1787 financial problems had dominated policy, they were now being subordinated to political considerations.*

The part played by the emigrés and the effectiveness of counter-revolutionary activities within France must both be seen in their true light. In Turin, where he had been living since September 1789, the Comte d'Artois had set up a kind of 'shadow cabinet'. Calonne, the true inspiration behind this group, was in London. The group had two objectives: to abduct the king and royal family, and to instigate a revolt in those provinces that were alleged to have remained loyal to the monarchy. Both were doomed to failure. An attempt to abduct the king in February 1790 was to cost the unfortunate Marquis de Favras his life. A grand plan for an uprising in south-eastern France combined with an invasion of troops from Piedmont, scheduled to take place in December, ended in fiasco. Without new support the counter-revolution was powerless, though it might still succeed in creating widespread unrest among a population obsessed with fears of some perpetual aristocratic plot. However, the counter-revolution was to receive unexpected and unwitting support from the Constituent Assembly when the deputies approved the Civil Constitution of the Clergy. In the nineteenth century the theocratic and anti-clerical schools spread the idea that there had always been a basic conflict between the Catholic Church and the Revolution, but the men of 1789 were certainly not aware of any such conflict; the deputies of the Assembly, clerics and laymen, were either professing Catholics or Catholic in their education. There was no clash between the old faith of France and the new cult of 'nation'. Yet, under the Old Regime the Church had traditionally been more closely associated with the monarchy than with Rome, and the Revolution had inherited the Caesaro-Papalist tradition; at the same time it had learnt tolerance from the philosophy of Enlightenment. To accept the principle of freedom of conscience meant recognising the rights of the Protestant and Jewish minorities. Now that the royal power had been stripped of its sacred aura, the deputies of the Assembly decided they could afford to imitate the example of the Emperor Joseph II, but the Civil Constitution of the Clergy, which the Assembly approved without consulting Rome, was condemned by the Pope and struck right at the consciences of Frenchmen. There was schism not only within the Church but also among the laity. The counter-revolutionaries found themselves reinforced by large numbers of rebellious priests and their flocks: the Assembly had unwittingly helped to swell the ranks of the opposition.

Less than a year later the revolutionaries were beginning to divide among themselves. These divisions were caused not only by personal ambitions or group rivalries, but also by a change in the general political scene which was reflected in the formation of factions each pleading their own particular interests. In the electoral districts and fraternal societies of Paris the working classes were trying to obtain a hearing for their grievances. Labourers and journeymen, who as 'passive' citizens were excluded from the official arenas of political activity, were not yet able to join in the chorus of protest. But the intelligentsia of the lower bourgeoisie bore a grudge against the silvermark qualification which prevented them from obtaining membership of the Assembly; the privileged classes, which included both the nobility and those bourgeois citizens who had made their own fortunes, suddenly found their political monopoly in jeopardy. The split within the Patriot party, which formed a majority in the Assembly, was rendered complete by the debates on the colonies in May 1791; deputies took sides against one another, some of them joining the 'Friends of the Negroes', others the 'Friends of the Colonists', and the final outcome of the debates was the formation of a 'Tory' party around Barnave and the Lameth brothers. The new 'Tories', whose loyalty was to the spirit of the Declaration of Rights rather than to the letter of the revolutionary manifesto, were anxious to restore stability to political life, and the logical step now was to approach the king. But on 20 June 1791 Louis XVI escaped from the Tuileries and fled from Paris; he was hoping to reach Metz, but got no further than Varennes.

With the flight of the king a myth had been finally destroyed. Louis had always been a reluctant constitutional monarch, but now had at last shown his hand. The flight to Varennes, the arrest, and then the return to a silent Paris were enough to dispel any illusions the people may have had. There was little point in Barnave suggesting to an anxious Assembly that the royal family had been forcibly abducted, nor in Louis himself swearing fidelity to the revised Constitution. The one element vital to any kind of conservative political structure – a king who was both loved and respected by his people – was missing. Neither the

Constituent Assembly nor the Legislative Assembly, which succeeded it on 1 October 1791, could now function as a centre of decision-making. The real sources of power were henceforth to be found in the Jacobin Club, which the moderates had deserted, in the popular press and in the streets of Paris.

France was soon to be involved in war with Austria. The 'Right' had certainly wanted open conflict, and Louis XVI and his queen had high hopes that the defeat of France would leave a frightened nation longing once again for royal protection. Apart from a handful of moderates who gathered round Barnave, both liberal nobles and conservative bourgeois shared La Fayette's opinion that a short military campaign would be enough to bring the political clubs to heel. But the revolutionaries were even more eager to take up arms; Robespierre's opposition to war was an isolated case. For the revolutionaries as a whole, with Brissot and the Girondins as their heroes, was presented the opportunity of advancing their cause dramatically. The revolutionary movement had been under a cloud of unrest and uncertainty for some time; this cloud was soon to be dispersed, and with it vanished the last chance of a peaceful revolution.

The man who showed the greater foresight in the short term was not Robespierre, but Barnave, who had predicted that early defeats inflicted on France would lead to a violent eruption of the masses and the end of the monarchy. With the king suspected of treachery, the generals refusing to fight and the Brissotins hesitating in their allegiance, the people launched a great campaign of self-defence in which 'patriotism' became the key slogan. All those Frenchmen for whom revolution meant both 'nation' and 'equality' united in a common assault on the rich, whom they suspected of betraying their country. The flood of patriotic sentiment epitomised by the Marseillaise, *the storming of the Tuileries, and the proclamation of* la Patrie en danger, *was not just a resurgence of old emotions: it was a second Revolution.*

THE IMMEDIATE PROBLEMS

On its return to Paris, the Assembly had to solve a three-fold financial problem: the Treasury had to be replenished, the Old Regime's debts had to be redeemed, and provisions had to be made for settling the debts which the Assembly had imprudently taken upon itself.

This was not really a budgetary problem. Public expenditure did not appear to have increased greatly: from 731 millions in 1789 it rose only to 822 millions in 1791, and in the meantime the short-term loans effected by Necker had been repaid. The problem lay, not with the budget, but with the Treasury. Resort to old expedients was impossible: by suppressing venality of offices the Assembly had cut off an important source of revenue, since it could no longer count on the advances (*prescriptions*) formerly made to the Treasury by bankers in anticipation of taxes. Neither was it practicable to ask for advances from the Caisse d'Escompte, for in November Necker had to admit that his overdraft was already above twenty-five millions. The new rulers of France had to find money without striking at the foundations of the new social order – the bourgeoisie and its clientele.

The king himself owned much of the land of France: in fact, a great many *cahiers* had demanded that ownership of the royal estates be transferred to the state, but they would not have produced much in the way of revenue. There were also the vast properties owned by the Church and valued at some three thousand million *livres*. It was a bishop, Talleyrand, who actually proposed that ecclesiastical properties be nationalised. The arguments he put forward, however ill-founded juridically and historically, made a direct appeal to lawyers inculcated with the principle of state-control which had been the very essence of royal absolutism. 'The clergy,' said Talleyrand, 'is not a proprietor like other proprietors, since the estates it administers, which it cannot dispose of itself, have been given, not for the personal advantage of individuals, but to enable the clergy to carry out its duties.' Talleyrand's interpretation of the Church's purely managerial control of its lands unleashed a torrent of abuse from the right wing of the clergy. The Abbé Maury vilified the usurers and Jews who were getting ready to grab the donations of the faithful and appealed to the self-interest of bourgeois property-owners: 'Our properties are the guarantee of your own. Today it is we who are being attacked, but make no mistake about it, if we are stripped of our properties it will soon be your turn.' But his protests were in vain: on 2 November 1789 the Assembly transferred ecclesiastical possessions to the state, and these formed by far the larger part of what was henceforth to be known as 'national' property.

The next problem was how to convert the Church's properties into funds. On 19 December an 'extraordinary treasury' was created for the purpose of selling a first slice of ecclesiastical lands to the value of four hundred million *livres*. At the same time a sort of Treasury bond was issued bearing interest at five per cent and of a minimum denomination of five thousand *livres*: this was the assignat in its first form. The bonds were to be backed by the proceeds of the sale of Church lands. However, this first attempt at a solution failed; though the state's immediate creditors had to accept the assignats whether they liked it or not, the general public viewed them with suspicion. Gradually the assignat became a paper-currency note. On 17 April interest was lowered to three per cent and the note became compulsory legal tender. On 29 September the interest on the note was abolished altogether and a fresh issue of over one thousand million *livres* was made. The minimum denomination of assignats was lowered to two hundred *livres* (16 August), then to fifty (8 October) and finally to five (6 May 1791). The consequences of making the assignat a bank-note should not be assessed solely in technical terms. Undoubtedly, by authorising the exchange of these paper-notes against metal currency the Assembly did legalise a system of two separate prices for goods, and this led to a decline in the value of money. The *livre* had already depreciated in the foreign exchange market before the issue of the assignat (it had fallen by nearly ten per cent by October 1789), and now the official value of the assignat at home declined, until by the spring of 1791 it had fallen by about fifteen per cent. Also, even though inflation had given a temporary stimulus to industry and the exchange market, it impoverished those on fixed incomes (wage-earners, salaried employees and investors in state loans).

Until the autumn of 1791, however, there was no serious financial crisis. But the uncertainty of the political scene, and above all, the outbreak of war, caused the depreciation of the *livre*, which had hitherto been only barely perceptible, to develop into galloping inflation. In fact, the nationalisation and sale of Church lands and the issue of the assignat were never intended to be purely fiscal manoeuvres. The Assembly had aimed at creating a strong body of new property-owners wholly committed to the Revolution, and thereby strengthening the alliances of the Third Estate. National property was auctioned by municipal authorities in lots as small as five hundred *livres*, with generous facilities for payment. The peasants and the bourgeois who bought the lands came to identify themselves more closely with the new social order. It is not really surprising that a politician like Jean Jaurès should have been sensitive to this aspect of the Assembly's financial policies: 'The assignat bank-note saved the Revolution.'

The greater part of the clergy and the faithful had openly espoused the cause of patriotism. Neither the decrees of August abolishing the tithe, nor the nationalisation of ecclesiastical lands on 2 November, had any marked effect on relations between Church and state. Sieyès and the Abbé Gregoire did protest, admittedly, but their allegiance was first and foremost to the Revolution. In any case, on 13 April 1790 the state introduced a special budget for the upkeep of the Church and its clergy, which meant that most of the lower clergy would be better off than before. Yet it must be remembered that the Church and clergy were not one and the same thing; though temporal in its organisation, the Church was a mystical body whose head and members were inseparable, and soon a rift began to form between the Church and the new state on two particular issues – religious toleration and the intervention of the temporal power in the spiritual domain.

The Declaration of the Rights of Man had not included any mention of freedom of worship, nor even any specific reference to freedom of conscience. But in affirming that no man was to be challenged on account of his religious opinions, it had been responsible for tolerance becoming a fact of French society, a fact to which nobody had taken exception. When, however, the Assembly granted Protestants (December 1789) and the 'Portuguese' Jews of south-western France (January 1790) the full rights of citizenship, the Church had some misgivings, for the clergy were afraid that tolerance might result in the general secularisation of the kingdom.

Of much greater significance was the claim advanced by jurists to the right of sovereignty of decision-making in matters concerning both the spiritual and the temporal; these jurists had been trained to respect the traditions of Caesaro-Papalism, which is not be confused with clerical Gallicanism. This claim was sometimes voiced in haughty language: 'We certainly have the power to change religion, but we shall not choose to do so' said Camus, who was in fact a defender of the Church. It was a claim that seemed to be borne out by fact. As early as 28 October 1789 the swearing of new monastic vows had been suspended, and on 13 February 1790 vows were prohibited and religious communities dissolved, except for those engaged in charitable works and education. The bishop of Clermont was distressed by what was happening: 'What seems to me to be illegitimate in this exercise of authority is the fact that it is taking upon itself to remove barriers it did not put up in the first place; without seeking the co-operation of the Church it is granting freedom to men whose vows were freely taken.' Barnave was contemptuous of such scruples: 'The fact that the existence of monks is incompatible with the needs of society is in itself enough to justify their suppression.' These two concepts, one based on social usefulness, the other on the primacy of spiritual and eternal values, were clearly irreconcilable.

On 12 July 1790 the Assembly went much further. In decreeing the Civil Constitution of the Clergy it attempted to make Catholic worship part of the general structure of public life. The dioceses were reduced from one hundred and thirty to eighty-three, to coincide with the number of departments. Parish priests and bishops were to be elected by 'active' citizens; candidates for the office of parish priest had to have been in the ministry for five years, and candidates for the office of bishop for fifteen years. All the clergy, who were now paid by the state, would have to take the oath of loyalty to the Constitution. Spiritual investiture was no longer to be dependent on the Pope: priests would be consecrated by their bishops, and bishops by a metropolitan archbishop or another bishop. Catholicism was to remain the state religion.

In itself this reform was quite acceptable to the Church. Indeed, had the Church not supported the equally radical reorganisation which Joseph II had imposed on his states? Apart from the majority of the bishops, who opposed the reform on principle as yet another stage in the social revolution, most of the clergy were ready to agree to the Civil Constitution; in fact, it was on the advice of Champion de Cicé and Boisgelin that Louis XVI countersigned the decree. But the Church insisted on one vital condition: a reform of this kind could not depend on a unilateral decision by the state, but must be approved by a spiritual authority. The Assembly rejected the suggestion of a national synod; even if it had agreed to the idea, it is doubtful whether such a synod would have approved of the Civil Constitution. However Gallican it may have been, the French Church was too closely committed to the spiritual supremacy of the Roman pontiff to agree to initiating a reform which had not received even his tacit approval. Pius VI felt nothing but antipathy towards the innovators of the French Revolution. He was an aristocrat, advised by the French ambassador in Rome, Cardinal de Bernis, who was opposing his country's cause; Pius was upset by what had been happening at Avignon, and in a secret consistory had already condemned the principles of the Declaration of Rights. He made no public pronouncement on the Civil Constitution of the Clergy until 10 March 1791, when he anathematised its contents as flouting 'the most sacred dogmas and the most solemn discipline'.

The Constituent Assembly had not waited for Pius VI's pronouncement. The deputies, responsible as they were for public order, had no intention of allowing uncertainty and unrest to develop, for this would have been playing into the hands of the enemies of the Revolution. Conscious of their mission as the builders of a new world, they resented being obstructed by the old. A decree issued on 27 November 1790 gave priests exercising public office two months in which to swear the oath of loyalty to the Constitution, and therefore to the Civil Constitution of the Clergy incorporated in it. The result was schism. One third of the clerical deputies in the Assembly agreed to take the oath in January 1791. In the country as a whole, however, only seven bishops (three of them *in partibus*) took the oath. Some of them refused on social rather than religious grounds; Dillon, the archbishop of Narbonne, made this witty comment: 'My God, if I had only been a bishop I might have given way like the others, but I am a gentleman.' The majority of bishops, even those committed to the Revolution, were loath to break their own sacred vows of obedience to Rome. Of the lower clergy, it seems that at first about half swore the oath and thereby became 'constitutional' priests; later, when the papal letters of denunciation were published, there were many retractions. As time went by new divisions were to appear. Some priests, who had themselves taken the oath, refused to admit 'intruders' to their churches (the 'intruders' were newly-ordained priests appointed by the 'constitutional' bishops without having received canonical investiture). In

spite of the Assembly's attempt to pacify the clergy by granting freedom of worship to rebellious priests in May 1791, the schism was to
cause a mighty cleavage in people's allegiances. Among the revolutionaries, all rebellious priests and their supporters were suspected of
aristocratisme and counter-revolutionary sympathies. The split in the
clergy had provided counter-revolutionary strategy with a formidable
band of auxiliaries.

It is tempting to think of the counter-revolution as a single, unified
movement. In reality it comprised as many different elements as the
Revolution itself. There was the great tradition of liberal aristocracy
going back to Fénelon and Boulainvilliers; side by side with this were
the traditions of enlightened despotism and pure absolutism. After the
events of summer '89 there had been two 'emigrations'. From Turin,
where he had taken refuge on 15 September 1789, the Comte d'Artois
directed the first emigration, which was political and subversive, under
the guidance of Calonne. The cream of the nobility assisted him,
handing out money in large quantities, speaking its mind openly and
repudiating revolutionary France. Other emigré nobles in the Netherlands, the Rhineland and Switzerland showed no hostility to their
country of origin. It was not until 1791 that the emigrés began to
form anything like a united front. Then all the minor provincial nobles
who had departed from France penniless, out of loyalty to their king,
gathered round the Prince de Condé in Worms and formed a courage-
ous and dignified body of resistance. In Coblenz, where Artois had
settled, the old Versailles nobility resurrected the frivolous and extravagant life of the court, as they had done in Turin. In Coblenz
and Worms the old distinctions of court nobility and provincial
nobility were thus revived, reopening an old feud.

Counter-revolutionary activity within France itself represented a
more serious threat to the new regime in Paris. Throughout 1790 the
Turin Committee was involved in two plots: the king was to be rescued
from the Tuileries, and armed insurrections were to be organised in
certain provinces. Two attempts to rescue Louis xvi had already
failed. On the first occasion (October 1789) a Farmer General named
Augeard conceived a scheme to help the king escape, but was betrayed
by informers. Then the Marquis de Favras, possibly at the instigation
of the Comte de Provence, made a similar attempt the following
December, but was arrested and hanged in February 1790. As for the
insurrections in the provinces, a number of leagues of nobles were
formed, but their conspiracies came to nothing.

It is dangerous here to confuse actual causes with psychology. The
widespread apprehension which had seized France at the time of the
Great Fear had not suddenly vanished in October 1789: throughout
1790, especially in the eastern provinces, the general suspicion of an

Caricature of Louis XVI, dated 2 June 1791, eighteen days before his attempted flight. Since the end of May he had virtually been a prisoner.

'aristocratic conspiracy', to be combined with a foreign military invasion, continued to cause panic among the people, and panic sometimes led to violence. The aristocratic conspiracy was one of the myths which play their own very real part in the making of history. It helped to develop republicanism both in theory and practice.

THE KING'S FLIGHT

The spring of 1791 saw the confrontation between the two sections of the Patriot party. The political rights which the Assembly granted to the freed negroes and mulattoes of Santo Domingo exasperated the right wing, which was also becoming increasingly disturbed by popular agitation, and so a 'Tory' party was formed whose purpose was to end the Revolution, revise the Constitution and gain the co-operation of the king. But, in their attempt to win over the king, Barnave and his friends were to come up against the same obstacle that had thwarted the 'Monarchiens' – the attitude of the royal court.

The king's intentions were never really understood by contemporaries. An attempt was often made to distinguish between Louis' aspirations and those of Marie-Antoinette, but the traditional image of the 'Austrian woman' pulling her weak-willed husband along the tortuous path back to absolutism does not stand up to an analysis of documents. The intentions of both the king and his queen were made clear on 23 June 1789: they were prepared to accept certain limitations of royal absolutism and agreed to the drawing-up of a Constitution, but they refused to abolish social privilege, except in taxation. Liberty, yes; equality, no.

In October 1789 Louis had sent a secret letter to his cousin, the king of Spain, in which he had disowned the decrees which the revolutionaries had compelled him to sign: 'I have chosen Your Majesty, the head of the second branch of our family, as the person to whom I entrust my solemn protests against all the decrees contrary to royal authority to which I have been compelled by force to assent since 15 July of this year. I beg Your Majesty to keep my protest secret until its publication becomes necessary.' What were the circumstances in which Louis envisaged publication? Flight from the Tuileries? The king and queen had both been mistrustful of the activities of the Comte d'Artois. Betraying a sad lack of political foresight, they both kept hoping that the Revolution would end by devouring its own offspring.

If the king and queen had felt this, why in October 1790, without forming any detailed plan of action, did they begin to think of the possibility of fleeing from France? They did so because they had misjudged the duration of the Revolution. Between February and May a number of events occurred which induced Louis to consider an early escape. Firstly, his aunts had emigrated in February, and in doing so aroused the suspicions of the revolutionaries. Then, on 18 April, when Louis tried to leave the Tuileries on his annual visit to Saint-Cloud, the crowds forced him to turn back. Convinced that there now remained only one possibility – flight – and anxious to force the hand of the foreign powers, whose inaction had angered him, the king at last made up his mind on 27 May: the escape was planned for 19 June, but at the last minute it was decided to postpone departure for another twenty-four hours.

Three men were responsible for the operation. The Baron de Breteuil, who had emigrated after the events of 14 July, took it on himself to obtain the compliance of the foreign powers. The Marquis de Bouillé, whose military career had taken him through the Seven Years' War and the American War of Independence, had made his reputation by quashing the army mutinies of August 1790. He was in

During the night of 20–21 June 1791 the king escaped from the Tuileries, but the presence of royal troops along the escape route aroused suspicion; this engraving shows the royal carriage being halted at Varennes.

command of the troops in Lorraine and Trois-Evêchés, and was thus chosen to take responsibility for the military preparations for the planned escape; in December he sent his son to explain the escape route to the king, suggesting the square at Montmédy as a convenient place of refuge. The most difficult part of the operation lay in the hands of Alexis de Fersen, who solved the problem of transport by buying a berline from a Russian baronness, Mme de Korff; he also had secret doors made in the royal apartments. The plan was for the royal family to leave the palace through an apartment on the ground-floor, which the Duc de Villequier had occupied before emigrating, and which looked onto both the courtyards at the Tuileries. The door of this apartment was not watched by National Guards, which raises the question of La Fayette's complicity: he may have wanted the queen to escape. Cunning and secrecy were vital for the success of the operation, but both were lacking, for informers had made details of the flight available to the popular press. The actual operation proved a failure because of the incompetence of the men chosen and the vigilance of the local populace of the villages through which the escape route was planned. When the king reached Varennes he was forced to admit his identity and was taken prisoner.

As soon as Paris learned of the king's arrest, the authorities, repre-

At Varennes Louis was forced to stay overnight in the house of a local official and finally admitted his identity (the engraving shows the local people pouring into the room where the king is seated at a table). Although he denied trying to leave the country Louis was arrested and taken back to Paris.

sented by the moderate La Fayette and Bailly, president of the Assembly, ordered Louis to be brought back, saying he had been 'abducted by the enemies of the Revolution'. The royal carriage re-entered Paris on 25 June amid a silent and hostile crowd. When, on 15 July, the Assembly's commission of inquiry proclaimed the king innocent, the Cordeliers Club and the fraternal societies (disowned by the Jacobins and democrat deputies, who insisted on observing legality) planned a great demonstration which took place two days later on the Champ-de-Mars. The National Guard opened fire on the crowd. This was the famous 'Champ-de-Mars Massacre' in which only about fifteen people were killed.

The split between moderates and democrats was now complete. The moderates deserted the Jacobin Club and set up their own club in the Feuillants monastery, also on the Rue Saint-Honoré. The democrats

The National Guards bring the king and queen back to Paris on 25 June 1791.
Large crowds gathered at the Tuileries to watch the return of the royal family.

Brissot (*below*), La Fayette (*below right*) and Louis XVI (*right*) were all in favour of war, though for different reasons; Robespierre (*opposite, right*) and Barnave (*opposite, left*) opposed the idea.

stayed with the Jacobin Club and managed to retain the support of the provincial Jacobin Clubs. The Constitution was revised and on 1 October 1791 the Constituent Assembly made way for a Legislative Assembly, composed entirely of new deputies. There were 260 Feuillants, 136 Jacobins and over 300 uncommitted deputies.

From this moment onwards the major problem facing France was the danger of war. Despite their misgivings at the way revolutionary ideas had spread from France, the sovereigns of Europe, and in particular the Emperor Leopold, had no inclination to intervene in French affairs. Leopold and the king of Prussia had been content to sign the Pillnitz declaration (25 August 1791), in which they expressed in rather vague terms their common desire to protect Louis XVI. In the eyes of the revolutionaries, this was unwarranted interference, but responsibility for the forthcoming conflict must be laid squarely on France. Louis XVI and Marie-Antoinette both wanted war because they were hoping that the defeat of France would be in their own interest. La Fayette and the moderate generals wanted war because they thought that a short, limited campaign would enable them to stabilise the Revolution. And, above all, a whole body of left-wing opinion, with Brissot as its chief spokesman, looked forward to the prospect of a great crusade of liberation. Robespierre, alone among the democrats, was against war; but the most clear-sighted opponents of the war-

policy were Barnave and his Feuillant friends, who foresaw that the war would bring the monarchy tumbling down in ruins and with it the whole liberal-bourgeois society which was so dear to their hearts. Louis XVI rid himself of their influence on 10 March and chose as his Foreign Minister a man eager for conflict – Dumouriez; on 20 April 1792 the Assembly formally approved a declaration of war on 'the king of Bohemia and Hungary'.

FRANCE AT WAR

Never was a war so much a matter of politics and so unmilitary in execution. Dumouriez, the new Foreign Minister, planned a rapid offensive which he hoped would give the people of the Netherlands the opportunity to rise up in revolt. The generals, their eyes turned towards Paris, wanted to concentrate on defence; on the eve of the declaration of war they sent the government a note demanding that internal disorder be suppressed and religious freedom respected. As for Dumouriez' 'offensive', Dillon, who was supposed to take Tournai, retreated as soon as he caught sight of the Austrians, and his troops, thinking they had been betrayed, disbanded and killed their commander. Biron, who had set off to capture Mons, also gave the order to retreat despite his superior numbers. Rochambeau resigned and La Fayette was naïve enough to write to the Minister for War on 6 May saying: 'I cannot conceive how war was ever declared without any kind of preparation.' On 18 May the three army generals decided to cease hostilities.

This was to lead inevitably to charges of treachery from the democrats. In the case of La Fayette, who had been relentlessly denounced by Marat and Robespierre, their suspicions were well-founded: on 17 May 1792 La Fayette had sent an emissary to the enemy, proposing a cessation of hostilities to enable the foreign troops to march on Paris. But the populace directed its attacks chiefly at the royal household and the 'Austrian committee' (meaning Barnave and his friends) which it believed had been advising the king.

For nearly a month Brissot and the government tried to cover up for the generals, but to no avail; the army would not move and officers were deserting in increasing numbers. Then the Brissotins tried to intimidate the king. Taking up the people's denunciation of the 'Austrian committee', they had three decrees approved by the Legislative Assembly: the first (27 May) concerned the rebellious priests who had opposed the Civil Constitution of the Clergy, the second (29 May) dissolved the king's personal guard, and the third (8 June) provided for twenty thousand *fédérés* to be encamped near Paris. But Louis would not be intimidated: he vetoed the first and third of the decrees, dismissed the Girondin government and on 12 June 1792 called on the Feuillants to form a ministry.

THE SWELL OF DISCONTENT

The war had coincided with a grave economic crisis; this time the cause was not a bad harvest, as in 1789, but the decline in the value of the assignat (by June 1792 it had fallen to fifty-seven per cent of its face value), the refusal of the peasants to sell their grain for worthless currency and the sudden rise in price of goods from the colonies, resulting from the slave revolts in Santo Domingo. Apart from the peasant uprisings, which had been endemic since the preceding summer, the year 1792 brought general food riots. On 3 March the mayor of Étampes, Simoneau, was killed by an angry mob demanding that

Of the leading Feuillants
Barnave was the one most
hated by the Jacobins, as
this caricature makes clear.

The monarchists despised
Feuillants and Jacobins
equally, for both parties
represented the same ideal:
the Revolution of 1789.

L'HOMME
DE LA COUR.
1791.

L'HOMME
DU PEUPLE.
1789.

1at.

BARNAVE.
Tantôt froid, tantôt chaud, tantôt blanc, tantôt noir,
A droite maintenant, mais autrefois à gauche,
Je vous disais bonjour, et je vous dis bonsoir.

Danse qu'ils Danseront

1at.

Pas de Deux entre un Jacobin et un Feuillant

prices be fixed. In Paris, on 20 January, the inhabitants of the suburbs had started to force grocers to lower the price of sugar, and on 14 February the washerwomen of the Gobelins pillaged shops.

Now, for the first time, a popular movement was born, independent of other factions, demanding not only economic reform but also genuine political democracy. This was not a proletarian movement, since it was made up not only of wage-earning working men, but also of journeymen, craftsmen and small shopkeepers. These men did not want higher wages, but fixed prices: their hatred was directed at monopolists and those bourgeois suspected of conniving with the enemy. They came to be known as the *sans-culottes*, not because they wore trousers, which were still rare at this period, but because they despised the breeches (*culottes*) worn by the rich, both nobles and bourgeois.

On the economic plane, the bourgeoisie remained united in its opposition to the demands of the *sans-culottes*. Men as different in their political views as Barnave and Robespierre were at one in their adherence to the doctrine of a free economy and in their hostility to any kind of price-fixing, which would merely serve as a reminder of the hated Old Regime and a threat to private property. But the problem was also political: there was a danger that popular agitation might end by shattering the unity of the Third Estate, and the bourgeoisie had to decide whether to preserve that unity at all costs, or deliberately to risk an open breach.

Among the Feuillants, popular unrest served only to strengthen the determination to smash the democratic movement. In their eyes the 'people' was the abstract 'nation' of the Declaration of Rights.

'The people,' wrote a Feuillant journalist, 'is the union of all the individuals who make up the nation. Factions misuse the word to persuade two hundred ignorant men that they are the people and therefore the sovereign power in the land.' But the lower orders of the populace had been roused and would now have to be kept in their place by force. Dupont de Nemours put the Feuillant case quite unambiguously: 'The suppression of the clubs will restore peace; all that is necessary is to destroy the machinery of insurrection.'

In the Assembly and the Jacobin Club, the bourgeois majority distinguished between the economic and political aspects of the demands of the *sans-culottes*. Many thought, with Pétion, that 'the bourgeoisie and the people together brought about the Revolution' and that 'only their unity can preserve it'. In June the deputies made one concession to the peasants by abolishing, without redemption, any casual dues to which the seigneur could not prove a title; but they dismissed any possibility of fixing prices, punished Simoneau's murderers and organised a national day of remembrance for him.

Robespierre and Marat showed greater foresight. Without trying to excuse the rioters who had killed Simoneau, Robespierre objected to the dead man being honoured officially; he even went so far as to publish in his journal a petition drawn up by Dolivier, a priest from the Étampes region, who was pleading for the fixing of prices. Robespierre, more aware than many of the mounting wave of popular feeling that was threatening to engulf the bourgeois revolution in which he had pinned his faith, was ready to make concessions in order to avoid further chaos.

Discontent was swelling among the Parisian populace. On 29 May the Faubourg Saint-Marceau had mobilised the strains of *Ça ira*. On 20 June a great demonstration was held. The ringleaders were men of obscure origins, though they are known to have included one Santerre, a rich brewer from the Faubourg Saint-Antoine. Setting off at about five o'clock in the morning from the Faubourgs Saint-Marceau and Saint-Antoine, the armed *sans-culottes* marched to the Assembly and compelled that body to accept their petitioners formally; the procession of pikes and red bonnets lasted over an hour. Then the mob smashed a door separating the Manège from the Tuileries gardens, massed in the Place du Carrousel, and then made its way into the palace. Louis, who had squeezed himself into the embrasure of a window, resisted the demonstrators' cries of 'Down with the veto!' for over two hours. He put on the *sans-culotte* red bonnet, drank to the nation, but would not give way on the veto. At eight o'clock, after Pétion had made a rather belated appearance, the Tuileries palace was evacuated. The demonstrators continued their march in the Faubourg Saint-Antoine, where shops and workrooms were shut down for a week afterwards.

The day had not been without results. The immediate effect was to restore the spirits of timid royalists, for the demonstrators seemed to have failed in their objective. Dupont de Nemours filed a petition which is believed to have borne twenty thousand signatures. On the 28th La Fayette, leaving his army, called on the Assembly to disperse the clubs. Pétion was suspended from office. But not a single Section was to disown the events of 20 June. The revolutionary movement, far from being checked, was stronger than ever before.

Both the Sections of Paris and the provincial municipalities decided to ignore the royal veto, and on 2 July the Assembly authorised their initiative: on the pretext of celebrating the fall of the Bastille, the *fédérés* planned to converge on Paris. Forced into the camp of the opposition, the Girondins made common cause with Robespierre. On 3 July, in the Assembly, Vergniaud made a formal indictment of the king; three days later, Paris heard that Prussia had joined the war, and on the 11th, the Assembly proclaimed a state of emergency: all

The crowd forces its way into the Tuileries palace. After resisting for two hours the king finally agreed to put on the red cap of the *sans-culottes*, but refused to withdraw his veto.

administrative bodies, all municipal councils, were henceforth to be in permanent session; the entire National Guard was called to arms; fresh battalions of volunteers were levied. But the real significance of this was political rather than military: the Assembly had assumed sovereign executive authority.

The citizens of France were now being recruited not merely to fight the Prussians: they had to resist the enemy within the state. This was made still clearer by the arrival in Paris of the *fédérés* who, from 8 July onwards, poured into the capital, bringing with them an even more violent attitude towards the question of executive power than the Parisians themselves had maintained. On 27 June, the general council of Marseilles had demanded that the executive should be appointed by the people, and answerable to them. When the Marseillais battalions entered the city on 30 July, they brought with them a reputation for extremism. The song they were singing as they arrived in Paris, which was to be known as the *Marseillaise*, was not in fact their own, but the army captain who had composed it at Strasbourg for the army of the Rhine had put into it all the patriotic passion of 1792. The people's love of their country and their hatred of 'tyrants', traitors and the accomplices of Bouillé gave the couplets of Rouget de l'Isle a particular historical colouring which will always be associated with the momentous events of 10 August 1792, the day on which the 'second' Revolution took place.

THE SECOND REVOLUTION: THE DOWNFALL OF THE MONARCHY

On 1 August, news reached Paris of the manifesto signed five days earlier by the Duke of Brunswick, the commander of the foreign armies. The capital responded with another insurrection. Parisians were already being incited to revolt by the *fédérés*, who on 17 July had filed a petition demanding that the king be suspended and had then demanded that a National Convention be elected by universal suffrage. It was the Sections of Paris, however, that played the decisive role, engineering their own special revolution: the 'passive' citizens of the capital now erupted onto the political scene, seizing control of the Sections, which they kept in permanent session, and organising a Central Bureau (at the Hôtel de Ville) to work in liaison with the Central Committee set up by the *fédérés*.

While preparations for the insurrection were being made quite openly, the bourgeois democrats found themselves once again divided into two camps. Brissot and his friends tried to influence the king and to prevent the situation exploding by a change of ministers. Robespierre, who until now had been an inflexible advocate of legality, realised that the oncoming flood was irreversible. Anxious above all not to destroy the unity of bourgeoisie and people, and to pave the way for some new form of legal government, he made a long speech on 29 July, in which he used the slogans of the *fédérés* and the Sections, demanding the abolition of the monarchy and the election of a National Convention by universal suffrage. Like the other democrat leaders, Robespierre did not take part personally in the revolt of 10 August.

During the night of the 9th–10th the tocsin was sounded, and the delegates appointed by the Sections began to arrive at the Hôtel de Ville; in the small hours of the morning they formed a revolutionary Commune and dismissed the official Commune or Municipality. Mandat, commander-in-chief of the National Guard, was killed and replaced by the popular Santerre. The Tuileries was now enclosed by a vast pincer movement as two columns, one from the Faubourg Saint-Antoine, and the other from the left bank (supported by the *fédérés* from Marseilles and Brest), converged on the palace. The first column arrived too late, for on the advice of Roederer, who had been

The revolt of 10 August, led by Santerre. The demonstrators surrounded the Tuileries and opened fire on the palace, but the king had already left.

disturbed by the very cool reception he had received from the National Guards, Louis XVI had gone with his family to the Manège. After he had left, firing broke out between loyal Swiss Guards and demonstrators; the *sans-culottes* of Saint-Marguerite arrived just in time to overcome the Swiss. Even the Manège could not offer the royal family much protection. Under pressure from *sans-culottes* armed with pikes, the Legislative Assembly decided to suspend the monarchy and replace the king by a provisional Executive Council which was to rule until a National Convention could be elected by universal suffrage.

The demonstrators of 10 August were by no means the dregs of the populace. Out of the three hundred and seventy-six dead and wounded, nearly a quarter were *fédérés*, all of whom were provincial bourgeois; the Parisians who had been killed or wounded included tradesmen, craftsmen and members of the wage-earning class. Once again the suburbs of Paris had distinguished themselves.

The uprising of 10 August 1792 brought a grand climax to the sequence of events that had started with the king's flight to Varennes. It put an end to the political programme of the Feuillants, who had hoped to consolidate the achievements of 1789 by founding a stable

The rebels at the Manège, where the king and queen had taken refuge (they can be seen behind the iron-grille window on the right).

social order on the principles of liberty and bourgeois property, and by accepting the principle of equality only as an equality of opportunity, and not as an equality of rights. Barnave, Duport, Lameth and Dupont de Nemours were removed from the political scene, either temporarily or permanently. La Fayette tried unsuccessfully to make his troops march on Paris; in the end he was forced to seek refuge among the enemies of the regime he had himself helped to establish. The failure of the Feuillants was due largely to the king's inaction. Louis, brought up in the tradition of absolutism and the conviction that his will alone was law, and committed irrevocably to the aristocratic cause, had not assented to any reforms since his programme of 23 June 1789. His authority was now reduced to nothing; already the prisoner of the new regime, he was soon to be made its sacrificial victim. By not daring to effect a change of dynasty in 1789, as the English had done in 1688, the liberal bourgeoisie had committed suicide.

Power was now in the hands of the democratic elements of the bourgeoisie. These democrats, who came from the middle and lower ranks of the bourgeoisie, did not have the innate respect for *élites* that

The song later to be known as the *Marseillaise* was composed by Rouget de l'Isle and was first heard at Mme Dietrich's salon in April 1792 (it was sung by the *fédérés* of Marseilles as they marched into Paris on 30 July 1792).

had induced the Feuillants to seek the support of a fringe of liberal nobles. But they did share the respect of the upper bourgeoisie for property and, although they had to make use of popular support in their struggle against the aristocracy and the powers of Europe, they had no intention of allowing themselves to be outflanked or of relinquishing control of the government.

However, the lower orders of both town and country wanted social democracy. The peasants were eager to free themselves once and for all from whatever seigneurial obligations still bound them, and to obtain a larger share of the spoils which the bourgeoisie had seized by nationalising ecclesiastical and royal properties. In Paris shopkeepers, craftsmen, journeymen and wage-earning workers had begun to indulge in the old egalitarian dreams of the Catholic League and the Fronde. The *sans-culottes* had become an independent force to be respected and feared. For them the victory of 10 August had been incomplete, and so they tried with ever greater determination to influence the course of French politics, as if hoping to accelerate the course of history, as if the newly released forces of bourgeois emancipation could be pushed back within the narrow bounds of medieval life. If war had not helped to give the *sans-culottes* some kind of ideological unity, their movement would probably have soon lost its way. Revolutionary patriotism had become a religion and already had its martyrs. Before long, as France lost ground in the war with Prussia, it was also to have its Inquisition and its public executions.

6

THE GIRONDE AND
REVOLUTIONARY
ROMANTICISM

T*he people's revolution of 10 August, and the war against Prussia and Austria, had brought a temporary halt to the great advance of the bourgeoisie that was eventually to lead to the peaceful liberalism of the nineteenth century. With the demise of the Feuillants, the intellectual élites of eighteenth-century Enlightenment had vanished from the political scene, leaving in their place men who owed everything to circumstance and who were to find themselves taking on responsibilities for which neither their educational background nor their political experience fitted them. For almost a whole year, French politics were to be dominated by two factions. The Jacobin democrats of Paris, who had established the revolutionary Commune of 10 August, sat high up at the back of the National Convention and thus came to be known as the 'Mountain'. These 'Montagnards' were a minority group, and for a long time the sympathies of the bourgeoisie were with their opponents, known at the time as the Brissotins, or Girondins, a term which historians generally use to refer to them.*

At first, however, the distinction between Girondins and Montagnards was not at all clear-cut. Socially, both factions belonged largely to the middle bourgeoisie; politically, they were both committed to the democratic movement; intellectually, they were nearly all equally contemptuous of religion and its priests (in this respect Robespierre was not typical of the Montagnards). Both factions were small in numbers, but by a combination of various forces – party spirit, ministerial solidarity and pure chance – they were soon to find themselves bitterly opposed in a mighty political struggle.

The history of the Girondins is inextricably bound up with the vicissitudes of the war against Prussia and Austria. Brissot and his group had been responsible for planning the war and setting it in motion. The question now was whether they would be able to impose the measures necessary for victory: if only they could bring the war to a successful conclusion, they seemed to have every chance of retaining power. But their hatred for the Parisian democrats of the Mountain, who were their rivals for power, led them to reject the drastic measures they themselves had been advocating. Wanting both war and revolution, but unwilling to resort to the policies necessary for the success of either, the Girondins provoked alternating reactions from the bourgeoisie and the masses, according to circumstances. In periods of comparative calm, when the counter-revolutionary menace seemed to have subsided, they enjoyed the support of the large majority of deputies in the Convention, who were exasperated by the suspicious, inquisitorial vigilance of the democrat leaders; but whenever the French armies suffered a setback, and the survival of France and the Revolution were at stake, they lost support.

The uprising of 10 August had not rid France of the threat of invasion. At the end of August the Austro-Prussian armies crossed the frontiers; Longwy and then Verdun capitulated. Meanwhile an 'aristocratic plot' was being hatched in Brittany and Vendée. In spite of Danton's attempts to unite the activities of the Legislative Assembly and the Paris Commune against the enemy, the timidity of the Girondins meant that it was up to the Parisian deputies to take the initiative in safeguarding public security. France now had a foretaste of the measures which the revolutionary government introduced a year later: repression took many forms, as 'suspects' were hunted down and refractory priests were forced to submit; national defence became a priority and grain was to be requisitioned and inventoried. Out-manoeuvred, the Girondins let the Assembly do as it pleased and even gave it reluctant support. However, the slowness with which the Extraordinary Tribunal, founded on 17 August, went about its business, caused an explosion of fury in Paris, and from 2 to 4 September the sans-culottes *forced their way into prisons and murdered rebel priests and common criminals. At first the Girondins tried to make excuses for the massacres without actually seeming to approve of them, but they soon changed their tactics and attempted to take advantage of the anti-terrorist reaction that was spreading through the country, by using it as a weapon against the Commune. They labelled their adversaries as* septembriseurs.

The National Convention took over from the Legislative Assembly on 21 September. Paris apart, the Girondins had benefited electorally from the reputation they had built up in the previous Assembly. They immediately established their leadership over the mass of uncommitted deputies who formed the 'Marsh' or 'Plain' and whose allegiance was first and foremost to the Revolution. The French victory at Valmy, quickly followed by the evacuation of foreign troops and the invasion of Belgium, the left bank of the Rhine, Nice and Savoy, gave new strength to the anti-terrorist reaction. The Girondins, in full control of the Convention, were now in a position to take the willing Danton into their administration and, forgetting the past, restore unity to the democratic movement. But the most powerful of them allowed the petty rancour of the Roland household and their own sense of exclusiveness to get the better of political considerations, with the result that feuds and insults continued to dominate the Convention. By monopolising committees, they deprived many deputies of the Plain of the oppor-

tunity of political office, so that men like Couthon and Lebas gradually went over to the rival faction, the Mountain. At the same time, by relentlessly attacking the Parisian democrats and their heroes, the Girondins exposed themselves to the accusation of being 'federalists'. Their leadership of the Convention produced nothing in the way of constructive policies. They were not prepared to associate themselves wholeheartedly with the sentence of death which the Convention passed on Louis XVI, but they could do nothing to prevent his execution. The Girondins have often been accused by historians of incompetent management of the war, but they showed themselves to be even less capable of bringing about the peace which some of them felt to be essential. The result was that France soon found herself at war with the armies of the 'Coalition', an alliance in which Britain played the key role for twenty years.

The spring of 1793 proved fatal for the Girondin faction, as divisions among its members multiplied. Once again military defeat and the treachery of the generals threatened France's security. Custine evacuated the left bank of the Rhine; Dumouriez lost Belgium and then went over to the enemy, taking with him the future Louis-Philippe. The conscription of three hundred thousand men, ordered by the Convention, led to an insurrection in the Vendée which seemed to sweep all resistance aside. In Paris the sans-culottes, exasperated by high prices, seemed to be planning another revolt. The Girondins refused to grant the concessions to which they had agreed after the uprising of 10 August. In March and April the Plain defied them and approved a series of revolutionary measures put forward by the Montagnards. The more they were threatened, the more inflexible the Girondins became, unwittingly gathering behind them all the royalist and counter-revolutionary elements in France. By the end of May Marseilles and Lyons were in a state of open rebellion. At the same time Isnard tried to frighten Paris with a repetition of the threats contained in the Duke of Brunswick's manifesto.

A sans-culotte uprising was planned quite openly; Robespierre and Marat, who had done everything they could to contain the rebels, had to let events take their course. On 31 May the sans-culottes were offered only partial concessions. On 2 June the National Convention, surrounded by eighty thousand armed men, gave its approval for the arrest of the twenty-nine leading Girondin deputies. The Girondins were finished as a political force.

Contemporaries tended to regard the Brissotin or Girondin faction as a solid phalanx, but each member of the movement had his own individual part to play in the history of the Revolution. In their social origins they were hardly distinguishable from the Montagnards: most of them, as journalists and lawyers, had the same background as the Parisian democrats. They are said to have felt a physical repugnance for the common people, and have been accused of worldliness. However, even if these charges are justified, there is nothing to suggest that their public life suffered as a result. Robespierre found the coarseness of the populace just as distasteful as did Vergniaud, and both Danton and Desmoulins indulged in the life of salon and boudoir. It would be a mistake to put too much trust in the view of Girondin habits mirrored by the instinctive hatred which the sans-culottes of Paris felt for the well-to-do and the world of social pleasures.

The Girondins showed little political originality. In their basic principles, there was little to distinguish them from other democratic factions. It is true that, by resigning themselves to a final break between bourgeoisie and people, they eventually found themselves in an unwanted alliance with the enemies of the Revolution. However, they moved in that direction not through premeditated policy, but through the sheer bitterness of their rivalry with the Montagnards.

The real originality of the Gironde was of a more personal, human kind, for it produced a certain type of politician who stood out from the main body of revolutionaries. Very much the children of their century, the Girondins had an immense appetite for liberty, a great capacity for optimism and for enjoying life. Above all, they embodied one of the fundamental ideals of the Revolution – the desire to sweep away the old social hierarchies and replace them by a world of opportunity, in which men of talent and eloquence could make their mark. This is why the very name 'Girondin' conjures up an image of eternal youth, irresponsible perhaps, but infinitely appealing.

THE GIRONDINS IN POWER

The Girondin faction was by no means homogeneous in its origins; when this group first appeared on the political scene, before the declaration of war, it was Brissot who dominated the debates in the Legislative Assembly. But he already had gathered around him four young friends united by their social origins, their careers and their political views. They were all deputies from the department of the Gironde, owing everything, or very nearly everything, to the Revolution. Three of them were lawyers; the fourth, Ducos, was a merchant, but even he had long been associated with the legal profession. The eldest of the four, Vergniaud, was thirty-six when the Bastille was captured. He was a Girondin by adoption, for his family lived in Limoges, and he had enjoyed the protection of Turgot, who had known his parents when intendant at Limoges. Thanks to Turgot the young Pierre Vergniaud had been awarded a scholarship so that he could complete his studies at the Collège du Plessis in Paris. After three years in Paris he began frequenting the salons and introduced himself into the literary world. His parents then sent him to Bordeaux to study law. He became secretary to Dupaty and thereby came into contact with the enlightened circles of the Girondin capital. By 1789, he was a lawyer with a local reputation, like Robespierre at Arras, and as a member of the town's academy made several attempts to write poetry, though without much success. The Revolution brought him a career as an administrator and politician. A captain in the National Guard and a member of the Jacobin Club in Bordeaux,

(*Above*) Marguerite-Elie
Guadet, elected to the
Assembly with Vergniaud.
(*Left*) Pierre-Victurnien
Vergniaud, the greatest
orator among the Girondins.

he was elected to the department of the Gironde and then to the
Legislative Assembly. Vergniaud was the greatest orator of the
Gironde, and probably of the entire Assembly, but his laziness of
temperament and intellectual independence made him unsuited for
the role of parliamentary leader. On a number of occasions, and particularly in the National Convention, he refused to associate himself
with the attacks launched by his friends against the left-wing deputies.

The reason for Vergniaud's reticence was that he was more aware
than the other Girondins of the need to preserve the unity of the
democrat movement. Later, however, he was to use all his powers of
eloquence in a counter-attack on Couthon and Robespierre: 'We are
being accused and denounced, as we were on 2 September, by a
violent mob of assassins! But we know that Tiberius Gracchus perished
at the hands of a demented people whose interests he had constantly
defended. We are not afraid of sharing his fate: our blood is at the disposal of the people; our only regret is that we cannot offer them more.'

The early career of Marguerite-Élie Guadet, another of the group,
also owed much to the system of patronage so characteristic of the Old
Regime. Born at Saint-Émilion in 1755, Guadet was the son of a minor
official and owed the opportunity to study law to the generosity of
some wealthy local citizens. The Revolution made this young lawyer

(*Above*) Armand Gensonné,
nicknamed 'the drake of the
Gironde' because of a speech
impediment.
(*Right*) Antoine-Nicolas Caritat
de Condorcet.

a member of the department of the Gironde and then president of the
local criminal court. Elected to the Assembly with Vergniaud, Guadet
showed a greater capacity for hard work and a more serious frame of
mind than his colleague; but he was a mediocre orator, and soon
yielded to the temptations of personal abuse in debates. Armand
Gensonné, the third of the lawyers in the group that formed round
Brissot, had a conventional social background. By 1798, he was
already well established as a lawyer. A defect in pronunciation caused
him to be nicknamed 'the drake of the Gironde'. But the effectiveness
with which he pleaded his cases in court, the seriousness of his approach and the clarity of his arguments quickly brought him to the
forefront of public life. Later, in the Convention, he also indulged in
the verbal slanging matches conducted by his Girondin colleagues.

Brilliant but inconsistent, these young Girondins longed for a republic in which talent would be the supreme criterion of success. By their
own personal charm and by frequenting the salons where they were
so popular, they attracted a wide and varied following; some of their
admirers were merely men with ambitions or grudges, but they also
had an immense appeal for educated men who refused to regard
democracy and culture as incompatible.

The most independent of the Girondins' sympathisers was Condorcet. His political career had been a fluctuating affair. A member
of the Society of '89, Condorcet was a friend of La Fayette and Sieyès
and had urged them to join the Brissotin faction when war became

imminent. The flight of Louis XVI persuaded him to commit himself politically to the idea of a republic, though to a republic of enlightenment and not the rule of demagogues. Although he was a friend of Brissot, he nevertheless condemned the Girondins' onslaught against Robespierre in the early days of the Convention. The Constitution which he put forward at that time was designed to appeal to the extreme left wing of the democratic movement, but the Mountain repudiated him and so he remained the friend of the Girondins.

A number of politicians had spontaneously gathered round Brissot and the orators of the Gironde during the life of the Legislative Assembly. Later, in the National Convention, others joined them. One of the first to attach himself to their faction in the Legislative Assembly was a manufacturer from the south called Isnard, whose blustering eloquence soon passed from extreme left-wing propaganda to a contemptuous denunciation of Parisian democracy. Among those who joined the Girondins in the Convention was Pétion, a friend of Robespierre who lost popularity because of his hesitation at the time of the uprising of 10 August. He supported the Gironde because he shared their grudges.

Foreigners played an important part in Girondin activities. Paris was teeming with political refugees who were eager to add their own grievances and desire for revenge to the flames of revolutionary France; indeed, in a sense, Girondin Paris became the centre of the European revolution. Among these refugees from abroad was the Swiss banker Clavière, who had been banished from Geneva in 1782 for expressing democratic ideas, and became Minister of Finances.

Ultimately the Girondins were known among their enemies as the

Maximin Isnard, a manufacturer from the south.

Étienne Clavière, a Swiss Girondin.

'Rolandins'; those Girondins who were close friends of the Roland household had formed a small nucleus within their faction which was to have a fatal influence on the Gironde as a political force. Yet Jean-Marie Roland de la Platière seemed ill-qualified to play the part of a faction leader. He was already well into middle age at the outbreak of the Revolution (he was born in 1734). His family had had close links with the *noblesse de robe*, and under the Old Regime Roland had held high public office as an inspector of factories; he was naturally in close touch with the economists of the time, and himself wrote a number of books.

Roland had married late in life, in 1780. His wife, Jeanne-Manon Phlipon, was a young woman of humbler social origins. The gentle and passionate Jeanne-Manon had come under various influences: from Rousseau she absorbed the deistic philosophy which appealed to her naturally mystical temperament, and from Plutarch and Corneille she derived a yearning for personal fame. Maybe it was not really fame that she desired, but simply the freedom to be an individual human being. The obstacles which eighteenth-century society placed in the way of talent were made even more insuperable for women by countless social taboos. In such circumstances it would hardly have been surprising if, in Jeanne-Manon Phlipon, the century's obsession with individualism had been sublimated in a longing for some extraordinary personal destiny. It is highly unlikely that her marriage with Roland, twenty years her senior, in any way satisfied these longings. For her, too, the Revolution brought the long awaited opportunity to escape from the tedium and routine of provincial life. At her salon in the Rue Guénégaud she gathered together some of the most outstanding personalities of the left. In the spring of 1792 Roland was appointed Minister of the Interior and Jeanne-Manon left the Rue Guénégaud for the sumptuous mansion that stood on the present-day site of the Banque de France. When the Girondin ministry was dismissed in June, she became embittered by her husband's loss of power and status. And so, when Roland was given back his position after the events of 10 August, Manon was determined to take the opportunity of wielding political influence herself. Until the uprising of 10 August she seems to have been fully aware of the need for unity among the democrats; she did everything she could to win Robespierre over to the Girondin cause, and she reproached Brissot and his friends for trying to come to terms with the king and for being so reluctant to give the movement bold leadership. But her jealousy of Danton, whose forceful personality overshadowed all the other members of the Executive Council, eventually filled her with intense loathing for the Montagnards. In itself her hatred of the left would have been quite harmless, but Manon made sure that the circle of young friends and

Portrait of Mme Manon Roland painted by Mme Labille-Guiard.

admirers who frequented her salon subscribed to her views; the novelist Louvet, the impetuous Barbaroux and the love-lorn Buzot all joined battle on her behalf. By the sheer violence and persistence of their verbal onslaughts these friends of the Roland household were to bring discredit on the entire Girondin movement.

THE PARIS COMMUNE VERSUS THE
NATIONAL CONVENTION

In the days following the revolt of 10 August, the Gironde established control over the Legislative Assembly, which had been deserted by the right wing, but it found itself confronted by a new power, the revolutionary Paris Commune, which was dominated by bourgeois democrats who were later to form the Mountain, the left-wing opposition in the National Convention. Executive power was entrusted to a provisional Executive Council of six ministers, with Danton as its dominant personality.

These two rival authorities found compromise difficult. Despite the feebleness of counter-revolutionary activity, the masses were frightened and compelled the Commune, and then the reluctant Assembly, to adopt a series of repressive measures. This was the first Terror, with its house-searching and arrests, its Extraordinary Tribunal (17 August), the measures taken against refractory priests, the institution of a civil registry of births, marriages and deaths, and the legalisation of divorce. Although the bourgeoisie unanimously rejected the urban population's demands for fixed maximum prices it did make the peasants wide concessions (division of national property into small lots for purchase, abolition of seigneurial dues, granting of sole ownership of communal properties to village communities).

The invasion of France by foreign troops made the militants intensify their demands for repressive measures and at the same time provoked an explosion of revolutionary patriotism. Once the frontiers had been crossed, Longwy and then Verdun surrendered, and Paris itself was threatened. During those troublesome days Danton was the embodiment of patriotic passion and revolutionary solidarity. On two occasions in particular his eloquence shook the Assembly. 'Everything belongs to the nation when the nation is in danger' he proclaimed on 28 August. Then, on 2 September, he made his most famous speech: 'Everything is in turmoil and all are ready to take up arms. . . . When the tocsin sounds it will not be a signal of alarm, but the signal to charge against the enemies of our country. To defeat them, gentlemen, we need men of daring: with such men France will be saved.' In this feverish atmosphere, in which Parisians enrolled in their thousands to defend their country, panic and hatred of the enemy within led to the massacre of eleven to fourteen hundred prisoners shut up in the city's various jails. The assassins who slaughtered indiscriminately common criminals, rebellious priests and 'aristocrats', were not from the lowest orders of the population, but included those same shopkeepers and craftsmen who had taken part in all the great revolutionary uprisings.

Danton, Minister of Justice and member of the Executive Council, became the guiding force behind the government's war policy.

For a while the authorities found themselves out-manoeuvred and embarrassed by the results of their appeals to patriotism. But the massacres were not used as a political weapon until the 'democrats' of the Commune tried to turn the angry populace against the Girondin leaders. At this moment, Danton intervened. But the Girondins nourished an intense hatred for the men who had attempted to make the September massacres the basis of a political manoeuvre. Soon the French victory at Valmy and the lull that followed gave them the chance to take their revenge.

After the fall of Longwy the war had followed a somewhat uncertain course. Dumouriez, who was now the chief general of the Army of the North, insisted on carrying out the plan to invade Belgium which

157

The massacres of 2 September 1792, in the abbey of Saint-Germain-des-Prés, where 300 prisoners were killed.

he had worked out as Foreign Minister. Even as late as 29 August he assembled a council of war and declared his intention to enter Belgium in order to prevent the Duke of Brunswick from continuing his march on Paris. But the orders he received from the Executive Council and the capture of Verdun forced him to abandon his plan of invasion. He was ordered to position his troops behind the Argonne, the 'Thermopylae of France', and Kellermann was to join him there with the Army of the Centre. Dumouriez appealed to the patriotism of the local inhabitants and positioned his army with great care. The Duke of Brunswick, commanding the Coalition army, appeared to be in no hurry to engage in battle. His troops, divided into separate corps, were advancing slowly and concentrating on securing control of key passes. Brunswick finally arrived in front of the Argonne on 7 September. On the 14th one of his lieutenants captured the Croix-au-Bois pass, which meant that Dumouriez had to retreat to Sainte-Menehould. On the 19th Kellermann's troops joined up with those of Dumouriez. The king of Prussia, spurred on by the impatient French *emigrés*, ordered Brunswick to engage in battle. Turning their backs on the road to Paris, the Prussians now had to fight on a reversed front.

On the morning of 20 September the Prussian vanguard was greeted
with a burst of artillery fire as it arrived in front of the height of Valmy.
At one o'clock in the afternoon the Prussian infantry was given the
order to attack the French positions. The French cannons could do
nothing to halt the Prussian advance. It was then that Kellermann's
famous cry of 'Long live the Nation!' was heard. On hearing the
French army singing the *Ça ira* the Prussian infantry hesitated.
Brunswick ordered a halt and by the evening artillery fire had ceased.
Even as a military operation the battle of Valmy was not without
importance. It was in fact one of the first military engagements in
which artillery fire played a major part. The legend of the 'operetta
battle' should therefore be forgotten once and for all. But it is true
that the psychological and moral effects of the battle were of greater
importance. In a phrase that has become famous, Goethe pointed to
the battle of Valmy as the beginning of 'a new era in the history of
the world': Kellermann's appeal to the 'nation' in arms was one of
the first signs of the change that was to take place in the rules of war.

On the day of the French victory at Valmy, the Legislative Assembly
made way for the National Convention.

THE NATIONAL CONVENTION

The National Convention, the third assembly to emerge from the Revolution, gathered on 20 September 1792 in the Manège. Why a 'Convention'? This term, of English origin and popularised by the American struggle for independence, signified a governing body assuming special powers with a view to drawing up a new Constitution and in the meantime exercising all the prerogatives of sovereignty. In theory, elections should have been held in two stages and by universal suffrage; but, in fact, all the opponents of 10 August, including the aristocrats and the Feuillants, were refused the vote or voluntarily stood aside. In Paris, where voting took place orally and in public, all those who had signed the old royalist petitions were barred from taking part. Moreover, the 'passive' citizens of France either were unaware of their civil rights, or were afraid to use them. And so the deputies of the most audacious parliament in the history of France were elected by a politically committed minority of citizens.

The members of the Convention belonged, with two exceptions, to the bourgeoisie. Many of them – nearly two hundred and fifty out of a total of seven hundred and forty-nine – were lawyers. The significant feature of the new assembly was that it contained most of the political *élite* produced by three years of revolution: some four hundred deputies had been members of provincial and local administrations, ninety-six had sat in the Constituent Assembly and one hundred and eighty-nine in the Legislative Assembly. The French bourgeoisie may have lost some of its leading politicians in the course of those three years, but it still seemed able to provide an abundance of men competent to take over government.

In this latter part of September 1792 the old political cleavages were not quite so clear. Among the hundred or so Jacobin deputies there were to be found both Girondins and Montagnards; the elimination of the Gironde and exclusive domination of the Mountain in the Convention proved to be a gradual process. It should be pointed out that, except in Paris, the electors had not voted for or against the rival parties, but for or against the democratic revolution set in motion by the uprising of 10 August. In Eure, where the Girondin Buzot and the Lindet brothers were elected as a group; in Marseilles, where the influence of a man like Barbaroux did not prevent future Montagnards from dominating the scene; indeed almost everywhere, the democratic movement presented a united front. As they had controlled the Legislative Assembly and the Executive Council, the Girondins were naturally the best known candidates at the elections, and their leaders were elected simultaneously in several departments: Carra seven times, Brissot three and Condorcet twice. In Paris itself, however, there was no question of compromise and the city's deputies included Robespierre and Danton and also the leaders of the Commune: Fabre d'Églantine, Collot d'Herbois, Billaud-Varenne and Camille Desmoulins. Marat was elected in spite of murmurings from numerous Montagnards, and the Duc d'Orléans, now known as Philippe Égalité, in spite of Robespierre's opposition. At first the Girondins, who numbered about two hundred against the Mountain's hundred, seemed to be in control of the Convention. They possessed the advantages of talent and of being well known public figures. The war they had advocated was no longer an embarrassment to them, for the victory at Valmy had removed the danger of defeat, for the time being at least. Confronting a political class which had been deprived of its most distinguished and experienced spokesmen, the Feuillants, by the uprising of 10 August, they proceeded to display their inexhaustible eloquence with the slightly offensive confidence of upstarts. Nothing, however, is more awkward in parliamentary government than the ability to charm an assembly without being at the head of the majority party, and the Girondins were far from being in the majority. The largest body of deputies in the Convention formed what came to be known as the 'Plain' (by contrast with the 'Mountain'), though their enemies referred to them scornfully as the 'Marsh'. The deputies of the Plain embodied the continuity of the bourgeois revolution. Their leaders, men like Barère, Cambon and Sieyès, felt a close affinity to the Girondins when defending property and freedom against the excesses of the left wing. But their chief enemy remained the aristocracy, the forces of counter-revolution; in moments of crisis the Plain gave its support to the Mountain's demands for drastic measures. Many members of the Plain agreed with Couthon, the paralytic deputy for the department of Cantal, who considered that there were two extremist parties, 'a party of men with exaggerated principles, and a party of cunning intriguers full of ambition'. By establishing their supremacy in the Convention and monopolising positions on committees, the Girondins were to offend the pride of many deputies and to lose the sympathies of men like Sieyès, who agreed with their ideas but was loath to submit to domination by a group of young lawyers.

Was agreement between the factions possible? The early sessions of the Convention seemed to suggest that it was possible. Danton ardently defended the cause of unity, and on several occasions had discussions with the Girondin leaders; on 21 September he succeeded in winning the Convention's unanimous rejection of dictatorial powers and 'agrarian law', which constituted a threat to liberty and private property and against which the Girondins had incessantly warned the nation. On the evening of the 21st the Convention also declared itself unanimously in favour of abolishing the monarchy. 'Kings,' cried

Grégoire, 'are in the moral order what monsters are in the physical order. The history of kings is a martyrology of nations.' The Republic had not yet been proclaimed: this was done indirectly on the following day, when it was decided that decrees should be dated from 'Year I of the Republic'.

The olive-branch held out by Danton was spurned by the Girondins. On 23 September Roland and his friends tried to exploit their parliamentary position to crush the Parisian democrats, their Commune and 'triumvirs' (Marat, Robespierre and Danton). The battle continued throughout October, but it brought the Girondins little success. They demanded that a 'departmental guard' be formed to protect the members of the Convention and reduce Paris, in the words of Lasource, 'to one eighty-third share of influence' (France was divided into eighty-three departments); but the Convention would not back their proposal and, though some departments sent *fédérés*, the latter did not assume the role expected of them. The Girondins managed to have the members of the Commune's general council replaced, but, though the new mayor, Chambon, was a moderate, the council remained *sans-culotte* or Jacobin; Chaumette was appointed as its attorney (*procureur*) and Hébert as his assistant. The Girondins had attacked the 'triumvirs' ceaselessly and with great passion, but while Danton found his position weakened because he had been unable to account for the secret funds he had controlled as a minister, neither Robespierre nor Marat suffered any loss of reputation. The Girondins' policy of aggression against the left wing was already half-way to failure.

In two respects, however, their policy was successful. The revulsion of public opinion against the terrorist excesses of September was intensified after the victory at Valmy, and the Girondins took measures to stimulate the change in mood: prisoners were set free, passports were restored, the press regained some of its former freedom and then, on 29 November, the Extraordinary Tribunal, set up on 17 August, was abolished. They were similarly successful in their measures against grain and trade controls: the decree of 8 December repealed the laws concerning the requisition and inventorying of grain and restored freedom of trade. The Girondins knew that, by resisting terrorism and economic controls, they would be able to exploit the fears of a united bourgeoisie.

THE TRIAL OF THE KING

What was to be done with the king? Since 10 August Louis XVI had been shut up with his wife, his sister Madame Elisabeth, and his two children in the medieval keep of the Temple. The Commune had made itself responsible for guarding the royal family, ignoring Roland's objections, and the king was gradually isolated from his family until on 11 December he was forbidden to associate with the young dauphin.

Should the king be put on trial? On 20 November a secret iron chest was discovered in the Tuileries and in it were found various documents revealing the king's association with the counter-revolution. A trial now became inevitable. In the Convention the deputies were divided into three camps: on the left Saint-Just and Robespierre, almost isolated from the rest of the assembly (even from their own colleagues of the Mountain), were opposed to a trial. In a long speech on 13 November Saint-Just had maintained that Louis XVI was guilty by the very fact of being a king, and that he should therefore not be tried, but simply punished forthwith. 'I say that the king must be punished as an enemy; we must fight him, not put him on trial. . . . What kind of law can possibly exist between humanity and a king?' About two weeks later, Robespierre came to a similar conclusion, though by a more rigorous process of reasoning: to put the king on trial, according to Robespierre, would be to put those who had deposed him on trial at the same time, and this would mean subjecting the Revolution to some kind of court of appeal. 'If the king is not guilty, those who have deposed him are. To put him on trial would be like a judicial inquiry submitting a case to a higher court for decision'. Robespierre too was in favour of sentence without trial.

The majority of deputies, though appreciating the strength of these arguments, rejected their conclusions. In their eyes Louis was guilty, but a regular trial was necessary so that public opinion both in France and abroad should be left in no doubt of the legitimacy of the verdict. Marat would not support Robespierre and Saint-Just. 'Louis Capet,' he wrote, 'had to be brought to trial. Such a step was necessary for the benefit of the people, for it is vital that all members of the Republic be convinced, even if this means employing different methods of argument for different types of mind.' On 5 December the Convention decided that there would be a trial and that it would judge the king itself. On 10 December the indictment 'enumerating the crimes of Louis XVI' was presented to the Convention; there must have been some deputies on the right who were against the trial, but they kept their silence.

On 11 December 1792 Louis XVI was brought for the first time before the Convention. He was allowed to choose his defenders, and selected Tronchet and the faithful Malesherbes, who instructed a young advocate by the name of de Sèze to plead the king's case. On 26 December, in the presence of the king, de Sèze developed a line of argument that was juridically irreproachable, but politically very weak. He began by pointing out that the inviolability of the king was laid down in the 1791 Constitution, and by insisting that if the king was to be tried nevertheless, he must be tried not as king, but as an ordinary citizen with the normal guarantees of two juries (an indictment jury and a trial jury), the hearing of witnesses and expert examination of documents. 'I look for judges among you, and I find only prosecutors.' He then defended the 'liberal' beginnings of Louis xvɪ's reign and denied that the king had been guilty of collusion with foreign powers. The assembly felt that the true political nature of the trial was being hidden behind a smoke-screen of procedure. 'Justice,' cried Saint-Just, 'cannot prevent great crimes from being concealed. A crime may not be seen to be committed, but its effects are no less real.'

The Girondins had done everything possible to delay the trial without actually opposing it. They had tried to wreck it with a general denunciation of the Bourbons, hoping to compromise the Montagnards with Philippe Égalité, formerly the Duc d'Orléans; in fact, on 16 September all Bourbons had been banished from the country. Once the trial had started they demanded that the judgement of the Convention be submitted to the people for their approval or disapproval. Vergniaud proclaimed: 'It was the people who, by the Constitution of 1791, gave the king his inviolability, and it is the people who should decide whether that inviolability must be taken away.' But the Girondins' demand for a referendum was rejected on two counts: firstly, on principle, for an appeal to the people would call in question the whole system of parliamentary representation which the Girondins had themselves defended so vigorously against the Paris Sections; secondly, for a political reason, for to submit the fate of the king to the primary assemblies would mean unleashing civil war. In a speech on 4 January Barère replied to Vergniaud. Like all Barère's interventions, this reply was decisive. In fact, Barère's voice seemed to echo the thoughts of the vast majority of the assembly: he was speaking on behalf of the Plain and refusing to be associated with the manoeuvres of the Girondins.

The critical debates began on 14 January. The deputies were to vote individually, as their names were called out, on three questions: the guilt of the king, the popular referendum and the penalty to be imposed. The assembly was nearly unanimous in deciding the king to be guilty. The proposal for a referendum was rejected by four hundred and twenty-three votes to two hundred and eighty-six. The Girondins fought their main battle on the question of the penalty to be imposed. Lanjuinais demanded that a majority of two-thirds be accepted, but Danton persuaded the deputies to reject his suggestion. Then Mailhe, the first deputy to vote on the question of the penalty, asked for a sentence of death, but with a stay of execution, and a number of Girondins imitated his example. The result of the vote was three hundred and sixty-six in favour of death out of a total of seven hundred and twenty-one votes cast, which represented a majority of five; but a second call of votes showed that, not counting those who had recommended a stay of execution, there was a majority of only one in favour of death without qualification. On 19 January a fourth vote was taken on the proposal for a stay of execution, but the motion was rejected by a majority of three hundred and eighty-three to three hundred and ten.

The details of the voting are not, however, as important as the deputies' motives in insisting that the king should die. The members of the Convention felt no personal animosity for Louis XVI. Even Robespierre admitted as much: 'I felt republican virtue wavering in my heart at the sight of the guilty man humiliated before the sovereign power.' The sentence passed on the king was a political decision. For the majority – the regicides – it was vital that any possibility of compromise should be banished once and for all, to prevent a counter-revolution which would demolish the political and social victories of 1789, and to reassure those who had bought national properties and those whose interests were bound up in other ways with the new regime. The regicides by demanding the execution of the king defied the counter-revolution and deliberately burned their boats behind them.

The motives of the 'appellants' (those who had supported a referendum) pose more of a problem. None of them were royalists. No doubt some of them, like Danton himself, hoped that, by showing clemency to the king, the Convention might be able to appease Europe; but calculations of this sort were a contradiction of Girondin foreign policy. It seems that, in their desire to refer the king's fate to the will of the people, these deputies were the prisoners of the policies they had adopted in September 1792, when they had deliberately encouraged the anti-terrorist reaction of bourgeois opinion and had received the support of the Convention in doing so. They thought they could save the king by appealing once more to the deep currents of that same bourgeois opinion, but this time they were deluding themselves, for the bourgeoisie was more concerned with self-preservation.

On 20 January 1793, at about two o'clock in the morning, Garat and Lebrun went to the Temple to inform Louis of the Convention's decisions. Louis made three requests: a delay of three days to prepare himself for death, permission to see his family privately, and permission to send for a non-juring priest, the Abbé Edgeworth de Firmont, who had been Madame Elisabeth's confessor. The Convention agreed to the second and third requests, and at about six o'clock Garat returned to the Temple with Edgeworth.

That evening Louis talked at length with his confessor and took leave of his family. Around eleven o'clock his servant brought him supper. 'The king,' the servant relates, 'ate with a good appetite; he had two wings of chicken, a few vegetables, two glasses of water and wine, and for dessert a small biscuit and a little Malaga wine.' Almost as soon as he laid down his head, Louis was fast asleep.

Woken up at five o'clock the following morning, he heard Mass said by Edgeworth and then declined to see his queen for the final meeting which he had promised her. He asked to be allowed to cut his own hair, but his request was refused. At about half past eight Santerre, the commander-in-chief of the National Guard, arrived to take him away. In the second court of the Temple a carriage, probably Clavière's, was waiting for him. The journey from the Rue du Temple to the Place de la Révolution took an hour and a half. It was raining and there was a mist in the streets; the doors of shops and the windows of private houses were closed by order of the authorities. A silent procession of some eighty thousand men, armed with rifles and pikes, followed the carriage.

On the Place de la Révolution, which was to become the Place de la Concorde, a scaffold had been erected facing the Tuileries, between the pedestal of the statue of Louis xv (where the obelisk now stands) and the Champs-Élysées. Twenty thousand armed men had taken up their positions on the square: legions of the National Guard, provincial *fédérés* and representatives of the Parisian Sections. The carriage came to a halt on the square at approximately ten o'clock. The king remained inside for a few minutes and then descended from the carriage and looked at the scaffold. He was allowed to remove his outer clothing himself, but had to have his hands tied. Leaning on Edgeworth he mounted the steps of the scaffold with drums beating. When he reached the platform he tried to resist and address the crowd. Royalist legend attributes these last words to the king: 'People, I die an innocent man! I forgive those responsible for my death and I pray God that my blood will not fall upon France.' But his voice was drowned by the crescendo of drums. At twenty minutes past ten the blade of the guillotine fell. The crowd started shouting patriotic slogans: 'Long live the Nation!', 'Long live the Republic!', 'Long live Liberty!', 'Long live Equality!'. As the body was taken away to the cemetery at the Madeleine the mob began to dance the farandole round the scaffold.

The death of the king caused little stir in the country as a whole. Certainly, there was intense despair among royalists. On the day before the execution, a former member of the royal bodyguard, Pierre de Paris, had assassinated a deputy, Lepeletier, who had voted for the king's death; and in the provinces there were signs of discontent here and there: in Orléans and Lyon mourning was worn, and a demonstration was held at Montbrison. On the whole, however, royalist sentiment appeared to have been numbed, and the general mood was

The guillotine was set up on the Place de la Révolution (now the Place de la Concorde). On 21 January 1793, surrounded by 20,000 soldiers and 3,000–4,000 *sans-culottes*, Louis xvi died, proclaiming his innocence to the end. As his head was shown to the crowds there were joyous cries of 'Vive la Nation!'

of apathy rather than indignation. On the revolutionary side, reaction was equally mild; except in Paris and in the assemblies, Louis xvi's fate aroused little feeling. This silence of an entire nation on the death of its monarch marks a major turning-point in the history of popular sensibilities. When Louis' head fell into the dust, the concept of a king as the anointed one of God, the healer of scrofula and worker of miracles, died for ever. Twenty years later, France restored its monarchy, but it was unable to revive the sacred mystique of royalty. In the meantime, the execution of the king was to have more influence on France's relations with Europe than on internal problems.

FOREIGN AND CIVIL WAR

The French victories that followed Valmy in the autumn of 1792 posed new problems for the leaders of the conquering nation. Savoy and Nice were occupied at the end of September, the towns of the Rhine and the Main in October, and Belgium was conquered by Dumouriez after the decisive battle of Jemappes (6 November). Everything seemed to point to a policy of concentration of French troops along the Rhine and the occupation of Holland. But Dumouriez let the opportunity pass by, and the Prussians were able to recapture Frankfort and the right bank of the Rhine. The real problem, however, was whether or not to seek peace, and, if not, what to do with the conquered countries. All France's political factions were afraid that peace might be the prelude to counter-revolution. Some, like Brissot, appeared to favour the creation of a system of 'sister-republics'. The majority, however, supported a policy of annexation for various reasons: they foresaw the difficulties involved in maintaining what would turn out to be disguised protectorates, and they supported the financial arguments defended by Cambon (was France going to have to bear the cost of the war alone?), and the rather fanciful theory of 'natural frontiers' championed by Danton and later by Carnot. Gradually, therefore, Savoy, Nice and Belgium were annexed (November 1792–January 1793).

Such a policy was bound to arouse the hostility of Britain. With a French fleet at Anvers, the Scheldt open to navigation and the welcome given in Paris to visiting British democrats, Pitt had good reason to prepare for a war: the execution of Louis xvi merely provided a legal pretext. But, once again, it was revolutionary France that opened hostilities. Although many French politicians could see the dangers of war, they were swept aside by the old blind hatred felt by their compatriots for a country that seemed to epitomise egotism and mercantile wealth, and whose reliance on credit and foreign trade made it vulnerable. On 1 February 1793 the Convention declared war on Britain

The battle of Jemappes, 6 November 1792, where Dumouriez won a great victory that enabled him to conquer Belgium.

and Holland. The 'Coalition' was joined by the Italian and German princes and by Charles IV of Spain.

To defeat the Coalition the Girondins would have had to be prepared to employ every means available. However, by the spring of 1793, the 'natural frontiers' policy had been abandoned, and the armies of the Republic occupied only Mainz. The generals were guilty of both treachery and incompetence, the populations of the annexed countries were resisting, and soldiers, frustrated by the attitude of their leaders, were deserting; but the Girondins tried to cover up these deficiencies because of their hatred for their Montagnard rivals, and refused to agree to the national government suggested by Danton and the deputies of the Plain. The treachery of Dumouriez, who went over to the enemy on 5 April, put them in an even more difficult position.

Meanwhile, at home the conscription of three hundred thousand men announced on 23 February 1793 caused widespread discontent largely owing to the arbitrary basis of selection. The Convention, reluctant to resort to compulsory military service for the nation as a whole, had resolved to follow the system employed on previous occasions: each department of France would provide a fixed contingent of troops made up of bachelors and widowers between the ages of twenty and forty; volunteers would be called up first, but article 11 of the decree laid down that, if there were not enough volunteers, citizens would have to make up the contingent, using whatever method of election was favoured by the majority. This meant that political rivalries would inevitably play a part in the selection of conscripts. At the same time, all members of administrative bodies were to be exempt, which naturally benefited the bourgeoisie. It is hardly surprising, in such circumstances, that trouble should have broken out here and there. In the district of Hazebrouck, in Alsace, and in Puy-de-Dôme uprisings occurred, and in Orléans a deputy, Léonard Bourdon, was attacked and seriously wounded. Except in Vendée, however, the revolts were suppressed without much difficulty, which suggests that the real origins of the Vendéan insurrection cannot be ascribed simply to resentment aroused by conscription.

The term 'Vendéan' is in any case rather misleading. The area affected by the peasant revolt did not include the whole of the department of Vendée; in fact, it overlapped into the neighbouring departments of Deux-Sèvres, Maine-et-Loire and Loire-Inférieure. Geographically, it covered the whole of the wooded regions with their primitive rock formations of granite and shale, while the limestone 'plains' remained loyal to the regime. In his brilliant *Tableau politique de la France de l'Ouest* André Siegfried made the geological distinction of 'Primary' and 'Secondary' regions one of the determining factors of French political history: his thesis was that, while the former appear to have favoured traditionalist, pro-clerical sentiments, the latter have been characterised by liberal, anti-clerical attitudes. This is an attractive theory, but one which has recently been contradicted by reference to the department of Sarthe, also in western France. Undoubtedly, in wooded districts, where populations were scattered, where there were no natural links between town and country, and where communications with other regions were poor, there would be a tendency for peasants, priests and seigneurs to form more closely-knit social groups than would be found in other parts of France. But there is a danger of interpreting the past in terms of the present and of forgetting that it was the Vendéan wars that were largely responsible for determining the present-day physiognomy of western France. The peasants of Vendée had in fact welcomed the early reforms introduced by the revolutionary regime. To attempt to explain the causes of the Vendéan wars solely in terms of geography would therefore be a mistake.

It would be equally unjustifiable to explain the Vendéan wars purely in terms of religion. Here again, there is a danger of assuming that features of eighteenth-century Vendée were similar to those of today: in fact, the distinctive quality of local patriotism which colours the religious faith of present-day Vendéans has derived directly from the events of the Revolution. Admittedly, these western regions of France had seen the Reformation solidly established in the sixteenth century, and in the seventeenth had witnessed the Counter-Reformation in its most intense form. Taken in hand once more by the missions, they had produced a clergy that was close in origins to the peasantry and an atmosphere of Tridentine Catholicism which found expression in the multitude of crosses and Calvaries that sprang up everywhere. Moreover, the Civil Constitution of the Clergy found some of its fiercest opponents in Vendée, and large numbers of refractory priests were imprisoned or banished in 1792. Nevertheless, there is no reason to think that religious feeling was any stronger in Vendée than it was in the other parts of France which remained loyal to the regime; the Vendéans certainly did not take up arms to defend their priests.

Apart from immediate causes and the fact that the peasantry's avowed purpose was to devote itself to God and the monarchy, little is known of the origins of the Vendéan uprising. One thing is clear, however: the contrast between the social alliances typical of this uprising and those characteristic of the Revolution as a whole. Instead of the usual bourgeois-peasant alliance against feudalism, there was an alliance of peasantry and nobility against bourgeoisie. The Vendéan peasants' hatred for the bourgeoisie of the towns may have been due to suspicions that the latter was taking too much of the recently nationalised wealth. Deprived of their spoils, and apparently having everything to lose by the advance of the revolutionary cause, they turned for protection to their old masters, the seigneurs and the Church.

The first disturbances occurred on 3 March, as soon as news was heard of the Convention's decision to conscript troops. Between the 3rd and the 9th uprisings broke out at Cholet, Chemillé and Clisson, and throughout the Mauges. At first the revolts were disorderly affairs, easily suppressed, and caused the authorities little anxiety. However, on the 11th, in over a hundred villages scattered over three departments, armed bodies were organised with a rapidity that rules out any question of spontaneous rebellion. These uprisings were not the work of the nobility: there certainly was an aristocratic conspiracy to engineer a general revolt throughout western France, but the leaders of this conspiracy were taken unawares by the peasant uprisings. The organisers appear to have been those men whom Mathiez scornfully describes as the 'nobles' valets' – the servants and dependents of the privileged orders who had been deprived of their former position by the Revolution. In the Mauges the rebellions were led by men like Cathelineau and Stofflet, a former gamekeeper, and in the Marais of Brittany by Gaston, a former wigmaker. Around them gathered an anonymous network of former tax-farmers, stewards and officers of seigneurial justice. Soon the rebels turned to the nobles to direct their military operations: men like Charette in the Marais, and Bonchamp and d'Elbée in the Mauges; in Poitou, at the beginning of April, Lescure and La Rochejaquelein appeared on the scene. As the nobles began to join the movement, rebel priests came out of their hiding-places and started to mobilise the faithful against the 'godless' of the towns.

Their enemies accused these priests of being ignorant peasants, but this was unjust, for they included men like the parish priest of Saint-Laud d'Angers, the Abbé Bernier, men who were later to gain high positions in the Church. At the beginning of June, Bernier joined the rebel leaders. Later, he renounced the royalist cause and negotiated for Bonaparte the Concordat which reconciled the Church with modern France. He was rewarded with the bishopric of Orléans.

The main insurrection began simultaneously in three regions. In the Marais, the capture of Machecoul on 11 March was followed by the massacre of local officials, 'constitutional' priests and National Guards: over five hundred people were killed within a month. By the end of March the insurgents were in control of the whole area, except for the coast where the nobles' initiative was rapid and highly success-ful, Clisson and Mortagne were occupied on 10 March, and then Saint-Fulgent was taken. The central rebel army set up its head-quarters at Quatre-Chemins-de-l'Oie and established control of com-munications. The Republican troops led by General Macé, which had marched from La Rochelle, were defeated at Pont-Charrault on 19 March. In the Mauges military operations were not brought under a unified command quite so quickly: on 12 and 13 March Saint-Florent was captured and sacked before Bonchamp had taken command in that area; on the 13th d'Elbée was at Beaupréau and Stofflet at Vezins; Cathelineau was marching on Jalais and, with Stofflet's reinforcements, took possession of Chemillé. Cholet was pillaged on the 14th. It was at this point that the movement acquired a semblance of unity, with the 'Grand Catholic and Royal Army' covering the entire Mauges region under the nominal command of Cathelineau. In reality this 'army' was merely a conglomeration of local units which were skilful enough at waging guerilla warfare in the wooded districts, but were not really able to co-ordinate their efforts effectively. Cathelineau's position as commander-in-chief seems to have been little more than a formality.

The Convention's attempts to suppress the revolt failed. On 19 March it unanimously approved a decree punishing all armed rebels with death and confiscation of property, but the decree was ineffective because all the offensives of the Republican army failed. On 11 April Berruyer was defeated by d'Elbée at Chemillé, and on the 13th La Rochejaquelin repulsed Quétineau at les Aubiers. But the regime's worst rebuff occurred on 5 May, when Quétineau surrendered in Thouars. Morale in Paris was at a low ebb. Just when Dumouriez had betrayed his country and left it exposed to the threat of invasion, the Vendéan insurrection had stuck a knife in the back of the Revolution.

The threat of invasion and the Vendéan insurrection had coincided

After the capture of Chemillé on 11 April 1793 the Vendéan leader, d'Elbée, is said to have stopped his men from massacring prisoners.

with a resurgence of popular agitation caused primarily by the constant rise of prices. The harvest of 1792 had not been at all bad. Once again, currency was at the root of the trouble. The new issues of money (eight hundred million *livres* on 1 February), combined with political events and the two-tier price system (goods were priced both in coin and paper money) reduced the value of the assignat still further: by the end of January its official value had dropped to fifty-five per cent of the face value, and by the beginning of April to forty-three per cent; its real value in terms of purchasing power was even less. Other factors were contributing to the rise of prices: the peasants, anticipating that prices would continue to go up, were delaying the sale of their produce, thereby reducing the quantity of food available on the market. The rise of prices operated very unequally in different parts of the country; the worst-hit area seems to have been the south-east, where prices were over three times as high as in 1789. Admittedly, wages were also going up; conscription had reduced manpower and, with the help of popular pressure, had increased the cost of labour. But the gap between wages in the capital and wages in the provinces was widening. In the provinces, where the average daily wage was twenty *sous*, the price of a pound of bread ranged from six to eight *sous*; in Paris, which was privileged because the price of bread had been pegged at three *sous* a pound, wages were over forty *sous* a day.

The populace was unanimous in its demands: it wanted grain supplies to be controlled by the use of inventories and requisitions, maximum prices to be fixed, and the assignat to be made compulsory currency. The spokesmen of the populace were agitators of obscure origins, the Enragés: in Lyons the movement was led by Leclerc, and in Paris by Varlet and Jacques Roux. Roux, who was a priest was the son of an army officer and came from the old province of Périgord; after teaching at a seminary, he became a curate at Saint-Nicolas-des-Champs, and was the idol of the Gravilliers Section. He made himself the champion of the poor both in the Commune, of which he was a member, and in his own district, where he went from house to house canvassing for support. Roux belonged to the long line of French priests who, throughout the Middle Ages and the Old Regime, had involved themselves closely with the common people and had championed their causes. The Enragés were not really a threat in themselves, but the disturbances which occurred in February 1793 gave their violent propaganda new significance. On the 25th a riot broke out in the Halles district of Paris and spread to other parts of the city, with women sacking grocers' shops. On the 26th the National Guard quelled the rioters. Following the example of Varlet, Jacques Roux defended them to the Commune: 'The grocers have only been made to give back to the people what they have been taking from them for a long time by charging high prices'.

At first the bourgeoisie unanimously and categorically repudiated the demands of the populace. Both Montagnards and Girondins were agreed in principle on the necessity of a free economy. In November 1792 Saint-Just had defended financial orthodoxy and economic freedom with the same enthusiasm as Roland, and had been denounced by a popular placard which read: 'The people knows that the orators who do all the haranguing and make all the finest speeches in the assemblies dine well every day. Citizen Saint-Just is one of this number'. The rioting was attributed to intrigue. The Girondins suspected the Montagnards, who in their turn denounced the aristocrats and the moderates. Many shared the view expressed by Robespierre on 25 February: 'I do not say the people are guilty of a crime, or even of attempting a crime; but when the people rise up in revolt, should they not have some worthy purpose in view, something better than paltry merchandise?' Robespierre's words show how vast a gap there was between the populace in reality and the populace as it existed in the imagination of the revolutionary bourgeoisie. For the bourgeoisie the revolution was primarily a matter of politics, but for the people, politics and economics were one and the same thing. The Parisian mobs represented no less grave a threat to the authority of the Convention than the uprisings in Vendée. It mattered little that popular resentment had crystallised round two opposite poles – in Vendée the rustic myth of a golden age of Catholicism and seigneurial rule, and in Paris the even more mythical concept of equality. For the bourgeoisie the danger was the same, since both movements seemed likely to isolate it as a class.

THE VICTORY OF PARIS AND THE DOWNFALL OF THE GIRONDINS

The two outstanding features of the political scene between the beginning of March and the end of May 1793 were the voting by the Convention of emergency measures similar to those soon to be taken by the Revolutionary government, and the bitter struggle between the Girondin and Montagnard factions. Why had the Convention approved measures to which the Girondins were opposed, and some of which even the Montagnards rejected?

Three new developments had caused the Revolution to be blown still further off course. Firstly, the *sans-culottes* were becoming increasingly troublesome. The general economic distress, the invasion of Belgium and the feebleness of the government had engendered a mood of permanent unrest and continual rioting in the capital. As a result of the demonstrations on 4 May the first law of the *maximum* (i.e. maximum price-fixing) was voted. As always, the mob-leaders were men of obscure background, and their demands were always the same: punishment of traitors and moderates, surveillance of suspects and taxes on the rich. And yet, though the pressure exerted by the masses was very real, it would be a mistake to think that the Convention had allowed itself to be forced by popular agitation into taking drastic measures – though this, in fact, was the view of the Girondins at the time, and Marxist historians have, oddly enough, adopted a similar interpretation. In voting for the measures of March to May 1793 the deputies were not acting from fear. The activities of the populace had merely served to reveal that, for the time being at least, bourgeois liberalism and public safety were incompatible. The Convention simply had to face facts and take the painful steps which the situation demanded.

The second factor which influenced the Convention's decision to adopt its repressive measures was the shift to the left in the policies of the Mountain faction: the Montagnard deputies, afraid of being outflanked by the bourgeoisie, found themselves compelled by circumstances to modify their position by gradually incorporating a number of *sans-culotte* demands in their political programme. In a letter to Barère, Jean Bon Saint-André wrote: 'If you want the poor to help you bring the Revolution to completion, you must first of all help them to live.' On the political plane, while Danton made every effort to bring about a 'left-wing coalition' which would unite the republican factions, Robespierre was quite ready to accept the programme urged by the *sans-culottes*, which largely coincided with his own anti-bourgeois suspicions (the elimination of the Girondins, the setting-up of a revolutionary tribunal, and the subordination of the generals to the government). Robespierre was at the same time a firm believer in parliamentary authority, and wanted to restrict the role of the populace to that of a pressure-group, leaving the Convention to reform itself. On the economic plane, however, the Montagnards were at first unwilling to approve the measures proposed by the Convention; only in late April did they begin openly to support temporary restrictions on property-rights.

As the Mountain faction drew closer to the *sans-culottes*, the deputies of the Plain drew closer to the Mountain, thereby bringing about the third modification of the political scene in the early months of 1793. Faced with the Vendéan insurrection and the threat of foreign invasion, many deputies of the Plain (the large body of previously uncommitted deputies who formed the 'centre' of the Convention), while sharing the Girondins' hatred of Robespierre and Marat, decided to vote with the Montagnards in favour of repressive measures. Reproaching the right-wing Girondins for opposing the emergency measures and the left-wing Montagnards for encouraging *sans-culotte* agitation, Barère pin-pointed the three fundamental facts which the Convention should recognise: in a state of emergency no government could rule by normal methods, and therefore revolutionary measures should be accepted; the bourgeoisie must not isolate itself from the people, and therefore the people's demands should be satisfied; but the bourgeoisie must remain the controlling body in this alliance, and so the Convention must take the initiative by introducing the necessary measures.

The measures were voted by the Convention between 10 March and 20 May. Like those adopted after the revolution of 10 August 1792, they were formulated with three objectives in mind: to provide for the surveillance and punishment of suspects, to meet the economic demands of the *sans-culottes*, and to make government more effective. On 11 March a Revolutionary Tribunal was set up for the trial of suspects. Danton, anxious to avoid a repetition of the September massacres, justified the creation of the Tribunal in these words: 'To free the people from the necessity of harsh deeds we must ourselves be harsh.' On 21 March watch-committees were instituted: each municipality was to have its own committee for the surveillance of foreigners and suspected traitors, and it was these committees that were soon to provide victims for the Revolutionary Tribunal. On 28 March the laws against emigrés were codified and made more severe: henceforth emigrés were banished under pain of death and their possessions confiscated. Economic measures followed later: assignats were made obligatory currency on 11 April, a maximum-price system for grain and flour was established on 4 May, and a compulsory loan of one thousand million *livres* was imposed on the wealthy on 20 May.

The real problem confronting the Convention was the exercise of power. Technically, the problem appeared to have been solved by three measures which the deputies approved during March and April. On 11 March government agents or 'representatives on mission' were sent out to the departments, officially to speed up the conscription of three hundred thousand men, but in fact they were entrusted with a wide range of special powers. On 9 April agents, endowed with unlimited powers, were sent out to the armies, and became the forerunners of the political commissars of the Red Army. Most important of all, on 6 April the Committee of General Defence made way for the Committee of Public Safety, a body which was to act in secret, supervising and speeding up the activities of the Executive Council, and was empowered to put its decisions into effect without delay. When the Girondins accused the government of instituting a dictatorship, Marat replied: 'Violence must be used to establish liberty, and the time has come to organise a brief despotism of liberty in order to crush the despotism of kings.'

However, the question of power was not really technical, but political. Who was to hold the reigns of government? The Girondins could rely on the sympathy of the deputies but were not able to command support for important decisions. There were two other possibilities, one put forward by Robespierre, the other by Danton. Robespierre's solution was to hand over control to the Montagnards, who had never hesitated to advocate violence as a revolutionary tool. His proposal had the advantage of simplicity, but, in the absence of a unified parliamentary majority, it would have meant imposing an administration on an unwilling Convention and relying on the support of the *sans-culottes* as a permanent instrument of blackmail. The solution put forward by Danton and backed by the great politicians of the Plain was the formation of a kind of Republican Front from which all extremists would be excluded: this Front would constitute a parliamentary majority that would include both Girondin sympathisers and those Montagnards not committed to Robespierre. At first it seemed that Danton's solution was to be preferred; of the nine members of the Committee of Public Safety appointed on 11 April seven, with Barère at their head, were deputies from the 'centre'; initially, the Mountain was represented only by Danton and his friend Delacroix. For a government of this sort to survive, the factions would have had to call a truce to partisan passions, but neither the Girondins nor the Montagnards had the slightest intention of coming to terms.

At the beginning of April, Danton, Robespierre and Marat violently attacked the Girondins, who responded by bringing Marat to the Revolutionary Tribunal. But Marat was acquitted and brought back to the Convention in triumph. The Girondins were more successful in the provinces, and with the support of the moderates gained control of Marseilles and Lyons. As Michelet put it, they were becoming a 'royalist' party and therefore no further compromise was possible.

On 10 May the Convention moved from the Manège to the Tuileries, where the old theatre had been converted into an assembly hall. It was here that the Girondins were to fight their last parliamentary battles. Their plan was to smash the power of the Parisian authorities, call for armed forces from the departments and, in the event of failure, take refuge in Bourges. They were counting on a large majority in the Convention, since nearly all the agents sent out 'on mission' were Montagnards. However, the memoirs written by Girondins show that their leaders were by no means united.

On 18 May Guadet denounced the Parisian authorities, 'anarchic authorities greedy for money and power', and proposed to abolish them immediately. The Convention contented itself with electing a Commission of Twelve to investigate the activities of the Commune. All twelve were Girondins. On 24 May they had Hébert and Varlet arrested. On the 25th, when a delegation came from the Commune to demand that the two men be released, Isnard's reply was violent: 'If ever the Convention were to be degraded, if ever these insurrections which have been going on since 10 March should cause any harm to the nation's parliament, I tell you in the name of all France that Paris would be annihilated, and soon men would be searching the banks of the Seine for signs of the city.' Isnard's threats, calling to mind the Duke of Brunswick's manifesto of July 1792, were the signal for a *sans-culotte* uprising.

Like all the previous uprisings in the capital, that of 31 May was the work of unidentified agitators, the 'nameless, characterless phantoms' described by Michelet. The initiative came from the Cité Section, which on 28 May invited the other Sections to send representatives to the former Archbishop's Palace, where an unofficial electoral committee had been sitting for several weeks. On the 29th two bodies met at the palace: an assembly of delegates from the Sections (only thirty-three of the forty-eight Parisian Sections were represented) and a mysterious Committee of Six, which was to play the decisive role in the insurrection. In the evening of the 30th there was another meeting at the palace, and the original Committee of Six was enlarged, first to nine and then to eleven members, all of them salaried employees, artisans or shopkeepers.

Marat was sent before the Revolutionary Tribunal on 24 April 1793. However, the Tribunal was under the control of the Montagnards, and Marat was acquitted, crowned with a laurel-wreath and carried triumphantly from the Palais de Justice to the Convention.

Neither the Montagnards nor the Commune wished to see the revolt become an uncontrolled riot. In the Convention Danton tried to prevent a full-scale explosion by having the deputies vote for the abolition of the Commission of Twelve, but on the following day the Commission was reinstated; however, Hébert, Varlet and their friends had been released. A speech made by Robespierre on the 26th is often quoted: 'When all laws have been violated, when despotism is at its height and when good faith and decency are trampled underfoot, then is the time for the people to rise up. This moment has come.' But the conclusion of the speech is much more cautious: 'I call on all Montagnard deputies to rally together and fight the aristocracy, and I tell them they have but one alternative: either to resist the forces of intrigue with all their might, or to tender their resignation.' For Robespierre parliamentary action was still vital. He was asking for 'moral insurrection', pressure from the masses to make the Convention purge itself. The same sentiments prevailed at the Commune, where Hébert and Chaumette did all they could to control the *sans-culotte* movement, and where the mayor, Pache, was regarded as a traitor by the extremists. The Department of Paris, whose *procureur-syndic*, Lullier, was a friend of Robespierre, summoned the delegates of the Sections to the Jacobin Club on the 30th, with the intention of blocking any initiative that might be taken by the Revolutionary Committee formed at the Archbishop's Palace.

But the Revolutionary Committee forestalled the Department. During the night of 30–31 May it suspended the Commune and then reinstated it immediately, rebaptising it in the name of the 'sovereign people'. The Committee appointed, as head of the National Guard, an excise official named Hanriot, who had been in command of the Sans-Culotte Section (the Jardin des Plantes quarter). As dawn broke the tocsin began to ring and drums began to beat; but the Revolutionary Committee encountered difficulties, since neither the Commune nor the assembly convoked at the Jacobin Club by the Department of Paris would give it effective support. Several Sections, notably the Butte des Moulins and the Marais, condemned the insurrection, while others merely refused to take part. The movement needed experienced ringleaders, like Roux and Varlet, to boost its numbers.

At about five o'clock in the evening the Convention was surrounded by the mob, and a variety of petitions were presented. The last, which had been prepared by the Revolutionary Committee, but was actually presented to the Convention by representatives of the Commune, was the most violent in its demands: it urged the arrest of the twenty-two 'appellants' (those deputies who had voted in favour of an 'appeal to the people' to decide the king's fate), the members of the Commission of Twelve and the ministers Clavière and Lebrun; it demanded that a *sans-culotte* army be organised and paid to hunt down and punish suspects, and that a tax be imposed on the rich; it also proposed that for the time being only *sans-culottes* should have the right to vote. The Montagnard deputies supported the petition's demand for arrest and trial of suspects, but the majority of the Convention was content to vote for the suppression of the Commission of Twelve. For both the insurgents and the Montagnards, the revolt of 31 May had been a failure.

The Revolutionary Committee had no intention of disarming. During the night of 31 May–1 June, it ordered the arrest of suspects: Roland had managed to escape, and so his wife was arrested instead. The decisive revolt took place on 2 June, a Sunday, and therefore large numbers of workers were able to take part. A crowd of eighty thousand men beseiged the Convention in the early afternoon. The deputies, assembled behind their president, Hérault de Séchelles, tried in vain to leave the gardens of the palace, but were forced to return, threatened by Hanriot's cannons. They finally accepted Couthon's suggestion that the twenty-nine-Girondin deputies, together with the ministers Clavière and Lebrun, should be arrested at their homes. There was nothing grandly tragic in the manner of the Gironde's downfall, only farce, humiliation and fear.

The events of 2 June 1793 did not have the same significance as the uprising of 10 August 1792 in the history of the Revolution. Not a single major development engendered by the revolutionary war had been reversed; the Revolution simply drifted further off the course it had been set by eighteenth-century thought, and the masses continued to take advantage of the situation to impose their economic and political formulae on a reluctant bourgeoisie.

In two respects, however, the events of 2 June marked a turning-point. With the downfall of the Gironde the romance of revolution vanished for ever. For over a year the Girondins had endowed the Revolution with an aura of charm, youthfulness and enthusiasm which had seemed to perpetuate the sweet and gentle atmosphere of the great city of Bordeaux from which many of them had originated. But the mood of France had turned against illusion; the country was being invaded, Vendée had risen up in arms and the *sans-culottes* of Paris were ready to take extreme action. Reluctantly the Convention took leave of these young men whose eloquence and talent it had admired and envied. There were other men ready to take over the responsibilities of power. The Convention was an inexhaustible source of talent and seemed always able to produce the right men at the right moment: in times of peace and hope, the Girondins; in times of hardship and danger, the Montagnards; later, when happier days returned to France, the quiet, cautious, but eminently capable deputies of the

The events of 2 June 1793 culminated in the banishment of the Girondin leaders. The deputies of the Convention walked out of the assembly hall *en masse* and tried to find a way out of the Tuileries gardens, but everywhere their path was blocked by troops and eventually they returned to the assembly hall.

Plain. To interpret this succession of administrations simply in terms of social origins would be to allow historical judgement to be clouded by illusion or prejudice. The factor which distinguished the successive roles played by the Gironde, the Mountain and the Plain was not social background, but political circumstance.

However, the revolt of 2 June involved more than a change of government. The whole bourgeois revolution, even in its most democratic convictions, rested on a belief in the virtue of the parliamentary system; this new theory of government and the old popular passion for direct rule were quite incompatible. The revolt of 2 June had struck a grave blow at parliamentary ideals. No matter what Danton and the majority of Montagnards may have felt, the Convention had not merely been subjected to the 'moral insurrection' of which Robespierre had spoken: its deputies had been made prisoners physically, and for the first time armed force had been used against the nation's parliament. The fact that the armed mobs of 2 June were plebeian rather than military in origin is of little significance. Michelet realised that the events of that Sunday were a foretaste of 'both Fructidor and Brumaire'. In this sense it was not only the Gironde but the Revolution itself which had suffered defeat.

7

A TIME OF ANGUISH

No period of the Revolution has aroused as much passionate controversy as that extending from 2 June 1793 to the spring of 1794. In many respects, however, this period had less influence on the formation of modern France than other, shorter episodes – the summer of 1789, for instance, or the early months of the Consulate. There is no real justification for the special place given to the Terror by some historians; its fascination is something based on emotions of admiration or contempt rather than serious analysis. The revolutions of nineteenth-century France and twentieth-century Russia have helped to build this brief episode into a myth. Obviously, by its very nature, the Terror has lent itself to emotional judgements: in the past both Danton and Robespierre have had their admirers and their enemies, and now Hébert has become the controversial figure. Admittedly, this kind of biased historical writing has not modified the general outlines of the Revolution, but it has singled out two dominant themes – revolutionary dictatorship and popular democracy. In assessing the significance of the achievements and ambitions of the French politicians of Year II of the Republic, there has been a tendency to give priority to anything that appears to contain the seed of subsequent historical developments. The year 1793, which marked the critical stage of the bourgeois revolution, has been either glorified as the precursor of 1871, or condemned as the signpost to 1917. This form of perspective is wildly distorting.

It is clear, by considering the attitude of the deputies of the Mountain during the summer of 1793, that the Terror was not the result of a conscious choice freely made. Counter-revolution threatened, both in Vendée and on the frontiers of France, and the 'federalist' insurrection seemed likely to split the revolutionary movement into two hostile camps. Yet, in the days that followed the revolt of 2 June the general political atmosphere was relaxed enough to enable twenty Girondin deputies, threatened with arrest, to escape from their homes. The summer passed without the organisation of any form of revolutionary dictatorship.

183

The bourgeoisie, faithful to its liberating mission, was loath to have recourse to the restrictive measures it had always struggled to resist. However, it was now compelled by the mobs to adopt terrorist policies. The upheavals of September forced the Convention to vote for the formation of a revolutionary army, the Law of Suspects and the fixing of maximum prices and wages, and the constant pressure exerted by the sans-culottes *hastened the co-ordination of revolutionary measures during October, November and December. It is therefore not without reason that more recent historians, and in particular Albert Soboul, have interpreted the endless agitation of the Parisian populace as a prime factor in the birth of the Terror.*

But was popular pressure enough in itself to bring about the Terror? It was hardly a new phenomenon in the history of France. The belief in the virtue of coercion as an instrument of justice, a kind of magical solution to social problems, was one of the most permanent features of the long martyrdom of the lower classes. This traditional aspiration of Frenchmen, buried and apparently forgotten in times when the stability of society, or of the nation, was not in jeopardy, always reappeared in a crisis. The special feature of the situation in 1793 was not so much the people's demands for repressive measures, as the sheer intensity of the crisis threatening France: the prospect of imminent chaos caused the masses to press harder than ever for economic and political controls, and at the same time persuaded the bourgeoisie to accede to their demands. As Barère put it in the famous decree of 23 August authorising a mass conscription, the Republic was just one vast besieged city. Lyons was in the hands of the royalists, Toulon lay under British control (it surrendered on 27 August), Condé, Valenciennes and Mainz were occupied by the Prussians, the Vendéans were victorious in Saumur, Nantes, Châtillon-sur-Sèvre and Vihiers, and the populace was demanding food. The bourgeois revolution had lost its bearings and now was isolated. Circumstances made it necessary to resort to the methods of Roman antiquity – dictatorship for the sake of public safety. But, since the bourgeoisie was not going to abandon parliamentary government, which had been its supreme political achievement, it was to be a dictatorship controlled by the Convention. The sans-culottes *were to suffer just as much as the aristocrats from the Convention's repressive measures. On 9 September their Sections were prohibited from sitting in permanent assembly; the* maximum général, *approved on 29 September, imposed controls on wages as well as prices, which helped to split the popular front; during the autumn and winter the government introduced measures to make militant action more and more difficult and hazardous; and then, with the 'drama of Germinal' and the execution of Hébert, the* sans-culotte *movement lost its politically autonomous character. Dictatorial methods, made necessary by the force of circumstances, were relaxed when the situation began to improve; controls on profits were eased after the events of Germinal, and restrictions on bourgeois property-rights ceased on 9 Thermidor. Far from being an inevitable part of the revolutionary process, the dictatorship of Year II bears all the marks of contingency, of a nation that had found itself in dire straits.*

A Time of Anguish

'Robespierrism is democracy.' This quotation from Babeuf, dating from February 1796, was the guiding inspiration of Jacobin historians right up to the time when distinctions began to be made between 'bourgeois' democracy and 'popular' democracy, between direct government and representative or parliamentary government, between Jacobinism and sans-culotterie. *It is certainly true that, since the capture of the Tuileries on 10 August 1792, the men who had taken control of the Revolution had considerably widened the political horizons opened up by that event. The revolution of 10 August had heralded the new era of political democracy. In the fields of universal suffrage, education and public assistance, the Convention paved the way for the achievements of the nineteenth century. The Declaration of Rights of 1793, the Constitution which followed it (but which was never to be put into effect) and the decrees of Ventôse form an impressive body of reforms. However, allowances must be made for the part played by tactics and circumstance in the reforming activity of the Convention. Although the 1793 Declaration of Rights proclaimed the rights of employment, education and public assistance, it did not impose on the rights of property-ownership any of the restrictions envisaged by Robespierre in the proposals he put forward on 24 April: in April Robespierre had been anxious to win the support of the* sans-culottes, *but now it was a matter of disarming Girondin propaganda by guaranteeing the property-rights of the bourgeoisie. The men of 1793 were not planners; Saint-Just said as much himself: 'The force of circumstances may lead us to things we had not expected.' Jaurès is right in placing the intellectually creative phase of the Revolution before the downfall of the Gironde; it was Condorcet who, in April 1792, had elaborated the Revolution's most broadly democratic plan for education; and, by comparison with the Constitution drawn up by the same Condorcet, the draft which the Montagnards submitted for the approval of the Convention on 23 June 1793 was very much a backward step. All the Revolution's great ideas had been developed before the revolt of 2 June. The Montagnards' strength lay not in intellectual originality nor in a vision of a future democracy, but in their capacity for effective action and their tactical skill.*

Some historians have attempted to make the Parisian sans-culotte *movement the forerunner of subsequent historical movements. Ten years ago Daniel Guérin saw in the conflict between the* sans-culottes *and the revolutionary government the embryo of a proletarian revolution within the bourgeois revolution. It has not been difficult to show that such an interpretation cannot be reconciled either with the economic and social reforms demanded by the* sans-culottes, *or with the social and professional composition of the movement (wage-earners working in industry were in a small minority compared with all the journeymen, shopkeepers and self-employed craftsmen). What united the* sans-culottes *as agitators was the struggle to persuade the government to introduce price-controls; their dream was of an ideal society in which property-ownership would be general, but limited to personal needs; in other words, they repudiated the concentration of wealth fundamental to capitalism. Their concept of the ideal*

185

society was essentially reactionary, and was inspired by a nostalgia for the old Utopian dream of a 'golden age'. It should not be forgotten that a fair proportion of the Parisian population at the end of the eighteenth century consisted of peasants; some of them were seasonal migrants who came to the capital in search of temporary employment, but there was also quite a large community of permanent settlers. Many of these peasants had owned the little plots of land they had cultivated, and they may well have infected the revolutionary mentality of the Parisian sans-culottes *with something of their own deep-rooted attachment to the principle of small-scale property-ownership.*

According to their most recent historian, the delegates of the Section assemblies (the sectionnaires) *were the Revolution's politically most advanced group: 'to them the principle of popular sovereignty, in the full sense of that term, implied that the Sections were autonomous and permanently constituted and possessed the right to authorise legislation, to control the activities of the nation's elected representatives and, when necessary, to dismiss them: the Sections were moving gradually towards direct government and popular democracy.' Yet, if the temptation to argue from hypothesis is disregarded, and one simply considers how far the method of militant* sectionnaires *were in fact comparable with the methods of twentieth-century democracy, such a theory will be seen to be disproved. The* sans-culotte *militants of the Sections were always a minority, and the methods by which they gained control of their assemblies bear a strange resemblance to those used two hundred years earlier by the Parisians of the Catholic League. The militants' insistence on oral voting in public sessions, their conviction that informing was a civic duty, their abhorrence of anything that might jeopardise unity, and their readiness to resort to violence were symptomatic of a fundamental characteristic of group psychology: the more they realised they were a minority, the more they claimed to represent the 'consensus' of opinion, and when they finally saw that persuasion was impossible they began to think in terms of coercion. The two passions that have always burned in the breasts of popular agitators – the demand for equality and the insistence on the punishment of the 'guilty' – had been rekindled by the Revolution. The guillotine, the 'scythe of equality', seemed to satisfy both these passions; but the revolutionaries were deluding themselves in thinking that it could solve the problems of French society. The legacy bequeathed to modern France by the revolutionary government of 1793–4 must be sought not so much in the part it played in the organisation of the modern French state, as in certain social, political and psychological features of contemporary France which can be seen to date from that period.*

There is one myth which has been particularly difficult to destroy, and which has been propagated chiefly by opponents of the French revolutionary tradition – the notion that the Jacobins were the architects of state-control and centralisation. Admittedly, the Jacobins found themselves forced by circumstances to depart temporarily from the dual ideal of decentralisation and elective office which the bourgeoisie had laid down in the 1791 Constitution. The decree of 14 Frimaire Year II (4 December 1793) subordinated all elected authorities to the govern-

ment committees and restricted the powers of the districts and municipalities by imposing on them 'national agents' who were directly answerable to Paris. But this return to centralisation was the result of exceptional circumstances, and in any case lasted only briefly; even in Year II centralised control was imposed only at a superficial level: the Jacobin movement, like the Gironde, displayed a tendency towards 'federalism', with the result that the popular societies, clubs and government agents were able to take power into their own hands and interpret the central authority's directives as they thought fit. It was not the agents of the Committee of Public Safety who were responsible for the framework of the modern French state, but Bonaparte's prefects. Brumaire 1799 was still some years ahead.

The most significant feature of the political scene in 1793 was not the dictatorship of one man, but the importance attached to parliamentary methods of government. Instead of allowing historical perspectives to be distorted by the image of the guillotine and its host of victims, one should study the activities of the Convention and the Jacobin Club and the day to day manoeuvrings of Robespierre. This 'very great tactician', as Michelet dubbed him, was first and foremost a great parliamentary leader. As early as June 1793 Robespierre had predicted the course which events were to take: 'We would have been victorious four years ago if only we had not neglected the instruments of guile and stratagem.' The Girondins had shown little capacity for political manoeuvre. In government Robespierre showed even greater skill than in opposition. His majority was small, however; he had to look for temporary allies among men who would before long become his adversaries; he had to defend himself against attack by diverting attention to the vices of financial speculation and the threat from abroad; he waited for his enemies to come into the open so that he could isolate them and then, when the opportunity presented itself, annihilate them. For nearly a year Robespierre succeeded in defending the policies of an often divided government to a reluctant Convention. As leader of the Montagnard administration he laid the foundations of the modern technique of 'managing' a parliamentary assembly.

At the same time the reorganisation of peasant society was nearing completion. The decree of 17 July 1793, which abolished without indemnity all remaining seigneurial rights, freed rural property-ownership from its last fetters. The decree of 3 June authorised the sale of emigré properties in small lots, with generous facilities for payment. The decree of 10 June envisaged the division of communal lands on an individual basis. In fact, this law was never really put into practice, as it would have resulted in land being chopped up into tiny portions; but the very fact that communal lands were preserved, combined with the spread of peasant ownership, was to contribute to the stability of rural life in the nineteenth century, though it also meant that agricultural techniques were to remain archaic. For a long time, the alliances which the bourgeoisie were obliged to form in Year II of the Republic proved to be an obstacle to agrarian capitalism and to the progress of crop-growing methods.

But the true value of the Jacobin heritage is to be seen in the realm of human intellect and sensibility. Even today '1793' stirs the emotions of Frenchmen. Some see merely the blood, the priests in hiding, the death of André Chénier; they repudiate 1793 wholly, without reservations, incapable of perceiving anything good in the events of that year – their attitude is beyond reason and intelligence. Others – and they are in the majority – are prepared to argue against Danton or Robespierre and to deplore the cult of the Supreme Being or the law of Prairial, without allowing their distaste for individual politicians or particular events to diminish a very deep and warm affection for the achievements of 1793. For them '93' means the nation of France driving back the invading armies of the Coalition, the great festival of Equality, the vengeance of the oppressed:

> '*Il faut raccourcir les géants*
> *Et rendre les petits plus grands*
> *Tous à la même hauteur*
> *Voilà le vrai bonheur.*'

THE SANS-CULOTTES

What exactly was a *sans-culotte*? A writer, defending the events of summer 1793, composed the following portrait:

He is someone who goes everywhere on foot, has no millions, just like all the rest of you, no manors, no valets to serve him, and who lives very simply with his wife and children, if he has any, on the fourth or fifth floor. He is a useful fellow, for he can plough a field, forge iron, saw wood, use a file, cover a roof, make shoes and is willing to spill his last drop of blood for the welfare of the Republic.

The *sans-culotte* had a distinctive style of dress and behaviour. Scorning the knee-breeches (*culottes*) and silk stockings worn by the rich, he wore instead a kind of straight trouser and a short jacket, the *carmagnole*. The red cap, probably introduced into popular circles by the cultivated bourgeoisie, was a tremendous success; although Robespierre disapproved of it and the bourgeois were openly contemptuous, the cap became the symbol of militant revolution and came to be worn generally during the summer of 1793. The pike which the *sans-culotte* usually carried represented the power of the people in arms.

The *sans-culotte* did not say 'monsieur' but 'citoyen' ('citizen'). He was determined that the familiar form 'tu' should replace the polite 'vous', which he regarded as a 'left-over from feudalism'. When addressing a petition to a deputy he would sign himself 'Ton égal en droits' ('Your equal in rights'). He disapproved of officers wearing epaulettes and wanted them to be made to eat from mess-tins with the ordinary soldiers. A devotee of equality, he was also virtuous: one

The *sans-culottes* considered 'Equality' to be the most important word in the revolutionary slogan 'Liberty, Equality, Fraternity'. Here, coal-men and 'Chevaliers de Saint-Louis' are seen together handing in their Old Regime medals at the town hall: as a sign of equality their names are recorded on the same register.

sans-culotte petition demanded that 'prostitutes should be compelled to live together in special national institutions where the air is healthy and should be given women's work to occupy them'; another petition demanded a law against gaming-houses and places of debauchery. Details like these provide the key to the *sans-culotte* mentality: a passion for egalitarianism and repressive action by the state. Anything that offended this passion was a sign of *aristocratisme* and counter-revolution. A haughty or scornful attitude, or the possession of a certain wealth, was enough to make a person guilty of *aristocratisme*. 'All rich people are aristocrats – great merchants and monopolists, bankers, swindling shopkeepers, everybody involved in chicanery and everybody who has possessions'. To be cultivated and 'enlightened' was to be suspect of lacking civic virtue and therefore liable to immediate arrest. The desire to 'level down' was often mingled with xenophobia; anyone who married a foreigner was an 'enemy of the French, an emigré at heart'; anyone who wore a garment made of foreign material was accused of decking himself out 'in the liveries of our enemies in order to keep our own dear artisans in poverty'.

189

Informing, which had been considered dishonourable under the Old Regime, became a virtue and duty under the Republic. Above all, the guillotine stirred the imagination of the *sans-culottes*. Many men who in their private lives were of a calm and gentle temperament were transformed at the sight of the scaffold. True, the populace regarded the Terror as a legitimate and necessary means for the defence of the Revolution, but one is surely justified in looking beyond conscious motives? The guillotine, variously known as the 'national chopper', the 'people's axe' and the 'scythe of equality', was the magic remedy of a people who had suffered centuries of hunger. 'The guillotine is hungry, it has been fasting for too long,' one *sans-culotte* shouted; a woman was heard to say she would willingly eat the heart of anyone who opposed the *sans-culottes*. During the famine of Ventôse a shoemaker advised people to go to the prisons, cut the throats of the prisoners, then roast and eat them, saying that 'if they want to make patriots eat cats, then they will be eaten like dogs'. Such vivid and original images must surely have sprung from memories of a whole history of humiliation of which we can know nothing.

The *sans-culottes* were echoing the demands of urban movements of earlier centuries. They wanted equality of situation, not of opportunity; equality of civic obligations, not of civic rights. The militants, always a minority, used the Parisian Sections as their platform to intimidate and impose their will. They 'regenerated' Sections by replacing moderates with their own sympathisers. By autumn 1793, non-participation in Section assemblies, or refusal to accept public office, was liable to result in arrest.

For these militants, sovereignty of the people meant the right of primary assemblies to authorise legislation, to control the activities of national deputies and, when necessary, to dismiss them, to supervise public officials, and in time of need to start insurrections. They replaced the principle of unlimited property-ownership with that of 'equality of possessions', restricting property to the 'extent of physical needs'. The only concrete item in this programme was the demand for maximum-price controls. In fact, it was only their common plight as consumers that united the *sans-culottes*. As producers they had little in common, earning their livings in widely varied occupations. Most of them were employed in crafts, working at home and selling their labour to merchants.

By Year II of the Republic, the militants of the movement were beginning to make their influence felt. They had created through their committees a 'sub-intelligentsia of shopkeepers and artisans', a petty bourgeois élite. The economic crisis provided an opportunity to 'break through'. They opposed a parliamentary regime because they were jealous of the 'men of talent' whom four years of revolution had placed

Engraving illustrating the great diversity of the sans-culotte *movement: on the extreme left, the cap, trousers and pike represent the idealised* sans-culotte; *the carter, market porter, cobbler and joiner (left to right) represent some of the many different occupations which the movement embraced.*

in the nation's assemblies and in the leading positions of power. It was a question of political rivalry rather than class struggle. A new stratum of society was eager to take over the reins of government. It was to wait a hundred years to realise its ambitions.

THE COMMITTEE OF PUBLIC SAFETY

Faced with the demands of the *sans-culottes*, the Montagnards were far from being a united political force. The events of 2 June 1793 had left control of the nation in the hands of the Committee of Public Safety, which had been established by the Convention on 7 April and strengthened at the end of May. Of the nine original members of the Committee, seven were deputies of the Plain and only two, Danton and Delacroix, represented the Mountain. For the time being it was Danton who dominated the Committee.

Was Danton the most realistic of the Convention's politicians, or merely a venal opportunist? By being oversimplified thus the 'Danton problem' has been distorted rather than clarified. Documentary evidence has left no doubt of his venality, but what exactly does this prove? The emphasis has been laid on Danton's services to the revolutionary cause, and the part he played in the counter-revolution has never been proved. History, after all, is not a matter of moral judgements. In more than one respect Danton resembled Mirabeau. He had the same strength of temperament, which caused him to declare, not without complacency: 'Nature has endowed me with the form of an athlete and the fierce physiognomy of Liberty.' He shared Mirabeau's love of life and pleasure, his genius for improvisation and his gift for swaying a crowd with his eloquence.

Danton revealed his true self in moments of grave crisis. His powerful oratory was aimed not at provoking the internal conflicts and schisms, which Robespierre considered beneficial to the currents of revolution, but at the necessity of unity against the common enemy. His strategy – the key to all the apparent contradictions in his political attitudes – was to present as broad a front as possible to the enemy and to avoid any divisions within the revolutionary movement. But, whenever he was unable to resist the tide of opinion, he went along with it. Though a champion of the Revolution, he was always prepared to negotiate with the opposition, and was even ready to grant the queen her freedom. Danton has been praised by some and censured by others. When all is said and done, was he not simply the victim, like Robespierre after him, of circumstances beyond his control? He found himself in the dilemma of knowing that to strive for peace was the intelligent thing to do, but that to speak openly of peace meant alienating revolutionary opinion.

In the early summer of '93, when France was suffering one military defeat after another, Danton was feeling the strain of political life. On 4 July Marat launched an attack on what he called the 'Committee of Public Ruin'. The uncovering of a supposed plot, in which Dillon was said to be involved, put Danton in a compromising position. He was weary and wanted to devote his time and energy to the young wife he had recently married. His withdrawal from the political arena may even have been a calculated manoeuvre: perhaps he felt that, as power had compromised him, he should now leave the others to compromise themselves, and concentrate on 'purifying' himself. On 10 July, at his own request, the Convention removed him from the Committee of Public Safety, which was reconstituted. Though he was re-elected to the Convention on 5 September, Danton refused to take an active part in the administration. Jaurès saw how dangerous such an attitude was, both for the majority in the Convention and for Danton himself: when a politician of outstanding ability spurns power there is always a possibility that he will sooner or later become a focal point for the forces of opposition.

Three days after Danton removed himself from the Committee of

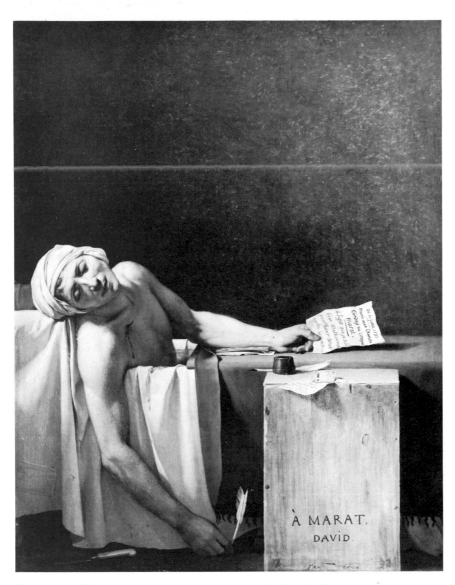

The death of Marat, 13 July 1793, painted by J.-L. David. Charlotte Corday stabbed Marat in his bath, believing she was striking down a tyrant; but, in fact, she merely made a martyr of a man whose reputation was waning.

Public Safety, Marat was stabbed to death by Charlotte Corday. This young woman from Caen (she was only twenty-five) had read too much Plutarch; she believed she was striking down a tyrant, but in fact she was responsible for creating a cult. In 1789 Jean-Paul Marat seemed to have little future. He was then forty-five and his life so far had been a succession of disappointments. Born in the principality of Neuchâtel of an Italian father, a defrocked priest who had been converted to Calvinism, Marat travelled, moving from Bordeaux to Paris and then from Paris to London, where he stayed ten years and acquired a certain social status as a doctor and writer. When he returned to Paris in 1776 he enjoyed only a brief success. Dismissed from his position as physician to the bodyguard of the Comte d'Artois in 1784, he then became embroiled with scientific circles over his very unsophisticated opinions on heat and electricity. Sick and in debt, he had not been able to derive any practical advantage from his travel experiences or from his studies and writings. But this store of intellectual riches was to find unlimited opportunities for expression when the Revolution came.

Within four years Marat had become the 'Friend of the People' (as editor of *l'Ami du peuple*), and his rapid climb to fame was hardly surprising. He had prophesied the flight of the king and the defection of La Fayette long in advance. His constant vigilance and the image he acquired of a perpetual fugitive from authority earned him a reputation as an invaluable, if perhaps excessively critical spokesman of the revolutionary cause. At the Cordeliers Club and in the Sections he stirred popular passions with his speeches and writings. His popularity caused him to be elected to the Convention, although many Montagnards were reluctant to accept him as one of themselves, and Robespierre gave him a cool reception. In his Memoirs Levasseur shows quite clearly what kind of role the Mountain intended Marat to play in the Convention: 'Marat never had any influence on the Convention. . . . His wildness was quite harmless, but it represented democratic zeal at its highest possible pitch of intensity. . . . Marat served as a sort of safety valve against the dangers of popular democracy being controlled by self-interested demagogues in the pay of foreign powers.' In other words, he was less dangerous inside the Convention than outside it; he was the guarantee of revolutionary orthodoxy and served to protect the Mountain against trouble from the left.

Yet, when death struck, Marat was also beginning to suffer the strains of political life. This democrat had nothing but contempt for economics. The great surge of revolt which, in February 1793, ended in the mobs sacking shops and demanding price-controls seemed to Marat to be merely a counter-revolutionary manoeuvre. On 4 July he violently denounced Roux, Leclerc and the rest of the 'Enragés'. He may have simply been anxious to destroy a rival faction, but the real reason for his attitude was probably his inability to understand the motives of the common people. Thanks to Charlotte Corday, death was to restore a mythical purity to the Marat legend. Immediately a cult grew up around the heart of the 'Friend of the People', which

Charlotte Corday in a tumbril on her way to the scaffold. To the end she maintained a dignified composure.

the Cordeliers took and kept. At the end of July a civic ceremony was held to 'raise an altar to the heart of the incorruptible Marat'.

For the Convention, however, Marat's death meant that the way was now open for all demagogues and extremists.

Apart from the Cordeliers Club, whose role will be discussed further on, the only likely source of extremist activity was the 'Enragés', who were finally eliminated in September 1793. The new Committee of Public Safety was a democratic coalition. Formed in stages from 10 July to 6 September, the Committee now had twelve members, all of them Montagnards or deputies of the 'centre' who had temporarily rallied to the policies of the Mountain. They had in common the advantages of youth (their average age was a little above thirty) and experience; they had all served their apprenticeship in previous assemblies or in high offices of state. The Committee's decisions were taken by agreement among its members, most of whom were responsible for a particular department. Billaud-Varenne and Collot d'Herbois, the last two to join the Committee and elected as a result of *sans-culotte* pressure, were entrusted with the supervision of the 'representatives on mission', Lindet was in charge of Supplies and Transport, Prieur of the Côte d'Or was responsible for Munitions, Saint-Just and Carnot for War, Jean Bon Saint-André and Prieur of the Marne for the Navy; Barère made his presence felt everywhere, while Robespierre supervised the political aspects of the Committee's business.

That differences of opinion existed among the members of the Committee is not in doubt, and these differences were often fundamental, as later events were to show. But not too much should be made of divergences of policy at this stage; for the time being the Committee was concerned with the immediate problems, and its members were united in their determination to take whatever steps seemed necessary. Constitutional government was to be suspended and an emergency dictatorship established in its place: 'revolutionary government' now became the order of the day. The three men who were to dominate the regime were Couthon, the paralytic deputy of Puy-de-Dôme, Saint-Just, who wore the halo of youth, and, above all, Robespierre.

Rarely has a man been as wildly misrepresented as Maximilien Robespierre. The animosity of historians has transformed this scholarly man into a mere demagogue, the moderate politician into a bloodthirsty revolutionary, the skilful parliamentarian into a dictator, the fervent deist into a detractor of religion. Even historians well disposed towards the Revolution have hesitated to do Robespierre justice; Michelet, in particular, misunderstood his character, suspecting him of being a 'hypocrite' and a would-be 'priest', and allowing him only one good quality: his antipathy towards militarism. On the other hand, those who, like Mathiez, have idolised Robespierre, have probably done just as much to propagate the myth of his inhumanity. When he arrived in Versailles in May 1789, this little man with delicate features and elegant bearing was just a provincial advocate with no fortune and little in the way of reputation. Orphaned at the age of six, the young Robespierre had been able to obtain bursaries so that he could continue his studies at the Collège Louis-le-Grand and follow the family tradition by becoming a lawyer. These early years of study, in which the pleasures of intellectual pursuits had been tainted by poverty, left a deep impression on Robespierre, a mistrust of affluence and the easy life. He owed his electoral success to the support he received from the lower ranks of the Third Estate, who preferred him to a colleague backed by the well-to-do of Arras. His first speeches in the Constituent

Maximilien Robespierre, the 'Incorruptible'.

Assembly created little effect among the deputies at the time, but made a powerful impression in the press and the clubs, where by the end of 1790 he was beginning to outstrip the great Mirabeau. Only he voted against the introduction of martial law, and only he fought against the laws depriving 'passive' citizens and the negroes of the West Indies of the rights of full citizenship. He was also one of the few to object to the proposal that the people's rights be limited to presenting petitions to the Assembly. He was one of the very few to understand right at the outset that the strength of the Revolution lay in the alliance between the bourgeoisie and the people. His isolation in the Assembly and the hatred and sarcasm he aroused there, merely served to enhance his prestige among the Parisian populace. The deputy from Arras was establishing himself as the leader of revolutionary Paris. After the king's flight he concentrated on rearguard action, though he did succeed in having deputies of the Constituent Assembly prohibited from membership of the Legislative Assembly.

Robespierre now waged his major battles at the Jacobin Club, where he managed to secure the loyalty of members in spite of the defection of the Feuillants. He boldly opposed the war, and by so doing risked losing popularity. He condemned the army's treachery and its defeat, and then turned his invective against the court and the Girondins. Danton's withdrawal gave him the opportunity to assume governmental responsibility, and in late July he was co-opted onto the Committee of Public Safety. Robespierre did not try to dominate his colleagues, but he enjoyed a moral authority which he owed to his past record as an opponent of ministerial policies and to the fact that he had managed to avoid compromising himself politically. His genius and his weaknesses served him equally well. Far from being doctrinaire, Robespierre was an outstanding tactician, a politician with a remarkable flair for choosing the right moment, distinguishing between practical possibility and mere conjecture, and going along with popular or parliamentary opinion without allowing himself to be outmanoeuvred by either. He gave proof of this tactical skill after the king's flight to Varennes, when he advised against republican demonstrations and stood firmly by the Constitution which he had himself criticised as not being radical enough; and again before the uprisings of 10 August 1792 and 2 June 1793, when he associated himself with the revolutionary movement only at the very last minute, in order to be able to influence its outcome. He was to display this same skill as leader of the revolutionary government, when he had to deal with hostile factions and safeguard his majority by isolating his immediate rivals from their sympathisers. Even a natural meanness of temperament, which led him to indulge in personal attacks and jealous suspicions, helped him in times of crisis. The 'incorruptible Robespierre' could be quite unscrupulous. After the September massacres he tried to divert popular anger against his Girondin rivals, just at the time when Danton was attempting to divert it against the foreign enemy. In March 1793 he perfidiously attacked the Girondins for their 'constant opposition to the union of the nations with our republic': after having previously opposed the war, he was now lauding French victories purely as a political manoeuvre. His incessant denunciations delighted the populace, for they seemed to echo its own deep anxieties.

Robespierre, though a realistic and efficient leader, was to succumb to the same Utopian fantasies in which Saint-Just indulged. The problems involved in the exercise of power, the aloofness of the bourgeoisie and the inability of the people to understand the real issues at stake, served to confirm the ideals these two men had formed in childhood. They dreamed of creating a world of brotherly love in which people would be bound to one another by solemn declarations of friendship and in which children would live on a vegetarian diet; but their picture of the future as one long rustic idyll was to be shattered by the realities of the mercantile world of capitalism. 'What is the source of the trouble? The bourgeois.' Robespierre had written these words on the eve of the revolution of 2 June. Their political significance has been emphasised often enough, but their metaphysical overtones are of even greater importance: for Robespierre and Saint-Just the bourgeois revolution which they had helped to bring into being contained the seed of absolute evil – the vices of affluence, atheism and self-interest which they found so detestable. 'I look on opulence not only as the price paid for crime, but as the punishment of crime, and I wish to be poor to avoid being unhappy', said Robespierre. 'Everybody wants a republic, but nobody wants poverty or virtue', said Saint-Just. Both men realised that institutions could never take the place of fundamental virtues. The cult of virtue led consequently to pessimism. 'Virtue was always in a minority on earth.' The Christian idea of the Fall was superimposed, in a secularised form, on the conviction that the mediaeval tradition of community life and human brotherhood had been broken by the new morality of self-interest and utility.

During the summer of 1793 the Committee of Public Safety had to face up to four dangers. It would be easy to exaggerate the seriousness of the threat posed by the Girondin resistance, which has sometimes been described as a 'federalist insurrection'. In both the west and the south the movement proved ineffective, except at Toulon, which surrendered to the British on 27 August, and at Lyons, which was taken by the royalists. The government faced a graver problem in the Vendéan uprising; the three royalist armies captured Saumur in June and then, on 18 July, won a great victory over the republican troops at Vihiers. The Convention immediately decided on the systematic destruction of the Vendéans. The problem of France's weakened frontiers was even more important, since the direction of the foreign war, at both the political and the military levels, had become entangled in general confusion and disagreement over policy. After Condé, Valenciennes surrendered on 28 July. The Austrians occupied Lower Alsace. Sardinian troops invaded the valleys of the Maurienne, the Tarentaise and the Faucigny, and Paoli surrendered Corsica to the British.

But the Revolution was also being threatened at its very centre by the dangers of extremism. Inflation had aggravated the food-shortage (the assignat had lost seventy per cent of its face value) and basic necessities, such as meat and soap, were unobtainable in many places; the people were demanding general price-controls (the 'general maximum') and legislation against hoarders. This time they were being led by the Cordeliers, a faction that was even more menacing than the 'Enragés' had ever been. Under Hébert, whose journal, *le Père Duchesne*, was enjoying a prodigious success, Vincent, the secretary-general at the Ministry of War, and Chaumette, *procureur-général* of the Paris Commune, an active minority of agitators was organised, and on 5 September the Convention was surrounded by the armed Sections demanding new ultra-revolutionary measures (the creation of a 'revolutionary army', the arrest of suspects and a purge of committees). The deputies had to yield on all three points, but retained the most important thing – the control of power.

THE DICTATORSHIP OF THE REVOLUTIONARY GOVERNMENT

Confronted by a general crisis in which the Revolution was being threatened from all directions – by the peasants of Vendée, the armies of the Coalition and the *sans-culottes* of Paris – the Committee of Public Safety instructed the Convention to approve a series of drastic measures which initiated the Terror.

The Constitution voted on 24 June was a hasty, improvised affair: the Girondins were accusing the Montagnards of being dictators and the Montagnards were anxious to show the nation this was not so. Although the rights of employment, public assistance, education and insurrection were ratified, no reservations were attached to property-ownership. However, the text of the Constitution was never put into practice, for on 11 August discussion on it was adjourned. On 10 October, at the instigation of Saint-Just, a decree proclaimed that 'the provisional government of France will be revolutionary until peace is restored'. Later, when local committees and certain government agents had begun to take too much power into their own hands, the law of

Jean-Baptiste Jourdan (*left*), born in 1762, became a brigadier-general at the age of 31 years. Lazare Hoche (*right*), son of one of the king's stablemen, was made a brigadier-general at the age of 25 years.

14 Frimaire (4 December) was introduced to strengthen the authority of the Committee of Public Safety: a war dictatorship had been established.

The course which the war had been taking demanded a complete reorganisation of methods of recruitment: to rely on a professional army or even on selective conscription was useless, and so it was decided to mobilise all available resources. This was the famous *levée en masse* which the Convention voted on 23 August after an outstanding speech by Barère. The decree laid down that henceforth generals would be answerable to the civil power, and at the same time paved the way for wholesale purges and the promotion of comparatively unknown officers like Jourdan and Hoche.

The *sans-culottes* insisted that these measures be accompanied by the imposition of a system of organised repression, and gradually the Convention gave way to their demands. The Terror, established as the order of the day on 5 September, was made more effective. On 17 September the Law of Suspects was decreed. The reconstituted Revolutionary Tribunal became the scene of endless trials and sentences of death. Among the most famous trials were those of Marie-Antoinette on 16 October, Philippe Égalité (the former Duc d'Orléans) in November, twenty-two Girondins and two Feuillants, Barnave and Bailly. In the view of the Montagnards, and particularly Robespierre, an organised and limited Terror was the only means of avoiding a

A crucial moment at the trial of Marie-Antoinette. She proclaims her innocence of the charges laid against her.

repetition of the massacres perpetrated by the Parisian mobs on earlier occasions.

On two points the government refused to give in completely to the demands of the militant minorities. In June and July it had been agreed that communal lands should be divided up individually among the peasants, and that all remaining seigneurial rights should be abolished without indemnity. But the urban populations' demands for price-controls were only partially granted. Although the 'general maximum' for prices and wages was approved on 29 September, its application proved to be no easy thing, since it had divided the formerly united front of the *sans-culotte* movement. Moreover, the revolutionary government refused to countenance any further economic controls, which would have undermined its own bourgeois foundations. These foundations were already being imperilled by another new development, the 'dechristianisation' movement. The Convention made no fuss about approving the revolutionary calendar which was introduced in place of the old Christian calendar (6 and 24 October);

202

This inkpot, representing the *sans-culotte* red cap crushing a priest, is one example of the anti-clerical propaganda of the Hébertists.

The confiscation of the clergy's wealth spread from the provinces to Paris. Here, gold, silver and other ornaments taken from churches are seen being brought to the Convention.

The Republican calendar: the traditional names of the months were replaced with new names representing the different cycles of Nature.

but when certain representatives on mission, notably Fouché in the department of Nièvre, decided to go a step further and convert churches into 'Temples of Reason' and their example was followed in Paris by foreign exiles, Robespierre resolved to put a brake on the dechristianisation campaign. On 16 Frimaire (6 December) the Convention reaffirmed the principle of freedom of worship.

By the end of the autumn of 1793 the revolutionary government's measures had brought a lull in the conflict between the Republic and its enemies at home and abroad. The Committee of Public Safety, which in the words of Barère had made 'a pact with death', had sent its own members (Carnot to the Army of the North, Saint-Just to the eastern front) to boost the morale of the troops and their commanding officers, with the result that France gained victories at Wattignies (16 October) and Landau (27 December). These were not decisive victories, since the enemy had not been routed on either occasion, but they did remove the immediate threat of invasion. The centres of counter-revolutionary activity within France were liquidated. Lyons, occupied on 9 October, was renamed Ville-Affranchie. Toulon was recaptured on 19 December. Only Vendée remained to be quelled. After Kléber had crushed the Vendéans at Cholet on 17 October, La Rochejaquelin, who had been appointed commander-in-chief of the royalist army, crossed the Loire to the north but failed in an attempt to capture Granville (13 November), and on 13 December his troops were cut to pieces in the centre of Le Mans. All that was left of the 'Grand Catholic and Royal Army' was a few scattered bands.

And so the autumn of 1793 ended with a pause in revolutionary ferment; but this relaxation of tensions heralded new dangers for the government, for it gave men time in which to reconsider their positions and revive forgotten grudges, and made the Republic of Virtue and the Terror seem less tolerable.

THE STRUGGLE AGAINST THE FACTIONS

The period of relative stability which extended through the winter of 1793–4 saw a number of dramatic schisms within the Montagnard coalition. The pretext for the confrontation was a case of financial corruption (speculation in the shares of the old East India Company) involving foreign bankers connected with the Hébertist faction (Perregaux, Proly and Walter) and also a number of deputies known to have had dealings with Danton, among them Delaunay, Chabot, Basire, Julien de Toulouse and Fabre d'Églantine. On 24 Brumaire (17 November) the Committee of Public Safety ordered the arrest of all concerned except for Fabre d'Églantine, whom Robespierre spared. While anxious to keep aloof from the factions of 'moderatism' and 'exaggeration', Robespierre needed Danton's support in his struggle against the chief source of danger, the extremist left wing. Returning to Paris on 20 November, Danton flew to Robespierre's assistance and, with the help of Camille Desmoulins, who on 5 December launched a new journal, the *Vieux Cordelier*, began a vigorous campaign against the ultra-terrorist and dechristianising Hébertists.

However, Robespierre also had to keep an eye on the other wing of his majority, all those deputies who had been implicated in the Terror and the policy of revolutionary war. To make matters more difficult, in the Committee itself, Collot d'Herbois and Billaud-Varenne defended the left-wing extremists and counter-attacked by having Fabre d'Églantine arrested on 12 January 1794. For the first time Robespierre found himself in a very weak position. While continuing to proclaim Virtue and Terror as principles of revolutionary government, he was soon compelled to resort to a series of purges.

The immediate threat came from the left-wing extremists. In February and March the activities of the Cordeliers were intensified under the double stimulus of economic hardship and political discontent. The Sections and the Cordeliers Club, which was led by Hébert and Vincent, demanded a wholesale redistribution of property and public offices. In an attempt to thwart the Cordeliers, Saint-Just presented a decree on 8 Ventôse (26 February) proposing the confiscation of the properties of suspects, which were to be handed over to the needy. In a few dramatic sentences he evoked the great millenarian dream of the poor. In reality this was just a manoeuvre to isolate the Cordeliers from the masses. The Cordeliers, however, were bent on securing power and on 12 Ventôse (2 March) Ronsin spoke of another insurrection. But the affair was ill-prepared and many Sections were reluctant to participate. The government was determined to prevent an uprising; the leaders of the Cordeliers were arrested during the night of 23–24 Ventôse (13–14 March) and were put on trial on 1–4 Germinal. Along with the genuine militants like Hébert, Vincent and Ronsin, a number of foreigners (Clootz, Proly, Pereira, Desfieux) and a police informer were arrested in Brumaire and were also tried. Chaumette and Hébert's widow were to perish in another rounding-up of suspects. On 16 Germinal (5 April) Danton and his friends were executed.

The elimination of the Cordeliers from the Committee marked the first stage in the return to bourgeois liberalism. Nevertheless, the contradiction which had troubled Danton remained unresolved; the bourgeoisie was eager to see liberal government restored but was reluctant to give up the fruits of war. Between Germinal and Thermidor, Robespierre strengthened the position of the bourgeoisie, but, committed to the Terror and unable to make peace, his government took refuge in dictatorship and fantasy. In the words of Saint-Just, the Revolution had 'frozen' – men of talent were dismissed, independent institutions vanished and bureaucracy was rampant. By intensifying dictatorship, the Committee was forging a double-edged weapon – useful for dealing with the *sans-culottes*, but not readily acceptable to the moderate deputies of the Plain.

On the economic plane, however, the bourgeoisie was well satisfied, for the government was anxious to reassure the merchant class. Although hoarding remained technically a crime, it was now liable only to fines. The 'maximum' imposed on prices remained, but the Committee authorised numerous exemptions, granting special subsidies to suppliers. In contrast, the condition of the wage-earner was deteriorating. The new bureaucracy intended to apply the 'general maximum'

The famous 'Tricoteuses', the Parisian 'knitting-women' who watched the executions of the Terror. In fact, only a minority of French women regarded the Revolution as an opportunity of obtaining equality of the sexes, and their struggle for political rights was to be in vain.

strictly and a new limit was imposed on wages which in practice amounted to a reduction in the cost of labour. But politically the Committee of Public Safety was drifting further and further from reality, intensifying its bloody repression. The law of 22 Prairial suppressed all guarantees of justice and its definition of 'enemy of the Revolution' was so vague that it could be made to apply to anybody. Robespierre's government, lacking any definite political programme, was clinging to the only instrument at its disposal. Between 10 June and 27 July, 1,285 persons were condemned to death, including André Chénier. The Great Terror sickened the whole nation – the masses no less than the bourgeoisie.

'Virtue' was no longer an adequate foundation for the Republic: Robespierre now decided that morality needed reinforcing with metaphysics. On 18 Floréal (7 May) he told the deputies that the struggle between factions was the result of moral depravity, which in its turn stemmed from atheism. He was not speaking as a philosopher, but as a politician: 'To the legislator everything that is useful and good is truth. The idea of the Supreme Being and the immortality of the soul is a constant reminder of justice; that idea is therefore social and republican.' The Convention's decree proclaimed that 'the French people recognises the existence of the Supreme Being and the immortality of the soul.' It instituted four great republican festivals and prescribed the celebration of a civic virtue every 'decade' (the ten-day week of the new calendar). On 20 Prairial (8 June) David, the painter, who was a member of the Convention, proclaimed the great festival of the Supreme Being and Nature; Robespierre, a bouquet of flowers in his hand, presided at the ceremony, surrounded by a long procession stretching from the Tuileries to the Champ-de-Mars. Messages of congratulations were sent to Robespierre both from abroad and by people in France. Though the festival might have seemed to be the prelude to a religious restoration, it merely served to make the government even more remote from the nation it was ruling.

THE VICTORIES OF YEAR II

For months the war effort had been slackening off. Troops had been clothed and equipped by a variety of means, but obtaining a sufficient quantity of arms was proving difficult owing to the lack of certain raw materials. At the château of Meudon, France's leading scientists, men like Chaptal, Monge and Berthollet, were devoting their energies to their country's defence. The army, now boasting five hundred thousand men, had been made a more effective force by amalgamation, better discipline and firmer leadership. Nonetheless, during the winter of 1793–4 a number of generals had been dismissed and replaced. Hoche, suspected of Hébertism, was arrested in Ventôse: 'We have proof that General Hoche is a traitor', wrote Robespierre.

Carnot had drawn up a general plan of campaign. The armies on the 'secondary' fronts were to content themselves with limited actions. Carnot's instructions resulted in a clash with Dumerbion, commander-in-chief of the Armies of the Alps and Italy who, supported by Bona-parte, wanted to invade Piedmont. The Army of the eastern Pyrenees, under Dugommier, seized a number of strongpoints in Catalonia, while in the west Müller repulsed the Spaniards. But the main front lay to the north; three armies were to co-ordinate their efforts here: Pichegru with the Army of the North (150,000 men) was to launch an assault along the seaboard of Flanders, Charbonnier (Army of the Ardennes) was to lead a diversion against Charleroi and Jourdan (Army of the Moselle) was to act likewise against Liège. The plan was badly executed. Pichegru was unable to prevent Cobourg from taking Landrecies (30 April) and despite the victory of Tourcoing (18 May), failed to get to close grips with the enemy. There was a serious differ-ence of opinion between Carnot, who wanted to reinforce the left flank along the seaboard of Flanders, and Saint-Just, who wanted to force the crossing of the Sambre. On 8 June Saint-Just gave Jourdan the combined command of the Armies of the Moselle and the Ardennes; he personally supervised the fighting at the Sambre. On the 25th Charleroi was taken. On the 26th (8 Messidor Year II) Jourdan de-feated Cobourg at Fleurus and his army was renamed the 'Sambre-and-Meuse'. Pichegru joined up with Jourdan in Brussels (10 July) and then set off for the north, leaving him to advance towards the Meuse. On 27 July (9 Thermidor), the day when Robespierre and his government fell, Pichegru entered Anvers and Jourdan entered Liège. Robespierre was no longer needed, for the spring of 1794 had been a time of victory for France.

9 THERMIDOR

Robespierre found himself confronted with discontent at all levels. The government agents or 'proconsuls', who had been recalled from the provinces for terrorist excesses or financial extortion, did not like being told that they would be punished like common rogues. Tallien, whose mistress had been in prison since Prairial, Fouché, Barras and Fréron complained incessantly, but few would listen to them because of their dubious records. A more serious threat to Robespierre's government was the jealousy of the Committee of General Security; Amar and Vadier belonged to the extremist, dechristianising wing of the Montagnard party; they detested Robespierre for his assump-tion of the role of high priest of the Supreme Being and for setting up

After a brutal struggle lasting 14 hours the battle of Fleurus, 24 June 1794, was won by the French under Jourdan (on the white horse).

a Bureau of Police over which they had no control. But the great Committee of Public Safety was itself divided; since 15 Messidor, Robespierre had absented himself from its meetings; on 5 Thermidor, at the request of Saint-Just, he agreed to be present at a general session, but did not return for subsequent sessions; he was concentrating his attention on the Convention, and on 8 Thermidor (26 July) laid his grievances before the deputies without actually naming his enemies.

It is not clear who led the anti-Robespierre movement. Much importance has been attached to Carnot's role in the conspiracy. It is true that Carnot had had several violent clashes with Saint-Just (over Jourdan) and with Robespierre (over Bonaparte), and he had been supported by the 'technicians' of the Committee, Lindet and Prieur of the Côte-d'Or. But the fate of Robespierre on 9 Thermidor depended on three men: Barère, who was the link with the Plain, the guaran-

9 Thermidor at the Convention: Tallien brandishes a dagger, while Robespierre is prevented from taking the floor.

tee of the Revolution's continuity and legality, Billaud-Varenne and Collot d'Herbois, who, as the representatives of the Terror and committed to the success of the war, gave the conspiracy the sanction of the new regime. Danton's gamble had failed: he had wanted liberty and peace, but without the security that military victory would bring. Now liberty had been made possible by the successes of the French armies, and all political groups were hoping to achieve their own particular ends. Robespierre owed his downfall to his obstinacy in trying to follow two contradictory policies: terrorist government with military victory. During the night of 8–9 Thermidor the details of the conspiracy were planned: Collot d'Herbois, who was president of the Convention, was to prevent Robespierre and Saint-Just from speaking to the assembly on the following day; agreement was reached with the deputies of the Plain, who were to hand over Robespierre in exchange for the lifting of the Terror.

On 9 Thermidor, around eleven o'clock in the morning, the Convention opened its session for the day. At noon Saint-Just began speaking, but was interrupted by Tallien; Billaud-Varenne then attacked Robespierre, who tried to take the rostrum, but Collot d'Herbois refused him permission to speak and then started ringing

The Hôtel de Ville, on the night of 9–10 Thermidor, where Robespierre and his friends were hiding. Augustin Robespierre tried to commit suicide by throwing himself out of a window (shown to the right of the picture).

his bell to drown Robespierre's voice. Barère then had the deputies vote a decree depriving Hanriot of command of the National Guard. At the proposal of Louchet a motion of indictment against Robespierre, Saint-Just and Couthon was passed. Augustin Robespierre and Lebas asked to be included in the indictment. 'The Republic is lost, brigands have triumphed.' The prisoners were led away to the Committee of General Security.

The last act of the drama of 9 Thermidor took place on the Place de Grève. As soon as Hanriot and the Commune were alerted they ordered the tocsin to be sounded and the Sections to be mobilised for the late afternoon. The five captives, taken to various prisons in the city, were soon released, but were slow to make their way to the Hôtel de Ville (renamed the 'Maison commune'); Couthon was the last to arrive, around one o'clock in the morning. They were dispirited and undecided: these parliamentarians had never had active experience of insurrection. The Commune's attempt to mobilise the Sections met with little response, for only sixteen Sections out of the total forty-eight sent men.

· The Convention was not slow to act, however. Barras was put in command of the armed forces and gathered contingents from the

The wound in the jaw which Robespierre received gave rise to a variety of explanations. This engraving illustrates the version given by the gendarme Méda, who claimed to have fired the shot himself. The next day Robespierre was executed without trial.

western and central Sections. The insurgents were outlawed. In the meantime, the troops which had been defending the Hôtel de Ville were disbanding. At about two o'clock the force commanded by Barras penetrated the Hôtel de Ville. Augustin Robespierre threw himself out of a window; Lebas shot himself; Maximilien Robespierre was wounded (or wounded himself) in the jaw. On the following day, 10 Thermidor, the leader of the Terror and the Republic of Virtue was executed without trial, together with twenty-one of his supporters. Workers who the day before had been demonstrating for a wage-increase were heard to shout as they passed: 'F . . . le maximum'.

8

THERMIDOR YEAR III

T he Convention survived Robespierre by fifteen months. On the surface
nothing seemed to have changed. It was the same assembly conducting
the same war against a Europe of kings and aristocrats. And yet
nothing was really quite as it had been before 9 Thermidor. On the 10th Paris
danced and sang: the inhabitants had begun to breathe a different air. As the
first few months went by, the Convention, despite difficult moments, gradually
drew nearer to its ideal: government by a property-owning élite.

The Thermidorean period has come to be regarded as a rather mournful phase
in the history of France. Politically, it brought only failure, for the regime to
which it gave birth was soon to crumble undramatically and ingloriously under
the mild assault of Bonaparte's troops. The contrasting images of the poverty
of the masses and the wealth insolently displayed by bourgeois upstarts seem
permanently to have coloured historical judgement. In the reign of Louis-Philippe,
when moralising attitudes were bound up with nostalgia for Robespierre's
Republic of Virtue, the immorality of Thermidor was to be condemned from all
quarters.

Historians have stressed two major themes in this stage of French history:
the 'reaction' and the 'return to 1789'. The phrase 'Thermidorean reaction',
used to describe the politicians toppled from power in Germinal Year III, was
taken up by Aulard and Mathiez, but in a rather different sense from the
original. In eighteenth-century dictionaries 'reaction' was only a term in physics.
After Thermidor, in the Dictionary of the French Academy published in 1798,
the word appeared for the first time with a new meaning: 'Reaction. Used
figuratively of a party avenging itself and taking action in its turn.' It is significant that this definition has none of the political and social overtones that later
came to be associated with 'reaction'. Nowadays the word conjures up what the
nineteenth century expressed as 'resistance to movement'. The 'reaction' of
Thermidor was not of this kind. Not only did the revolutionary movement con-

tinue to advance, it went beyond itself in seeking to consolidate its conquests – the fundamental liberties and property-ownership without privilege. It might be argued that the Thermidoreans were 'reactionary' (in the modern sense) in refusing the demands of the lower classes for a share in the government of their city. True, but the reluctance of governments to give power to the masses was a deep current which formed part of the logic of the Revolution of Enlightenment, and which had already resumed its course in Germinal Year II. Boissy d'Anglas was merely carrying on where Robespierre had left off.

Was Thermidor a return to 1789? There can be no doubt that, after the brief episode of Year II, the bourgeoisie began to direct their energies once more to the objectives they had never lost from view: economic freedom, individualism in property-ownership and franchise based on a property qualification. To this extent Thermidor re-established the Revolution's link with 1789. But what a difference there was between the fall of the Bastille and the execution of Robespierre! The summer of 1794 bore little similarity to that of 1789; men's hearts had undergone a transformation, the blood did not move as freely through their veins. Barnave and the authors of the Declaration of Rights of '89 had been full of optimism: they had been confident of the people's ability to overthrow the Old Regime. Five years later a 'Declaration of Duties' was being proposed. 'No-one can be a man of property without wholeheartedly and religiously upholding law.' The bourgeoisie's concern to defend its vested interests was accompanied by a certain timid caution understandable in men who had witnessed the riots over the 'maximum', the Parisian uprisings and the havoc wrought by the guillotine. 'A country governed by property-owners represents social order. A country governed by non-property-owners represents a state of nature.' The philosophy of Boissy d'Anglas bore the mark of experience. When Dupont de Nemours said: 'It is obvious that property-owners are a country's leading citizens, since everyone depends on them for food and accommodation', was he echoing the theories of the Physiocrats, or was he simply remembering 10 August 1792? The deputies of the Convention in 1795 were rather like young men who leave their families, sow their wild oats and then return to settle down soberly in a lawyer's office. But the social scene had changed. The exclusiveness of the old bourgeoisie was being broken down. Salons were opening their doors to upstarts, speculators, manufacturers and contractors. The new bourgeois were just as determined as the old had been to consolidate their wealth, but they had known none of the intellectual delights of the time of the Enlightenment.

After the coup d'état *of 9 Thermidor the victors were anxious to limit re-organisation to a change of personnel. Their policy was to claim that all the evils of the Terror were attributable to Robespierre. The* Journal des hommes libres *of 13 Thermidor denounced the 'cult of personality' in these terms: 'No, liberty cannot perish; never will another man dare to attempt to destroy it, for I hope that Frenchmen will renounce the habit of worshipping and idolising individuals, a habit that has nearly been their undoing.' Barère predicted: 'The strength of the revolutionary government will be increased a hundredfold by the downfall of the tyrant who was hindering its progress.' Illusions of this sort were to prove difficult to sustain. The interplay of political forces in the Convention and the sudden re-awakening of public opinion soon swept them away.*

The coalition which had toppled Robespierre on 9 Thermidor was deeply divided. The decisive role in the coup *had been played by the members of the two great committees – Billaud-Varenne, Collot d'Herbois and Barère of the Committee of Public Safety, Amar and Vadier of the Committee of General Security. They had been supported by those politicians committed to a war of conquest and to dechristianisation. They had few real friends, and even their colleagues, Carnot and Lindet, quickly resolved to keep their distance. The men who gained from 9 Thermidor and were greeted as public heroes were Tallien, Barras, Fréron and Merlin de Thionville. Their contemporaries called them 'Old Cordeliers' or 'Dantonists'. These former government agents, who had been responsible for brutal repression in the provinces, had suddenly switched from the camp of the terrorists to that of the 'Indulgents', as the Dantonist moderates had come to be known. The majority of the Convention, though united in its repudiation of Robespierre, was divided on the future. The Plain, where Girondin sympathisers could now emerge from their enforced silence, was joined by a number of Montagnards like Thibaudeau and Cambacérès. The Mountain gradually lost more and more of its deputies, though Levasseur, Duhem and Ramps put themselves at the head of a hard core of Robespierrists who were prepared to fight to the last.*

All groups were intent on power. The Committee of Public Safety was determined to hold on to its control of the nation and to continue the old policy without Robespierre. The Thermidoreans, as Tallien and his friends were now called, were equally determined to wrest power from the Committee. The Girondins wanted to recall their colleagues exiled on 31 May 1793 so that they could wield greater influence in the Convention, while the Plain and its Montagnard converts were also anxious to take over the executive. In this kind of situation the hopes expressed by Barère were doomed to disappointment. Within a few weeks the Convention had abolished the two indispensable supports of the revolutionary government – centralisation of power and the guillotine.

But the Terror could not be lifted without jeopardising the positions of the men responsible for it. The fiction of the 'cult of personality' was soon forgotten as people began to ask themselves on whose shoulders blame should be laid. The majority of the Convention was in favour of forgetting the past, but in a period of revolution it is impossible to avoid looking back. Public opinion was simply not prepared to let bygones be bygones.

The fall of Robespierre had brought more than mere relief to the people of France: it had provoked a mighty explosion of repressed emotions. 'Everywhere,' a journalist of 12 Thermidor wrote, 'the terrible fear that has been tormenting people's minds is giving way to joy.' The young Charles de Lacretelle gave his own account of the reaction of Parisians: 'People were hugging each other in the streets and at places of entertainment, and they were so surprised to find themselves still alive that their joy almost turned to frenzy.' Paris developed a mania for dancing which Gardel was to depict in his ballet, la Dansomanie.

There was a spontaneous surge of popular opinion demanding the release of political prisoners and the punishment of terrorists. The movement began on 15 Thermidor, when friends and relatives of detainees agitated at the general assemblies of the Sections. On 9 Fructidor a former member of the Commune of 10 August, Méhée de la Touche, published a pamphlet that enjoyed immediate success. It was entitled la Queue de Robespierre: *what good had been done by cutting off Robespierre's head, asked La Touche, since his 'tail' (Billaud-Varenne, Collot d'Herbois and Barère) was still wagging?*

The bourgeoisie was at one with the populace in repudiating the terrorist regime of Robespierre and his Committee. Mathiez interpreted this alliance of sympathy between bourgeoisie and people as justification of Robespierre's policy towards the factions. Georges Lefebvre, while insisting on the sincerity of the neo-Hébertist agitators, concluded: 'Their collusion with the reactors [i.e. the 'reactionary' bourgeoisie] is not in doubt.' But is this not to fail to take into account the very real feelings of disgust and nausea which Robespierre's regime had aroused among the French people as a whole? At the Electoral Club, which met in the Archbishop's Palace, and in the Museum Section sans-culotte *leaders savagely attacked the government of Year II.* In his Journal de la liberté de la presse *Babeuf lauded Tallien and Fréron, branded Robespierre as 'Maximilien the Cruel' and reproached the Convention for being too merciful to the terrorists. In his eyes Year II had brought the counter-revolution. Varlet, another dema-gogue, imprisoned for singing the praises of Lecointre, saw the revolutionary government as 'a government bent on destroying the nation, a social monstrosity, a Machiavellian masterpiece'.*

In the Convention Lecointre, carried along on this wave of public sentiment, indicted Barère, Billaud-Varenne, Collot d'Herbois, Vadier, Amar and David (26 August), but the deputies, far from siding with him, condemned his denunciation as calumny. Thibaudeau saw the embarrassing position in which the Convention found itself. If it refused to punish the men of the Terror it would appear to be condoning their crimes, but if it brought them to trial it would be indicting itself, since it had given the Committee's measures its approval, either by formal vote or by its silence. It was now that the moderates of the Plain came into their own. On 1 September Barère, Billaud-Varenne and Collot d'Herbois resigned from the Committee of Public Safety, but then Tallien, compromised by Lecointre's denunciation, was also forced to resign. With their position in jeopardy, the Thermidoreans decided to look for support outside the Convention, in the streets, the press and the theatres of Paris.

Fréron and Merlin de Thionville had had a certain amount of experience of the tactics of minority movements. They began to organise the kind of popular pressure which the sans-culottes *had so successfully applied against the Con-vention in 1792–3, but on a different social base. The first leaders of Fréron's 'Gilded Youth', as the movement was called, were actors, singers, dancers and* musicians. '*The movement attracted all the young people of the higher classes of Parisian society*', wrote Duval. '*It also included notaries' clerks, advocates' clerks, merchants' clerks – in short, everybody belonging to the respectable bourgeoisie.*' The '*Gilded Youth*' also included numerous absentees from military service and former revolutionary agitators like the famous Saint-Huruge. Armed with sticks and recognisable by their square collars and their long tresses of hair, these young men met in the city's various gardens, and in particular at the Café des Canonniers (*formerly the Café de Chartres*) and at the Maison-Egalité (*formerly the Palais-Royal*).

The ground was taken from under the Jacobin press on *1 Fructidor*, when the Committee of Public Safety decided to suppress subscriptions to journals. A new, moderate press took its place and according to Lacretelle was controlled by a common policy laid down by the leading editors. The theatres assumed a political role. '*It was now a matter of which theatres would accept and perform plays which heaped scorn and execration on the criminals whose iron yoke held us down for so long.*' The salons wielded a more discreet but more effective influence on parliamentary opinion. At the gatherings of the beautiful Thérésa, now Mme Tallien and known among Parisians as '*Notre-Dame du Bon Secours*', and those of de Vaines and Le Hoc, the deputies mingled with bankers, contractors and the survivors of the old nobility. The temptations put before the deputies were strikingly described by Thibaudeau: '*The deputies were caressed and pampered only with a view to obtaining favours and corrupting their political integrity. To their faces they were flattered with every kind of allurement, but behind their backs they were made fun of. . . . If some pretty woman made a jest about the Revolution how could the deputies take offence? Their republicanism was not strong enough to overcome their fear of displeasing the ladies or appearing ridiculous in their presence.*'

Social habits were undergoing a gradual change as the strict rules of revolutionary times fell into disuse. The red cap of the sans-culottes, *despised by the Gilded Youth,* was going out of fashion. The cockade, though still obligatory, was becoming more and more discredited, and police records show numerous cases of this law being broken. The use of the familiar '*tu*' form instead of '*vous*' was frowned on. The word sans-culotte was regarded with contempt; a journalist wrote: '*it only serves to remind the French people of the wild and barbarous acts perpetrated against them. . . . The honour of the nation seems to demand that this word vanish for ever from our dictionaries.*' Though '*citizen*' was still the official form of address, the old '*monsieur*' began to be used once more at the salons. In *January 1795* anti-terrorism found its anthem, le Réveil du peuple, *with music composed by Gaveaux to the words of Souriguères, words which called for vengeance on the* 'atrocious horde of assassins and brigands'.

The Convention was inevitably caught up in the movement of public opinion. Gradually it gave ground, though not without bold resistance. As a result of the trial of a hundred and thirty-two inhabitants of Nantes who had been sent to Paris before *9 Thermidor*, the atrocities committed by Carrier, a representative *on mission, were made public. On 22 Vendémiaire (13 October) Carrier was formally indicted. In November the Gilded Youth directed their onslaught against the Jacobin Club, and on the 11th the Convention yielded and ordered the Club to be closed down. In December, a few days before Carrier's execution, it was decided to reinstate the seventy-three Girondin deputies who had protested against the events of 31 May 1793. A violent attack was launched against the members of the old Committee of Public Safety, and on 7 Nivôse (27 December), despite the opposition of Carnot and Lindet, the Convention agreed to elect a commission to prepare charges against Collot d'Herbois, Billaud-Varenne, Vadier and Barère. Dissatisfied with the Convention's slowness to act, Fréron's bands of Gilded Youth conducted a twofold campaign in January 1795. First they declared war in the theatres, forcing actors suspected of Jacobinism to sing* le Réveil du peuple *and to make public 'confessions'. Then they started tearing down the busts of Marat from public places and throwing them into the sewers. On 21 Pluviôse (9 February) the Convention had to give way: the remains of Marat and those of all 'martyrs of the Revolution' were removed from the Panthéon. On 12 Ventôse (2 March) it approved the arrest and indictment of Collot d'Herbois, Billaud-Varenne, Vadier and Barère, and the four terrorists were put on trial on 2 Germinal. At the same time all banished Girondins were recalled from exile.*

The Jacobins had been helpless in the face of this sustained offensive. Their defeat was due more to the general revulsion against the Terror and the passivity of the masses than to the activities of Fréron's Gilded Youth. Levasseur admits this in his Memoirs: 'A great many Frenchmen who had been our allies now regarded us as fools, fanatics, even criminals.' The people of the suburbs and the Sections had withdrawn its support from Jacobinism. Even on the economic plane the populace ceased after Thermidor to have any confidence in the virtues of coercion. On 10 Vendémiaire the Electoral Club presented the Convention with a demand for freedom of trade and the end of requisitioning. This has been misinterpreted as proof of collusion with the moderates. A recent book by Kare Tönnesson confirms the following police report of 17 Vendémiaire: 'The majority of the people wishes trade to be freed from all restrictions, including those on exports and hoarding; it believes that goods would go up in price at first but would be forced down again by competition.' There can be no doubt that there was a stage in the Revolution when economic freedom was actually being demanded by the masses.

During the winter of 1794–5 two movements of very unequal importance served to modify the attitude of the lower classes: one was political and mainly affected the Sections; the other was economic and involved the masses of the populace.

In January 1795 the militants of the Gilded Youth movement had tried to fraternise with the working population of the suburbs. However, though they had a certain measure of success, nothing could conceal the growing antagonism of the Sections towards their movement. It was now not only terrorism that was being hounded, but everything related to the sans-culotte *movement as a whole. The pressure of moderate opinion only served to bring Jacobins and* sans-culottes *together. The political debate was no longer between Robespierrists and defenders of the rights of man, but between the partisans of the republic of the rich and those of the republic of the poor, between the bourgeoisie as represented by the Gilded Youth and the* sans-culottes.

The alliance of Jacobins and sans-culottes *would probably have led to nothing if poverty had not by now reached tragic proportions. The abolition of price-controls decreed on 4 Nivôse Year IV (24 December 1794) had been well-received at first, but very soon the collapse of the assignat brought about the ruin of the majority of wage-earners, artisans and small shopkeepers. During this particularly harsh winter the price of fuel went up at the same rate as food prices. Above all, there was one striking difference between the economic situation of 1794–5 and that of the previous year: the existence of a 'free' market where supplies were plentiful, but where the populace found themselves able to buy less and less with their money, served to emphasise the distinction between rich and poor.*

Popular discontent seized upon two slogans: 'Bread and the Constitution of 1793'. The Thermidoreans displayed considerable skill in ensuring that their repressive measures were directed at demonstrators and Montagnard deputies alike. On 12 Germinal (1 April) a crowd of women, building workmen and artisans formed in the central Sections of Paris and succeeded in occupying the assembly hall of the Convention for four hours. With the help of National Guards from the western Sections the Committees were able to restore order without much difficulty. Barère, Collot d'Herbois and Billaud-Varenne were deported to Guiana and eight Montagnard deputies (including Thuriot and Lecointre) were arrested. Paris was put under martial law and sixteen hundred militants were put in prison. On 1 Prairial (20 May) the tocsin was sounded in the suburbs. The Convention was again invaded by the populace, and the deputy Féraud was assassinated. Within three days order was restored and the Faubourg Saint-Antoine was forced to surrender.

The last few months of the Convention saw a widening of the rift between the victors of Thermidor and their right-wing allies, who now favoured a constitutional monarchy and comprised Girondin deputies recalled from exile, journalists and the Gilded Youth. The current of young Parisian opinion which Tallien and Fréron had directed against the Montagnards was henceforth to be turned against the Thermidoreans.

Freedom of worship, proclaimed in February, might well have contributed to political stabilisation, but in the absence of a strong government it merely served to encourage the royalist movement. Until the spring of 1795 there had been no general reaction against the royalist revival and the White Terror which had been unleashed in the south of France. Thibaudeau explains the reasons for this silence: 'For the Republic's sake, I was much more afraid of the terrorists of Year II than of the royal terrorists of Year III.' The majority of royalist journalists were Feuillants who wanted a constitutional monarchy, not a restoration of the Old Regime. But the death of the dauphin in the prison of the Temple on 8 June meant that the claimant to the crown was now the Comte de Provence, who assumed the name of Louis XVIII and published a counter-revolutionary manifesto at Verona. The Quiberon Bay expedition (27 June), with which the constitutional monarchists refused to associate themselves, ended in failure and aggravated the rift between the right wing and the Thermidoreans. The Thermidoreans appealed to the revolutionary patriotism of France, let the military and the Jacobins persecute the Gilded Youth and tried to impose the Marseillaise *as a national anthem. The right wing protested at the 'massacres' of Quiberon Bay and dragged up the terrorist records of Tallien, Fréron and Chénier.*

The Plain did all it could to avoid a final break. On 8 August it even allowed the arrest of ten Montagnard deputies, among them Fouché. It appealed for a union of 'patriots of '89, constitutional monarchists and republican democrats'. It readily assented to the Constitution put forward by Boissy d'Anglas (2 August), which was designed to satisfy both Thermidoreans and constitutional monarchists. The reintroduction of property-qualification as the basis of the franchise and a restriction of civil rights were to prevent any further interventions by the populace in the political arena. The decentralisation of power – two legislative assemblies and an executive directory – would rule out the possibility of dictatorship. But the vital question was control of the new legislative assemblies, and the Plain was determined to preserve its majority. By the decrees of 5 and 13 Fructidor (22 and 31 August) it was laid down that two-thirds of the deputies of the new legislature would be chosen from among the deputies of the Convention, and that if the electorate did not respect this figure, the re-elected deputies of the old Convention would complete their numbers by co-opting their former colleagues. 'These decrees,' wrote Mme de Staël, 'broke the treaty that had been tacitly signed between the Convention and honnêtes gens.' *Former deputies of the Constituent and Legislative Assemblies and moderate journalists anxious to play a political role found they were on safe ground in objecting to the Convention's insistence on perpetuating itself. On 13 Vendémiaire Year IV (5 October 1795) the western Sections of Paris rose up in revolt: the mobs included large shopkeepers, members of the liberal professions and public officials, men who were not intending to restore the Old Regime, but were simply eager to see the last of deputies who had been clinging to power for too long. Barras, turning for support to army officers who had been struck off the list for having Jacobin views, appointed Bonaparte as his commander-in-chief and managed to restore order without much trouble.*

Vendémiaire led to a certain revival of revolutionary energies. Officers who had been dismissed after Thermidor were reinstated, imprisoned Jacobins were set free, the White Terror that had been raging in the south was suppressed and eventually imprisoned deputies were included in a general amnesty. Tallien and Fréron, who failed to secure re-election, would have liked to go much further by indicting the leaders of the right wing, declaring the elections null and void and returning to the policies of the old Committee of Public Safety. The Plain refused to follow them, and showed moderation in its treatment of the rebels of Vendémiaire (there were only two executions). Faced with the danger of a resurgence of the Terror of 1793–4, Thibaudeau publicly reminded Tallien that he had defended the September massacres. When the Convention was dissolved on 26 October 1795 the Plain had succeeded in eliminating from power nearly all the members of the Thermidorean plot; but it had only been able to regain control of the executive by jeopardising the success of the new legislative councils and the Directory.

What brought about the final decline of the National Convention? The most obvious cause was the weakness of parliamentary authority in the face of the double peril of royalism and terrorism. Contemporary observers realised this full well: 'It was not easy for the Convention to steer a middle course between the two rocks that were threatening its existence. A just and strong man might have been able to succeed, but the task was quite beyond an assembly at war with itself. But to explain the Convention's decline in terms of external forces is not convincing. Public opinion would not have tolerated a new Terror, and the moderate royalists wanted to consolidate the conquests of 1789 by establishing a constitutional monarchy. Neither terrorists nor royalists were a serious threat to the foundations of the new regime.

Was it the war, then, that brought about the Convention's loss of authority? It had undoubtedly led the Republic further and further from its original course. With the royalists advocating the frontiers of 1789, and the army refusing to give up the spoils of victory, the Thermidoreans had to resign themselves to pursuing the policy of natural frontiers proposed by Sieyès and Reubell, and in these circumstances a general peace was no more than a dream. Since 1792, experience had shown that the pursuit of a war policy made it impossible for a constitutional regime to function properly. For the time being, however, there were no serious doubts about the justification of French foreign policy.

It was parliament itself that was being challenged. The Convention had lost touch with public opinion; it no longer enjoyed the majority support which is the only true basis of legitimate authority. The lower classes, hit by drought and famine, had ceased to exercise any influence on government policy. This naturally delighted the bourgeoisie, as did these lines from the Gazette française*: 'As for the populace, it seems to have lost the habit of thinking in order to concentrate on the great problems of satisfying its physical needs; it appears stunned by its recent experience of unlimited sovereignty, which it exercised in such a bizarre fashion.' But bourgeois opinion itself was divided and fragmented; it was no longer to be found in the Convention, and yet the Convention was simply the mirror of the bourgeoisie's own disunity. The gap between the electorate and its representatives was widening not because they had nothing in common, but because, on the contrary, they shared the same defects. Public opinion expected its deputies to show the way, and not merely reflect its own weaknesses.*

223

The divisions within the Convention related not so much to the future as to the recent past. It has not been sufficiently stressed that the great debates of the Thermidorean period were retrospective in character. In reading the speeches of deputies and books of memoirs one cannot help noticing this obsession with the past. The deputies of the Convention were constantly haunted by two spectres: the banishment of the Girondins on 31 May 1793 and the Terror. In his Memoirs Levasseur returns to these themes frequently and at length: 'Yes, the Gironde was republican. . . . Yes, its banishment was unfortunate' but 'by repudiating 31 May the Thermidoreans were saying that we had merely been a gathering of factions: by publishing this imprudent decree they were forging a weapon against themselves.' And Thibaudeau had this to say: 'To repair the outrage committed on 31 May against the inviolability of the nation's representatives the Convention was to strike yet another blow at that very same principle.' On the day when it accepted the violation of the representative principle France's young parliamentary authority had undermined its own legitimacy, and the damage done on 31 May 1793 was to weigh heavily on the Thermidoreans. But memories of the Terror were to be an even greater burden. Babeuf actually went so far as to say that the Terror had simply been the counter-revolution at work. A statement of this kind is understandable coming from a man who had never been personally involved in the administration of the Terror and had known only its prisons. But the deputies of the Convention, who had voted for the great terrorist measures of 1793–4, were not in a position to exorcise the past so easily. Thibaudeau, one of the deputies who had voted for the measures, made this agonising reappraisal: 'The Terror of '93 was not a necessary consequence of the Revolution, but an unfortunate deviation from it. It did more harm than good to the foundations of the Republic because no-one dared admit responsibility for it.' Thermidor Year III was a time when men tried to forget something that simply could not be forgotten.

THE THERMIDOREANS

The events of 9 Thermidor did not constitute a revolution. Indubitably, the removal of the 'triumvirate' of Robespierre, Saint-Just and Couthon was spontaneously and joyously welcomed by public opinion: working men demonstrated their approval, the popular societies and Section assemblies sent countless messages of congratulations to the Convention, and the bourgeoisie was filled with new hope. But nothing definite seemed to have been achieved. The new regime's directives, worked out by the Committees and published in the press, were based on the condemnation of the 'cult of personality' and the exaltation of collective responsibility.

Slandering the dead and punishing the most seriously compromised survivors of the Robespierrist regime presented few problems. At the historic session of 9 Thermidor the leaders of the coalition in the

The two faces of the Thermidorean Convention. The coalition that brought about Robespierre's downfall appeared to favour both the *sans-culottes* and the Gilded Youth, but in fact the Thermidoreans were as opposed to the demands of the masses as to those of the monarchists.

Convention had fired the first shots: according to Billaud-Varenne the 'tyrant' was merely a moderate, and according to Vadier merely a protector of priests. These themes were taken up and enlarged by singers and journalists. One new song accused Robespierre of slandering the French armies. The press likened him to a tiger and to Cromwell. He was charged with planning a massacre like that of St Bartholomew's Day, 1572. Above all, he was denounced for his insatiable ambition and his desire for a royalist restoration. The issue of *le Sans-Culotte* of 12 Thermidor warned its readers: 'You will see the *fleur-de-lys* replacing the tricolour, a new high priest substituted for the one you have overthrown, and tyranny reimposed over your dying bodies.' On 20 Thermidor *le Journal de Perlet* announced startling revelations about the life of debauchery led by Robespierre and Couthon:

'The veil which the tyrant was careful to draw over his private life is slowly being removed, and we are discovering that the moral austerity and disinterestedness he spoke of ceaselessly were as foreign to him as the virtue whose name he constantly profaned. We are assured that he took possession of the house of the former princesse de Chimay at Issy . . . This was the Trianon of the successor of the Capets. . . To enhance his position in the eyes of his future royal colleagues the tyrant intended to force the hand of the young Capetian princess and marry her.' 'Principles, friends, principles; there is our slogan!'

But the 'principles' concerned were to be the Robespierrist principles of revolutionary government and terror. The first official pronouncements of the Thermidoreans made clear the form their regime would take. On 11 Thermidor Barère described the *coup d'état* of the 9th as 'a minor commotion which has in no way impaired the authority of the government in its political, administrative and revolutionary operations, either at home or abroad'; in other words, the changes to be expected from Robespierre's downfall were to be strictly limited. Barère promised indulgence for those guilty of 'involuntary error', but none for the aristocrats, who forfeited any right to clemency by their intriguing and whose 'errors' were crimes against the nation. The press fell into step the following day, declaring that the government of France, now that it was rid of its tyrants, was determined to continue its policy of terror towards aristocrats and all wicked men. A contemporary witness wrote of Barras and Tallien: 'I do not think that it was their deliberate intention to continue Robespierre's policies, but I suspect that they only wanted to lift the revolutionary waggon half-way out of the rut in which it had become stuck.'

The new regime's determination to continue its predecessor's repressive policies was not to be easily thwarted. In the provinces the watch committees and popular societies launched in Year II remained as part of the administrative system for nearly a month after the *coup d'état*. Moreover, executions were still taking place: General Moreau's father died at Brest on 13 Thermidor. Even in the Convention affirmations of loyalty to the 1793 Constitution were mingled with repressive tendencies. While re-opening the Jacobin Club on 11 Thermidor, Legendre warned public opinion: 'The aristocracy must not be allowed to triumph.' For some three months the soldiers of the republican army continued to receive copies of Audouin's *Journal universel* and Vatar's *Journal des hommes libres*, which defended the Robespierrist regime without supporting Robespierre himself (the Committee of Public Safety had taken out subscriptions to these journals on the army's behalf). Even when the administration had been decentralised and the members of the Committees had been replaced, the majority in the Convention did not intend to break with the past. On 20 September Robert Lindet was instructed to report on behalf of the Committees: as a member of Robespierre's Committee of Public Safety, Lindet represented the new regime's link with the old. The following day an official ceremony was held to accompany Marat's body to the Panthéon. On 9 October, in a proclamation to the French people, Cambacérès declared: 'The Convention, constant in its progress and resting on the will of the people, will preserve the government that has saved the Republic by establishing it on a regular basis.' Many Montagnard deputies shared Levasseur's view that it was quite enough to condemn Robespierre's excesses, without allowing revolutionary fervour to be dampened.

It is not difficult to see why *sans-culottes* and moderates were drawn briefly together in their common joy at finding life apparently safe once more. In his Memoirs, Charles de Lacretelle shows very clearly how disproportionately Robespierre's execution affected the mood of France, leaving the people with the feeling that genuine liberty had been restored by the death of one man. But was the execution of Robespierre to deliver the nation from its captivity? The answer to this lay with the Convention and, above all, with popular opinion.

The revolutionary government was likely to survive only if the anti-Robespierre coalition could hold together after its victory of 9 Thermidor. However, each of the political groups that had formed the coalition had its own problems and each was hoping for power. The members of the Robespierrist Committees, Collot d'Herbois, Billaud-Varenne, Vadier and Amar, were all determined to remain in office.

In the eyes of the masses, the men who deserved the credit for Robespierre's downfall were Tallien, Fréron, Barras, Merlin de Thionville, Legendre, Thuriot and Lecointre. These 'Thermidoreans', a strange medley of sincere Dantonists and repentant ultra-terrorists, had one definite ambition: to transform their moral victory into a political victory by seizing control of the machinery of government.

The shapeless mass of the Plain, the uncommitted 'centre' of the Convention, had expanded or contracted according to the demands of the particular situation. In the troubled times of Year II, when Robespierre declared that the Plain no longer existed, many deputies had moved up to the higher benches of the Mountain. The movement back to the Plain began on 10 Thermidor, and included a number of former Montagnards. This enlarged 'centre' represented the very essence and logic of the bourgeois revolution. It had only agreed to

hand over Robespierre so that it could take control of the executive:
it was not intending to leave power in the hands of the Thermidorean
conspirators, both wings of which it regarded as equally corrupt. The
deputies of the Plain were also inspired by less worthy motives, as they
sometimes unconsciously showed. Thibaudeau, a repentant Montagnard, quite innocently reveals his own ambitions: 'From that moment
a sudden transformation took place within me. Now one could
honourably make a career for oneself, and so I threw myself wholeheartedly into politics and began to play an active role.' Having previously remained silent, either from prudence, like Sieyès and Cambacérès, or from humility, like Thibaudeau, these genuine representatives of the old Third Estate were longing to speak out, control and
govern.

The right wing of the Convention filled out quite rapidly. Former
Girondin sympathisers, including Boissy d'Anglas, welcomed the men
of Thermidor into their fold: this was a calculated manoeuvre, producing a somewhat bizarre alliance that was to prove none too secure,
but which was advantageous to the Girondin cause.

Finally, loyal Montagnards gathered round Duhem, Ramps and
Levasseur. These Montagnards had little trust in the sincerity of
Robespierre's detractors, but in order to keep the fires of revolution
burning they were prepared to come to terms with those among them
who had occupied positions of power under Robespierre.

Clearly, the ambitions of these rival factions were totally irreconcilable.

Within a month of Robespierre's downfall it seemed that the
machinery of the Terror had been dismantled. Historians have described the processes of Thermidor as the 'destruction of centralisation'.
Yet, if one studies the decrees that were passed and then considers
how far they were put into effect, and if one concentrates on the spirit
rather than the letter of those decrees, it will be seen that the system
of power was essentially unchanged: it may have been 'broadened',
but the centre of decision-making had been consolidated.

The reorganisation of the administration was achieved in three
stages. On 11 Thermidor Barère proposed that three deputies be co-
opted in place of Robespierre, Couthon and Saint-Just. Immediately
Merlin de Thionville asked that the previous question be moved.
This was a revolution in itself: for the first time for over a year
deputies were daring to indulge in the normal procedures of parliamentary discussion. Tallien took the opportunity to put his own group's
demands to the assembly, repudiating a continued dictatorship by the
representatives of the Terror. At his suggestion the Convention passed
a decree stipulating that a quarter of the members of the two governing Committees were to be replaced every month, and went further

Allegory of violence and bloodshed under the Terror: among the heads carried by the Furies is that of Robespierre (with spectacles); the eye and ear at the top of the picture are the symbols of vigilant justice.

by laying down that outgoing members could not be re-elected before an interval of one month had elapsed. Two days later the Committees were reorganised. The heroes of Thermidor seemed to have achieved their purpose: Tallien and Thuriot entered the Committee of Public Safety, Merlin de Thionville and Legendre the Committee of General Security. Executive power was thus being divided between the two wings of the anti-Robespierre alliance.

The deputies of the re-formed Plain wanted to go further. What point would there be in the victory of 9 Thermidor, if they were not to be able to control the Terror's suspect heirs? On 11 Thermidor Cambon, who, with Barère, had been the guiding force behind the first Committee of Public Safety and who was hated by both left and right, put forward a solution: the government's executive committees, the equivalent of ministries, were each to be attached to a parliamentary committee. Cambon's proposals were amended and developed and received the Convention's approval on 7 Fructidor (24 August).

In theory the Committee of Public Safety was to have no more authority than the other committees; it handed over police responsibilities to the Committee of General Security, and the administration of the Interior and Justice to the Legislative Committee; it was left only with responsibility for foreign affairs and the army.

Paris received special attention. After 9 Thermidor its Commune was abolished. On 7 Fructidor the Convention reduced the powers of the Sections by replacing their watch-committees with committees each representing an *arrondissement*, thereby laying the foundations of the twelve sub-divisions of future Paris. A decree of 14 Thermidor (31 August) laid down a provisional scheme for municipal government: two commissions would be responsible for the essentials; the police and the collection of taxes. These commissions, appointed by the Convention, were to leave all other aspects of urban administration to the Convention's own committees.

But the decrees were not effective. Never was Paris so rigidly subordinated to the government as in the great summer of 'liberation'. In the provinces the *de facto* authorities – representatives on mission, departments, communes – continued to follow their own 'federalist' inclinations, paying little heed to the feeble echoes of the central power in Paris. Moreover, the Committee of Public Safety had not suddenly been reduced to the minor role so often attributed to it by historians. The orders issued by Aulard show just how much power it retained, even over committees not legally subject to its authority. Men had been replaced, but institutions had not greatly changed.

With anti-terrorist feeling growing there could be no longer any question of sharing power. Realising their positions were in jeopardy, the members of the old Committees tried to justify the past by perpetuating its methods. The Thermidoreans, on the other hand, decided to rely on public opinion. The two factions clashed on 26 Thermidor, over the releasing of suspects. On 11 Fructidor (28 August) Tallien contrasted 'the class that is afraid' and 'the class that is creating fear'. After being indicted by Lecointre, the three Robespierrists – Barère, Billaud-Varenne and Collot d'Herbois – left the Committee of Public Safety (1 September). In the short term, however, the Thermidoreans' gamble did not pay off. The Convention accused Lecointre of slander, and Tallien was himself compelled to resign from the Committee. The new members reached a secret agreement with the leaders of the old Committee and joined with Lindet in declaring: 'Let us not reproach ourselves either for our misfortunes or for our faults.' But they were forgetting two powerful sources of resistance: the men who had been excluded from power and, even more important, the pressure of public opinion, which despised the personalities of the new regime as much as the regime itself.

The swell of popular resentment was directed primarily at the prisons and the Revolutionary Tribunal, whose terrorist activities had affected all classes of society. On 15 Thermidor, at the first session of the Section assemblies since the downfall of Robespierre, relatives and friends of detainees gathered in a crowd to demand that prisoners be set free and attacked the watch-committees. Both in the suburbs and in the centre of Paris, people were demanding the release of the militants who had been imprisoned as Hébertists. Many of the prisons' inmates were harmless bourgeois citizens suspected merely of *aristocratisme*. Some were nobles – the Duc d'Aumont and the Duc de Valentinois, for instance – or generals of the republican army like Kellermann, the hero of Valmy. The Convention bowed under the onslaught. On 18 Thermidor (5 August) it approved two decrees. All detainees who did not come under the Law of Suspects (17 September 1793) were to be set free, and henceforth revolutionary committees and representatives on mission were obliged to give grounds for their arrests.

Paris was suddenly transformed. *Le Sans-Culotte* of 22 Thermidor read: 'From the prison doors all the way back to their homes citizens who have been released from their chains are being warmly greeted by the people . . . while their denouncers are left to feel only remorse, shame and dishonour.' In five days (18 to 23 Thermidor) the Committee of General Security released four hundred and seventy-eight prisoners, among them La Harpe and the actors of the Théâtre-Français who had been shut up in the Madelonnettes. Later (2 Fructidor), Tallien secured the release of Thérésa Cabarrus.

The Convention was disturbed by this wave of leniency. When it reorganised the Revolutionary Tribunal on 10 August it reaffirmed its intention of maintaining the Law of Suspects. To embarrass the new 'Indulgents', the Montagnards proposed that lists should be printed with the names of released prisoners and the deputies who had vouchsafed their patriotism; the Convention agreed to their proposal. Merlin de Thionville objected to the lists, which could obviously be used in future reprisals, but it was Tallien who foiled the Montagnards' scheme by persuading the assembly to agree that the names of denouncers should also be printed. The Convention did not want civil war, and so it rescinded its decisions. The watch-committees were reduced in numbers on 7 Fructidor: there was now only one to each district, and in Paris one to each *arrondissement*. But the advocates of repression felt that too much had been given away, while the moderates wanted much broader relaxations. In the words of Lacretelle, 'the prison gates were opening too slowly.' Was it going to be possible to abolish the old institutions without removing the men who had been responsible for them?

Wives, friends and children welcome the *modérés* at the prison gates in the autumn of 1794. Some *sans-culottes* had also been imprisoned.

During the troubled times of the Terror social life in Paris had inevitably dwindled. With the advent of Thermidor Year III, and in spite of the fact that France was still at war, people abandoned themselves once again to the world of pleasure and entertainment. Paris was suddenly seized with a passion for dancing. Georges Duval, then a lawyer's clerk, has left a colourful description of this feverish obsession of Parisians:

The dancing craze was quite sudden, spontaneous and frightening. Hardly had the scaffolds been overturned, with the draining-well under the Throne still showing its gaping mouth to frightened passers-by . . . and the ground was still soaking in the human blood that had been poured over it for two whole months, when public dances began to be organised all over the capital. . . . The joyful sounds of clarinet, violin, tambourine and flute summoned the survivors of the Terror to indulge in the pleasures of dancing.

The first public dance was held at Tivoli, on the right bank, in the garden of the one-time Farmer General, Boutin. Other gardens were used for the same purpose: the Marbeuf and the Élysée palace, where the orchestra was conducted by the negro Julien. The milliners of the

The Jacobin puritanism of the Terror was followed by a great freedom of morals. This flirtatious scene in a typical Parisian salon illustrates the revival of the woman's position in the new society.

Rue Saint-Honoré frequented the dances in the Jardin des Capucines, the young ladies of the Marais flocked to the Vauxhall gardens, while the clerks of the city gathered at the Ranelagh on Sundays. Well-to-do young people had their rendezvous at Frascati and the Pavillon de Hanovre. People danced in the Cité and on the left bank, from the Rue Dauphine to the Jardin des Carmes, from the Rue de Vaugirard through the old cemetery of Saint-Sulpice. Dances of a superior class were restricted to 'members', while in the suburbs any old barn was converted into a dance-hall. A particularly notorious occasion was the 'Dance of the Victims', at which the dancers aped the victims of the Terror.

THE GOVERNMENT AND THE PRESSURE OF OPINION

Tallien and Fréron, excluded from the Committees on 15 Fructidor, were deprived of their membership of the Jacobin Club two days later. They then made common cause with Boissy d'Anglas and the Giron-

A typical *muscadin* or 'Gilded Youth', with long sideboards, large cravat, tightly buttoned jacket and boots with long pointed toes.

dins they met at the dinners given by Formalaguès. The new right wing of the Convention was a strange collection of Girondins and Montagnard deserters, but its one hundred and fifty votes were not enough to give it a majority. Tallien and Fréron, as old Cordeliers, brought to the right wing their experience of the methods of active minorities, and set about mobilising popular opinion and the Parisian press.

The new agitators who dominated the streets of the capital came to be known as 'Fréron's Gilded Youth'. In organising the movement Fréron was assisted by Barras, Tallien, Goupilleau de Fontenay and Merlin de Thionville, all former Montagnards. But the rank and file of the Gilded Youth had no political past and no visions of the future. They repudiated the Revolution unreservedly. Many of them were absentees from military service and were proud of the fact. Clerks from notaries' offices and from the world of commerce also enrolled under Fréron's banner, with their employers' permission. The movement's leaders were drawn from the artistic professions: Quesnel and Henri were actors, Elleviou a singer, Souriguères a musician and

Trenitz a dancer. They took their propaganda from journalists like Martainville, Isidore Langlois and Dussault.

The care they took over their toilet, their long locks of hair and square collars infuriated the military and the Jacobins, who called them 'muscadins' (the French Academy's Dictionary of 1798 defines 'muscadin' as 'a small pastille containing musk'). Armed with sticks, they gathered at the Café des Canonniers (the old Café de Chartres) and at the Maison-Égalité (the Palais-Royal). Two or three times a week they drilled at the Tuileries, in the Champs-Élysées or at the Luxembourg. But their chief task was not to fight, but to patrol the streets, intimidate revolutionary opinion, impose their authority in places of entertainment and cafés and monopolise public platforms in the Section assemblies. From time to time they clashed with mobs in the Rue des Gravilliers or the Rue Grenier-Saint-Lazare, but they did not dare challenge the suburbs.

Police reports mention the Gilded Youth as early as 25 Fructidor (11 September): 'The *muscadins* are swarming everywhere.' Within two months, according to Lacretelle, they had made themselves 'the people of the tribunes, the "sovereign people", the dictators of the theatres, the oracles of the cafés, the orators of the Sections, the self-appointed magistrates of public opinion'.

Since the death of Hébert the press, though free in theory, had been monopolised by the government and its Jacobin supporters. On 10 Thermidor, a campaign was launched by both left and right in favour of total and effective freedom of the press. On the left, Legray persuaded the Museum Section to approve a motion to this effect, which was then presented to the Convention. On the right, the assault was led by Dussault who declared: 'A great revolution took place on 9 Thermidor: it is for us to consolidate that revolution and to use our paper and ink to stop the breaches which have already been made in it.'

For two months, popular and moderate opposition maintained a united front against the government. In the *Journal de la liberté de la presse*, Babeuf denounced 'Maximilien the Cruel' and condemned the government of 1793 as counter-revolutionary. Moderate opinion was expressed by equally powerful channels. The Bertin brothers gathered together leading journalists each week at a restaurant in the Place du Louvre. These journalists were former Feuillants and Girondins, who inclined towards a constitutional monarchy, but for the time being they were content to attack the politicians and institutions of the Terror. Fréron and Tallien both had their own journal – *l'Orateur du peuple*, which became a catalogue of denunciations against loyal Montagnards and Jacobins, and *l'Ami du citoyen*. Not since 1792 had the press played such an important part in politics.

Meanwhile the attack launched by Lecointre against Collot d'Herbois, Billaud-Varenne and Barère had misfired and Tallien had been forced to leave the Committee of Public Safety. The new right wing now decided to challenge Jacobin control of the Sections, to mobilise public opinion against the Jacobins and to compel the Plain to share power with it.

The offensive organised by the moderates in the Sections was boosted by two petitions drawn up in Fructidor and Vendémiaire, which put forward contradictory programmes and caused a general stir of agitation. One petition, neo-Hébertist in inspiration, was drawn up by the Museum Section under the guidance of Legray. It demanded free elections, especially for the municipality of Paris. The second petition, sent by the Jacobins of Dijon, protested against the indiscriminate release of prisoners and demanded the expulsion of nobles and priests from all public offices and the limitation of the freedom of the press. Four Sections supported the Museum petition, and eight the Dijon petition. Although the Sections as a whole did not support the petitions, the Convention took fright and ordered the arrest of Jacobin agitators after disturbances on 10 Vendémiaire. Encouraged by this, the moderates set about gaining control of the Sections: popular opinion was apathetic, and within two months most of the Sections had been 'de-Jacobinised'.

The Jacobin movement was finally wrecked by the revelation of Carrier's mass-drownings in Nantes. In January 1794 one hundred and forty-two inhabitants were arrested and sent to Paris for trial, but by September only ninety-four were left, the others having died on the way, or in prison. On 15 September the prisoners were acquitted, but public opinion continued to hound Carrier. A commission was appointed and decided to deprive him of his parliamentary immunity. The Montagnards had been quiet for some time but they now began to mount their attack upon the Jacobins. Billaud-Varenne warned on 13 Brumaire: 'The lion is not dead when it slumbers, and when it awakens it exterminates all its enemies'. On 19 and 21 Brumaire the Gilded Youth set about smashing windows of the old Jacobin monastery, and Jacobins were beaten up. The committees decided to close the Club with the approval of the Convention. The Thermidoreans took advantage of this revulsion of opinion to try to rescue minor positions, but only the Committee of General Security opened its doors to them, taking in Bentabole and Reubell. The battle for power was not yet over.

With the closing of the Jacobin Club and the removal of Marat's remains from the Panthéon, the balance of power had swung in favour of the moderates. Below the surface political regroupings were certainly taking place, and on 18 December Babeuf had taken up his pen

In Vendémiaire (1794) the Convention forbade the affiliation of political clubs. On 19 and 21 Brumaire bands of Gilded Youth raided the Jacobin Club in Paris, and immediately afterwards the Club was closed.

once more, this time against the Thermidoreans, proposing an alliance of *sans-culottes* and Montagnards. But the centre of the stage was dominated by the ghosts from the past: the Girondins, the dead king, the men responsible for the banishments of the previous year, and the shadow of Marat.

The right wing of the Convention intended to make Tallien and Fréron pay for their support by insisting on the reinstatement of the seventy-three deputies who had protested against the banishments of 31 May 1793 and whom Robespierre had saved from execution. Neither the Plain nor the Thermidoreans gave in immediately: by reinstating the seventy-three Girondin sympathisers the Convention would be questioning the legitimacy of 31 May 1793 and condemning itself in retrospect, for at the time it had given its approval to the banishments. In Vendémiaire Cambon, in an attempt to save Barère, imprudently accused the Dantonists of having organised the uprising of 31 May, whereupon the Thermidoreans defended the uprising: 'We had been suffering a long period of repression,' shouted Thuriot, 'when the revolution of 31 May came to save France.' Tallien expressed himself in these revealing words: 'In times of revolution men must not look back to the past.'

But, as Thibaudeau wisely commented, 'the country had not forgotten the past'. The revelation of Carrier's atrocities enabled Legendre and Lecointre to renew their accusations against the members of the old revolutionary committees (15 Frimaire, 5 December), and they succeeded in persuading the Convention to order an investigation of the accused men's dossiers. Both wings of the assembly had reason to think it would be in their interest to recall the seventy-three deputies: the Montagnards were hoping that a gesture of goodwill might remove the threat hanging over Barère and his friends, and the Thermidoreans did not object to having their majority increased, as long as the Girondins did not try to revive past quarrels. On 18 Frimaire (8 December) the Convention decided unanimously, without a debate, to recall seventy-eight deputies.

However, both Montagnards and Thermidoreans soon found their calculations had misfired. Almost as soon as they were back in the Convention, the Girondins withdrew their support from the Thermidoreans, when the latter refused to reinstate the twenty-one Girondin deputies who had been banished on 31 May 1793. On 7 Nivôse (27 December), in spite of Montagnard opposition, the Convention decided to indict Barère, Collot d'Herbois, Billaud-Varenne and Vadier.

The Thermidoreans were not keen to see reprisals carried any further. They had secured the removal of three members of the Committee of General Security, including David. At the proposal of Barras they decided to make the anniversary of the execution of Louis XVI (21 January) a national festival. They also had a royalist teacher of law brought before the Revolutionary Tribunal.

The initiative was now seized by the Gilded Youth. On 30 Nivôse (19 January) the singer Gaveaux gave the assembly of the Guillaume Tell Section a performance of a song he had just composed to words by Souriguères: *le Réveil du peuple*. Within a few days this hymn of vengeance had become a 'counter-Marseillaise':

'Quelle est cette lenteur barbare?
Hâte-toi peuple souverain
De rendre aux monstres du Ténare
Tous ces buveurs de sang humain.'

The Gilded Youth forced actors suspected of Jacobinism – Trial and Laïs of the Opéra, Vallière of the Théâtre Feydeau, Fusil and Talma of the Théâtre de la République – to sing Gaveaux' song and make a public 'confession'. On 12 Pluviôse (31 January) they started removing busts of Marat from theatres and other public places. The enemies of a religion always begin by killing its saints. Marat and Le Peletier were regarded as usurpers; even when dead they seemed to hold out a protecting hand over the past, mysteriously perpetuating its influence. One method of demolishing the myths of the past was to destroy

A violent reaction to the decision to transfer Marat's remains to the Panthéon: the Gilded Youth set about smashing busts of Marat in the theatres, public buildings and squares of Paris.

the memory of its heroes. Some busts were broken and others thrown into the sewers. The Convention ordered them to be put back, but to no purpose, for the mobs of youths immediately started all over again. Finally the deputies gave in. On 20 Pluviôse they decided that the Panthéon would be reserved for great men who had been dead for at least ten years, which meant that Marat's remains could be removed from the great temple of honour. The picture which David had painted in memory of Marat was taken down from the wall of the Convention's assembly hall.

The early successes of the Gilded Youth movement instilled confidence in the moderates, for they had strengthened their positions at all levels. The political transformation of Paris was now completed. Gradually the Sections that had shown the strongest Jacobin tendencies in the autumn passed into the hands of the moderates during the winter. There was a demand that the decrees of Year II be struck from the official registers and that commissions be appointed to investigate the activities of former office-holders. At the same time, committees were purged on various social pretexts – those engaged in trade were expelled, as 'uneducated wretches'.

Political plays were put on in the theatres. At the Théâtre Molière, the tradesmen of the Rue Saint-Denis wildly applauded Armand Charlemagne's *Le Souper des Jacobins*. In Floréal, Ducantel put on *l'Intérieur d'in comité révolutionnaire*, which attracted large audiences.

The Convention paid careful attention to these movements of public opinion. On 5 Ventôse, it decreed that all officials dismissed since Thermidor should be put under house-arrest under the surveillance of the municipal authorities. Seven days later, the Convention voted without debate for the indictment and immediate arrest of Barère, Collot d'Herbois, Billaud-Varenne and Vadier.

At the same time reparation was made to victims of Year II. Those who had left France after 31 May 1793 were authorised to return, providing they worked on the land or at a manual trade, to take possession of belongings left unsold, and to collect compensation for the rest. Those Girondins banished on 31 May 1793 were reinstated on 18 Ventôse, and the right wing, thus reinforced, succeeded in cancelling the proposed anniversary festival of 21 January. This wave of right-wing feeling provoked a reaction – the neo-Hébertist and Jacobin leaders joined forces and rallied to the defence of the 1793 Constitution.

On 2 Germinal the Convention began to debate the indictment of Barère, Collot d'Herbois and Billaud-Varenne – Vadier had escaped from Paris. The three men were vigorously defended – Carnot told the assembly that by condemning these men, it would condemn itself. The outcome was still uncertain when Merlin de Thionville proposed the Convention should be replaced by a new assembly, to be elected according to the 1793 Constitution, and which would decide the fate of the accused. Neither the Plain nor the Thermidoreans wanted anything to do with the 1793 Constitution, and refused to support Merlin – public opinion followed suit. Like it or not, the Convention was going to have to complete the task it had set itself.

ROYALIST INSURRECTION IN THE WEST

Even before 9 Thermidor the royalist movement had acquired a new vigour in western France. In Vendée, where the disaster of Savenay (23 December 1793) had left the old 'Catholic and Royal Army' in scattered fragments, a revival of the insurrection was caused by the brutal repression conducted by General Turreau. The bands led by Charette in the Marais, Sapinaud in the central district and Stofflet in the Mauges were rapidly swelled by the victims of Turreau's cruelty. To the north of the Loire in the spring of 1794 the 'Chouan' movement had begun to take root. The Chouans were a small minority who had to rely on surprise attacks, often at night. It has sometimes been suggested that the Chouan movement was an offshoot of the Vendéan expedition north of the Loire. A number of Vendéan rebel-leaders certainly joined the Chouans, but the latter had organised themselves well before this, at least as far back as September 1792, and as in Vendée, the mass conscription of three hundred thousand men decreed in March 1793 had resulted in the formation of a resistance movement of rebels who refused to enter military service. Local gentry such as La Bourdonnaye fought side by side with non-juring priests and smugglers under the leadership of the famous Jean Cottereau, otherwise known as Jean Chouan. All of them wore the coarse peasant breeches, short jacket and round hat immortalised by Marche-à-Terre in Balzac's novel, *Les Chouans*.

After the death of Robespierre the situation in the west changed in two important respects. Joseph de Puisaye, who had succeeded in unifying the Chouan movement, went to England, received the title of 'commander-in-chief of the Catholic Army of Brittany' from the Comte d'Artois and was then given the opportunity by Pitt to flood western France with counterfeit assignats. The second important change in the situation after Thermidor was the government's deci-sion, backed by the representatives on mission, to adopt a policy of clemency towards the rebels. Hoche and Canclaux, who were released from prison to command the armies of Brittany and Vendée, were in favour of such a policy. In September representatives on mission granted generous amnesties and entered into secret negotiations with some of the rebel-leaders. On 2 December 1794 the Convention approved a decree demanded by Carnot which promised a complete amnesty to all rebels who laid down their arms within a month. But the government still had to come to terms with the leaders.

Three pacts were made with the royalist insurgents. The first was the agreement reached between the government and Charette in the manor-house of La Jaunaye on 15 February 1795. The past was to be forgotten, and the rebels were promised compensation for destroyed properties and assistance in rebuilding houses and villages. All of them, even emigrés, were to be given back whatever had been confiscated by the government. The Vendéans were granted the privilege of per-forming their military service locally in their own territorial com-panies, which would be financed by the state. Freedom of worship was to be extended to all, even to those priests who had refused to swear to the Civil Constitution of the Clergy. A second agreement was signed in April with the Chouans, and a third in May with Stofflet.

The Thermidoreans' enemies considered that the Republic had surrendered to the royalists by signing these three pacts, and many historians have expressed the same view, insisting that Hoche and his

On 17 February 1795 a treaty was signed (near the château of La Jaunaye) which appeared to put an end to the Vendéan war. But were the Vendéan chiefs sincere, or were they merely playing for time?

colleagues had been duped by the rebels in a manoeuvre to gain time. The recent research conducted by Mr Hutt, an English historian, has shown the weakness of this theory. In fact, Hoche and the Thermidoreans realised well before Bonaparte that the only hope of putting an end to the insurrection in the west lay in dissociating the peasant masses from their royalist leaders and satisfying their religious needs. The government's concessions were based on a diagnosis which in the long term was to prove well-founded: if the Republic opened the Vendéan peasants' churches, guaranteed their personal security and showed itself capable of maintaining order, the fundamental causes of Vendéan hostility would cease to exist.

One thing at least had been achieved: the whole of France now enjoyed the genuine freedom of worship for which Grégoire had so far been clamouring in vain. The principle of freedom of worship was officially formulated in the decree of 3 Ventôse (21 February), though Boissy d'Anglas, who presented the decree to the Convention, incorporated in it a number of highly restrictive conditions: for him Christianity was 'by its very nature servile, in its essence the ally of despotism, intolerant and dominating, something which degrades the human race, the accomplice of all the crimes of kings'; since religious faith could not be destroyed, it must be controlled. Immediately there occurred a revival of religious life. Five bishops, including Grégoire, formed a 'committee of united bishops' which set about establishing 'constitutional' worship on firmer foundations. But those who gained most by the decree were the priests who had been able to remain loyal to Rome because they had not had to swear the oath to the Civil Constitution of the Clergy, or had only taken the 'little' oath (to 'liberty and equality'); on the other hand, those priests who had actually refused to take the oath were still excluded from the privileges laid down in the decree. The Abbé Sicard, released from prison in Bayonne in November 1794, helped the Abbé Jauffret to launch the *Annales religieuses, politiques et littéraires*, which became a rival to Grégoire's *Annales de la religion*. But freedom to worship was of little use without churches in which to practise that freedom. On 11 Prairial (30 May) Lanjuinais persuaded the Convention to authorise worship in all churches not served by 'rebel' priests. A few days later the restoration of religious liberty was celebrated with great splendour in fifteen of the capital's churches.

THE UPRISINGS OF GERMINAL AND PRAIRIAL

Until spring 1795, the artisans, small shopkeepers and labourers, who had supported the Cordeliers in 1793–4, had practically ceased to be an active political force. Admittedly they had supported Legray and Babeuf in the general revulsion against the regime of Terror after 9 Thermidor, but when, on 28 Frimaire, Babeuf called for an insurrection, he failed to rouse the people.

During the autumn and early part of the winter, the conditions of the masses worsened. Certain foodstuffs, such as butter and vegetables, were plentiful but very expensive. The gap between the official and black markets was widening so that while the poor were starving, those who could afford high prices helped profiteers to make their fortunes.

What caused the shortages of 1794–5? The peasants, encouraged by inflation, were ignoring requisitions and the government committees were reluctant to use force for fear of being charged with terrorist methods. But the causes lay much deeper than this: the imposition of economic controls had merely served to mask the effects of shortage and had done nothing to solve the basic problem. The growth of the army and war industries had altered the balance between producers and consumers, while the reduction of taxes had encouraged the peasantry to consume more of its own produce – in short, supply was far behind demand. Moreover, foreign grain arriving at the French Channel ports could not be transported to Paris because of the paralysing effect of the winter on communications.

At first the bourgeoisie and populace were united in opposition to the extension of economic controls in September. Seeing how plentiful goods were in the unofficial market, where price controls did not operate, the people thought that if controls were to be abolished in the official market, stability would eventually be restored. The masses had been converted temporarily to the idea of complete freedom of trade. The blame for all troubles was laid upon the speculators, the 'merchant aristocracy' and the employees of organisations in charge of food supplies.

The general body of manufacturers, merchants and contractors, were equally determined to sweep away the controls which war had imposed on the government of 1793–4 (Year II). Restrictions on foreign trade were lifted by a succession of measures. On 26 Vendémiaire import controls on manufactures were removed and on 6 Frimaire the abolition of import controls was extended to all goods except those from enemy countries. Once trade was thus freed, the whole system of price-controls was jeopardised – and the partisans of economic freedom succeeded in having the 'maximum' abolished on 4 Nivôse. The only restrictions which continued to operate were those affecting food supplies for the army and for Paris – here requisitioning remained.

The populace was rather frightened by its success in obtaining these economic relaxations. They now began to blame their economic plight upon the restoration of free trade. The winter and spring of 1795 were terrible, and the assignat collapsed, dragging down with it all those on fixed incomes. Goods became more expensive and basic foodstuffs scarcer on the official market.

The collapse of the assignat resulted from the re-opening of the exchange market which had revealed the true worth of paper-money. As prices rose more and more notes had to be printed to finance the war and state expenditure. Moreover, the public had lost confidence in paper-money and thus the assignat fell from thirty-one per cent of its nominal value in July 1794 to eight per cent by the following March.

Despite the effort of the government commission responsible for supplies, there was less and less food available on the official market. By January new consignments had begun to slow down and reserve stocks were quickly used up. The injustices of the economic situation became more obvious daily. The profiteers of the black market now

The collapse of the assignat accentuated the contrast between the misery of the starving poor and the wealth of the new rich.

joined the wealthy world of the manufacturers while the great mass of the people were poverty-stricken: the hungry now also included those on moderate fixed incomes, state employees, pensioners and *rentiers*. Gradually the populace turned in fury against the Convention. By the end of March, angry crowds were gathering daily in the streets and petitions phrased in menacing terms were organised and taken to the deputies in the Tuileries.

The uprising of 12 Germinal Year III (1 April 1795) was a pale reflection of the great uprisings of 1792 and 1793. Levasseur wrote: 'Paris was divided into two nations: on one side the people, and on the other the bourgeoisie.' But he omitted to mention that this time the people had been disarmed, disorientated and demoralised by famine, and that the bourgeoisie was too frightened to show much resistance.

Trouble had been brewing for the past two weeks. On 1 Germinal (21 March) the women of the Faubourg Saint-Antoine had led the delegates of the Sections to the Convention to demand the 1793 Constitution and a solution of the food crisis; at the Palais-Royal and the Tuileries, scuffles had broken out between bands of Gilded Youth and local artisans. After subsiding for a few days the movement erupted

245

again in the Gravilliers Section (7–9 Germinal). On the 10th the Section assemblies were the scenes of wild tumult; in the suburbs and the densely-populated eastern districts of Paris the delegates demanded bread, a democratic Constitution, the release of patriots and the re-opening of the fraternal societies. In the centre and the west the Sections were concerned not so much with the food shortage as with the punishment of Barère and his three colleagues, whose trial had at last begun. On the 11th a particularly threatening petition was put forward by the Quinze-Vingts Section. This was the signal for insur-rection.

The government committees were prepared for trouble. On 28 Ventôse the Convention had forbidden members of the National Guard to pay others to take over their duties; the purpose of this prohibition was to make sure the Guard included as many of the bourgeoisie as possible. On 1 Germinal a police decree laid down death or deportation as the penalty for anyone threatening violence against deputies. But the very severity of the penalties showed how weak the government's measures were in practice; the soldiers of the regular army could not be relied on, and in the National Guard whole battalions were either suspected of Jacobinism or were generally dis-organised. An attempt was made in the moderate Sections to form nuclei of reliable men who could be trusted with rifles; on the evening of the 11th two deputies ordered the Gilded Youth to assemble for the following day, while the Committee of General Security gave the order for armed detachments of one hundred and fifty men per Section to be formed.

As in the days of the Catholic League, it was in the Cité that the uprising began. On the morning of 12 Germinal the local women began stirring up feeling among the crowds gathered outside shops and persuaded their menfolk to assemble in front of Notre-Dame. The mob, under the command of Van Eck, former commander-in-chief of the Cité Section's battalion who had been dismissed after Thermi-dor, assembled illegally in the cathedral, now a Temple of Reason, and decided to make for the Convention. On the way the marchers were swelled by innumerable angry Parisians. The day before, a large number of workmen living in lodgings had been hit by a decree forcing them to buy food in the free market; they included stone-cutters, masons and others engaged in the building trade. Between one and two o'clock the mob forced its way into the Convention's assembly hall in the Tuileries without meeting any resistance from the Gilded Youth, who had been stationed in the royal courtyard that morning by Dumont and Tallien.

The demonstrators managed to stay inside the assembly hall for four hours. They interrupted Boissy d'Anglas, who was reading a report on the food situation, with cries of 'Bread! Bread!' They read out their petitions to the assembly and made no attempt to prevent right-wing deputies leaving. Eventually the Montagnards advised the mob to go home. Meanwhile, the crowds outside the building had continued to grow. As soon as trouble had broken out the Committee of General Security had sounded the alarm by ringing the one and only official tocsin in Paris, that of the Pavillon de l'Unité. However, the loyal battalions of the western Sections were slow in arriving. Some of them had had to pass through districts where mobs had formed, and many of their members had insisted on finishing their meals before taking up arms. By about six o'clock there were enough of them to clear the Tuileries of demonstrators without a shot being fired.

In several Sections, including the Panthéon, agitation continued through the night and illegal assemblies were held.

It is difficult to say just how spontaneous was the insurrection of Germinal. Barère and Dyzès claimed that the Thermidoreans deliberately provoked an uprising to make it easier to break the recently reinforced opposition of the left wing. The Thermidoreans in turn accused Bourdon of having instigated the movement. There is no evidence to support either of these charges. It is certain, however, that the uprising left the right wing much stronger in the short term. On the evening of 12 Germinal the Thermidoreans began exploiting their success. 'This day must be made complete,' exclaimed Dumont. Barère, Billaud-Varenne and Collot d'Herbois were deported to Guiana before their trial had finished. Vadier, sentenced along with the rest, could not be found. The arrest of eight Montagnard deputies, including Charles and Léonard Bourdon, was decreed. Around midnight martial law was imposed on Paris and General Pichegru, assisted by Barras and Merlin de Thionville, was appointed commander-in-chief of the Parisian army.

On 13 Germinal there were two further outbreaks. Early in the afternoon the Gravilliers Section refused to hand over Bourdon, and the battalion of the Temple Section had to be sent to arrest him. Then in the evening, trouble occurred when the three terrorists sentenced to deportation were being moved. Barère may have been right in thinking that the mob was intending to inflict its own more violent punishment on the three, or it may, on the contrary, have wanted to prevent their exile. The most likely explanation, however, is that the people of Paris simply panicked at the thought that the Convention might be following the example of the king's flight to Varennes four years earlier.

Repression continued. On 16 Germinal the arrest of eight more deputies was ordered, among them Cambon (who managed to escape),

Thuriot and Lecointre, who had only recently joined the Montagnards. On 21 Germinal (10 April) it was decided to withdraw all civic rights from 'all men known to have taken part in the horrors committed during the tyranny that preceded 9 Thermidor'. Sixteen hundred Parisian militants were affected by this decree.

During the next few months some Thermidoreans began to be disturbed by the swing to the right in government policy. On 12 Floréal (1 May) Chénier and Louvet embarked on a denunciation of royalism and, despite Tallien's opposition, persuaded the Convention to pass a decree against emigrés and refractory priests. Once again, an open split in the Thermidorean government was prevented by murmurings of trouble in the suburbs. In one month the major food shortage had become a famine. Distributions of rice did little to offset the scarcity of bread; eventually the ration of bread was cut to two ounces a day, though there was no shortage in the pastry-shops, where bread was being sold at twenty-six *sous* a pound. Malnutrition brought a rapid increase in disease and suicide as the masses desperately looked for a solution to their misery. Some began to indulge in memories of earlier days, recalling the Parisian women's march to Versailles in October 1789 and the improvement in the bread situation which had followed Louis xvi's enforced return to the capital; on 12 Floréal, women hopefully declared: 'We must be patient; we shall have a king before two weeks are up, and then we shan't be short of bread any more.' Some of the hungry populace even longed for the days of Robespierre, while the majority sought consolation in the Utopian programme of the neo-Hébertists, which had never been put to the test of reality.

Famine brought conspiracies, illegal assemblies and pamphlets in its wake. At the end of Floréal another insurrection was being quite openly prepared. On the 30th, the day on which the Section assemblies met, an anonymous pamphlet entitled *l'Insurrection du peuple pour obtenir du pain et reconquérir ses droits* provided the insurgents with their programme, the methods by which to achieve it, and a slogan to shout at the deputies of the Convention. The programme urged by the pamphlet was the restoration of the Constitution, the arrest of the present government, the release of imprisoned patriots and new elections. The Sections were urged to arm themselves and march on the Convention, and then to fraternise with government troops. The great slogan was 'Bread and the Constitution of 1793!'

At dawn on 1 Prairial (20 May) the tocsin roused the Faubourg Saint-Antoine and the Faubourg Saint-Marceau. Between five and nine o'clock it was sounded in the Sections of the east and centre, and in particular the Gravilliers, the Arsenal and the Arcis Sections. The routine was the same as in Germinal: first the women gathered to-

La Disette du pain. *An 4.*
Dans cette facheuse année, des femmes faisoient
cuire, dans les places publiques des choux et autres
racines qu'elles vendoient aux ouvriers, et aux pauvres
30 sous chaque assiétée, et n'en n'avoit pas qui vouloit..

Vendeur d'argent
au péron du palais Royal

Des Rentiers vendent leurs
derniers éfets.

Bad harvests, speculation by grain-hoarders, the abolition of the 'maximum' and monetary inflation caused a serious food crisis: bread and meat became very scarce.

gether, and then they called on their menfolk to march on the Convention. But this time the insurgents were careful to equip themselves with weapons (pikes and cannons) and to give themselves some kind of official leadership: as had happened in 1792 and 1793, several hours were wasted in trying to persuade responsible but reluctant citizens – battalion commanders and civil committee members – to give the uprising the prestige of their authority. At about one o'clock in the afternoon the suburbs began their descent onto the city. Inscribed on hats and jackets were the magic words: 'Bread or death!', 'Bread and the Constitution of 1793!'

By the time the Convention opened its session for the day at about eleven o'clock, the first groups of women were already occupying the public galleries. The deputies proceeded to outlaw the 'ringleaders', in other words the first twenty demonstrators to be arrested, and called 'all good citizens' to arms. The government Committees, which were sitting in the Hôtel de Brionne, to the north of the Carrousel, decided at one o'clock to order the troops surrounding Paris to assemble at the camp of Sablons, and at the same time to mobilise the National Guard. The Committees' delay in taking action has been interpreted by certain historians as a Machiavellian plot by the government to let the insurrection have time to get under way so that the political opposition in the Convention would be compromised. In fact, the Thermidoreans had reason to be apprehensive at the thought of summoning the National Guard. Many of its battalions, even though they were commanded by pro-government officers, consisted of men who would be wearing the rebels' slogans on their caps. The three battalions of the Faubourg Saint-Antoine actually set off without their officers to give the rebels their support, and on the way succeeded in persuading the Arsenal battalion to join them.

At about half past three they reached the Tuileries to find that the first band of attackers had been driven back with whips some two hours earlier. It was now that the decisive assault was made. Féraud, a deputy, was struck down by a pistol-shot when he tried to resist; his head was cut off with a knife and was then paraded round on a pike for some time, until eventually, at about seven o'clock that evening, it was presented to Boissy d'Anglas, who had been presiding over the session. As on 12 Germinal, the insurgents wasted several hours arguing and reading their pamphlets, forgetting all about the government Committees, which had instructed Raffet to bring the loyal battalions of the western Sections. At about nine o'clock the rebels demanded that the deputies recommence their deliberations and, while the crowds outside dispersed of their own accord, a number of Montagnards induced the assembly to approve some of the measures demanded from the public galleries, including the release of imprisoned 'patriots' and the deputies arrested in Germinal, and also the arrest of five more deputies. At half past eleven, two columns of National Guards entered the hall, one led by Raffet and Legendre, the other by Augis. The demonstrators tried at first to put up a resistance, but then scattered and escaped through the doors and windows of the hall.

No sooner had the Convention been delivered from the rebels than it voted for the arrest of fourteen Montagnard deputies, among them Prieur of the Marne, Romme and Bourbotte. Was it possible that the Thermidoreans had deliberately delayed the National Guard's arrival on the scene in order to make the elimination of the Montagnards all the easier? This is by no means impossible: the Thermidoreans, mindful of the events of 10 August 1792 and 31 May 1793, were convinced that the Mountain had organised this insurrection. But it must be remembered that they had been outmanoeuvred and only intervened when they knew they would win.

The uprising of 2 Prairial had shown up the great weakness of the traditional forces of law and order. The Convention had been surrounded by troops of the regular army – here Murat first entered French history – and also by battalions from the Sections, which on this occasion had been led by their regular commanders. In theory,

On 1 Prairial the insurgents invaded the Convention in the Tuileries, killed the deputy Féraud, put his head on a pike and presented it to Boissy d'Anglas, the new president of the Convention.

General Dubois could count on forty thousand men. But, when the battalions of the Faubourg Saint-Antoine trained their cannons at the Tuileries, the gunners of the other Sections decided to make common cause with them and began fraternising with the insurgents. When the Committees found themselves having to negotiate with the mob, they sent a dozen or so deputies to talk things over and promised to settle the food problem. Then, when night came, the crowds made their way back to the suburbs. If the uprising of 2 Prairial was a failure, its weakness was not so much numerical as political.

The revolts of Germinal and Prairial had certain features in common, but were also different in some respects. On both occasions there was the same lack of co-ordination, the same hesitancy shown by the populace when it actually came to seizing sovereignty. This shows just how important the leadership of bourgeois Montagnards and Hébertists had been in the uprisings of Year II. But the differences between Germinal and Prairial are quite marked. Not only was the movement in Prairial more radical, it had been given more precise directives (defection of the National Guard and fraternisation). It therefore seems that Kare Tönnesson may well be justified in adopting the view of Buonarroti, who suspected that the uprising had been planned not by the men who actually took part, but by the prisoners of Plessis. This would explain why an operation which seemed to have been carefully planned was executed so imperfectly.

In order to prevent any further trouble from the Faubourg Saint-Antoine, which had always been a hotbed of insurrection, the Committees formed an army of twenty thousand volunteers commanded by General Menou. The last barricades surrendered on 4 Prairial. The government immediately introduced a series of highly repressive measures: members of the Committees of Year II and former representatives on mission were arrested, the Sections were purged and thirty-six men were sentenced to death. On 29 Prairial six condemned Montagnard deputies, including Romme, tried to kill themselves; three of them succeeded, and the other three were dragged, bleeding, to the guillotine. The intervention of the army had proved decisive.

THE DISSOLUTION OF THE COALITION

On the day that brought the downfall of Robespierre, French armies had entered Liège and Anvers. The offensive had been resumed at the beginning of September, against the Austrians in the province of Liège, against the Prussians in the region of Trèves and against the Anglo-Dutch forces. The Army of the Sambre-and-Meuse crossed the Ourthe and the Roer, and the Army of the Rhine-and-Moselle entered the

Palatinate. On 6 October Cologne was taken, followed by Bonn on the 8th and then Coblenz. By the end of the month the Prussians were evacuating the left bank of the Rhine, abandoning Austrian garrisons at Luxembourg, Mainz and the bridge-head of Mannheim.

The most spectacular French success was Pichegru's conquest of Holland. His troops, followed by large numbers of emigré Dutch republicans, first seized the principal strongholds along the Meuse. As the rivers were ice-bound, Pichegru had no difficulty in crossing them: he led his troops across the Lower Meuse on 27 December, the Waal on 8 January and the Lek on 15 January. The Dutch, deserted by the British, ceased hostilities. For them the time had come for a 'French peace'.

The Republic now had an opportunity to make peace with all Europe. The Coalition which had formed against France in 1793 had been a superficial alliance and had been undermined from within by deep discord. Ferdinand III of Tuscany – a Habsburg – was the first to negotiate with the regicides.

For a large body of French opinion that had never accepted the violation of the old alliances, Prussia was still the power whose friendship mattered most. Moreover, the king of Prussia had every reason to want to extricate himself from the war with France. A desire for peace had manifested itself in several parts of the Empire, in particular at Wurtemberg and in Hesse-Bassel, and gave the Hohenzollerns a chance to resume their traditional role as a counterpoise to Viennese influence. Above all, Frederick William II was much more concerned about Poland than about France. Despite the advantageous terms he had obtained from Russia in the second partition of Poland (January 1793), he was still not satisfied. When Kosciuszko had rebelled in March 1794 he had sent troops to take Warsaw, but they were defeated and forced to raise their siege of the city on 6 September, leaving Suvorov's Cossacks to take possession (10 October). Catherine II, the real arbiter of Poland's destiny, showed her goodwill towards Austria by handing over Cracow, Lublin and Sandomir. Frederick William II, displeased by Catherine's gesture, agreed to negotiate with France. Talks began in October, but it was not until the signing of the treaty of St Petersburg on 8 January 1795, which divided Poland between Austria and Russia, that he decided to send an official negotiator, the Count von der Goltz, to Basle. Everything now depended on the price which France was expecting for peace.

Opinion in France was unanimous in wanting this peace, but was not agreed on the conditions that would be acceptable. At first the Committees showed a cautious attitude, remaining loyal to the policy of Robespierre. Few of their members shared the stubbornness of Sieyès and Reubell, who were still propounding the hazy dogma of 'natural frontiers', which had become so fashionable in the early months of 1793. Would not the Meuse be a satisfactory substitute for the Rhine? This was the opinion of Barthélemy, who was handling the negotiations at Basle, and it was also the opinion of Carnot. But logic carried little weight compared with the emotional appeal of a Republic with boundaries extending as far as the Rhine itself. Royalist and counterrevolutionary journalists were waging a campaign for the frontiers of 1789: the 'old frontiers' became the slogan of the enemies of the Thermidorean government. The government was anxious not to let the Jacobins monopolise patriotic sentiment at a time when it was having to cope with the after-effects of the Terror: it was afraid of pushing the army into the arms of the Jacobins and thereby losing the mainstay of its authority. Even more important, nationalism was now a great popular passion, a passion which it would have been unwise to suppress at a time when the masses were being deprived of their other great dreams of universal suffrage and direct democracy. In comparison with motives such as these, the interests of the bourgeoisie – which were to be an influential factor a year later – were of little significance. The Thermidoreans were fighting for survival, and the Rhine became their battle-cry.

Prussia eventually yielded on this issue and by the treaty of Basle (5 April 1795) recognised French occupation of the left bank of the Rhine until a general peace should be concluded. But, at the same time, she declined an alliance with France and secured the neutrality of North Germany.

The real victims of Thermidorean policy were the Dutch. They had done everything they could to please their occupiers. On 16 February, which saw the birth of the independent Batavian Republic, they expressed a desire to be regarded as a sister-republic by France, but their hopes were to be dashed. Sieyès and Reubell were sent to The Hague with instructions to bring the Dutch down to earth. By the treaty of 16 May 1795 (27 Floréal) they imposed a protectorate on Holland. By the terms of the treaty, France annexed Dutch Flanders, Maastricht and Vanloo, though she had not yet decided to annex Belgium: the 'union' of Belgium was not effected until 1 October (9 Vendémiaire Year IV. France was to keep an army of twenty-five thousand men in Holland and was to receive an indemnity of one hundred million florins; in addition, countless works of art found their way to Paris. In return France was offering Holland the protection of a close defensive and offensive alliance.

Peace negotiations with Spain were carried on as military hostilities continued, in an atmosphere worthy of fifteenth-century Florence. On 17 September Dugommier, commanding the Army of the eastern Pyrenees, drove the Spaniards from Bellegarde, their last stronghold on French territory, and invaded Catalonia. On the 20th he received a mysterious letter from Godoy, the Spanish chief minister, and with it an olive-branch. He sent letter and olive-branch to the government in Paris. Dugommier died before the capture of Figueras (28 November) and his successor, Pérignon, took Rosas on 3 February 1795. The negotiations had been floundering for some time when Moncey's capture of Bilbao accelerated matters. Peace was signed at Basle on 22 July 1795. By the treaty France gained the Spanish half of Santo Domingo, but in return undertook to evacuate Catalonia and the Basque country.

However, a general peace was not possible unless Britain and Austria accepted the French terms, which they did not: on the contrary, they strengthened their alliance and in May 1795 Francis II was able to mass two large armies, one commanded by Wurmser along the right bank of the Rhine, the other under Clerfayt between the Mein and the Ruhr. The armies of the Republic were not what they had been in Year II; their numbers had dwindled, since desertion was now easier. It has been estimated that in March 1795, out of a theoretical fighting force of one million, one hundred thousand men, there were only some three hundred and thirty-five thousand fighting on the frontiers, and of these only two hundred and ten thousand were engaged on the northern and eastern frontiers.

Everything depended on two men: Pichegru, appointed commander of the Rhine-and-Moselle, and Jourdan, who kept command of the Sambre-and-Meuse. The representatives on mission recommended a joint offensive by the two armies. Luxembourg was taken on 7 May, but Pichegru refused to move. It is difficult to say whether Pichegru was contemplating treachery; he was in touch with the Prince de Condé's emissaries in August and did not commit his troops to battle until the Convention had been dissolved in October. At this stage he was an embittered soldier with little affection for a Republic which did not know how to reward its heroes. On 6 September Jourdan managed to cross the Rhine near Dusseldorf, planning a turning movement in the direction of Mainz; but, as Pichegru had failed to support him, he was compelled to withdraw to the left bank of the Rhine on 1 October. Three days after the Convention made way for the Directory, the Austrians began to raise the siege of Mainz.

As the war with Europe continued, a new threat was presented to the government by a resurgence of royalist activity. In the provinces – and in particular at Lyons, in the Rhone valley, in Provence and in Languedoc – a campaign of repression known as the 'White Terror' was launched against politicians who had been active in the Revolution since 1792. The Convention did not give its sanction to the massacres, but it did nothing to stop them; as Thibaudeau himself ad-

Louis XVII, nominally king since his father's execution, was still imprisoned in the Temple. A number of deputies, including Barras, visited him to inquire after his health. His death, announced on 8 June 1795, was a great setback to the royalists.

mitted, it was convinced that the 'terrorists of Year II' were more to be feared than the 'royal terrorists of Year III'. Constitutional monarchists disapproved of the cruelties of the 'White Terror', which damaged their own cause. They had been gaining ground in public opinion, even in those quarters of political life which had hitherto been firmly bound up with the Revolution. They dreamed of completing the victories of 1789 by putting Louis XVI's son, a prisoner in the Temple, on the throne of France.

Their plan failed for two reasons. The death of the dauphin on 8 June 1795 was described by Mallet du Pan as 'the triumph of the Republicans'. The pretender, the former Comte de Provence who now took the title of Louis XVIII, published a proclamation at Verona on 24 June which ruled out any possibility of reconciliation. But the royalist movement suffered an even more disastrous setback when the emigrés in the entourage of the Comte d'Artois persuaded the British to let them land at Quiberon Bay (23 June) at the time of the Vendéan and Chouan insurrections. General Hoche, who had been warned of their plan, succeeded in blockading the Chouans and emigrés on the peninsula. Some of them managed to rejoin their ships, but the large majority were taken prisoner. The military commissions set up by Tallien showed no mercy: all but three of the seven hundred and fifty-one emigrés were shot.

The landing at Quiberon Bay and the ensuing executions had immediate political repercussions. In public opinion the break between the Thermidoreans and the right wing of the Convention was now complete. Although they had expressed their disapproval of the Quiberon Bay landing the constitutional monarchists could not forgive

the government, and particularly Tallien, for the mass execution of the prisoners. They resented the reawakening of republican patriotism, the reappearance of the *Marseillaise* and the release of former Jacobins – everything, in fact, which was part of the general reaction to the British intervention. But hardly anyone in the Convention wished to destroy the coalition between the Plain and the right wing. The Plain, moreover, was quite capable of protecting itself on the left: it had learned from Robespierre how to fight a battle on two fronts, though without the guillotine. Its slogan was the union of 'patriots of '89, constitutional monarchists, Jacobins, moderates, *exagérés*, democrats and republicans'. The right wing needed the support of the Plain if it was going to obtain the Convention's approval for a new Constitution.

THE CONSTITUTION OF YEAR III

There was no longer any question of putting into effect the Constitution of July 1793, which had been voted in great haste and largely for reasons of expediency. On 29 Germinal (11 April) a commission of eleven members had been appointed to prepare a new charter for France. Six of them had been Girondins, and one of the six, Daunou, was to be the chief inspiration behind the new Constitution. Durand de Mailhane and Boissy d'Anglas represented the Plain, Thibaudeau the 'repentant' Montagnards and Berlier the orthodox Montagnards. Rarely had a commission been more truly representative of that dynamic section of the bourgeoisie which, since 10 August 1792, had been seeking to restore stability to France. It worked for two months before submitting its report to the Convention (5 Messidor). Another two months were devoted to discussion, during which time the greatest stir was caused by the intervention of Sieyès. At last the Constitution preceded by a Declaration of Rights and a Declaration of Duties, was approved on 5 Fructidor (22 August).

The Constitution of 1795 was yet another attempt to realise the eighteenth-century ideal of enlightened bourgeois liberalism. The Declaration of Rights repeated the principles laid down in the Declaration of 1789, but in more definite terms and with firmer guarantees. The formulae which popular opinion had imposed on the Constitution of 1793 were swept aside, revealing the very essence of eighteenth-century political thought: for the Enlightenment the happiness of all was an end for which to strive, not a right to be claimed recklessly; public assistance bore too close a resemblance to the charities of 'feudal' times not to be regarded as an insult to the self-respect of the individual. The principle of equality was stripped of the distortions of the 'levelling-down' mentality: it was reaffirmed as an equality of opportunity, not an equality of immediate rights. In 1789, as

Lanjuinais lucidly explained, equality had been defined negatively, by reference to existing social orders and privileges. It must now be defined positively: 'Equality means the same law for all.' The 1795 Constitution marked a distinct advance on its predecessors, and was the foundation on which the entire structure of nineteenth-century French constitutional law was to be built.

Above all the risk of dictatorship had to be eliminated, and so the representative principle which had been violated on 31 May 1793 was protected by a host of theoretically insurmountable guarantees. The men who drew up the Constitution were not repudiating the Revolution, but were simply concerned to prevent insurrections by active minorities. Boissy d'Anglas made this illuminating statement: 'When insurrection is general it has no need of justification, but when it is only partial it is always wrong.' And so the right of insurrection, which had been implicit in the Declaration of 1789 because it was confused with the right of revolution, was omitted from the Declaration of 1795. It was in this same spirit that the Declaration of Duties proclaimed the responsibilities that inevitably went with equality, and above all the obligation to respect the laws laid down by the nation's representatives in parliament. To discourage intimidation and violence the Constitution introduced the secret ballot, a reform for which the working-class of nineteenth-century Britain was to strive so tirelessly.

The structure of power advocated in the Constitution was based on an idea of primary importance which Sieyès defined in a striking manner, and which represented the essence of true liberalism: the repudiation of the concept of sovereignty. Speaking of the sovereignty of the people, Sieyès declared: 'The only reason why this word has assumed such colossal importance in our imaginations is that the people of France, their minds still filled with the superstitions of royalism, have felt obliged to endow it with the whole gamut of high-sounding attributes and absolute powers which have given all usurped sovereignties their brilliance.' The State was to be neither the individual nor the mass of individuals, it was to be nothing, or at any rate it was to be subordinated to civilian society. The twentieth century has had difficulty in understanding this powerful aversion to the concept of State which was characteristic of the society of the Enlightenment. The separation of powers was merely one method of expressing this aversion; alternative theories were put forward, by Sieyès among others, but were rejected. The Convention's refusal to accept his suggestions was a painful blow to Sieyès, who always looked with contempt on the Constitution of 1795. The legislature was to be divided into two assemblies: the Council of Five Hundred, which was to be responsible for initiating legislation, and the Council of Elders, which was to pass the resolutions of the other Council into law. The executive was entrusted to a Directory of five members chosen by the Elders from a list submitted by the Five Hundred.

As far as the franchise was concerned, the main objective was stability. This meant repudiation of a genuinely democratic electoral system, but nevertheless the system proposed by the new Constitution was, for the Europe of 1795, remarkably broadly based. The vote was no longer to be dependent on the payment of a fixed amount of taxes, as in 1791; henceforth any adult Frenchman who had been living in the same place for at least a year, and who paid taxes, even voluntarily, was entitled to vote for 'electors' at the primary assemblies. As in the Constitution revised after the king's flight to Varennes, it was at this intermediate stage of the electoral system that the 'brake' was imposed. In order to be eligible for election to the secondary assemblies a man had to be able to fulfil certain tax and property qualifications which varied according to the size of the agglomeration. Restrictions were also imposed with regard to age: the 'electors' of the secondary assemblies had to be at least twenty-five, a member of the Council of Five Hundred at least thirty, and a member of the Council of Elders at least forty. To avoid the hazards of sudden shifts of public opinion, members of both the executive and the legislature were to be replaced in stages: every year one of the five Directors and one-third of the members of the two Councils were to be replaced. The Revolution's work of demolition had been done by others. The authors of the Constitution of Year III were intent on rebuilding France so that her revolutionary heritage might be preserved.

But the grave risk of civil war made even those deputies weary of the responsibilities of power realise that they could not give way to public opinion. What would happen if, as seemed quite possible, the electorate voted for men who were not committed to the revolutionary cause? Baudin said: 'The abdication of the Constituent Assembly shows clearly enough that the surest way of wrecking an untried Constitution is to leave it to be implemented by an entirely new legislature.' It is quite possible that in 1795 the opposite was true, but so strongly were the deputies influenced by the experience of the recent past that they decided to play safe: on 5 Fructidor (22 August) they decreed that the electorate would have to choose two-thirds of the new legislature from the members of the Convention. On 13 Fructidor a second decree laid down that if the electorate did not respect the two-thirds rule, the re-elected deputies of the Convention would themselves co-opt enough of their former colleagues to make up the requisite number. These decrees were the effect, and not the cause, of anti-parliamentary feeling.

Royalists and moderates now launched a campaign against the 'perpetuals', as the deputies of the Convention were contemptuously described. Their propaganda found a willing audience in a country bruised and battered by the events of recent years. Police reports record the gradual spread of discontent: 'The large majority seems to be in favour of the Constitution, but not the two-thirds decrees. Many people feel that not a single member of the Convention should be re-elected.' The most unpopular figures were Tallien, whose windows were broken on 21 Fructidor (7 September), and Marie-Joseph Chénier, who received this taunt at the Opéra: 'What have you done

Jean-Lambert Tallien, one of the group of politicians who brought about Robespierre's downfall and came to be known as the 'Thermidoreans'.

with your brother, Cain?' Indignation was especially fierce when the Convention decided that those who had been deprived of civic rights in Germinal and Prairial would be allowed to vote at the primary assemblies. In Paris the decree was ignored.

The deputies of the right wing maintained an attitude of caution. Their position was doubly reassuring: their opposition to the Thermidorean government was bringing them popularity, and this increased their chances of being re-elected in accordance with the two-thirds decree. But journalists and men of action had no such grounds for keeping quiet, and so they set about mobilising the Sections, at first by legal methods and then by more devious means.

The primary assemblies, summoned to a plebiscite on the Constitution and the two-thirds decrees, were held from 20 Fructidor (6 September) to 1 Vendémiaire Year IV (23 September). In Paris the Sections declared themselves in permanent session, and on 21 Fructidor the 'Bankers' Section' (the Le Peletier Section) proposed the constitution of an inter-Sectional central committee. Young men and journalists aped the revolutionary orators of 1789 and 1792. No effort was spared, and men were even sent to harangue the troops at Marly. Every Section but one – the Quinze-Vingts – rejected the two decrees. In the provinces the Constitution was accepted by all the departments except Mont-Tonnerre, but the two-thirds decrees were rejected by the departments of the Rhone valley, the west, Bas-Rhin and the region round Paris (including the department of Paris itself). However, on 1 Vendémiaire the Convention published the results of the plebiscite: 914,853 for the Constitution and 41,832 against, and 167,758 for the decrees and 95,373 against.

The right wing was now divided. Ultra-royalists scorned the agitation which the plebiscite had provoked. Brottier and des Pomelles, the agents of the Comte d'Antraigues, disapproved of a movement based on the sovereignty of the people's will. For opposite reasons the shrewder minds of the Convention and the salons advised against illegal action. Mme de Staël told the young Lacretelle that a campaign by the Sections might lead to civil war and wreck any chance of a gradual solution. 'To speak of the sovereignty of the people is something quite new for you,' she said to him; 'you are fumbling with a language which they know better than you and which they created for their own use.' Mme de Staël had put her finger on the real weakness of the royalist movement: to appeal directly to the people against the nation's elected representatives, to talk about the rights of the people, when in fact the royalists were thinking only of their own advantage, was hardly likely to win the sympathy of moderate bourgeois opinion. But the younger members of the movement, and especially its journalists, turned a deaf ear to the wisdom of their elders. They were determined to have their own insurrection.

13 VENDÉMIAIRE

Between 1 and 13 Vendémiaire (5 October) the Gilded Youth engaged in intense activity in the Sections. Richer Serizy handed over the Théâtre-Français and the left bank to Fiévée and set up his headquarters in the convent of the Filles-Saint-Thomas, where the assemblies of the Le Peletier Section were held. This was to be the centre of the insurrection. On 5 Vendémiaire the Le Peletier Section presented to the Convention a petition signed by twenty-two other Sections. When it learned on the 10th that trouble had broken out in the region of Dreux, and that the white flag had even been seen there, it called on the Sections to arm themselves and assemble the following day at the Théâtre-Français. But not many Sections responded and the assembly dispersed without having come to a decision.

The insurrection was given a fresh impetus on the evening of the 11th, when the Convention decided to entrust full powers to an extraordinary committee of five members, which was to include the fearsome Barras. At the same time the Convention called on the officers who had been dismissed for Jacobinism, the volunteers of the suburbs and the popular quarters, and former terrorists just out of prison, to form three battalions which were to be known as the 'Patriots of '89'. On 12 Vendémiaire it reintroduced the decree of 21 Germinal which had deprived terrorists of civic rights. With the spectre of the Terror reappearing, the Parisian public took fright; it was now only too willing to listen to the voices of the right-wing press. But the Convention was determined to free itself from the fetters that threatened to jeopardise its future: on the evening of the 12th, General Menou was dismissed and replaced by Barras, who gathered around him a number of

Vicomte de Barras, elected one of the five members of the extraordinary committee, formed in early Vendémiaire Year IV.

generals, including Brune, Carteaux and Bonaparte, who were unlikely to hold moderate sympathies. These generals had four to five thousand regular soldiers at their command and also fifteen hundred 'Patriots of '89'. On the other side, the insurgents' central committee, headed by Richer Serizy, appointed as its commander-in-chief a former Hébertist general, Danican.

On 13 Vendémiaire Paris was under arms for the last time. The insurgents numbered twenty to twenty-five thousand men, but they had no cannons to set against those brought by Murat during the night from the camp of Sablons (the Sections had given up their cannons in Prairial). During the morning the two sides manoeuvred their troops. On the left bank Danican succeeded in gaining control without engaging in combat. On the right bank, from the Louvre to the Tuileries,

Carteaux had placed his men in a protective curtain guarding the bridges, while in the Rue Saint-Honoré Bonaparte kept an eye on the church of Saint-Roch. Outside this church, at about half past four, fighting commenced. The two columns which Danican had organised on the opposite bank tried to penetrate the wall of enemy troops across the Pont-Royal and the Pont-Neuf, but they were dispersed by cannon-fire and Danican himself vanished. At Saint-Roch fighting continued until the morning of the 14th. All around the streets were empty. The uprising of Vendémiaire had cost three hundred dead and wounded, including members of the liberal professions, officials, *rentiers* and shopkeepers.

In the Convention the uprising had repercussions which, though predictable, were nonetheless dramatic. On the 17th Tallien and Legendre broke with the leaders of the right wing, accusing them of condoning the uprising by their silence. The moderates accepted this challenge and Lanjuinais spoke quite openly of the 'massacre of Vendémiaire'. His boldness was understandable, for the elections had begun and by the 20th it was clear that the voting was following a uniform trend: everywhere the electorate was repudiating the men who had been implicated in the events of 9 Thermidor Year II and choosing those outgoing members of the Convention who had been least involved in the governments of the recent past. The Thermidoreans now resorted to desperate tactics. On 23 Vendémiaire Tallien, speaking from the high benches of the Mountain, denounced Lanjuinais, Boissy d'Anglas, Lesage and Larivière as accomplices of the insurgents of the 13th. The Thermidoreans' plan was quite simple: they hoped to have the elections declared null and void and then establish an emergency regime.

The deputies of the Plain were too familiar with this kind of manoeuvre. In repressing the insurrection of 13 Vendémiaire they had taken care to separate the innocent from the guilty, and only two of the rebels had been executed. The officers who had been dismissed after 9 Thermidor were reinstated, but the 'Patriots of '89' were disbanded. Thibaudeau told Tallien that his defence of the September massacres deprived him of any right to interfere in the functioning of the new Constitution. The Plain had triumphed.

At its final session on 4 Brumaire (26 October) the parliament which had beheaded a king and established its mastery over the populace of Paris decided that the Place de la Révolution should be renamed the Place de la Concorde; it also granted an amnesty to those of its members whom it had consigned to prison. To the very end the Convention had found itself unable to banish the memories of the past.

9

THE
BOURGEOIS REPUBLIC

The Directory has received less attention from historians than any other period of the French Revolution. A brief examination of the average school text-book will show how unequal has been the importance attached to the different stages of the Revolution: the story begins dramatically with the explosion of 1789, develops with the European war and the Committee of Public Safety, and then suddenly stops short at the Directory. The four years that elapsed between 13 Vendémiaire Year IV and 18 Brumaire Year VIII are generally treated much more cursorily than the short period of the Gironde and the Mountain, and it is always the glorious Italian campaign which is allowed to dominate those four years, as if in an attempt to obliterate the squalor of the domestic scene and to pave the way for the splendours of the Empire.

Yet the lack of interest in the period of the Directory has been due not so much to nationalist sentiment on the part of Frenchmen, as to a particularly strong tradition of French public life that is still very much alive today – the prejudice against parliamentary institutions. The Directory, wedged between Year III and the Consulate, naturally tends to be regarded as a rather dull transitional stage separating two great peaks of the Revolution: coming after Robespierre and before Bonaparte, this group of very ordinary men who governed France collectively could boast neither a hero nor a saviour. Moreover, as a government of the 'centre', the Directory has attracted the scorn of both the revolutionary and the conservative traditions. It was too eager to repudiate Robespierre and the Jacobins and too fond of money and women to please left-wing opinion; and even today, after more than a hundred and fifty years, right-wing opinion stubbornly clings to the partisan judgement pronounced on the Directory by the France of the Consulate and the Empire, just as the Fourth Republic is now judged from the viewpoint of the Fifth Republic, obsessed with the image of the saviour leading the nation out of chaos.

Anti-parliamentary prejudice in France dates specifically from the period of *the Directory, and was both the cause and the consequence of that government's downfall. Let us define our terms at this point. If parliamentary government is defined as ministerial responsibility to an elected assembly, then the Directory was not a parliamentary regime, since it was based on a clear division of the executive and the legislature. Again, if parliamentary government is defined simply as representative government, then it must be remembered that revolutionary France had three representative assemblies before 1795. But the political compromise of the Constituent Assembly was paralysed by the monarchy, and during the period of the National Convention a temporary dictatorship was forced on France by the war with Europe. The Directory represents the first attempt in French history to establish a republic on the normal processes of representative institutions.*

The Constitution of 1795 (Year III) was very much a product of the eighteenth century. It upheld liberty, the promotion of talent and the rational organisation of social life; it aimed at a rigid separation of powers, a vast property-owning democracy and a more centralised administration. The five Directors were to govern, the two Councils to legislate and local authorities to be elected by property-owners and to be made ultimately responsible to a Directory commissioner. The Constitution was both a return to the France of the Feuillants, without the king and the nobles, and at the same time the forerunner of the Napoleonic system of prefectures. Bourgeois France hoped to found a system of government on the concerted abilities of all the nation's property-owners.

This attempt at parliamentary government, jeopardised at the outset by the 'two-thirds' decrees, ended in failure less than two years later, in Fructidor, when the two Councils were invaded by the troops of Hoche and Augereau. The coup d'état *of 18 Fructidor not only doomed to failure the Republic of the deputies, but also restored dictatorial government at the expense of legality. The situation resembled that of 2 June 1793 when the Girondins were expelled, but with one important difference: in Fructidor the legal government of France was challenged not by the people of Paris, but by the army.*

The Directory was not really a new regime, for it was inevitably the heir and prisoner of the past. The politicians were the same. Faced with a royalist revival and a resurgence of counter-revolutionary activity, the deputies of the Convention were determined that a large number of them should sit in the new legislative Councils – and had been confronted with the uprising of Vendémiaire as a result. The Convention, anxious not to repeat the mistake made by the Constituent Assembly when it had declared itself collectively ineligible for the Legislative Assembly, made sure that its deputies formed two-thirds of the Council of the Five Hundred and the Council of Elders; the new third, elected freely and for the most part royalist, was therefore helpless to influence the choice of the five Directors. The Thermidoreans elected men from their own ranks to all five positions. Already known popularly as the 'perpetuals', the Thermidoreans were bound together by their common heritage.

And yet this common heritage was as much a liability as an asset, for it included the recent drama of the Terror. Although the new regime officially repudiated 'terrorism', the extreme form of dictatorial government, it could not obliterate memories of 1793–4. On the extreme left, terrorism was still regarded as a necessary instrument of equality, not only against the nobles, but against the rich classes as a whole. The moderates, on the other hand, were so appalled by the thought of the Terror that they began to favour a restoration of the monarchy. Even within the Directory itself the events of Thermidor had not freed the old members of the Convention from the ideas of the past. On the left were Reubell and Barras, who had never had any scruples about legality when resisting royalist activity; on the right stood Carnot, elected to the Directory on his reputation as an 'organiser of victories', but who was anxious to have people forget his role in the Committee of Public Safety and to be regarded as one of the bourgeoisie; he and Letourneur were the advocates of 'order' and favoured a compromise with the constitutional monarchists; finally, in the centre of the Directory, was the hapless La Révellière-Lépeaux, tossed from one side to the other, the living symbol of the contradictions of the times: one of the Girondins who had been banished under the Terror, he was fanatically anti-terrorist, but remained loyal to the anti-clerical and annexationist policies of the Gironde. In the words of Albert Sorel, he was 'the vicaire savoyard in the government' (the vicaire savoyard was the fictitious personage through whom Rousseau made his 'profession of faith' in Émile).

This divided team included only one great politician – Barras. Once again the Revolution had found itself a leader among the survivors of the nobility. But was he in fact a leader? The ex-viscount stood out from among his pedestrian colleagues by his elegance and expensive tastes; above all, he possessed political flair, the ability to make quick decisions. But he was also lazy, giving himself up to worldly pleasures surrounded by his own little court of admirers: hardly a suitable leader for the new France, and yet the regime had no-one else to whom it could turn – except the generals, and they were intent on pursuing the war.

The Directory inherited not only the aftermath of the Terror, but also the endless European war, for neither Britain nor Austria had yet laid down their arms. By persuading Prussia to accept the French occupation of the left bank of the Rhine in the spring of 1795 and by annexing Belgium in the autumn, the Thermidoreans had appeared to commit themselves as a body to the revolutionary doctrine of 'natural frontiers' – in other words, to the pursuit of the war. Despite Carnot, who wanted to come to terms with Europe, they preferred to devote their energies to foreign adventure rather than to the internal stability of France. Since 1792 it had been patently obvious that a war against monarchic Europe and mercantile Britain would make it difficult for France to establish a truly republican system at home; but, at the same time, peace might also jeopardise the Republic, since this would be a victory for French royalism. At least the war kept the army happy, and now that Jacobinism was no longer an effective force the army was the Republic's only support. Formerly the preserve of the aristocracy, the army now offered a career to commoners, and neither officers nor soldiers had any intention of being deprived of opportunities for promotion by allowing the policy of conquest to be dropped. The war had another attraction for the Thermidoreans of the Directory: it was a profitable concern.

The decline of the assignat and the bad harvests of '94 and '95 had added financial and economic crisis to the burdens inherited by the new regime. For several years taxes had been slow to reach the Treasury's coffers and the Revolution had been financing its public expenditure, and particularly the war, not with the production of real wealth but by issuing paper-money. Towards the end of the life of the Convention, the disruptive effects of inflation were intensified when the Thermidoreans abandoned the policy of a controlled economy. The economic crisis of '95–'96, which increased government expenditure and compelled the Directory to buy cereals from abroad with metal currency, gave a further impetus to the decline of the assignat, which fell almost to zero. The peasants were paying their taxes in assignats and selling their produce for metal currency; this meant in fact that only a small proportion of produce was sold, and so the whole economic relationship between town and country was imperilled. In the face of such crises the Directory was no better equipped than the king of France had been; indeed, it was more vulnerable because the final collapse of the assignat occurred during the Directory's tenure of office, leaving the public convinced that the government of the day was responsible both for inflation and for famine. The only remedies which the Directory could offer were those employed by its predecessors of the Convention – the constant issues of paper-money, forced loans and then the sale of nationalised property, growing ever more rapid. Even if the war was able to finance itself with plunder, it could not cover the ordinary expenditure of the Republic.

But the Thermidoreans of the Directory had one clear advantage over the earlier governments of revolutionary France. They realised that it was no use trying to build the Republic on the foundations of 'virtue' advocated by the Enlightenment, but that conquest in war and self-interest were the soundest principles to follow. During the period of the Directory the modern alliance of politics and finance replaced the Robespierrist dream of a Spartan republic. It was surely no coincidence that Barras and Reubell, often considered as the two 'corrupt' members of the Directory, were also its most clear-sighted and energetic republicans.

The armies were without pay, food and clothing; the hospitals were not getting the supplies they needed, and the people had no bread. With no Treasury funds to tap, the government was reduced to expedients, printing the next day's assignats the night before. However, the impoverishment of the lower classes and the bankruptcy of the Treasury brought wealth to speculators. Vast profits were made by contractors supplying the armies and by foreign capitalists granting loans, and the sale of nationalised properties for worthless paper enabled men to convert their wages into real estate. And so the new financial élite found itself inextricably bound up with a vast body of small-scale property-owners who shared its own fears of a restoration of the monarchy and the nobility and the inevitable disputes over land-ownership that would ensue. But it was even more closely bound up with the regime. Barras himself said:

The office of deputy, previously regarded as a position of honour, was no longer being sought for the same motives that had inspired the early assemblies. It was regarded as a position of advantage to be obtained by devious means, a stepping-stone to wealth rather than glory. As the moral ideas of the Revolution grew weaker they were replaced by materialist ideas. People had already begun to talk of the practical age that was dawning.

The bourgeoisie was slowly establishing itself as the ruling class of France, though it still lacked social and political roots; its main strength for the time being lay not in itself, but in the weakness of its adversaries. To the left, the Jacobin movement had been stifled in Germinal and Prairial of Year III, and even the atrocious winter of 1795–6 had done nothing to revive it. The Babeuf plot certainly gave a new expression to the egalitarianism of the sans-culottes, but its advocacy of 'levelling', its social composition and the alliances it formed with the former deputies of the Convention made it little more than the death-rattle of popular terrorism, a posthumous reconciliation of the ghosts of Marat, the 'Enragés', Hébert and Robespierre. The plot, exaggerated out of all pro-portion by bourgeois counter-propaganda, in which Carnot played a major part, was easily suppressed with the help of police informers.

The chief threat to the Directory came from the right. The cannons of Vendémiaire had not destroyed the White Terror of vengeance unleashed in Thermidor. However, the country as a whole did not want to return to the Old Regime. Thermidor had brought public opinion back to the great dream of 1789: constitutional monarchy. At elections the well-to-do peasant and the bourgeois of the towns voted for moderate royalists who had little sympathy with the members of the old Convention. The new 'third' in the Councils was predominantly royalist. A pretender capable of taking advantage of such a situation might well have obtained a legal majority in the elections of Year VI. But Louis XVI's brother, who had proclaimed himself Louis XVIII, looked only to the past and to the Chouans. The schism within the Church intensified the ultra-royalist movement, for rebel priests were looking forward to the time when they would be rewarded for their long and bold resistance. Consequently, the period of the Directory brought no solution to the problem that had always confronted the constitutional monarchists: they were royalists without a king. They fought tirelessly against the 'perpetuals' of the two Councils, against anything associated with the Convention, and they bitterly opposed the last law decreed by that great assembly, the law of 3 Brumaire Year IV, which prohibited all relatives of emigrés from public office. But without a suitable candidate for the royal succession they were unable to reach any lasting agreement, either with moderate republicans such as Cadoudal, or with ultra-royalists such as Carnot.

The first parliamentary republic in the history of France, with no majority to lead it, managed to survive for a time because of the very feebleness of three conflicting forces at work within it. The Thermidoreans of the Directory were continually threatened from both right and left, but Jacobinism was dying as a political force and royalism remained divided and undecided; buttressed by financiers, the army and public apathy, the Thermidoreans at least knew what they wanted, which was to remain in power. On 13 Vendémiaire they had paid the price of their determination. Two years later they were to find themselves in a similar plight, but the manner of the army's intervention on that occasion showed clearly enough that they had more reason to fear their saviours than their enemies.

THE NEW INSTITUTIONS

The elections of Vendémiaire Year IV were fairly calm, possibly because the two-thirds decrees had deprived them of any real significance, and possibly because the three-stage electoral system and the preponderance of the bourgeoisie had tended to dilute political passions. In each department of France the secondary assemblies of property-owning 'electors', who had themselves been chosen by the voters of the communes and the cantons at the primary assemblies, had observed the rule by which two-thirds of the deputies of the new Councils were to be elected from members of the old Convention; however, as many of these former 'Conventionnels' were elected in several departments at the same time there were finally only three hundred and ninety-four of them, instead of the prescribed five hundred. As the deputies from the colonies had already been re-elected the remaining hundred or so 'Conventionnels' had to be co-opted to the Councils by their former colleagues. In choosing the other third, the electoral assemblies naturally avoided voting for outgoing members of the Convention.

There were consequently three categories of deputies in the two Councils of the Directory: the 'Conventionnels' who had been re-elected by the departments, the 'Conventionnels' who had been co-opted by their re-elected colleagues, and the new deputies who made up the other third. The first of these categories included moderates such as the ex-Girondin Lanjuinais and Boissy d'Anglas, and the new third was strongly royalist or counter-revolutionary, but this bias to the right was partly compensated by the contingent of co-opted deputies which strengthened the left wing of the new legislature.

The seven hundred and fifty deputies were asked to declare their ages and family circumstances; the names of all those over forty who were married or widowers were put in an urn and the first two hundred and fifty drawn by lot formed the Council of Elders; the rest went to the Council of Five Hundred.

The most striking feature of the new legislative Councils was the fact that they were dominated by the same men who had been governing

France since Robespierre's downfall in Thermidor Year III. Although many of them felt that reconciliation and compromise were essential if a stable regime was to be established, they were still too close in time to the violent upheavals of the past and still unable to forget the part which they themselves had played in those upheavals. Their presence in the Councils provided a certain continuity in the government of France, but they were divided in their attitudes to both past and future. Between a right wing of some hundred and fifty royalists, mostly liberal or constitutional monarchists, and a left wing of three hundred republicans, composed largely of those Thermidoreans who had been responsible for the executions at Quiberon Bay and the repression of the uprising of 13 Vendémiaire, control of the assemblies was exercised by the moderate Thermidoreans, who were hostile to dictatorial methods of government but were at the same time committed to the Revolution. These moderates, anxious to preserve an order which had scarcely yet been established, wished to show their loyalty to the new parliamentary institutions, but the insurrection of Vendémiaire had already proved how hazardous their task was to be.

The first duty of the Councils was to choose the five Directors who would exercise the executive power. The Council of Five Hundred was to draw up a list of fifty names from which the Council of Elders would select the five. Not wanting to leave anything to chance, the leaders of the majority in the assemblies (the 'majority' being the 'two-thirds', the deputies of the old Convention) gathered at the home of one of them to decide on a plan of action. They decided to make their colleagues' choice easier by drawing up a list of forty-five obscure names and five famous 'Conventionnels'. They were thus applying the principle of the two-thirds decree to the election of the executive. The Five Hundred added the name of Cambacérès to the list, but the Elders rejected this moderate royalist and left themselves with no choice but to elect the five well-known figures recommended by the group of deputies who had conferred in secret. The men elected as Directors, in the order of votes received, were La Révellière-Lépeaux, Reubell, Sieyès, Letourneur and Barras. Sieyès immediately refused to join the Directory, saying that he was not fitted for such a position; he had not been able to forgive the Convention for rejecting the Constitution he had drafted, and he maintained an attitude of aloofness from the new regime; throughout the period of the Directory he plotted surreptitiously against the men he despised until he succeeded in bringing about their downfall. A new list of ten candidates was drawn up in which the only name to stand out was that of Carnot. The Five Hundred again proposed Cambacérès, but the Elders elected Carnot. This man who had first-hand experience of the rivalries of the Committee of Public Safety was mistrustful of the Directory

Reubell   Carnot

and its collective powers, but he nevertheless agreed to accept his appointment.

The executive now lay in the hands of five regicide Directors, all of them former members of the Convention and therefore closely implicated in the upheavals of the past few years. As in the two legislative assemblies, the fact that they had shared the common experience of the past did not prevent them from being sharply and deeply divided. Carnot, elected to the Directory as the spokesman of Jacobinism, quickly established himself as its most moderate member. Letourneur stood by Carnot. La Révellière-Lépeaux, the former Girondin, shared their abhorrence of terrorist methods, but differed from them in his anti-clerical and annexationist views. The two most powerful personalities in the new executive were Reubell and Barras, who represented the left. Reubell was the advocate of the 'natural frontiers' policy, a man of no great intellect but with a strong loyalty to 1789 and 1793. Barras, the ex-viscount and ex-terrorist who had become the man of Thermidor and Vendémiaire, personified the continuity of the Thermidorean regime, governing the present in the name of the past and watching jealously over the power that had been seized on 9 Thermidor. For the time being, however, rivalries were put aside as the five men divided power among themselves. Letourneur took charge of the Navy and La Révellière-Lépeaux was made responsible for Education, the Arts and Manufactures. The three strong men of the

Letourneur   La Révellière-Lépeaux

Directory assumed all the more important posts: Carnot took over
the War Office, Barras the Police and the Interior, and Reubell controlled Diplomacy, Finances and Justice.

With its own affairs settled, the Directory turned its attention to
the appointment of the six ministers who were to be responsible for
the day-to-day routine of the executive. Five of the six were appointed

Barras

without much deliberation, but it took a little longer to appoint a Minister of Finances. The Directory soon demanded that a seventh ministry be set up, for Police, a sure sign of the regime's instability. The Directory, mindful of the Constitution and of its own powers, never associated the ministers with political decisions. It appointed Lagarde, a former member of the parlement of Douai, to the important post of Secretary General. It took some time for local government to be properly organised; the key men in this field were inevitably the commissioners appointed by the Directory to supervise municipal and departmental administration.

THE PACIFICATION OF THE WEST

When the Directory came into office the royalist threat suppressed on 13 Vendémiaire still presented a very real danger. Though a careful watch was kept on Paris, where the royalist press enjoyed a monopoly of public support, there were frequent outbreaks in the provinces, particularly at Amiens, Rouen and Avignon. But the chief problem was the insurrection in the west, where Charette had taken up arms again in June, on hearing of the arrival of the British squadron.

The crushing of the emigrés at Quiberon Bay prevented the Comte d'Artois from making his intended landing. Hoche, appointed commander of the Army of the West, now set about the task of 'pacification' with patient determination: his strategy represented a combination of military and political methods. Hoche had realised that two political concessions, freedom of worship and the ending of conscription, were essential if the war-weary peasants were to be persuaded to abandon their royalist leaders. But even when the Convention had granted these concessions, he had continued to apply military pressure on the peasantry; in fact, he even stepped up his campaign, organising mobile columns of troops which marched across the countryside disarming the peasants and forcing them to pay their taxes. He did not hesitate to order raids on produce and livestock, or to take hostages and have whole communes punished for attacks on property and its owners. As a result of such repressive measures the Vendéan leaders began to find themselves more and more isolated. Stofflet, who had taken up arms again in January 1796 at the command of the Comte d'Artois, was taken prisoner in February and shot immediately at Angers. In March even the elusive Charette, forced to take flight by Hoche's offensive, was captured in the Marais and was shot at Nantes. The last of the rebel leaders, d'Autichamp, surrendered in the spring. Hoche still had to contend with the Chouans, who were scattered between Sarthe and Brittany. His mobile columns enjoyed the same success there as in Vendée, and eventually the rebels were compelled

Foreign policy was one of the Directors' most important responsibilities. Here the president of the Directory gives an audience to ambassadors in the Luxembourg palace.

to hand over their arms to the republican troops. By the end of the spring of 1796, the civil war was over and the Directory disbanded the Army of the West. Any acts of brigandage that still occurred were the result of economic distress rather than political organisation.

ECONOMIC DISTRESS AND THE BABEUF CONSPIRACY

The financial crisis which the Convention had bequeathed to the Directory rapidly developed into a major catastrophe. As metal currency steadily vanished from circulation, assignats were printed in ever greater quantities and declined in value daily. At first the Directory resorted to the expedients used by its predecessors: in four months the numbers of assignats in circulation doubled. The majority in the Councils, reluctant to accept proposals that the assignat should be abolished and replaced by a bank-note issued by a bank of big financiers decided to administer a further inflationary boost to the assignat by authorising a forced loan of six hundred millions from the wealthy. This brought the Directory only a brief respite, however, and at the

Fluctuations in the respective value of paper-money and gold made the Bourse a centre of feverish activity. Only exchange-brokers were allowed inside the Bourse, but crowds of speculators gathered outside.

same time caused considerable political unpopularity. When this expedient had failed the regime found itself compelled to issue a new paper note, the *mandat territorial*, which was to be valid for the purchase of national lands. Within two weeks of its issue (18 March) the new note had lost two-thirds of its value. In February 1797 both assignats and *mandats* lost all monetary value, and so the great revolutionary experiment of paper-money ended with a return to metal currency. By enabling vast areas of national land to be bought up by the new possessors of wealth the experiment had resulted in the largest and most rapid transfer of property ever to have taken place in the history of France. The financial crisis was aggravated by the slow rate at which taxes were reaching the Treasury's coffers and by the expenditure necessitated by the European war and the food shortage. Eventually, the regime was forced to improvise from one day to the next, constantly inventing new expedients without being able to provide the resources needed to support them.

While speculators and contractors made huge fortunes out of the financial crisis, all those on fixed incomes suffered great hardship; the *rentiers* who had invested their money in government loans were practically ruined. The lower classes were even more severely hit by the combined effects of the financial and food crises. The harvests of '94 and 95 had been bad, and the winter of '95–'96 was the worst of the Revolution. Reduced to desperate straits, the poor resorted to brigandage and murder, killing many of those who had been able to

As holders of fixed incomes the *rentiers* were almost ruined by the financial crisis.

Beggars swarmed the streets during the winter of 1795–6, the worst winter of the Revolution.

buy national properties and torturing the inhabitants of isolated farms to find out where they had hidden their 'treasure'. Despite the measures taken by the Directory in Paris, popular resentment mounted against the government and the 'perpetuals' of the legislative Councils, who had taken the precaution of fixing their salaries in myriagrammes of grain. There was a resurgence of Jacobin activity, centred in the clubs and societies of Paris, which had multiplied since the autumn with the Directory's approval. Barras had supported the founding of the Panthéon Club, where Babeuf was soon to make a name for himself. The Panthéon Club, initially composed largely of Thermidorean bourgeois anxious to support the regime's growing anti-royalist tendencies, also included a number of ex-Robespierrists just out of prison, among them the Tuscan Buonarroti, an admirer of the 'Incorruptible Robespierre' and a commissioner to the Army of Italy. These former Maratists, Hébertists and Robespierrists now joined together in search of a new political platform for popular agitation. They found their leader in Babeuf.

Babeuf had welcomed the *coup d'état* of 9 Thermidor and had himself taken part in the anti-Robespierrist press campaign, but as the Thermidorean regime became more moderate he shifted his position and used his journal, *le Tribun du peuple*, to attack his recent protectors. He soon joined the Parisian terrorists in prison, but was set free in September when the royalists once again became the chief threat to the regime. Although Babeuf is generally regarded as the first com-

277

munist in French history, he was the heir of his country's recent past rather than a precursor of French communism. His propaganda was directed not at the proletarians of modern communism but at the former militants of the Parisian *sans-culottes*. Modern Italian historians have stressed the role which Buonarroti played in the development of Babeuf's ideology. Whether or not the programme of the 'Equals', as Babeuf's band of disciples was called, was in fact worked out together by the two men in the prison of the Plessis, on thing is certain: well before 1789, Babeuf had begun to feel a close link with the land-hungry peasantry and had indulged in the kind of criticism of private property which was one of the commonplaces of the philosophy of the Enlightenment. In Year IV he became known as 'Gracchus' Babeuf (the name evoked the agrarian legislation of the Gracchi in ancient Rome). His communism, based on the division of land and the equal distribution of crops through a communal store, displayed the fatal twofold obsession of pre-industrial economic thought – land, on the one hand, and poverty, on the other. The atrocious conditions of Year IV merely served to strengthen Babeuf's egalitarian demands. His ideology was based on the sharing of land and the equal distribution of produce. But Babeuf took his fundamental principles from Marat and Hébert: the enslaved populace was to be liberated by an insurrection conducted by an organised minority determined to establish the dictatorship of the people. A month after the Directory had instructed General Bonaparte to close down the Panthéon Club, a 'Secret Directory of Public Safety' of seven members was formed, including both Babeuf and Buonarroti. As the economic crisis worsened and as the masses tried to recover their breath after the repression of Prairial Year III, the secret committee set about organising its conspiracy.

Though concentrated in Paris, where Babeuf placed his agents in each of the *arrondissements* and among the troops, the conspiracy was joined in the provinces by the terrorist deputies of the Convention who had been declared ineligible for the new legislative assemblies. But the Directory was aware of what was going on. Barras relates in his Memoirs that his informers had warned him of Babeuf's schemes even before the closing of the Panthéon Club; but Barras, who detested the royalists and firmly believed in his policy of a united republic front, wanted to avoid taking action against the left; this cynic also felt a certain nostalgia for the heroic days of the past which made him reluctant to strike against his former colleagues of the Convention, and so he said nothing. It was Carnot who, warned of the imminent insurrection by one of Babeuf's military agents, persuaded the Directory to take action. Letourneur and La Révellière-Lépeaux both sided with Carnot; Reubell maintained a neutral attitude and Barras was forced

(*Right*) François-Noël Babeuf, who later changed his first name to Gracchus, was born of a poor family in 1760 at Saint-Quentin.

(*Above*) Filipo Buonarroti, a contemporary and friend of Babeuf, came from one of the best families in Pisa.

onto the defensive. Carnot was determined to exorcise his own past; as the Director responsible for national defence he was furious at the extent to which Babeuf's propaganda had spread through the army, and as an eighteenth-century bourgeois imbued with the superiority of men of 'talent' he regarded the new 'levellers' with abhorrence. At Carnot's insistence, the Directory deliberately exaggerated the importance of the Babeuf conspiracy until it acquired the dimensions of the modern 'red peril'.

The conspirators were rounded up by the police on 21 Floréal (10 May). The Directory informed the assemblies in a highly dramatic and alarmist manner. But at the time the public treated the conspiracy as just another terrorist faction that had been thwarted – quite understandably, since the real originators of the movement were overshadowed by the more famous figures of the old Convention, men like Drouet, Lindet, Vadier and Amar. Paradoxically, Carnot's deliberate campaign of panic later drew the attention of the people to the ideas contained in the manifesto of the 'Equals', giving communism its first popular audience and the French bourgeoisie its first great fright. Carnot himself signed the warrants for the arrest of two hundred and forty-five agitators. Babeuf and his friends were brought before the High Court, and after a long trial Babeuf and Darthé, an ex-Robespierrist, were sentenced to death and executed in May 1797. Nevertheless, through those of their comrades who were either acquitted or imprisoned, particularly Buonarroti, the manifesto of the 'Equals' was handed down to the Jacobin and socialist movements of the nineteenth century.

THE ROYALISTS AND THE ELECTIONS OF YEAR V

In the autumn of 1796 the Directory entered its first electoral year; at the beginning of the following spring, a third of the deputies of the two Councils and one of the Directors would have to be replaced. The forthcoming elections might well alter the whole balance of power, since half of the old 'Conventionnels' who had been re-elected in Year III would be leaving the assemblies. If the new third were as moderate as the new deputies of Year III it would have a majority in the Councils and would therefore be able to dictate the choice of the new Director.

The Directory was divided. The Babeuf affair had isolated Reubell and Barras and ruined their hopes of organising a united republican front against the royalists. By bringing social issues back into politics and attempting to overthrow the regime, Babeuf had unwittingly strengthened Carnot's position and encouraged the men in power to rally together. For the present Carnot's repressive policy was sup-

ported by the majority in the Directory and also in the Councils, where
the republican deputies were considering the coming elections and
the likelihood of their majority being reversed. In an attempt to forestall the electorate, a large number of republican deputies began to
disassociate themselves from the left and form a conservative 'centre'.
The obvious intention behind the policy of the new centre in the Councils was to make overtures to the constitutional monarchists; Barras
and Reubell regarded the manoeuvre as a dangerous concession to the
ultra-royalist movement which was still smouldering in the west and
south of France. The success of the centre alliance depended on the
government's ability to act with firmness; failing firm action, the
situation would inevitably develop into a struggle for power that
would enable the royalists to infiltrate the regime from the inside by
having themselves elected to the Councils.

Luckily for the Directory, the royalists were just as divided as the
government's supporters. Louis xvi's brothers were as intransigent as
ever; while they were pleased to see the progress being made by the
constitutional monarchists, they maintained their own extremist
position, making use of an agency in Paris that was receiving money
from Britain to finance plots against the Directory. On the other hand,
the majority of the moderate royalists who assembled at Clichy preferred to use the coming elections to establish a constitutional monarchy legally, but they had no suitable candidate they could put forward as king. Many of them realised that, by supporting Louis xvi's
brothers, they would be taking an even graver risk than their Feuillant
predecessors had taken; in 1791 the Feuillants had some reason to
hope that they could persuade Louis xvi to accept his new role of
constitutional monarch, but the moderates of Clichy knew that to put
Louis xviii on the throne would mean establishing a monarchy of
vengeance and White Terror. At the same time, the Republic was of
too recent origin and too closely associated with the other Terror for
them to feel able to trust the regicides of the Directory, Barras or even
Carnot. Their hope of reconciling France was to find a liberal prince
to put on the throne, but they had looked in vain for a foreign dynasty;
the cause of the Duc d'Orléans had been brought into disrepute by his
father, Philippe Égalité; the legitimate succession had been broken by
martyrdom. The moderates thus found themselves in an ambiguous
position: they wanted order at home and peace abroad, and a reconciliation of the France of nationalised property and the old France of
the aristocracy; but they were the prisoners of their time, condemned
to choose between the Republic of the Thermidoreans and the
monarchy of the Chouans.

As the 'Clichyens' had been unable to find a new dynasty for the
throne of France, the two branches of the royalist movement were not

separated by so wide a gulf as in the nineteenth century: the ultra-royalists, based abroad for the greater part, were led by the Comte d'Artois, who controlled his agents and conspirators from a distance; the constitutional monarchists, on the other hand, operated largely within France and were intent on infiltrating the regime by the legal channel of elections; but both movements were bound up with British money and the brothers of Louis XVI. The Comte de Provence, who had taken the title of Louis XVIII, associated himself with a plan intended to deceive the men of Clichy: a great electoral campaign was to be launched under the cover of a Philanthropic Institute founded that same year (1796), and every attempt was to be made to reassure moderate opinion – the candidates put forward by the Institute were to be 'respectable' bourgeois citizens anxious for stability and peace and nothing more. But in fact the campaign was controlled by a select few whose purpose was to bring about the restoration of the pretender. The princes were supporting the subversive activities of the Abbé Brottier, who had taken it into his head to place agents in the army with a view to instigating a military *coup* against the Directory. Brottier made approaches to Colonel Malo, commander of the 21st Dragoons, but Malo informed on the conspirators in January 1797. Brottier and one of his accomplices, Duverne de Presle, were sentenced to ten years imprisonment; La Villeurnois, another accomplice, was sentenced to one year, and the rest were acquitted. Despite the comparative leniency with which the conspirators had been treated, the majority of the Directory had recognised the danger and found legal pretexts for keeping all detainees in prison. A first breach had been forced in the centre alliance in the Councils, and both royalists and supporters of the Directory now became more and more passionately involved in preparations for the elections.

The Catholic Church played an important part in the progress made by the royalists during the summer and autumn of 1796, for it still exercised a powerful influence over popular sensibility and bourgeois opinion. Neither the revolutionary religion with its *décadi* ceremonies (the 'Sunday' of the ten-day week or 'decade' of the Republican calendar) nor the cult of theophilanthropy practised by a number of distinguished anti-clericals and freemasons had been able to oust the traditional faith of France. The peasants remained loyal to their God and to their priests, and even in the more enlightened sectors of society, Catholicism and the Revolution had gradually come to be regarded as less incompatible since the end of the Terror; moderate republicans and constitutional monarchists both looked on the traditional Catholic faith as a pillar of social order, an easy guarantee of the people's good behaviour.

In the Directory this view was shared by Carnot, whose support of

A rather fierce caricature of royalists (emigrés who had returned and 'White Jacobins') promenading in the Boulevard des Italiens.

the centre alliance led him to seek a compromise with the Church. Between May and September the new majority in the Councils approved a series of laws which made the position of rebel priests somewhat easier, and Cochon, the Minister of Police, urged that they be treated with patience and tolerance. In June the victorious Bonaparte signed an armistice with Pope Pius VI, and Carnot took this opportunity to seek a religious peace with Rome, anticipating the policy that was to result in the Concordat of 1801. Carnot was not making any concessions to the Church; he merely wanted the support of the Pope in settling the religious question in France. In July Pius VI sent a delegate to Paris to negotiate terms; but the Directory, where Reubell and Delacroix were in charge of foreign policy, insisted on the annulment of all papal decrees concerning French affairs which had been issued since 1789, and in particular the bull condemning the Civil Constitution of the Clergy. The papal delegate would not agree to the demands of the Directors and the talks came to nothing.

In reality no-one in France had ever wanted a compromise with Rome. Rebel priests and constitutional monarchists were afraid that any such move would be to their detriment; the ultra-royalists were quite understandably counting on the electoral support of a Church hostile to the Revolution and everything it stood for; and in the Directory Reubell, Barras and La Révellière were united in wanting to keep religion out of the struggle for power. By the beginning of 1797 the policy of the centre alliance had floundered; the suppression of the Brottier plot sounded its death-knell. The combined forces of anti-clericalism and annexationist opinion had taken control of the executive out of Carnot's hands, and it was Barras who now dominated the Directory. But everything still depended on the results of the March elections.

The Directors had made their own preparations for the elections, which they had every reason to fear. On 7 Ventôse Year IV (25 February 1797) they withdrew the right to vote at primary assemblies from all Frenchmen whose names had appeared on the lists of emigrés. On 25 Ventôse (15 March) they asked the Councils to decree that the electors of the secondary assemblies (chosen by the primary assemblies) must swear the oath professing hatred 'of royalty and anarchy' which had already been imposed on all public servants of the Republic. However, the Councils rejected this attempt to put electors on the same footing as officials and compromised by substituting a declaration of loyalty to the Constitution, which the royalists were quite prepared to make. In a final attempt to thwart the electorate the 'Conventionnels' in the Councils tried to make sure that the outgoing third, which was to be drawn by lot from among themselves, would be as small as possible by including the names of deputies who had died or resigned.

But the efforts of the Directory were futile against the proselytism of rebel priests, the vast propaganda campaign launched by the royalists and the spontaneous moderatism of bourgeois opinion – after all, it was the bourgeoisie that was being asked to elect the new deputies. The bourgeoisie was not longing for a return to the Old Regime and royal absolutism; but, having secured the abolition of privilege at the cost of the Terror, which it still remembered with deep fear, it passionately wanted to see the end of civil and religious discord and yearned for stability in commerce and peace abroad. It did not consider the Republic, still stained with the blood of the Terror, to be the best form of government for France. Traditional monarchy, on the other hand, had the weight of centuries behind it and had a great appeal for a sector of society that was weary of strife. Consciously or not, bourgeois moderatism was the prisoner of an organised royalist onslaught. The Directory also suffered the repercussions of the anti-terrorist repression that had followed the Babeuf conspiracy, and in many departments of France the royalists had gained control of the primary assemblies. Of the two hundred and sixteen outgoing deputies, only eleven were re-elected to the Councils, and two of these, including Boissy d'Anglas, belonged to the Clichy moderates. In all but about ten departments royalists were elected. Was the Directory going to admit defeat?

THE *COUP D'ÉTAT* OF 18 FRUCTIDOR

The new Councils assembled on 1 Prairial after Letourneur had been named as the outgoing Director by drawing of lots. It became clear at once that the control of power would be in the hands of the royalists, three of whom were appointed to important positions, having already been singled out for office by the Clichy moderates: Pichegru was elected President of the Council of Five Hundred, Barbé-Marbois President of the Council of Elders, and the diplomat Barthélemy replaced Letourneur in the Directory. However, though the right wing in the assemblies was united against the executive, it was divided and uncertain about the future, wavering between the temptation to bring about a rapid restoration of the monarchy by a *coup d'état* and the alternative policy of a progressive alliance with republican moderates like Thibaudeau and Carnot.

The spring of 1797 thus found the two political camps in Paris as divided and uncertain as the country itself. Emigrés and refractory priests were returning in large numbers and counter-revolutionary violence was breaking out once again; those who had bought nationalised property were becoming apprehensive, the towns were restless and the army was losing patience. In the Councils the right wing voted for the quashing of the law of 3 Brumaire Year IV and approved a number of measures in favour of refractory priests; most important of all, it tried to bring the executive to its knees by transferring some of its financial powers to the Treasury and by refusing to approve estimates; the latter was a double-edged weapon, as it induced the state's countless creditors to side with the Directory.

The Directory was the first to decide on aggression and the use of force, which Reubell had been advocating since March. La Révellière, angered by the relaxation of the laws against rebel priests, joined him in June, ignoring the royalists' pleas to support them. Barras, disturbed by the situation, took every possible precaution for the future, entering into contact both with the royalist agency in Paris and with Britain. But he was playing a double game: at the end of May he had secretly sent one of his friends, Fabre de l'Aude, to talk with Bonaparte in Milan and make sure that the Army of Italy would support him against the Councils. Fabre de l'Aude brought back from Milan not only the promise of Bonaparte's support, but also proof of Pichegru's treachery and the royalist conspiracy revealed by papers seized from the Comte d'Antraigues. And so, by the beginning of the summer of 1797 the 'triumvirs' of the Directory were resolved on their course of action: ruling out any likelihood of winning popular support, they were committed to military intervention.

The armies were republican in their sympathies, for they had acquired their wealth and glory in the war against the Europe of kings. In the summer of 1797 they enthusiastically applauded the addresses in which their leaders attacked the Councils. However, though the three armies of the Republic were ready to defend the regime, two of their commanders did not seem willing to give their support unconditionally. Moreau, in command of the Army of the Rhine-and-Moselle, hesitated all summer, without succumbing to royalist advances, but without actually denouncing them. In Italy Bonaparte took advantage of the Directory's weakness to obtain approval for his own personal strategy, and in particular the occupation of Venice; attacked in the Councils, he retaliated with a dramatic proclamation to his army on 14 July: '... We are separated from France by mountains, but if necessary you will cross them with the speed of an eagle to preserve the Constitution, to defend liberty and to protect the government and the republicans...' He sent Augereau to Paris to buttress the Directory, but at the same time took care to keep in touch with the other side by writing to Carnot and approaching Barthélemy through his faithful friend, Lavalette, who advised him to wait. Hoche, commander of the Army of the Sambre-and-Meuse, was the only general openly to commit himself to the defence of the regime. On 1 July, under the cover of a movement of troops to Brest in preparation for an expedition against Ireland, he dispatched nine thousand men for Paris. By mid-July his cavalry was at La Ferté-Alais, near Corbeil, in the 'constitutional radius' which the army was theoretically prohibited from entering. The right wing in the Councils heard of the advance, and realised the final crisis was imminent.

On 14 July the 'triumvirs' appeared to yield to Carnot's demand for a ministerial reshuffle that would favour the right, but in fact the intention of the three Directors was exactly the opposite of what Carnot was hoping for: Benezech, Cochon and Petiet, all Carnot's men, were dismissed, but Merlin and Ramel, detested by the right, were kept in their ministries. Hoche took over War, François de Neufchâteau the Interior and Talleyrand Foreign Affairs. Petiet then informed the Councils of the presence near Paris of Hoche's troops, and in so doing sparked off the crisis.

The royalist majority wanted to retaliate by entrusting the military

Hoche, commander of the army of the Sambre-and-Meuse in February 1797.

command of Paris to Pichegru and by indicting the Directory. It was counting on Carnot's support, but Carnot refused: Barras, who was now resorting to every possible kind of manoeuvre, had just informed him of the papers seized from the Comte d'Antraigues and the treachery of Pichegru. Reluctant to have anything to do either with the illegal 'republican' movement or with the royalist conspiracy, Carnot decided to stand aside from the conflict. The Councils maintained their offensive, but in August Hoche's troops gradually established themselves in the capital; the energetic Augereau, released by Bonaparte, took command of the Paris division and Chérin, one of Hoche's generals, was put at the head of the guard entrusted with the protection of the Directory. Finally, on 7 Fructidor (25 August), La Révellière succeeded Carnot as president of the Directory. Everything was now ready for the *coup*.

When the Councils resolved on 17 Fructidor to indict the 'triumvirs' it was too late: during the night of 17–18 Fructidor (4–5 September) Paris was occupied by the army. At dawn Augereau arrested Pichegru, his friends in the Councils and Barthélemy; Carnot went into hiding and eventually managed to flee the country. There were no violent upheavals. The *coup d'état* of 18 Fructidor was a model of the politico-military *putsch*, and bore unmistakable signs of the tactical genius of Barras.

On the morning of 18 Fructidor a great proclamation by the Directory – or what was left of the Directory – covered the walls of the city: in justification of the *coup* it mentioned the Anglo-royalist conspiracy, the revelations made by the men accused in the Brottier plot and the papers taken from the Comte d'Antraigues. Beside the proclamation a decree laid down that anyone guilty of wishing to restore the monarchy or the 1793 Constitution would be shot without trial. With the collapse of parliamentary institutions France had returned to dictatorial government. This time it was the army that seized control – the military glory achieved in the European war had brought its almost inevitable consequences.

The two assemblies sat on 18 Fructidor in the new premises assigned to them – the Five Hundred in the Odéon, the Elders in the School of Medicine; the few deputies who attended were dispirited. As on 2 June 1793, the deputies admitted total defeat by approving two emergency laws demanded by the triumphant Directors. The more important of these laws, voted on the 19th, comprised a long series of measures for 'public safety'; it quashed the elections in forty-nine departments and provided for the deportation to Guiana of fifty-three deputies, two Directors (Barthélemy and Carnot), the ex-minister Cochon and a number of other prominent royalists. Nearly a third of the deputies of the legislative assemblies were thus deprived of office: Normandy, Brittany, the Parisian region and the North had no parliamentary representation at all. At the same time the elections of local administrations and judiciaries were quashed, and the Directory reserved for itself the right to make appointments; a second series of harsh measures was directed against emigrés who had returned and refractory priests, who were now liable to execution or deportation; finally, the controversial law of 3 Brumaire Year IV was re-introduced. On 22 Fructidor the Councils passed a second law which gave the police control of the press and named forty-two journals whose editors were to be deported.

Barras had won the day, but everyone realised that this was the end of the institutions of Year III. Parliamentary government had failed, and was now to be replaced by the old hazards and uncertainties.

10

THE NAPOLEONIC CAMPAIGNS

The coup d'état *of 18 Fructidor made it clear that henceforward control of internal problems was to be exercised by the army. Where first La Fayette and then Dumouriez had failed, Augereau had been successful. How had this been possible? The campaign of 1796–7 brought a threefold change in the political scene: the foreign policy of the Directory had altered course, Bonaparte had won his independence and Italy had again assumed a role of importance in European history.*

It is tempting to make the diplomacy of the Directory fit into a coherent system. The interpretation which Albert Sorel put forward in L'Europe et la Révolution française, *and which was later taken up by Jacques Bainville, was based on two dominant themes – the continuity of Directory policy and the inevitability of the war. Sorel maintained that the struggle for natural frontiers, which the Revolution inherited from the Old Regime, contained all the seeds of the Napoleonic drama up to 1815. However, historical research has proved this theory to be largely false. Should one then conclude, with Raymond Guyot, that the Italian war was set in motion by the personal ambitions of Bonaparte and the violation of natural frontiers? But this does not explain why the Directory followed Bonaparte, sacrificing a policy which might have succeeded in favour of a pointless adventure.*

In fact, the choice confronting the Directory was by no means as clear-cut as this. In October 1795 the diplomatic attitudes of French politicians were fluctuating and uncertain. The majority readily accused the right, royalist or moderate, of wishing to revert to the frontiers of 1789, but no politician had advocated such a solution. The policy of natural frontiers, on the other hand, was urged by a large section of public opinion and had an uncompromising spokesman in Reubell. But Austria would have demanded compensation before complying with such demands. Moreover, there existed another section of republican opinion, which was the heir to the Girondin policies of 1793 and was more interested in revolutionary expansion than in military conquest. La Révellière and Sieyès were both much drawn to the idea of a great crusade which, they hoped, would girdle France with sister-republics.

Whatever the fluctuations of policy, the outcome was the same: the war was to be pursued. The decision was hardly a response to public opinion, for the bourgeoisie appears to have been generally in favour of peace. Louis Madelin and Albert Sorel have ascribed less noble motives to the Directory: according to Madelin, the real motive for the war was to keep the French armies occupied; in Sorel's view, the generals had made themselves indispensable by becoming the 'treasurers of the nation'. It would be a mistake to make too much of these theories. The plundering of Italy certainly kept the armies and their camp-followers alive, but it contributed nothing to France's internal budget. And fear of the sword was no stronger in 1796 than in 1793.

The real foundations of the Directory's war policy were the links which the Revolution and the Terror had forged between war and republic, on the one hand, and between peace and monarchy, on the other. The 'triumvirate' and the majority of the old Convention feared peace less in itself than as the first stage in a restoration of the monarchy, the danger of which they probably over-estimated. The regicides inevitably identified expansion with the Republic, and the Republic with themselves. To pursue the war offered them the most effective protection against the right wing, and at the same time the least dangerous means of defending themselves against the left. The suburbs of Paris were now disarmed, but passions still smouldered. The people had been deprived of their opportunity for active revolt; should they now be denied their military conquests?

The Army of Italy was a lesser evil for the Directory: it would provide support for the regime against the royalists without involving compromise with the terrorists. And so the Italian campaign can be seen to have been rooted in the Directory's desire to avoid internal troubles. In fact, the campaign was to prolong and aggravate those troubles, for it made the two fundamental weaknesses of the regime – royalism and terrorism – into a force essential to its own survival, but only in order to crush that force more effectively.

Yet the deviations in the foreign policy of the Directory cannot be explained without first taking into account the victory of Lodi and Arcola. Propaganda very soon embellished reality, transforming what was often a difficult campaign into one long triumphal march, and a clever strategist into an epic hero. The danger in refuting this legend lies in erring in the opposite direction and ignoring history: according to Guglielmo Ferrero, Bonaparte was, until Leoben, merely the faithful executant of a policy decided in Paris, a man with no original notions of strategy who derived his military education from Guibert (Guibert's works on military strategy had undermined the humanitarian rules of limited war so dear to the eighteenth century and had ushered in the holocaust of revolution). Bonaparte, argued Ferrero, was a mediocre tactician whose success in carrying out a plan of campaign worked out for him by others had depended on the ruthless violation of neutral states and the cowardice of his opponents. Sorel saw Bonaparte as a protagonist in the struggle for natural frontiers; Ferrero regarded him as no more than a grain of sand lifted up by the Italian storm.

It is not difficult to show the weakness of Ferrero's thesis. Although Bonaparte had no doubt read Guibert, his military education was not acquired from any single source: he had received an excellent all-round training in strategy. Admittedly, he was not always able to apply in detail the strategy which he had prepared, but this is hardly surprising, for the art of war consists in modifying plans according to circumstances and profiting by the enemy's mistakes. Unlike Guibert, Bonaparte attached the greatest importance to numerical superiority, and he knew how to make the best use of large forces in manoeuvring and exploiting early successes to the full. His military genius cannot be called in question.

Bonaparte's rise to power was quite exceptional by any standards. He and his family are known to have enriched themselves with Italian spoils, but Bonaparte was no common embezzler; he was later to declare at St Helena: 'Self-interest is the key only to vulgar actions.' His personal experience of poverty had taught him that riches were indispensable to power. One can sympathise with Michelet's indignation at the publicity campaign which Bonaparte himself launched through his proclamations and letters. Marcel Reinhard, in publishing the correspondence of the aide-de-camp Sulkowski, revealed to what extent this Paris-operated propaganda machine exaggerated the general's successes and concealed his failures. But propaganda alone was not enough to create a legend. Contemporary accounts tell of the wave of popularity that surrounded Bonaparte, who himself recounted how he felt a sudden awareness of his mission on the night of Lodi: 'That night I saw myself for the first time no longer as a mere general, but as a man called to influence the destiny of a people. I saw myself in History.' Yet Bonaparte scorned men of clear-cut ambitions. 'I have no ambition at all,' he once said. He used Italy as he was soon to use France: as a theatre in which to play out his own drama.

In Italy, which for three centuries had been regarded as a pawn of rival dynasties, Bonaparte found favourable conditions for a regime he was soon to impose on France. Most Frenchmen who knew Italy in the revolutionary period showed scepticism, if not downright contempt, for the Italian 'patriots'. More moderate opinion considered the Italians not yet ready for liberty, a short-sighted view shared by many historians, for whom Buonarroti and the Italian exiles in France were but rootless individuals, and the Italian Jacobins simply idle dreamers isolated from their own people. Recent historical studies have shown these judgements to be at fault. A deep current of sympathy for the Revolution manifested itself among the Italian people from 1789 to 1796, and in Italy Jacobinism found a more solid basis than in any other country of Europe. It is true, on the other hand, that the political divisions of the Italian peninsula and the lack of communications between town and country conspired to block the path of Italian Jacobinism and to prevent the Italian revolution from taking the violent and egalitarian form which the French revolution had taken. But the Directory feared the Italian Jacobins, linked as they were with Babeuf and the neo-terrorists, and many shared Carnot's view that a unified Italian republic would be a rival to France. Above all, the French army would have to live on the conquered territories, and its presence would inevitably arouse the hostility of the Italians. Stendhal observed: 'The good people of Milan did not know that the presence of an army, even a liberating army, is always a calamity.' The drama of Italian Jacobinism lay in these contradictions.

Liberty, however, was not to be confused with Jacobinism. For many liberal nobles in Italy, and for the bourgeois who made up a new and growing patrician society, liberty was the ultimate realisation of the aims of enlightened despotism: it was the ideal of the Constituent Assembly of '89, tempered by the experience of '93, a regime of property-owners founded on the liberty of the individual and on civil equality. Bonaparte discerned this at a glance, and saw in it a model to apply to France. In a letter to the Directory he confessed his preference for an 'aristo-democratic' republic, an ideal which he brought to reality by organising an administration of eminent men closely subjected to the executive power, namely himself. Basically, as Albert Sorel perceived, these Italian 'patricians' resembled the Feuillants of '89 and the future republicans of Brumaire.

The Italian campaign had reached the point of no return. The Directory had made, or at least had countenanced, the decisive step towards an unlimited war. Bonaparte had emerged triumphant from the battles of Lodi and Arcola, and in him the world was soon to behold the last, the greatest and perhaps the only enlightened despot.

If the war had been inspired by conventional motives, the treaty of Campo Formio might well have been the prelude to a general peace. However, other forces were involved. Firstly the sovereigns and aristocracies of Europe regarded the France of 1798 as the country of Jacobin egalitarianism, the land of the regicides and the incarnation of Satan and absolute Evil. Secondly, Revolutionary opinion saw the continued existence of Europe's thrones as a scandal. Thirdly, British dominion of the seas was to be crushed at all costs.

The conflict between Britain and France was of long standing, but the Revolution had introduced a new phase in Anglo-French enmity. War offered French manufacturers and artisans the opportunity of revenge against the trade agreement of 1786, which had lowered import duties on British goods entering France. After the treaty of Campo Formio French hostility was concentrated wholly against 'Perfidious Albion'. A loan was floated to finance the war and enjoyed a great response, even among Frenchmen of modest means. According to the reports of French diplomats Britain had reached a crisis: without allies and driven from the Mediterranean by the capture of Leghorn and the Franco-Spanish treaty, she was being threatened at home by mutinies in the navy and, in particular, by the Irish rebellion. France intended to attack on three fronts: Bonaparte would command the invading army; the diplomats would make certain that Britain remained politically isolated; and the economic blockade that

Britain had been directing at France would be turned against her in an intensified form.

There seemed every reason to hope that a military landing in Britain would succeed. Moreover, the British economy was vulnerable to a policy of organised blockade. Britain's export industries depended largely on European markets, and cereals and naval munitions had to be imported. Finally, the weaknesses of the British banking and financial system, though exaggerated by the French, were nevertheless very real.

The whole operation was jeopardized, however, as soon as secondary motives were allowed to interfere with the primary objective of defeating Britain. For the blockade to be effective it was essential that France should come to an understanding with the United States, but the protectionist attitude of French industrialists and the dishonesty of Talleyrand caused Franco-American negotiations to break down. Instead of landing in Britain, Bonaparte insisted on the expedition to Egypt, thereby reopening the Eastern Question, putting Russia on the alert and giving Pitt the best available army in Europe.

Since 1793 economic ambitions had never been absent from the strategy of revolutionary expansion, and after Campo Formio those ambitions became more grandiose. The generals, not content with levies, resorted to pillage. At the same time, France established agreements with the sister-republics which were economically advantageous to herself. But the French government was still mainly preoccupied with maintaining its protectionist policy. The law of 10 Brumaire Year V (31 October 1796) had prohibited ships of neutral countries from bringing British goods into France. The law of 29 Nivôse Year VI (18 January 1798) decreed that any neutral ship carrying British merchandise, or which had merely called at a British port, was to be seized immediately. The United States retaliated by revoking all agreements previously made with France and by sending out their pirates to harass French shipping.

How far were French territorial conquests a direct consequence of this policy of economic expansion? Undoubtedly, certain military projects were closely connected with the blockade; but during this period the French government made no sustained attempt to establish military control of the coasts of Europe: its policies in no way foreshadowed those adopted by Bonaparte after 1807. French military and political expansion was still inspired primarily by revolutionary mystique and the personal initiatives of generals and contractors. Constitutions modelled on that of Year III were dictated from Paris and imposed in turn on Rome, Switzerland and the Milanese. But the protectorates were soon infected with the political instability that had seized Paris. While the campaign of conquest of 1798 had not been sufficiently committed to create a permanent rearrangement of political boundaries, it had aggravated discontent in Europe.

The Imperial Diet had yielded to French demands for control of the left bank of the Rhine and the secularization of the Papal States, but the emperor would not give his sanction. Should France now negotiate directly with Austria?

Francois de Neufchâteau was sent as envoy to Seltz, but with no guarantees to offer. There remained Prussia, the supreme hope of the French government. But Prussia had no intention of abandoning a profitable neutrality in exchange for a dubious alliance.

In such a situation the slightest sign of weakness on the part of France would be fatal. Nelson's victory at Aboukir (August 1798) struck the first blow. In November, the Neapolitan army entered Rome. In December, Russia and Britain reaffirmed their alliance. Hostilities between France and Austria resumed even before the two countries were officially at war again (March 1799). In the spring and summer of 1799 the French armies suffered a series of disasters, but their victories of the autumn showed Europe that the Republic still knew how to fight, even if it had proved incapable of making peace.

It is easier to discern the weaknesses of French policy at this period than to understand its underlying causes. The policy of the Directory cannot be attributed simply to the doctrine of 'natural frontiers', nor should it be interpreted merely as a continuation of a traditional rivalry for colonial power. French diplomacy would seem to have been conditioned largely by economic pressure, ideological necessity and internal instability.

Manufacturers, who had lost their overseas markets and hoped that military conquests would provide new outlets, succeeded in bringing pressure to bear on the government. Yet to suggest that the bourgeoisie of 1798 was intent on establishing economic supremacy in Europe would be misleading. French industrialists and financiers, far from preaching war, longed for peace. Reubell and La Révellière regarded prohibitive legislation and blockade primarily as political weapons in a war designed to promote national greatness. Ideology exercised an even greater influence on Directory policy than did economics. The coup d'état *of 18 Fructidor had reawakened the crusading spirit of 1793. The Directory had been accused of deliberately provoking this resurgence of propaganda, which in fact it made every effort to check. On the other hand, the aristocratic powers of Europe repudiated the new France. Talleyrand shrewdly observed: 'Our enemies regard the treaties which they sign with us merely as truces of the kind the Muslims make with the enemies of their faith.' The Directors cannot be held solely responsible for the war.*

However, neither can they be wholly exonerated. Historians have tended to present Barras, Reubell and La Révellière as incompetent men who did not know what they were doing, but this is to treat the myths propagated by the Brumaireans as established fact. When Bonaparte returned from Egypt he set the example for this kind of distortion, accusing the Directors of having attempted to revolutionize the whole of Europe and having sent him into the desert merely to be rid of him. Yet Reubell had sanctioned neither the Italian venture nor the Egyptian expedition. La Révellière, though a champion of the 'sister-republics', opposed the extremism of the European Jacobins. To the very end the Directors wanted to explore the possibilities of peace. Their policies, compared with those of the Brumaireans, Talleyrand and Sieyès, lacked neither prudence nor insight.

But the regime had lost all authority. The coup d'état *of 18 Fructidor and the treaty of Campo Formio had confronted the Directory with two great menaces: Bonaparte and neo-Jacobinism. As Georges Lefebvre has shown, Bonaparte's Egyptian expedition was 'the starting-point of the second Coalition'. In Italy, Switzerland and Holland the generals united with the Jacobins, and on 30 Prairial Year VII took their revenge for their defeat of 22 Floréal Year VI (see Chapter 12). The victors of Prairial then blamed the fallen government for the defeats which they themselves had brought about.*

The new ruling alliance found its justification in the contradictions of anti-Directory opinion. It reflected the mood of the country, expressing, though incapable of resolving, the conflicting desires of Frenchmen – peace with expansion, brotherhood with exploitation, a Republic whose indivisibility did not preclude foreign adventure. The European war and the absence of a suitable candidate for a constitutional monarchy were the two chief causes of the temporary failure of the liberal Revolution. France's inability to make peace and to find a king provided Bonaparte with his opportunity, which he seized on 18 Brumaire.

THE ARMY OF ITALY AND ITS GENERAL

In the first six months of the Directory the military situation was unfavourable, but the diplomatic position was by no means hopeless. After a good start, the German campaign soon failed. After Pichegru had been won over to the cause of Louis XVIII by Condé's agents, he had remained inactive, and had forced Jourdan to give ground. When the armistice was signed in January 1796 the Austrians had reconquered Mannheim and part of the Palatinate. In Italy the victory of Loano was short-lived, for Scherer was unable to profit by his success. The armies dwindled; sickness and desolation had reduced by nearly a half the eight hundred thousand men who had marched under the republican flag in Thermidor Year II, and payment in worthless assignats encouraged indiscipline and pillage among the remainder. The situation was aggravated by the disorganisation of transport and a chaotic system of administration and provisioning.

Could France make peace? Since July 1795, North Germany and Prussia had guaranteed her their neutrality; and, in the Holy Roman Empire as a whole, Austria was having difficulty in maintaining a state of war, while in Italy her relations with Turin were poor. Austria had certainly strengthened her alliance with Russia and Britain on 28 September, but Catherine II gave no more than encouragement, while Pitt, faced with financial crisis and famine, was in favour of negotiations. The Republic was not prepared to compromise, and all attempts at bargaining during the winter failed; and so the campaign of spring '96 had to be prepared.

Plans of campaign were drawn up in the historical and topographical department directed by Clarke and Dupont. Carnot then had these plans adopted after consulting the generals. As in 1795, the main offensive against Austria was to be made in Germany by the Sambre-and-Meuse Army under Jourdan and by the Rhine-and-Moselle Army under Moreau, who replaced his friend Pichegru. These armies were to cross the Rhine and march towards the Danube, but no plan was made to co-ordinate their movements. For the Army of Italy under its commander Scherer, Carnot adopted the plan of campaign put forward by the general of the Interior, Bonaparte, who had been submitting his proposals in various memoranda over the previous two years. Bonaparte's plan was summarised in a note on 29 Nivôse Year IV (19 January 1796) as follows: to take the offensive against Piedmont, force the Turin court to leave the Coalition and invade Lombardy. Following these recommendations Carnot sent instructions to Scherer, who disapproved of them and resigned his commission. He was replaced by Bonaparte on 2 March. Barras boasts in his Memoirs that he was responsible for this decision, but according to La Révellière it was a unanimous decision of the Directory.

The annexation of Corsica gave Napoleon, the second son of Charles Bonaparte, a supreme opportunity to pursue a military career. Although he had been a friend of Paoli, Charles Bonaparte abandoned the cause of independence and allied himself with the occupying army; as a result he was able in 1778 to obtain bursaries for his two elder sons from the fund which Versailles reserved for the sons of the impoverished provincial nobility. At Autun, Brienne (1779–84) and the Champ-de-Mars military college, Napoleon received a thorough education. However, unlike most of his comrades of the minor nobility, he felt no sense of loyalty to France's doomed regime; he dreamed only of Corsica and detested the country which he found himself obliged to serve. From 1786 to 1793 he led a garrison life at Valence, Auxonne and then back again at Valence, interrupted by long stays in Corsica. At the time of the battle of Valmy he was on his way back to his native island, a decision which at the time appeared to have been a mistake, for the Bonapartes in Corsica had staked their all on the Revolution. When a general uprising in April 1793 forced the French to flee from Corsica the Bonaparte family was also compelled to leave, and Napoleon found himself back in the country from which he had vainly tried to escape.

During the summer of 1793, while on a mission to Avignon as captain in the 4th regiment of artillery of the Army of Italy, Bonaparte witnessed the civil war raging in the south of France. In August he composed a short treatise defending Montagnard policies which won him the favour of the representatives on mission; one of these was

Bonaparte in 1798.

Saliceti, who was supervising the siege of Toulon and chanced to meet Bonaparte just as the artillery commander of the siege was wounded. Saliceti immediately appointed Bonaparte as artillery commander, and at the end of September Bonaparte was promoted from captain to major. Bonaparte had studied the fortifications of Toulon during previous visits, and realised at once that everything depended on driving the Anglo-Spanish fleet from the roadstead by using cannons. Under the newly-appointed Dugommier, who replaced the unco-operative Carteaux and Doppet as seige-commander, Bonaparte's strategy was put into effect: the fleet left the roadstead on 17 December, republican troops entered the town on the 19th and on the 23rd Bonaparte was promoted to rank of brigadier-general. On 7 February 1794 he was appointed artillery commander of the Army of Italy.

The anti-terrorist reaction which followed the fall of Robespierre affected Bonaparte along with many other young officers who had owed their promotion to the 'tyrants'. The representatives on mission to the Army of the Alps were anxious to appear zealous, and denounced the man whom Saliceti now called 'Robespierre's man', 'their plan-maker, whom we had to obey'. He was accused of involvement with a foreign plot in Genoa, imprisoned on 6 August in the Fort Carré at Antibes and stripped of his command. He was released shortly afterwards – 14 September – but he was now only a suspect officer without definite duties. Even his participation in the campaign which led to the taking of Cairo (24 September) was detrimental to him. The Army of Italy, corrupted with Jacobinism and a desire for plunder, was not liked in Paris.

Bonaparte had become an embarrassment to his former friends. Saliceti, who, in spite of his fear of a compromising friendship, was always anxious to promote Corsican solidarity, tried to force destiny by giving him the mission of recapturing Corsica from Paoli and the British. Bonaparte wanted nothing better, but was doubtful about France's naval capacity. At Toulon he waited for the departure of the first vessels, which soon returned after facing the fire of the British fleet, and he was again reduced to patrolling the coast. In March 1795 he was given a new assignment, command of artillery of the Army of the West. Bonaparte had no scruples about fighting the Vendéans: he therefore accepted, and went to Paris. However, Aubry, a former Girondin who was then in charge of the War Office, altered Napoleon's posting in a fit of vengeance, and the proud artilleryman found himself given command of an infantry brigade. Without openly refusing to obey, he postponed his departure under various pretexts. For a time he thought all would be well: in August 1795 Doulcet de Pontécoulant replaced Aubry and chose Bonaparte as head of the topographical office where plans of campaign were drawn up. Bonaparte at once returned to his Italian projects and drew up two memoranda outlining his ideas for an offensive in Piedmont and Lombardy. But Doulcet did not remain on the Committee of Public Safety for long, and his protégé was struck off the strength of the army, 'in view of his refusal to take up the post assigned to him' (15 September).

These were difficult weeks. Romantic imagination tended to picture him as the officer on half-pay, trailing wearily through the streets of Paris with his two acolytes Junot and Marmont, glad to pick up any crumbs from a bourgeois table. But Bonaparte was not stricken with poverty; he could still afford to send money to his mother, and had indeed been worse off at Valence. He could not, however, bear not to be loved. Désirée Clary, the young Marseillaise whose sister had married Joseph Bonaparte, did not reply to the letters in which he poured out his dreams to her.

The uprising of 13 Vendémiaire was to bring him both renown and love. Barras had known him since the siege of Toulon, and had seen him in Paris haunting government corridors in search of a job. He needed the officers whose careers had been jeopardised by Thermidor, in order to put down the royalist rebellion. Bonaparte was given command of the artillery on 13 Vendémiaire and in fact exercised the functions of chief-of-staff. He now began to emerge from the shadows. Thanks to Barras, and also to Fréron – lover of his sister Pauline – his name was acclaimed by the Convention. He was reinstated into the army and promoted to the rank of divisional commander ten days later, and on 3 Brumaire (25 October) he succeeded Barras as commander-in-chief of the Army of the Interior.

This twenty-six-year-old general had had little real experience of women: brief adventures and unrequited adolescent passions had left a great void in the proud, solitary young man whose imagination had been fed by so much nocturnal reading. As Elie Faure rightly said, he was 'an obvious victim for the first woman who smiled at him without irony or disdain'. He could hardly fail to be charmed by Josephine de Beauharnais. It matters little whether her son Eugene was responsible for their meeting, as some said, or whether they met in the salon of Barras, one of her many lovers. He was immediately attracted by this Creole, who revealed to him the delights of mature femininity, and he became her lover. She continued to fascinate him, and he wanted to marry her. This shows the touching sincerity of his love for Josephine, the fading courtesan who moved in the shady world of Thermidorean society, possessing only her children and her debts. Even the blindest prejudice could not attribute his motives to ambition and a desire for social climbing. He was completely under her spell, everything about her dazzled him: 'My mind is full of thoughts of you when I awake,' he wrote. 'Your picture and the memory of yesterday's intoxicating evening have left me in turmoil.' Josephine at first found him 'drôle', then became a little alarmed by such an absorbing passion. Finally she accepted the advice of Barras, who was delighted to see the mistress of whom he had wearied firmly settled in the arms of his protégé, and agreed to the marriage. On 9 March the commander-in-chief of the Army of Italy married 'citizen Beauharnais' in the presence of Tallien and Barras. Three days later Bonaparte set off for Italy.

ITALY AND HER CONQUERORS

At this time Italy was a patchwork of territories divided by the rigid barriers which the dynastic rivals had maintained for two centuries. To the north, seven dominions divided the foothills of the Alps, Piedmont and the plains. Two oligarchic republics had outlived their past greatness: Genoa, with poor and restricted territory, and the Venetian Republic, which stretched from Venetia to the Ionian islands. Emilia was cut into three: Ferdinand of Bourbon held Parma, Piacenza and Guastalla; the last of the Estes of Modena had married his only daughter to a Habsburg: Bologna, Ferrara, Ravenna and Forli, known as the Legations, made up the northern part of the Papal States. Two divisions stand out: Lombardy had belonged to Austria since 1713 and was reduced on its western side in 1748, when it had been obliged to cede Alessandria and Novara to Piedmont, but it was extended eastwards by the acquisition of Mantua. The state of Savoy, or kingdom of Sardinia, bore its two names uneasily: Savoy, with Nice, had only belonged to France since 1792, and Sardinia was a backward dependency of Piedmont. Unlike the rest of northern Italy this state was not an ancient free town which had slowly absorbed the surrounding country, but a group of fiefs united by a dynasty.

It is easy to find the similarities between the Italy of 1796 and the France of Louis xvi, and also the great differences between the two countries. Urban centres existed in the north, where a newly-found prosperity had fostered a desire for liberty and reform; but these centres were isolated from one another by the political diversity of the country, and were even more isolated from the landless peasant class: the type of property-owning alliance formed by the French bourgeoisie and peasantry in 1789 appeared impossible in Italy. It was no doubt for these very reasons that Italy had been the natural home of enlightened despotism in the eighteenth century. The liberals, with the support of innovating monarchs or ministers – Leopold in Tuscany, Tanucci in Naples, du Tillot at Parma – had been able to secure reforms, in particular the limitation of the privileges and wealth of the clergy, without overthrowing the existing social order.

Josephine de Beauharnais brought both passionate love and the elegance of the salons into Bonaparte's life. On 9 March 1796 they were married.

However, the French Revolution had brought with it fundamental social and political changes. To prevent the disease spreading to Italy, her sovereigns reacted by immediately quelling the slightest sign of revolutionary tendencies, and arrests and trials, involving even those holding the most moderate views, increased sharply. Those princes who had hitherto supported a Jansenist clergy were alarmed by the Civil Constitution of the Clergy decreed in France and left the Jansenists to the mercy of the Roman Curia. This wave of reaction merely served to intensify the movement of reform: the earlier champions of enlightened despotism now assumed more advanced positions, similar to those of the Constituent Assembly of 1789. Others even cherished dreams of a democratic Italian republic.

The democratic ideal was more widely held among Italians than has often been allowed. The repercussions of the French Revolution among Italians were too strong to be attributed merely to propaganda from Paris. At Dronero (Piedmont) in 1791 the inhabitants rose up with cries of 'Long live Paris, long live France!', and at Odogna (Abruzzi) the municipality told the royal commissioners that it wanted to be responsible for its own administration, like the French communes. In December 1793 at Rionero (Basilicata), a crowd invaded the village square proclaiming: 'We want to do as the French have done.' Italian historians are therefore right to challenge the traditional view that the masses were either apathetic or positively hostile towards the Revolution. It was the occupation of 1796–7 that provoked Italian antipathy.

The Jacobin patriot movement derived its main impulse from the masonic lodges linked with the Marseille lodge. These lodges founded clubs in Turin and Naples which were responsible for a number of conspiracies. Certain Jacobins who were being sought by the police took refuge in France and grouped themselves around Buonarroti.

The Jacobin movement was to be of major importance in Italy's future. Candeloro wrote: 'For the first time men from every state in Italy came together to struggle and sacrifice their lives for political reform and for independence and unity.' In the short term, however, the movement was doomed to failure for two reasons: internal conditions in Italy favoured a gradual and moderate process of reform rather than a revolutionary upheaval; and secondly, everything depended on France. For the French government, as also for enlightened opinion, Italy was merely a diplomatic pawn and a country ripe for exploitation: France intended to turn Italian Jacobinism to her own advantage.

THE VICTORIES OF BONAPARTE

Bonaparte rejoined his army at Nice on 29 March. This army comprised some forty-five thousand men, 'all the rabble of Provence and Languedoc' (Alfieri), with leaders in whom courage was mingled with a desire for plunder, like Masséna, or who were anxious, like Augereau, to achieve personal glory. The new general-in-chief asserted his authority in his first words to them: 'Soldiers, you are nearly naked. . . . I shall lead you out into the world's most fertile plains. . . .'

He planned to separate the Piedmontese from their Austrian allies

On 15 May 1796 the French made a triumphal entry into Milan through the *Porta Romana* and were welcomed by enthusiastic crowds.

in a rapid offensive. The Austrians were the first to attack (10 April) but were quickly repulsed, and Bonaparte concentrated his assault on the Piedmontese. On 28 April Victor Amadeus was obliged to sign the armistice of Cherasco. Bonaparte was now free to enter Lombardy, and after defeating the Austrians at Lodi (10 May), he made a triumphant entry into Milan on 15 May. The government then ordered him to take an expeditionary corps into central Italy and abdicate the command of his troops in Lombardy to Kellermann. By threatening resignation Bonaparte forced the Directory to change its mind, but in June he agreed to advance to Emilia and Tuscany, in order to hold those rich territories to ransom and compel their sovereigns to agree to some form of compromise. In the armistice of Bologna (23 June) Pius VI gave Bologna and Ferrara to France, promised to pay her twenty-one million *lire* and to surrender a hundred great works of art. The grand duke of Tuscany received Bonaparte at Florence after the occupation of Leghorn.

The raid into central Italy represents a major step in Bonaparte's career. The general, who had successfully challenged the Pope's domination and had been received to dinner by a Habsburg, could no longer be content to let his wings be clipped by a government of 'lawyers'. Henceforward he treated directives from Paris less seriously. In Emilia he found a political situation which differed radically from that of the area around Milan, where he had been forced to let the democrats have their way. The liberal aristocracy and the prosperous enlightened bourgeoisie controlled Emilia, and Bonaparte saw here an opportunity to establish his 'aristo-democratic republic'. Only a small proportion of the plunder seized in central and northern Italy reached the Directory: Bonaparte now began to accumulate the fortune that was later to be essential to his rise to power.

The people of Italy, however, did not accept such treatment passively, and already in May trouble had broken out in the Pavia district and had been rigorously stamped out. At Bologna, according to a letter written by Sulkowski, anti-French elements were to be found among the 'exaggerated' republicans. Even these early revolts reveal the dilemma characteristic of Italian Jacobinism, torn between the desire for revolution and love of their native country. But the immediate threat came from the Austrians, who were holding Mantua.

The Italian campaign was hereafter hinged on one operation, the siege of Mantua, which was occupied by an Austrian corps of thirteen thousand men. At the end of July Wurmser came down from the Tyrol in a first attempt to raise the siege. Bonaparte had to abandon his siege equipment, but Wurmser was forced to retreat back to the Tyrol after Castiglione (5 August). Owing to shortage of equipment and the exhausted condition of his army, Bonaparte waited three weeks before resuming the offensive. Wurmser was then obliged to take refuge in Mantua.

The other battle-fronts of the Republic were now showing signs of weakness. It must be remembered that Italy was only a secondary theatre of operations for Carnot and his colleagues, whose main objectives were to invade Britain and to threaten Vienna by the Danube. The expedition which set out to land in Ireland was broken up by a storm; and after initial successes in August, the Sambre-and-Meuse and Rhine-and-Moselle Armies, commanded by Jourdan and Moreau, met the resistance of the Archduke Charles, the finest of the imperial generals, and were forced to retreat just as Bonaparte was about to win his decisive victories (September–December).

November was nonetheless a difficult time for Bonaparte. An army of fifty thousand men under the Hungarian Alvintzi was preparing to lift the siege of Mantua. For fifteen days (1–15 November) the French army suffered a series of reversals, and its morale reached a low ebb. In spite of the tradition spread by Bonaparte's family, the victory of Arcola (17 November) was merely a difficult minor engagement of no decisive significance. But while Carnot seemed prepared to make peace, Bonaparte took his army systematically in hand, and when Alvintzi attacked, won the brilliant victory of Rivoli (14 January). On 2 February Wurmser capitulated and surrendered Mantua. French Italy was no longer in jeopardy. Bonaparte then imposed the treaty of Tolentino on the Pope, and thereby acquired Romagna and

Although J.-L. David signed the petition demanding that Italian works of art remain in Italy, famous paintings by Mantegna, Luini, Giorgione and Perugino, to name but a few, were taken to Paris in the name of 'Patriotism'. *Above: Christ on the Mount of Olives*, by Mantegna.

fifteen millions, after which he took the offensive against the Archduke Charles, with a considerably strengthened army of sixty-five thousand men. In March the French advanced into Friuli and the Tyrol. After the occupation of Klagenfurt (26 March), Bonaparte suddenly offered an armistice to his sorely-pressed enemy.

Why did Bonaparte suggest an armistice? He knew public opinion wanted peace, and he was anxious to obtain terms that would highlight his personal successes; the Armies of the Rhine, however, were renewing the offensive. By the armistice of Leoben (18 April) Austria lost Belgium and the Milanese, and secretly agreed to concessions in Italy at the expense of the neutral Venetian Republic. One of the main aims of Directory policy – control of the left bank of the Rhine – had to be postponed. To make up for this the victorious general told the Directory: 'The states of Venice will soon be at our disposal'; and accordingly, on the pretext of anti-French activity in Venetian territory, particularly in Verona, which may well have been provoked intentionally, he declared that a state of war existed between Venice and France, and proceeded to expel the city's government. Meanwhile, Bonaparte reorganised occupied Italy to form a Cisalpine Republic uniting Lombardy, Modena, Massa, Carrara, the Legations and Romagna, and supported the moderates of the prosperous middle-class, the heirs of enlightened despotism, against the Jacobin democrats. In the Cisalpine Republic can be traced the main features of Bonaparte's ideal of government – an administration of distinguished men under the strict control of the executive power. Whether peace could be made depended on events in Paris: the *coup d'état* of 18 Fructidor, for which his faithful general Augereau was largely responsible, put the Directory in Bonaparte's debt, and he took advantage of this to dictate the terms of the treaty of Campo Formio. By this treaty, Venetian territories as far as the Adige were ceded to Austria in exchange for an eastern extension of the Cisalpine Republic and a promise – subject to the ratification of the Imperial Diet – to cede the left bank of the Rhine (18 October). The treaty, which erased the Venetian Republic from the map of Europe, was accepted by the Directory with great misgivings; nevertheless it satisfied French public opinion.

The Italian campaign was closely linked with the preparations for the *coup d'état* of Fructidor and its consequences, and thus had a profound influence on the fate of the regime of Year III: it had temporarily ruled out the possibility of achieving internal stability, which only a rational and permanent peace could have fostered.

In retrospect it is tempting to interpret history in terms of 'inevitable' forces, but it would be a mistake to imagine the Directory as a contemptibly feeble civil power giving way to the victorious soldier, Bonaparte. The Directory included statesmen of intelligence and decision and the Army of Italy never pretended that its mission was to save society.

The relationship between France and her armies had certainly changed since Valmy and Jemappes. The last conscription had taken place in 1793, and since then opportunities for desertion had resulted in the growth of a force which, for the first time, virtually consisted of volunteers, an army half-way between the professional corps of Louis XVI's royal army and the conscripted army of 1793. This was a professional army in a sense, but the rules of the profession had changed: whether or not commanders were obeyed now depended on what opportunities for plunder and promotion they could offer. At the same time it was an army that shared the nation's conflicting desires; it longed for a republic without orators, a social order from which the more fanatical advocates of order would be eliminated, and the kind of conqueror's peace which merely made war all the more inevitable. It was far from being an army of praetorians, and when it intervened in Fructidor (1797) and again in Brumaire (1799) it did so only at the invitation of the civil power.

The generals themselves, when urged to intervene in political conflicts, showed little confidence in the chances of a military government. In Thibaudeau's Memoirs Kléber and Bernadotte are seen to have been hesitant and timid on the eve of the *coup d'état* of Fructidor. It has often been said that fortune favoured Bonaparte in eliminating his most dangerous rivals just at the right moment; but it is forgotten that none of his rivals saw himself as an emperor. They were not without ambition, but they were more familiar with the field of battle than with the corridors of power. Poor Moreau was dismissed for keeping the papers proving the treachery of his friend Pichegru, naïvely imagining that he might become a second Monck. The death of Hoche in September occurred just in time to prevent his legend from being demolished. Soubol called him 'the bold and blameless warrior, the knight-errant of hope'. In fact, Hoche's career showed the same mixture of frustrated authoritarianism and unsatisfied political ambition that characterised all the generals of 1797. Like the men under their command, they were discontented but at the same time too clear-sighted to think that France would accept a military dictatorship.

Bonaparte was very different. Quite apart from possessing that indefinable quality called genius, he had a remarkable understanding of the nature of power. In Italy he had given his soldiers all the booty they wanted; but he had also learnt that a general only becomes a statesman when he really asserts himself over the military by acting in his civilian capacity. He liked to change into civilian clothes from time to time. In 1802 he spoke of this to the Council of State: 'I told those of the military who had scruples, that military government would never take root in France. . . . I govern not as a soldier, but because the nation sees in me the civic qualities necessary for government.' He was also too wise to underrate a consensus of intellectual opinion. His favourite companions for conversation at Mombello were Monge and Berthollet; and he chose to send Monge to Paris, accompanied by Berthier, solemnly bearing the treaty of Campo Formio. On 28 December, after Carnot had been ejected from the Institute by the triumvirate of Fructidor, Bonaparte took his place.

In his civilian capacity as member of the Directory Carnot, the poor and painstaking captain of engineers, had succeeded in organising military victories. He had failed in his premature dream of bringing stability to France, a dream which could only be realised after peace had first been achieved. He never really understood the needs and desires of the social and intellectual world from which he had emerged. The new intellectuals of France preferred Bonaparte, the general whose glorious campaign in Italy concealed a career founded on *coup d'état* and opportunism. Perhaps they showed the greater foresight; they may have glimpsed in this offspring of the Corsican gentry the

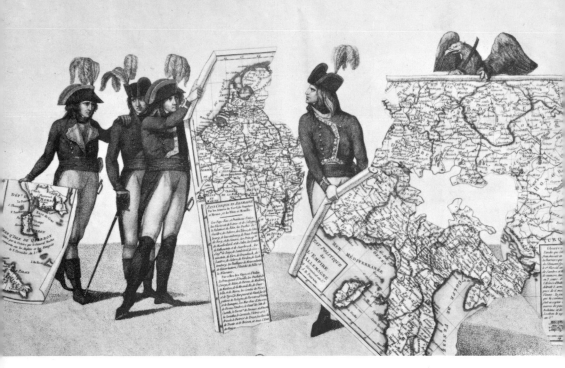

Engraving designed to glorify Bonaparte at the expense of his rivals. Bonaparte's success in Italy eclipsed the victories of the other generals. *Left to right*: Pichegru, Moreau, Hoche and Bonaparte.

personification of all their regrets and hopes, the symbol of a pure and peaceful Revolution and of a Europe dominated by the French Enlightenment.

THE CONQUEST OF EGYPT

The signing of the treaty of Campo Formio left Britain the only power still at war with the Republic. French politicians and public opinion viewed the idea of a peace settlement with horror. On 26 October 1797 the Directory published a violent proclamation of war and appointed Bonaparte as general-in-chief of the Army of Britain. It was decided to concentrate a fleet of sixty-three men-of-war and some fifty frigates at Brest for the spring of 1798, and Admiral Brueys was to join it with the Mediterranean squadron. On 8 February Bonaparte set out for Dunkirk, leaving Desaix and Kléber to inspect the ports of Brittany and Normandy. The wars of the eighteenth century had shown the tactical superiority of the British navy, but since 1793 there had been no full-scale sea battles, for the British had been content to blockade the Brest and Toulon squadrons in their anchorages. The French fleet was almost intact, and mutinies aboard British ships in the spring gave encouragement to French hopes. But these hopes were soon to prove unrealistic. The British blockade had prevented the French navy from obtaining supplies from abroad, and emigration had weakened the navy more than the army. The turning-point of the war at sea was the battle of Camperdown on 11 October: the Dutch fleet under De Winter was attacked by Duncan as it left Texel and was completely destroyed. This success gave a great boost to British confidence. Bonaparte and his lieutenants returned from their tours of inspection in downcast mood. Bonaparte realised that it would be foolish to attack Britain without mastery of the sea and advised either that peace be made or that France concentrate her offensives elsewhere, against Hanover or Egypt. Britain could now breathe freely again.

Talleyrand was responsible for the Directory's decision to undertake the hazardous expedition to the East. He had been repeatedly advocating French intervention in Egypt for several months, and Bonaparte had been discussing plans with him. Bonaparte's motives were probably largely personal. If the Army of Britain remained inactive, he might rapidly lose his popularity and become too involved in domestic affairs. A swift and victorious campaign in the East would keep him in the limelight and would leave him politically uncommitted on his return. At first Reubell and Barras were opposed to the Egyptian campaign, but eventually they gave it their support. The Directors were probably glad of an opportunity to be rid of Bonaparte for a while, for he had by now acquired the status of a party leader; but it must also be borne in mind that Talleyrand and Bonaparte had promised them that the expedition would be short and would be directed not against Turkey, but against Britain. Thus the Directors were relieved of the responsibility for a decision that was to reopen the Eastern Question and set up a Second Coalition against France.

The expedition was ready by May. Bonaparte left Toulon on the 19th and arrived off Malta on 19 June with a fleet of over three hundred ships and an army of thirty-eight thousand men and thirty-three generals. The island put up no resistance. Re-embarking for Egypt, Bonaparte and his fleet appeared off Alexandria on 1 July; the troops landed during the night and occupied the city the following day.

Egypt had been a province of the Ottoman Empire since 1517 and was governed by a pasha appointed by the Sublime Porte. But the Mameluke Beys had established themselves as a rival power, and two of them, Mourad and Ibrahim, exercised genuine sovereignty. Bonaparte used Talleyrand's arguments to justify his landing in a letter to the pasha and in a proclamation to the people of Alexandria, in which he stated that he had come to restore to the Egyptians the rights taken from them by the Mameluke usurpers, and that he fully respected the claims of the sultan. Kléber remained in Alexandria with three thousand men, while Desaix led the other divisions across the desert

The Battle of the Pyramids, which was fought on 21 July 1798 and lasted nineteen hours, was to decide Egypt's fate. Bonaparte placed his troops in square formations with his artillery at the corners; some of the enemy were pushed back into the Nile.

towards Cairo. The Mamelukes were easily defeated at Romanieh on 16 July, and in a second engagement three days later at Chobreis Mourad was routed as Ibrahim evacuated Cairo and headed for the Red Sea. Bonaparte pursued Ibrahim and defeated him at Salalieh on 11 August. Bonaparte had conquered Egypt but had failed to destroy the Mamelukes; and in the meantime the French army had fallen into a trap.

Britain had been fully aware of the preparations being made at Toulon, even if she did not know their purpose. On 9 May Rear-Admiral Nelson had been sent to keep a watch on the French fleet. He passed close to Bonaparte's ships several times and even reached Alexandria on 28 June, two days before the French landing. Thinking the enemy was heading further north, Nelson proceeded towards

Syria and then reached Sicily. Leaving Syracuse on 25 July for Morea, he discovered the destination of the French expedition from a captured brig. On 1 August he arrived off the anchorage of Aboukir, where Brueys' fleet lay at anchor some distance from the coastal batteries. Bonaparte had ordered Brueys to take soundings in the port of Alexandria, but Brueys reckoned it was not practicable to enter the old harbour and decided instead to anchor off Aboukir. Nelson sent some of his ships between the coast and the French fleet and was thus able to isolate them from one another, surround them and attack broadside on. All the French fleet was sunk except for the *Guillaume Tell* and the *Généreux*.

The battle of the Nile was not only important strategically, for within a few weeks France was isolated in the Mediterranean. Bonaparte had played a dangerous game with the sultan: while protesting peaceful intentions he had tried to raise up the Greeks of Morea and the Albanians of Ali Pasha of Janina against him. The sultan made approaches to Tsar Paul I after Aboukir and opened the Straits for him on 20 August; on 30 August, he signed a military pact with the tsar with a view to retaking the Ionian islands and finally, on 9 September, declared war on France. Ali Pasha of Tebelen massacred the French garrisons in Albania, the Russo-Turkish fleet took Cerigo, Zante and Cephalonia, while Vaubois found himself besieged by Nelson in Malta. The Second Coalition had been formed.

Bonaparte's Egyptian policy has long been regarded by historians – at any rate by French historians – as a far-sighted enterprise which was to lead to the opening-up of Egypt to modern civilisation and progress; however, in many respects it merely offered traditional answers to traditional problems. This was not the first occasion that the land of the Nile had fallen subject to a conquering minority, foreign not only in race but also in civilisation and religion. All previous invaders had been faced with the same problems: maintaining a native administration, dealing tolerantly with the religious question and avoiding friction, levying taxes, putting down revolts, and winning the support of the nation's élite.

On the advice of a specialist in Oriental affairs, Venture de Paradis, Bonaparte set up everywhere councils of notables, and offered concessions to Islam. But the financial demands he made on the Egyptian people were insatiable, and when public hostility found an outlet in the Cairo revolt (22 October) it became clear that the philanthropic motives which Bonaparte had proclaimed were simply a mask intended to conceal the reality of foreign occupation.

And yet the Egyptian campaign illustrates the common historical paradox of a barbarous act of aggression which ultimately encourages the spread of civilisation; it led to the founding of the Egyptian Institute of Sciences and Arts, the experiments of Monge, Berthollet and Geoffroy Saint-Hilaire and attempts to industrialise the land of the Pharaohs. Even if the civilising process did not lead to lasting achievements in Egypt it had a profound influence on the intelligentsia of France after 1815.

THE REVOLT OF EUROPE

Even before Bonaparte had left Toulon, the Republic had exceeded the frontiers agreed upon in the treaty of Campo Formio. The occupation of Switzerland was carried out in February, on the pretext of revolutions in the Vaudois, Basle and Lucerne. Apart from Mülhausen and Geneva, it was intended that Switzerland should now form a single republic. The situation in Italy was more complicated: the Jacobins of the Cisalpine, backed by French soldiers and civilians, were trying to stir up revolt in Piedmont, Tuscany and the Papal States, but found themselves opposed by Directory policy which was unanimously against a unified Italian republic. Their only victory came as a result of the accidental death of General Duphot in Rome, when the French occupied the city and created a wholly artificial 'Roman Republic' (February).

The Directory cannot be held responsible for this policy: indeed they did all they could to thwart it, and saved Tuscany, Piedmont and Genoa from a fate similar to that of Rome. The real responsibility lay with an assorted group of men including Bonapartists, Jacobins and corrupt army suppliers, who imposed a policy favourable to themselves but which cut at the very roots of revolutionary ideals.

The occupation was accompanied by political and financial demands which were completely inconsistent with the concept of revolutionary brotherhood. Within a year, the Cisalpine had two constitutions and four *coups d'état*. Switzerland and Holland suffered from repercussions of the upheavals in Paris. The growth of 'revisionist' ideas in France was shown by the strengthening of executive power, while among her sister-republics Italy, and to a lesser extent Switzerland, were being systematically exploited.

The revolts that broke out in 1798 and especially in 1799 against the administration and the armies of the Republic indicated the general discontent felt in occupied Europe. It is tempting to see two factions at work: on the one hand, the anti-revolutionaries, and on the other, those who wanted to use against France the very principles which she had claimed to stand for – unity, liberty and equality. However, such a distinction would be only partially true. Everywhere except in France 'patriot' was an equivocal term. A letter from a deputy in Vaud in June 1798 makes this clear:

> In God's name make the French subject to some authority other than their own whims and fancies, for they are becoming more and more barbarous. . . . Everyone is indignant about the behaviour of the French, and the best news you could give us here would be to declare war on them: this is the pitch to which feelings among our people have risen, and when I say 'our people' I mean not only the 'patriots' but also their enemies.

Many revolts broke out against the foreign domination: in April 1798 there was revolt in the little mountain cantons of Zug, Uri, Unterwald and Schwytz, in the Valais in May, in Nidwalden in September and in the Oberland in April 1799. The same basic patriotism combined with latent hostility existed among the Dutch and Zealand sailors, who mutinied in 1799.

Liberal and democratic minorities made more elaborate efforts to make themselves politically independent of France. The moderates, who carried on the tradition of enlightened despotism, were tempted to use the Republic's diplomatic and military problems as an excuse not to link themselves with France. In the Cisalpine, Melzi, who was envoy at Rastatt in 1798, and Marescalchi, ambassador in Vienna, tried to obtain the approval of Austria and France for an extension of territory on the Piedmont side in exchange for the conversion of the Republic into a kingdom which could be offered to one of the Spanish Bourbons. France prevented these plans from maturing, but the ideas that had prompted them continued to flourish. The same feelings were current in the Dutch Directory, which tried to obtain a separate peace at the time of the Anglo-Russian landing in 1799.

Most of the anti-French uprisings of 1798 and 1799 combined reaction against extortion and pillage with motives related to those that had sparked off the revolt in Vendée – passionate attachments to the Christian faith and, as was the case in the Belgian departments, a refusal to submit to conscription. The occupation of Rome and the Pope's exile had been welcomed by revolutionary opinion as a promise of appeasement. Roger Ducos said: 'The peace of the world will date from 26 Pluviôse year VI: on this date the fanaticism which is at the root of every war was stamped out.' But these idealistic notions bore little relation to reality.

As in Vendée in 1793, conscription in Belgium led to revolts among the rural population. As soon as the Jourdan law of September 1798 became known, peasants on the left bank of the Scheldt began to cut down the Trees of Liberty and replace them with crosses, burn civil registers and molest Republican partisans. Within a few days, during the later part of October, the peasant war spread throughout the region between Anvers and Ghent. The towns remained loyal to the French, however, and strict measures were taken by the authorities to put down the revolt, which then broke out in Luxembourg. There the insurgents were able to take the town of Hasselt, and they were only quelled after heavy fighting. Many priests were afterwards deported to the Ile de Ré.

These outbreaks became almost continuous in the Papal States, where they were accompanied by anti-semitic demonstrations, since most of the Jews had allied themselves with the Republic. Even before they reached Rome, the French troops were attacked by peasants led by their priests, notably in the Masaccio district. In the Trastevere on 25 February the population seized the opportunity offered by the mutiny against Masséna and rose up and massacred some Jews, with shouts of 'Viva Gesú Cristo!' and 'Viva María!'. In April the Trasimene department rose up and thereafter revolt became endemic in

Italy. The French retreat in the summer of 1799 suffered badly from guerilla attacks. The movement was at its most violent in Tuscany where an army based on Arezzo terrorised the surrounding area: this was led by a strange trio, a former officer named Lorenzo Mari, his wife who was known as the 'Pucelle du Valdarno', and her English lover, Windham. When Sienna was taken Jews were burned alive or murdered. The superficial order created by the Republic was crumbling everywhere: but nowhere were disturbances as violent as in the kingdom of Naples.

The occupation of Rome had led King Ferdinand iv of Naples to consider taking advantage of the chance offered to seize Benevento and Pontecorvo, two papal fiefs enclaved in his territory. The Republic was prepared to negotiate, but the wise advice of Gallo, the sovereign's Minister for Foreign Affairs, was outweighed by hatred of the Revolution, coupled with the influence of Lady Hamilton and Nelson. A treaty with Austria was signed in May and strengthened by a secret agreement in July 1798. On 23 November after Aboukir and Nelson's triumphant return, the Neapolitan army, led by the Austrian general Mack, invaded the territory of the Roman Republic. Championnet had left only one garrison in the Castel Sant'Angelo at Rome, and so Ferdinand iv was able to enter the city without difficulty on 29 November, and allowed his troops to assist the population in slaughtering Jews and Jacobins.

Once again French revolutionary opinion steeled itself against the danger which threatened it. 'War! War! This has been the constant cry of France and her army for the last six months' (*le Rédacteur*). On 6 December the Councils declared war on the kings of the Two Sicilies and Sardinia. While Joubert's troops occupied Piedmont, Championnet forced Mack to abandon Rome on 12 December and entered the kingdom of Naples. His lieutenants Lemoine and Duhesme encountered armed peasant resistance in Abruzzi, while Championnet himself pursued the Neapolitan army, which had been put to flight. Panic seized the court at Naples, and the sovereigns took refuge in Palermo. On 11 January Mack decided to sign a truce with Championnet: the French were only to occupy the northern half of the kingdom and were to receive an idemnity of ten millions.

The truce was not observed. The *lazzaroni*, who were determined to continue the war, roamed the streets of Naples and forced Prince Moliterno to become their leader. Meanwhile the patriots and exiles who were following the French army implored Championnet to intervene; he agreed to do so and ordered his men to resume their march. Moliterno left the *lazzaroni* to their fate and took refuge in the Castel Sant' Elmo, while they fought in the streets of Naples for three days. On the evening of 23 January Championnet was at last able to take full possession of the city. Maria Carolina had good reason to write: 'The common people are still the least bad.'

The Directory had no intention of making Naples a vassal republic; the civil commissioner Faipoult had been given the task of maintaining a provisional French administration, but Championnet refused to obey his instructions, and in a decree on 24 January he officially recognised the Neapolitan Republic. The new regime was established without difficulty in every province except southern Calabria. Faipoult did not want to see the republic in control of its own finances and proposed to confiscate all its public funds. He was expelled by the military and complained to the Directory, which recalled and court-martialled Championnet. The social policy of the Naples administration and the continued pillaging combined to alienate the common people from the regime in which they had at first held such high hopes. The disillusioned peasants turned against the rich and formed robber bands led by men like the notorious Fra Diavolo. Making the most of this situation, Cardinal Ruffo, one of Ferdinand iv's counsellors, landed near Reggio and raised a 'Christian Army of the Holy Faith' which occupied the whole of Calabria in two months. Ruffo did away with the new taxes and turned a blind eye to looting and the burning of mansions. Just when the insurrection was beginning to subside, the war in Europe forced the French to leave the south of the peninsula and hand over the Neapolitan patriots to the vengeful fury of Maria Carolina and Nelson.

The cessions agreed upon in the secret clauses of the treaties of Basle, 1795, and Campo Formio, 1797, were subjected by Austria and Prussia to the decision of the Imperial Diet. In November 1797 negotiations were opened at Rastatt, but these came to nothing because no party was prepared to make the concessions necessary for peace. On Bonaparte's initiative France had gone far beyond the zones of influence allowed her by the earlier treaties. The emperor refused to sacrifice his vassals. Although the Directory did all it could to keep the peace, war broke out again early in March. There was a spontaneous resurgence of revolutionary patriotism which was further encouraged by the murder of the French delegates at Rastatt (28 April). But it was undermined by internal conflicts: the very factions which had launched the Republic on its adventure – the Bonapartists, the generals and the Jacobins – were now critical of the government they had overthrown on 30 Prairial. The deciding factor in the 1799 campaign was the intervention of the Russian troops under Suvorov. While the British landed in Holland, Suvorov was able to occupy northern Italy, except Liguria. This offered no threat to the Republic, but Bonaparte now had an opportunity to play the part of the 'supreme saviour'. He was not trying to imitate Alexander, in spite of the legend he later

The king of Prussia (1), the emperor of Russia (2) and the emperor of Austria (3) show their apprehension at French expansion. The artist has mistakenly included the Parthenopaean Republic (Republic of Naples), which was not formed until January 1799.

circulated at St Helena: he decided to take the offensive as a preventive measure when he saw a Turkish army assembling in Syria to invade Egypt. However, all factors conspired to force him to leave Egypt, for his career was foundering there: he was beaten at Acre and forced into a retreat as arduous as the 1812 retreat from Moscow, according to Sorel; and there was latent revolt among the Mamelukes. The newspapers which his British enemies sent him (a short-sighted policy) finally persuaded him to return to France. On 22 August he set sail without warning, leaving Kléber in command of the Army of Egypt.

THE FINAL VICTORIES OF THE REPUBLIC

The French victories of autumn 1799 were facilitated by disagreements between the members of the Coalition and by the Republic's war effort. The only ambition uniting the Coalition was the destruction of the Revolution. On all other issues it was divided. The tsar of all the Russias set himself up as the champion of divine right: his sole aim was to re-establish religion and restore monarchy. He disapproved of his allies' territorial objectives, and wrote to his ambassador in Vienna: 'Guided by my honour, I hurried to the rescue of humanity and de-

317

voted thousands of men to preserving its well-being. But, when I resolved to reduce the present French colossus to nothing, I never contemplated allowing another to take its place and become in its turn the terror of neighbouring princes and the invader of their states.' This bitter letter referred to the emperor and the king of Naples. In Italy, the Austrians were not prepared to let Suvorov re-establish the administration of the king of Sardinia: they proposed to annex or divide up Piedmont, and with the monarchs of Palermo they intended to dismember the Papal States. Paul I was most exasperated by the Neapolitan designs on Malta, where Vaubois was resisting Nelson's fleet. Pitt's cabinet was not deceived, however: behind her defence of 'principles', Russia had interests of her own to consider. By the Turkish alliance she already controlled the Straits and the Ionian islands; there now existed the risk that she might appeal to the Order of St John of Jerusalem to help her to acquire control of Malta, the Gibraltar of the eastern Mediterranean. The Habsburg monarchy resented Suvorov's presence in Italy and feared Anglo-Russian plans for Holland, and therefore intended to protect the Netherlands. All these doubts and suspicions resulted in a general reorganisation of military command. The Archduke Charles was ordered down to the Lower Rhine to survey operations in Holland, leaving Switzerland to Suvorov, who was to be replaced in Italy by the Austrian, Melas. Each power was thereby granted political satisfaction: Austria could keep the Russians under observation, since they had moved from Italy to Holland; the tsar would have the honour of being the first to march on Paris; Britain gained satisfaction as it was of paramount importance to her that France be destroyed. From a military point of view this was folly, for between the decision to reorganise (31 July) and Suvorov's departure (24 September) the French had gained time, a valuable ally.

By the equivocal *coup d'état* of Prairial (see Ch. 12, p. 391) the French had also won over to their cause a number of conflicting factions which were temporarily united in the war effort. The Jacobins now had their last opportunity to play out the drama of Year II before they were brought to heel. The generals, who held a naïve belief in their own power, and especially Bernadotte, who was proving himself an efficient War Minister, now had a chance to prove to France that Public Safety could manage without a Robespierre. Jourdan introduced mass conscription, and despite desertions, exemptions and absenteeism, more than a hundred thousand men were called up. A forced loan was raised to finance the war and the 'great nation', watched secretly by the future conspirators of Brumaire, regained some of the vitality of 1793.

However, recovery did not originate in Italy. On Joubert's death

Championnet was chosen to direct operations there. He was defeated at Genola (4 November), surrendered Coni (5 December) and yielded to Gouvion-Saint-Cyr the honour of holding Genoa for the Republic. All the major events took place in Switzerland and Holland. The Archduke Charles did not want to wait for Suvorov in Switzerland and he therefore made a vain attempt to drive back Masséna's army. Masséna meanwhile strengthened his positions, sent Lecourbe to drive the Austrians from the St Gothard Pass and attacked before Suvorov arrived. The 'second battle of Zurich' was in fact a series of successful assaults made on the enemy between 23 and 27 September. Korsakov's Russian corps and Hotze's Austrian army were driven back to the other side of the Rhine. Lecourbe put so many obstacles in Suvorov's path that the old Russian leader ordered a retreat on 5 October, disheartened and furious with his Austrian allies. He was vindicated by the tsar, and operations were completed at the end of the month, by which time Holland was lost. The Duke of York, with forty-five thousand men, had hoped to break through the Franco-Dutch defence of Brune and Daendels, but he was beaten at Bergen (19 September), although he later managed to force the republicans back at Alkmaar (2 October). The Anglo-Russian assault was overcome at Castricum on 6 October, and the Duke of York was now isolated. On 18 October he accepted an armistice whereby he agreed to re-embark. By the time Bonaparte took over power, the Coalition had been divided and reduced to a defensive position. On the morning of 18 Brumaire Gohier had every reason to declare the Republic triumphant.

It is easy to see why the popularity and the legend of Bonaparte grew so fast: he had arrived at exactly the right moment to save his country from anarchy and danger from abroad. But the popular image of the general without a failure to his name took no account of the repeated assaults made on civil authority in Egypt and the disaster of Aboukir. The victories of Zurich and Bergen had been won in the great man's absence; moreover, the newly-acclaimed hero of victory, peace and order had contributed more than anyone to disorder, to war and, indirectly, to defeat. Nonetheless, the hollow claims of the Napoleonic legend also contained a very simple truth. Bonaparte appeared to reconcile what were in fact irreconcilable aspirations. He enabled people to forget what was best forgotten in their past, and at the same time he personified everything of which they still dreamed. For them he represented Campo Formio without the Coalition, Vendémiaire without the scaffold, and the Republic without the Constitution or the men of Year III. He became the supreme saviour of a country that knew no other way of escaping from the contradictions of its deepest yearnings.

The Duke of York was unable to take advantage of early success against the Franco-Dutch forces and was defeated at Bergen and Castricum in October 1799.

11

THE NEW FRANCE

During the Directory, when the bloodbaths of the Terror had become a thing of the past, French society began to reveal the profound changes brought about by the Revolution, changes which gave that society an essentially modern character. At the collapse of the Old Regime, the phenomenon of the 'natural' family, with its high birth- and mortality-rates, had already ceased to exist. But a study of population figures for eighteenth-century France suggests a particularly sharp drop in the birth-rate for the decade 1790–1800: according to the census of 1792 and 1793, for example, there were three hundred and eighty-four births per hundred marriages, compared with four hundred and seventy-six for the period 1778–87. The difference between these figures is all the more significant because during the Revolution the average age at marriage was lower than it had been under the Old Regime.

As variations in population trends inevitably have a delayed effect, French society in the latter years of the eighteenth century did not suffer the consequences of its lower birth-rate; on the contrary, benefiting from the high birth-rate and reduced mortality-rate which had been characteristic of the century, France still had the largest population of any country in Europe and was therefore able to continue supplying men for the armies of revolutionary expansionism. But the fall in the birth-rate in the last ten years of the century points to a fundamental change in the mental climate of France, for it surely suggests a greater control of sexual behaviour and the rapid development of contraceptive techniques. Contraception had undoubtedly been practised for some considerable time among the educated classes and had become more widespread as living standards improved during the second half of the century; in the reigns of both Louis XV and Louis XVI demographers and moralists were already deploring its harmful effects, which they exaggerated. It seems, however, that contraception was not practised generally in France until the Revolution, indicating a profound break with the religious prohibitions of the past and a new attitude towards human values and *happiness. In France, the Malthusian Revolution had no chronological correlation with the Industrial Revolution, as it had in the other great countries of Europe. This demonstrated that France was more advanced intellectually than economically.*

The new trend was not only a sign of a secularised world; it was very much a part of the new France of the property-owners, men anxious to have smaller families so that each of their children would have the best possible chance of success in life. Property-ownership spread rapidly during the Revolution with the sale of nationalised land, especially in the rural areas. Georges Lefebvre has estimated that in northern France a third of the thirty thousand peasants who bought nationalised lands during the period of the Revolution had possessed nothing before 1789. Many peasants began their slow and painstaking accumulation of wealth by purchasing small plots of ground, just like old Grandet in Balzac's novel.

The spread of property-ownership in the towns is more difficult to assess statistically, but it was no less real: during the hard times of economic and financial crisis, a petty bourgeoisie of tradesmen and craftsmen had grown up; at the same time, the Revolution had brought a vast increase in the numbers of public officials and the abolition of venal offices had made positions in public service open to all. Though lawyers were less wealthy than they had been under Louis XVI and many rentiers were totally ruined, bourgeois France had begun to assume some of its essentially modern features. The country was becoming increasingly dominated by the wealth of the merchant and the tradesman and the political power of the deputy. Now that the barriers of social privilege had been swept away, an egalitarian society was slowly taking shape, a society in which opportunities for advancement depended largely on individual talent, the hazards of financial speculation and the vicissitudes of political life. And yet the new France resembled the old in more ways than men believed. The social pleasures of the Directory were not so very different from those of the Old Regime, and it was no mere coincidence that during these years Talleyrand regained some of his former zest for life.

Perhaps it is misleading to define a society by concentrating on its most dazzling features. After all, French society in the years following the First World War was not just the Paris of Cocteau. Similarly, in the period of the Directory, when Mme Tallien reigned supreme over all Paris, the Grandets of rural France were amassing their fortunes so that they could make their sons into 'messieurs'. But modern social history, in its concern with detailed statistics, is in danger of attaching too little importance to the Parisian scene which the Goncourts described so vividly. During the Directory, Paris finally established itself in the role of pre-eminence prepared for it by the intelligentsia and salons of the eighteenth century, a role in which it had already distinguished itself as the centre of all the great events of the Revolution. Versailles was now deserted, no more than a memory: the City had won its struggle against the Court. Paris and power were henceforth inseparable. At first the capital had used its newly-found supremacy as an instrument of terror. Now, with the years of tragedy past, it inherited the status that had formerly belonged to the court at Versailles: it became the centre of money, of women and of pleasure, the symbol of the ideal life of which provincial France dreamed.

The money spent on dining and entertaining in Paris belonged to a new class of rich men, for most of the wealth of the Old Regime had been plundered by the Terror and inflation. But fortunes were still built up in much the same way, by traditional methods of speculative trading, and in particular by taking advantage of the chaotic state of the Treasury, rather than by the profit-based methods of modern capitalism. The contractors of the Republic proved even more unscrupulous than their ancestors, the Farmers General of the Old Regime. The increase in public expenditure, the necessity of providing for the armies, the inefficiency of the tax-collecting system and monetary instability had created ideal conditions for speculation and profiteering of every kind; an oligarchy of financiers guaranteed the Treasury's debts and took a large part of the nation's wealth as security. Starting from nothing, these men set no limit to their ambitions, for they had no one to fear: in former times the king of France had wielded an authority over his creditors which the Republic could not possibly hope to emulate. Politics and finance had become more closely interdependent: Barras and Ouvrard were the first two representatives of the new alliance.

However, the money that was being made so easily and rapidly was not diverted into the productive fields of investment and savings; preserving its old aristocratic function, wealth was devoted to the pursuit of pleasure, as if the new society of bourgeois France unconsciously hoped to endow itself with the aura of nobility. Pleasure is not acquired as easily as power, and the bourgeoisie of the Directory could find no other way of enjoying itself than imitating the social habits of the Old Regime. But the setting had changed, for the great houses of the Faubourg Saint-Germain were now deserted or had been sold and the social life of the city had moved across to the right bank, where public dances had replaced the private functions of earlier days. Nearly all the most distinguished figures of the old society were abroad or in the provinces, although a few returned to Paris where they were welcomed in the more snobbish circles. The new society already had in its midst a number of deserters from the aristocracy who were able to set an example to the rest; men like Barras himself, formerly a viscount and now an irremovable Director, the new regent of a kingless France; and Talleyrand, the 'bishop' who had returned from America.

The frenzied cult of pleasure was not just a reaction against the puritan repression of the years of the Terror; it also expressed a yearning for social vengeance. When Bonaparte married Josephine de Beauharnais, whose name evoked an aristocratic past, he acted not as a vulgar opportunist, but as a man passionately in love who wanted to obliterate memories of a humiliated childhood. Thus women occupied an even more dominant position in the society of the Directory than under the Old Regime; they were the incarnation not only of pleasure and luxury, but of money and success. During the years which separated the religious and social prohibitions of the Old Regime and the restrictive severity of the Civil Code, women enjoyed a brief emancipation, revelling in the homage which the new society paid to feminine beauty and draping their bodies in scanty pseudo-classical garments. The astute Josephine, well aware of the passing of time and of youth, took many lovers who helped her to climb to the top ranks of society. She provided the link between the Revolution and the Empire. The true queen of Paris was Mme Tallien, a woman of sculptural beauty and the mistress of both Barras and Ouvrard. A ball without her was unthinkable.

The men who enjoyed the limelight in the society of the Directory were the intellectuals and the military. Here again, although the new revolutionary society had either destroyed the flower of the old nobility or driven it from the country, it had inherited the institutions of the old order: Sieyès and Bonaparte replaced Turgot and Choiseul as France's leading figures in the academic and military worlds. But the new men of France were much more powerful than their counterparts of the Old Regime had ever been. The jurists of royal absolutism had merely been clerks, but the deputies of the Revolution wielded vast powers; the king's marshals had hardly been more than courtiers, while the generals of the Republic were great liberating heroes. Liberty and military conquest had made all things possible. Money certainly played an open part in the political life of the Directory, but it did not rule supreme. The Revolution had reinforced an unwritten law of French history whereby businessmen refrain from taking part personally in the struggle for power.

The Terror had been the regime of the intellectuals and the sans-culottes. *The Directory was the republic of the academics and the generals. From the newly-founded Institute, and through the medium of secondary and higher education, the ideologists of the Directory spread the message of the eighteenth-century Enlightenment over bourgeois France. Voltaire, Condillac and Condorcet came into their own; their aim had been to banish superstition by education and to establish society on rational foundations. The Enlightenment now exercised greater influence over France than at any other period of the Revolution, and its ambition was to uproot the Church and put natural religion in its place. Much of modern France was born of these Utopian ideals and the upheavals which issued from them. But the national consciousness forged by the intellectuals of the Revolution was inevitably Messianic in character, for the banner of Enlightenment had become the banner of the French armies beyond the Rhine and the Alps. Thus the revolutionary war continued to perform the role invented for it by the Girondins, endowing the French soldier with the twofold prestige of arms and ideas. Victorious generals contributed more to the Republic's ideology than to its coffers. Yet their view of the Republic was less academic and less bourgeois than that of the intellectuals: they looked on France as the people itself, all that was durable amid the ephemeral victories of politicians.*

The way in which Parisian society abandoned itself wholly to the world of pleasure and entertainment was also a sign of its uncertainty with regard to the future. Since the execution of the king of France the Revolution had not been able to put in his place a political authority acceptable to the country as a whole. The Republic of Enlightenment preached by the academics of the Institute had no deep roots among the French people. It was still confronted by its natural adversaries, the Church and the royalists, more united than ever by the persecution they had suffered together. On the other hand, the Republic was finding increasing difficulty in uniting those who had benefited from the Revolution: many peasants, even those who had bought national land, still preferred to listen to their priest and resisted the attempts made by the bourgeois of the towns to substitute the new religion for their traditional Catholic faith. Moreover, while clerical control of primary education had been destroyed by abolishing all the Old Regime's country schools where children had been taught to read and write from holy books, the Republic had put nothing in their place; concentrating its attention entirely on secondary and higher education, on the towns and the children of the bourgeoisie, it had no alternative system of education to offer the inhabitants of rural France. The peasant, whose horizon extended no further than his slightly enlarged plot of land, still feared the return of the landowners of the Old Regime and wanted firmer guarantees of security than the endless coups d'état *in Paris could provide. Naturally mistrustful of his deputy and a prisoner of the monarchic tradition of power, the peasant would have liked to see what Mirabeau and so many others had longed for since 1789: a king committed to the Revolution.*

This was also the wish of many of the bourgeoisie who were looking for a new, conservative regime. After all the years of inflation, war and upheavals of various kinds, stability had become the dream of 1798, just as change had been the dream of 1789. This is always a sign that a revolution has succeeded.

POST-REVOLUTIONARY SOCIETY

Revolutionary France had inherited the passion of the eighteenth century for taking censuses. Questionnaires and inquiries, similar to those undertaken by Louis xvi's intendants, were conducted all over the country, so that it is possible to make a statistical comparison of population figures for the Old Regime and the period of the Revolution. In the spring of 1796 the Directory received a long report on the population of France which had been drawn up by the great mathematician Prony, who at the time was head of the surveying and planning department. In his calculations Prony had followed the common practice of basing censuses on the boundaries of Old France, though he had extended these a little to include Avignon, Comtat, Savoy and the Maritime Alps. He had imitated the method employed by Terray's and Necker's intendants, basing his figures on the average number of annual births. By this method he obtained a total of 28 million inhabitants. The national almanac for Year IV gave a total of 27.8 millions (31.8 millions including the Belgian departments, 32.9 millions including the colonies).

The France of the Directory was still one of the most densely populated countries in Europe, and showed no signs of the supposed effects of depopulation which the enemies of the Revolution had attributed to the war, emigration and, above all, the Terror. The most recent estimates put the total number of emigrés at one hundred and fifty thousand and the total for the guillotine's victims at about twenty thousand; moreover, in the eighteenth century the death-toll of war, both civil and foreign, was infinitely less than it has been in the present century. The figures just given are statistically insignificant when set against the general trend towards population-growth which was characteristic of the second half of the eighteenth century in France. The population of France in 1789 was about twenty-six millions; by 1795 the total for the same area (i.e. within the boundaries of 1789) was about twenty-seven and a half millions.

France remained essentially a rural nation, and towns of over two thousand inhabitants accounted for less than one-fifth of the total population. France recruited her armies from the peasantry; since the beginning of the Revolution over eight hundred and fifty thousand men had entered military service. The size of France's population was one of the keys to the course taken by the Revolution, and to Napoleon's rise to power.

A young Burgundian noble lady who had been imprisoned during the Terror, Mme de Chastenay, came back to Paris to spend the winter of 1796–7 with friends. She was to remember those months for the rest of her life:

Never had winter in Paris been so gay. As in the provinces, all the best people gathered at the subscription balls. All over France the pleasures of life were cultivated quite uninhibitedly. A long period of famine had come to an end, money had reappeared and with it an abundance of everything. The revolutionary regime was over once and for all. No-one now spoke of informers or gendarmes. I have never seen people enjoying themselves as much as this; masks were even worn on the highways – life was just one great carnival.

The eighteenth century had returned to France, with its masks, its merrymaking and its women. But Mme de Chastenay was too young to recognise that these were different faces concealed beneath the masks and different women reigning over a new society. The aristocracy of eighteenth-century France had passed on its social customs to the upstarts of the Revolution, and was now horrified to see this distorted and yet somehow faithful reflection of itself in the people's mad rush to indulge in pleasures once reserved for the privileged few.

The cult of pleasure began as a reaction against the repression and

Since Thermidor Year II the people of France had been dancing everywhere, in the streets, in disused churches, in hotels and palaces. The waltz, which had just arrived from Germany, now invaded the salons.

austerity of the Terror and its egalitarian principles. For the men and women of the new France the great ideal of a Republic founded on virtue was dead. Robespierre had dishonoured both Terror and Virtue. His successors were only too aware of the price paid for the Spartan Utopia of which Robespierre had dreamed, and in any case they were not even prepared to accept its underlying aims. They had wanted the Revolution so that they could live in style, not in poverty; now that they had taken possession of the high offices of state they were eager to conquer the world of pleasure. They were initiating themselves into one of the great secrets of the Old Regime. If they could enjoy themselves and entertain in the grand manner, and if their women were pretty, then their victory over the aristocracy would be complete. The occasional noble might make a timid appearance in their salons from time to time, but he would be in the alien world of the bourgeoisie.

The new society was being rebuilt on the ruins of the old world of the nobility, which had been either driven out of the country or destroyed by the terrible vengeance of the Terror. Within a few years vast numbers of nobles had fled from France, almost without resistance. The Thermidoreans were not anxious to see them return to their country and find their properties sold, for they would inevitably help the cause of the royalists. The Thermidoreans therefore allowed the law of 8 March 1793 to remain in force (the law had banished all

After the tensions of the early years of the Revolution, social life regained its former prominence during the Directory. Here men and women are seen playing cards.

emigrés permanently and authorised the execution of any who were captured); after the royalist uprising of 13 Vendémiaire they introduced the law of 3 Brumaire Year IV, which prohibited all relatives of emigrés from holding public office. These laws were often attacked by the Councils, but the Directory continued to apply them as political circumstances demanded; they were relaxed in Year V when many republican deputies joined together in forming a new conservative 'centre' in the Councils, but were reinforced after the *coup d'état* of 18 Fructidor. The only method by which an emigré could re-enter France legally was to have his name struck off the official list of exiles, and this was not easily done. On 13 February 1797, out of seventeen thousand requests submitted to the Directory, only fifteen hundred were granted. A number of nobles managed to obtain forged certificates of residence from sympathetic or corruptible officials.

However, not all the nobility had emigrated; many had simply gone into hiding, or had left France only temporarily. Mme de Staël, an indefatigable intermediary between the old aristocracy and the new bourgeoisie, made much of this subtle distinction, though it had no legal validity. In her eyes the 'emigrés' were the ultra-royalists, those who had left France at the beginning of the Revolution and who still dreamed of a restoration of the Old Regime; the others, those who had been driven from France by the Terror, were merely 'fugitives' and therefore were entitled to return home, where they would swell the ranks of 'respectable' society. It was on behalf of these 'fugitives', men like Narbonne and Talleyrand, that the baroness persistently interceded with the government, sometimes with success.

Mme de Staël was not alone in her efforts. There were a number of survivors of the old aristocracy in the new society of the Directory, and women in particular were able to wield something of their old political influence. Josephine de Beauharnais obtained many secret favours from Barras. Pasquier, the future chancellor, relates:

> It was usually the emigrés who took advantage of her generosity and zeal, either because they wanted to be spared from some military commission or other, or because they wanted her to support their requests for permission to return and for the restitution of their property. They were now beginning to return to France, having used up their resources and weary of the humiliation of depending on the help of foreigners. They were prepared to brave all kinds of danger in the hope of finding a few remnants of their property left or a few inheritances to claim, and in order to see their relatives and their native country once again.

A life of pleasure awaited the returning emigrés, a life which they knew better than the parvenus of the Revolution. Mme de Chastenay, still full of the joys of winter 1796–7, says:

> I have already said that the subscription balls were the highlight of the winter. Peace seemed so near, and a number of prominent Vendéans were even seen at the dances, and also, I think, Mme de Bonchamp. Everyone gathered now at the Tivoli and the Pavillon de Hanovre. The emigrés were especially keen to join in these events, under the cover of their forged passports and certificates of residence; they appeared in large numbers, still young and delighted to see Paris again, to find themselves enjoying its social life once more and to hear French spoken at the street-corners. It really was quite wonderful.

And Mathieu Molé, who was to be minister to Napoleon, Louis XVIII and Louis-Philippe, describes this same period: 'Life in Paris was very pleasant at this time, and though I did not go much into society I knew about everything that was going on. Most of the emigrés had returned home and were filling the gap which their absence had left in society. . . . Everybody was trying hard to forget the sufferings of the past. Misfortune seemed to have left a stain which everyone was anxious to remove as quickly as possible.'

But these accounts by eye-witnesses all date from the period of the 'centre' alliance in the Councils, and were written by members of a nobility which was already committed to a policy of reconciliation, and which in 1797 represented one of the mainstays of constitutional monarchism. This mood of optimism was to be shattered by the events of 18 Fructidor and the reintroduction of repressive measures against nobles and priests. The period of the Directory therefore marked only

The new society brought luxury and affluence with it. Many men made their fortunes in the years of the Directory.

the first hesitant signs of an aristocratic resurgence that was to gather momentum under the Consulate. The returning nobles were defeated men intent on rescuing what possessions they could; they simply had to accept the inevitable and come to terms with the new society.

While it included a fair proportion of the members of the old aristocracy, the society of the Directory was dominated by the new men of France, the politicians and the financiers. The close link established during this period between power and money gave the bourgeoisie of France a distinctly modern character, and at the same time aroused the hostility of both the right wing and the anti-capitalist left wing. The new 'republic of friends' was based on a social world of common interests, and to justify its assumption of the role previously played by the aristocracy and then by the 'populace' it invented a euphemistic title for itself: the *honnêtes gens* or 'respectable people'. The use of the adjective was a sign of a guilty conscience, for the new men of France were not always conspicuous for their honesty. Admittedly, they could plead extenuating circumstances: financial chaos, galloping inflation and all the temptations presented by the sale of nationalised land, by speculation and by the European war. But they had themselves been responsible for creating those circumstances. The downfall of Robespierre had paved the way for the restoration of chaotic freedom to an economy that was still lifeless.

331

This engraving symbolises the rise of a new wealthy class during the Directory. *Left* ('what I was'): the poor man leaves home; *centre* ('what I am'): having made his fortune, he is able to drive a lady in a coupé; *right* ('what I would have been'): the figure with the anchor over his shoulder shows what the man's fate would have been in normal times.

When the young Benjamin Constant arrived in Paris in May 1795 he felt completely at home in Thermidorean France. In a letter to his aunt he explained the technique of buying national property with almost worthless paper-money: 'National land is sold at an interest-rate of $\frac{3}{4}\%$; in other words, for 100 *livres-assignats* you have an income of 15 *sous* in kind or in cash; at the current rate of exchange 100 *livres-assignats* are worth 2.5 to 3 *livres* in metal currency; and so, for 3 *livres* at the very most you will have an income of 15 *sous*, which brings the rate of interest up to 25%.' This simple and highly profitable method of calculation was common practice at the time; the letters written by the deputy Rovère to his brother, a constitutional bishop, and by Le Paige, a member of the Council of Elders, to an administrator in Vosges, were both concerned primarily with the purchase of national property. In 1797 the failure of the experiment with the *mandat terri-torial* resulted in the wholesale squandering of national property, which was paid for at par, although the new currency had already collapsed. Vast numbers of Frenchmen became rich overnight, buying up the old châteaux of the aristocracy and the great houses of the Faubourg Saint-Germain in Paris. This new class of property-owners, which had everything to lose in the event of a royalist restoration, was perhaps the most powerful bond uniting the bourgeois Republic of the Directory; on 1 August 1797, during the period of uncertainty that followed the election of a new royalist 'third' to the Councils and preceded the *coup d'état* of 18 Fructidor, Benjamin Constant, living at the time in an old monastic building near Paris, sent this message of alarm to Lausanne: 'Since the new third was elected the government has been rocked to its foundations . . . everywhere purchasers of national property are being murdered or robbed . . .' But Augereau and the army were soon to restore order.

The chaotic state of the nation's finances produced even more dramatic changes of fortune and status than the indiscriminate sale of national property. It struck a powerful blow at the bourgeoisie of the liberal professions, which had already been hit by the abolition of venal offices, and it ruined the vast numbers of *rentiers* who had invested their money in fixed-interest government loans. But financial chaos was a paradise for debtors and speculators. Having abandoned direct state-control in an attempt to banish the hateful memories of the recent past, the Directory had to throw itself at the mercy of the finance companies, which attached exorbitant conditions to their guarantees of aid. The state's markets were put to tender without any previous publicity or open bidding, and as a result bribery, which had been rampant under the Old Regime, and direct intervention by politicians in commerce, became the order of the day. In his Memoirs the honest La Révellière expressed his indignation at the way in which Barras surrounded himself with money and women. But Barras was setting an example which was followed by all his protégés in the worlds of politics, business and pleasure, transferring his favours from Bonaparte to Ouvrard and from Josephine de Beauharnais to Mme Tallien, finally returning Josephine to Bonaparte and passing Mme Tallien on to Ouvrard.

The contractors who supplied the armies of the Republic were some of the wealthiest men in France at this time: Jean-Pierre Collot, who was bound up with Bonaparte and the Army of Italy and was to provide some of the funds which Bonaparte needed on 18 Brumaire; the Belgian Michel Simons, who contracted with Ouvrard to supply the French navy and was the lover of the famous actress, Mlle Lange; and Hanet-Cléry, the brother of Louis XVI's valet, who supplied the Armies of Germany and Switzerland. But supplying the Directory with grain and currency and taking a direct part in the government's financial manoeuvres (e.g. the liquidation of the *mandat*) presented equally great opportunities for contractors and financiers. In fact, the money that flowed through the upper reaches of Directory society was gained largely by this kind of financial operation rather than by the normal methods of bourgeois investment. The contractors and financiers had simply taken the place of the Farmers General of the Old Regime.

THE PROVINCES

During the Revolution the provincial life of France had sunk into even greater obscurity than under the Old Regime. Not only were the provinces overshadowed by the splendour of Paris, but they had also lost many of their illustrious names. In the old days the provinces had been able to maintain contact with Versailles through their great families, their governors and their bishops; the towns had been able to boast their own parlements and academies, and the countryside had been named after its châteaux and churches. A whole provincial society had existed which vanished along with the clergy, the nobility and the office-holders of the Old Regime. Ecclesiastical property had been sold and many of those who had bought religious buildings had turned them into profit-making enterprises, converting abbeys into factories and chapels into stables. Even when the buyer was an educated person his values were those of practical social utility, and he would scorn the 'Gothic' monuments of superstition. The very term 'Gothic', misused by many cultivated people, including Mme de Staël and later Stendhal, shows how great an abyss separated the worlds of enlightenment and barbarity in the minds of the educated.

Many of the provincial nobility had emigrated. Some of them were able to protect part of their property by divorcing their wives, who then received their dowries back and were less likely to be persecuted than their husbands; sometimes friends interceded anonymously on behalf of the emigrés and were able to prevent all their possessions from being taken by the state. But when a noble found himself able to return to France, or when he was released from prison or simply came out of hiding, he could not hope to regain his old social status. Deprived of his seigneurial rights and demoralised by the rout which his class had suffered, he was now an exile in his own country, reduced to the domestic routine of provincial life. 'We lunched together,' relates the Comte Molé; 'after lunch the women would gather round the drawing-room table with their needlework, and someone would read aloud from a book to provide a suitable subject for conversation. The men either joined the women in the drawing-roon, went for a walk or returned to their rooms. After dinner we did the same things . . . the evening usually ended with a little music.'

In the towns of provincial France society was caught up in the same passion for a life of gaiety, pleasure and dancing that had seized Paris, but as a collective reaction against the recent past rather than in conscious imitation of the capital. Provincial society had also been transformed by the wholesale destruction of the old privileges of rank and wealth. At Dijon, according to Mme de Chastenay, 'there were a few houses where members of the old parlement gathered, though with little pleasure, putting on affected airs of virtuous melancholy. I did not know any of them, not even vaguely. . . . It was common knowledge at the house I used to frequent that the young women found this social life hideously tedious.' The gatherings which Mme de Chastenay visited were held at the house of Mme Caristie, where there were 'few lawyers or persons in important positions, and none of the old parlement'. Mme de Chastenay describes her hostess as a 'truly lovable woman whose husband had made his fortune in business and was frankly something of an upstart. Her house was by far the most pleasant.' The Revolution had not only ruined the clergy and the nobility, but had impoverished many of the bourgeoisie of the Old Regime – the king's financiers, office-holders, *rentiers* and property-owners.

Those who had gained from the Revolution were the bourgeoisie and peasants who had bought nationalised property. The fever of speculation that had seized Paris was merely part of a nation-wide movement; in fact, in the provinces the transfer of the lands of the Church and nobility into the hands of the new property-owners was a much more radical and durable phenomenon than in Paris itself. The chaotic financial policies of the Directory, and in particular the fiasco of the *mandat territorial*, had enabled the bourgeoisie to buy up large areas of land to the detriment of the peasantry. Yet in most of the departments of France the prefects of the Consulate were to report an increase in the total number of peasants liable for land-assessment; Georges Lefebvre has estimated that in the north a third of the thirty thousand peasants who bought national lands held no lands at all in 1789. Although the massive expropriation of land during the Revolution mainly benefited the bourgeois of the towns and those peasants who were already quite prosperous, it did also enable a vast number of poorer peasants to become property-owners.

The peasants also benefited from the financial and economic situation. They bought land with assignats, paid their taxes in assignats and sold their grain for good metal currency. At the same time, the return to a free market enabled them to make large profits by charging high prices during the period of food-shortage in 1795–6, or at least to delay the sale of their produce. While the peasants made their profits or hoarded and waited for the right moment to sell, the inhabitants of the towns went hungry. Admittedly, not all peasants were in a position to enrich themselves in this way; there were large numbers of day-labourers who remained as poor as ever. But nevertheless it remains true that towards the end of the '90s there existed a whole class of property-owning peasants which had prospered by the Revolution and was ready to give its support to the regime that would offer it the strongest guarantees of protection. This class had little difficulty in choosing between the government of Barras and the promises of Bonaparte.

Relatively little is known about the way in which urban social structures evolved during the period. Statistics point to a general but slow advance by the lower classes and an increase in the number of small shopkeepers and artisans. The lower classes had been severely hit by inflation in 1795–6, but began to recover in the second half of the Directory, when deflationary policies caused prices to fall more than wages. At the same time, the prodigious growth of the machinery of the state during the revolutionary period had created a whole multitude of new positions which were rapidly filled by the petty bourgeoisie, later to be described by Balzac in his novel *les Employés*. But industry and commerce had made no progress: the French Revolution had not been an economic revolution. By the accident of war it had ruined the bourgeoisies of the Old Regime's great ports – Marseilles, Bordeaux and Nantes. Unintentionally, with the emigration of the nobility, the Revolution had closed up the traditional outlet of France's luxury-goods industry. Sometimes the old industries were replaced by new ones, but, despite the constant efforts of revolutionary governments from the Constituent Assembly to the Directory, there had been no real improvement either in the techniques of production or in the methods of mobilising capital. Provincial bourgeois society, where family life and thrift were regarded as supreme virtues, had undergone as profound a transformation as had Parisian society – thus paving the way for the Civil Code. Nevertheless in the economic sphere provincial France remained unchanged.

PARIS

Paris had at last triumphed over Versailles: the capital had become the life and soul of France. The city had been prepared for its new role by the eighteenth-century trend towards centralisation, the growing importance of urban life generally and the brilliance of its own literary salons; but in stripping Versailles of its old supremacy the Revolution had also given Paris control of politics and the positions of power. Under the Old Regime men had sought political favours by desperately trying to obtain a smile of approval from the king in some corner of the palace; in the nascent bourgeois society of the Directory those anxious for promotion sought their opportunities at the dinners attended by Barras and Sieyès in the capital.

At Versailles, the great palace was empty, its park overgrown with weeds, a silent memorial to the drama of the October Days in 1789 when the women had marched from Paris and forced the king to return with them to the city. But Paris itself had also undergone a transformation. Though still the same city architecturally, the Paris of Gabriel and his successors, it had been taken over by new masters. Church properties had been sold, particularly in the Cité and the Ile Saint-Louis, where hitherto had stood numerous abbeys and churches. Notre-Dame was deserted, but the smaller churches had been bought up, taken over as living-quarters or demolished. Saint-Éloi des Barnabites had been turned into a cannon foundry; Saint-Pierre-des-Arcis had been pulled down and a theatre built in its place. Outside Sainte-Madeleine and Saint-Germain-le-Vieux notices were put up saying 'For sale' or 'To let'. Similarly, on the hill of Sainte-Geneviève, from the Place Maubert to the Val-de-Grâce, monasteries and their gardens were now occupied by contractors busy making their fortunes amid the debris of the city's great architectural monuments.

The Paris of the nobility had also vanished. The Faubourg Saint-Germain, where the great noble families of eighteenth-century France had lived after abandoning the Marais quarter, had completely changed. Along the left bank between the Odéon and the Invalides, in the Rue de Varenne, the Rue de Tournon and the Rue de Grenelle, the magnificent houses which the nobility had been forced to quit were passed from hand to hand by property-speculators. Sometimes a house would be sold several times in a month without any of its buyers ever actually seeing it. Those houses that were not being bought and sold by speculators were used for commercial purposes: the Hôtel Biron in the Rue de Varenne had been converted into a public dance-hall, and the huge apartments of the Hôtel d'Orsay were being used as shops for ladies' fashions. The cult of money which dominated post-revolutionary society was a more powerful force than people realised at the time, obliterating a whole way of life and its art.

But the Parisian bourgeoisie used its money to shape its own urban world. This world reflected a trend that had begun in the last decades of the Old Regime, when the Farmers General and other financiers of the monarchy had started building themselves great houses and semi-rustic 'follies' on the right bank of the Seine, from the Chaussée-d'Antin to the Roule. The new rich of the Directory were merely following the example set by their predecessors.

The right bank became the centre of Parisian social life. Every evening the lights of the cafés sparkled from the gardens of the Élysée to the Place de la Révolution; the Champs-Élysées, planted with trees barely thirty years old and dotted with eating-houses and bars, became the fashionable place for walks. Elegant cabriolets moved rapidly along the Chemin du Roule, bringing Parisians to enjoy the pleasures of the city. The Élysée palace, the Hôtel Beaujon, the Hôtel Monceau with its *jardin anglais*, the Hôtel Biron, the Hôtel d'Aligre and the Hôtel Longueville were all used for public dances; everywhere the great

France was seized with Anglomania: the English 'buggy', a small open carriage, was often used by the *muscadins* for promenading in the streets of Paris.

A woman of fashion in evening-dress,
Greek hairstyle.

Hairstyle *à la Titus*, loose cut-away coat,
Hussar-style trousers.

Dress *à la Coblentz*, long shawl, English-
style hat.

Hat *à la Minerve*.

buildings erected by the aristocracy of the Old Regime for the sophisticated pleasures of the select few had been taken by the new bourgeoisie and turned into places of public entertainment.

The heart of the new Paris was the Chaussée-d'Antin, which had been built up piece by piece on land taken from the surrounding nurseries and market-gardens. Building had begun there in the reign of Louis xvi, when actresses had started erecting little rococo pavilions in semi-natural settings, but it was not until the revolutionary period that streets were laid and this became the fashionable quarter, developed by businessmen and building-contractors. Vast sums of money, acquired with little effort by the new wealthy class, were invested in sumptuous houses decorated with extravagant neo-classical luxury. 'In the modern drawing-rooms of Paris, I see nothing but tombs of ancient Romans', said one of Louis xvi's great architects. This ostentatious display of wealth, which sometimes degenerated into vulgarity, intensified the old class distinctions in the eastern quarters of Paris. The Revolution had erected a wall of fear between the rich and the poor of the city.

On 5 July 1797, a few months after returning to Paris, Talleyrand wrote to one of the friends he had left in America describing the Parisian social scene:

... What a difference there is between the Paris of the Constitution and the Paris of the Revolution! The revolutionary committees and prisons have gone and have been replaced by dancing, entertainments and firework-displays. . . . The women of the royal court have disappeared, but their place has been taken by the women of the new wealthy class; like their predecessors, these women are followed by whores who try to emulate their life of luxury and extravagance. Around these dangerous sirens swarm those bands of brainless creatures who used to be known as *petit-maîtres* and who are now called the *merveilleux*: they talk politics as they dance, sigh for the return of monarchy as they eat their ices and yawn with boredom as they watch a display of fireworks.

The former bishop, who had sound judgement in these matters, had discerned the common bond linking the old society with the new – the pre-eminence of women. The aristocracy of eighteenth-century France had been dominated by the women of the court, who had replaced war and the person of the king himself as the overriding influence in aristocratic life. In the world of the Directory women re-emerged triumphantly after having been temporarily cast aside by the Terror and popular puritanism. Society still had its whores: Mlle Lange replaced 'la Guimard', the eternal actress always ready to satisfy masculine vanity. The *'femme du monde'* had changed just as the Parisian world itself had changed: she was often a *parvenue*, and sometimes a coarse creature, more concerned to display her bodily charms than to attract men by her conversational ability: the society of the Directory saw the birth of the Parisian *demi-monde*.

As always, the men who wrote contemporary accounts of social behaviour during the period of the Directory tended to exaggerate the immorality of women in order to make their own position appear more respectable. The society of this period included a great many serious-minded women like Mme de Condorcet, and many faithful wives like Mme Récamier. But there can be no doubt that, during the years separating the Jacobin austerity of the Terror and the bourgeois virtue of the Civil Code, the new freedom which had been stimulated by divorce encouraged men and women to cultivate the life of pleasure. The women who reigned supreme during the Directory – Mme Tallien, Mme Hamelin and Josephine de Beauharnais – passed from one man to another, from financiers to politicians and from politicians to financiers. Marriage did not satisfy Josephine any more than it did the others. From the highest to the lowest levels of society prostitution flourished.

The new salons were lacking in style just as the new beauties were lacking in intelligence. Some salons deliberately excluded those of the old nobility who had not emigrated. At Auteuil, in the house of Cabanis, Mme de Condorcet carried on the tradition of the old literary salons by gathering men of learning together, but by doing so she cut herself off from the mainstream of Parisian society. The few women who had been part of the old society and wanted to continue 'as before' found their salons being frequented by a wide diversity of types – former Robespierrists, new deputies, generals promoted from the ranks and aristocrats who had rallied to the new regime. Mme de Staël, who could not help looking back to the days of the Necker salon, regarded the deputies who visited her gatherings as common men: to her they looked like yokels as they mingled with her 'well-bred' guests, succumbing reluctantly to the fascination of elegant manners and 'good company'. Her salon was one of the most hospitable in all Paris.

Many of the salons of the Directory – those held by Barras at the Luxembourg, Talleyrand at the Ministry of Foreign Affairs, Merlin at the Ministry of Justice and Sieyès in the Rue du Rocher – were restricted to the world of politics. The royalist salons, which included those of Mme de Vaines, the wife of a prominent official of the Old Regime, and the Marquise d'Esparbès, who could boast La Harpe among her guests, drew both the *élite* of Parisian society and the politicians of the opposition. One evening the guests at the salon of Mme de Montesson, the morganatic wife of Louis-Philippe d'Orléans, father of Philippe Égalité, fled when Mme Tallien, who had not been invited, suddenly appeared in their midst. The title of 'Queen of Paris' was no

The Directory style displays sobriety and a tendency towards the classical. The furniture, simple in its lines, retains the elegance of the Louis XVI style.

longer recognised in the closed society of the vanquished aristocracy. It was at the great balls given in the Hôtel Thelusson and in the other leading houses of the new society that the beautiful Mme Tallien was awarded this honour.

When Mme de Staël returned to Paris in the spring of 1795, reassured by the moderate policies of the Thermidoreans, she immediately engaged in feverish political activity. Revelling once again in the salon life which she had missed for so long, the baroness was anxious to revive the constitutional monarchist movement. But her old friends had gone, and so she began employing every means at her disposal to secure the return of the emigré Feuillants whose patroness she had been before the Terror. In her campaign she was assisted by Benjamin Constant, an unknown young Swiss of twenty-eight who had been her lover for a year and who was determined to make a reputation for

The elegant interiors of the Directory saw the return of the pre-Revolutionary
cabinet. A gold coffee-pot stands on the classical-style three-legged bronze table.

himself. But the uprising of Vendémiaire compromised the royalist cause, and the couple returned to Switzerland to stay in Necker's château.

In the spring of 1797 Constant returned to France alone: the baroness had been prohibited from entering France by a decree of the Directory, but she helped her lover by advancing him generous sums of money from her immense fortune. Constant very soon found his feet in a world that shared his desires – money and power. It is quite fascinating to observe this intelligent and intense young man's conquest of Paris. Speculating on national property with Necker's money, he bought himself an old ecclesiastical estate in the canton of Luzarches, to the north of Paris. He was now a property-owner and therefore committed to the Republic of Enlightenment, to which he was also drawn by his hatred of the clergy and his love of liberty. He took advantage of his new property-owning status to obtain French citizenship; he had already strengthened his claim to citizenship in the summer of 1796, at the time of the suppression of the Babeuf conspiracy, by publishing an essay of Thermidorean propaganda which held a political programme in its very title – *De la force du gouvernement actuel de la France et de la nécessité de s'y rallier*. The orthodoxy of Constant's argument is summed up in a single sentence from the essay: France had declared itself 'for liberty on 14 July, for the Republic on 11 August, and against anarchy on 9 Thermidor and 4 Prairial'. Or, in other words: 'I am not calling on any monarchic state to declare itself a republic, but I am entreating Frenchmen not to turn against their Republic.' Constant involved himself in the elections of spring 1797, but his French citizenship failed to secure him parliamentary eligibility; Reubell detested Constant because of his support of Barras, and a great many republicans mistrusted a man who had taken a baroness as his mistress.

At Christmas 1796 Mme de Staël was informed by Barras that she could return to France on condition that she stayed at Luzarches with Constant and kept quiet. She spent the winter there, awaiting the birth of a daughter (her husband, who was Swedish ambassador in Paris, claimed the child as his own). But there was no question of her keeping quiet! As she could not go to Paris (she did not return to the capital until May) her friends came out to Luzarches to see her – Montesquiou, Mathieu de Montmorency, Roederer and, above all, Talleyrand.

The 'bishop' owed his return to France to the intercession of Mme de Staël, who had been his lover several years previously in London. Since the autumn Talleyrand had passed through one of the most difficult periods of his brilliant career. Penniless and with no occupation, he quietly planned ways of acquiring a fortune and a position of influence. He held no political convictions, but he did have a past; he was free to attach himself to any of the political parties except the royalists. In the spring of 1797, after the royalist elections, he joined Benjamin Constant and the republicans of the Councils (Cabanis, Daunou, Chénier and Sieyès) in founding the 'Constitutional Circle', formed to support the Directory against the royalists. Talleyrand had declared his affiliations: the *coup d'état* of 18 Fructidor was to meet with his approval.

However, the indefatigable Mme de Staël, assisted by Constant, finally imposed Talleyrand on Barras and his reluctant colleagues. In the ministerial reshuffle of 14 July 1797 which marked the beginning

In 1786 Germaine Necker, daughter of Louis XVI's minister, married Baron de Staël. Her salon became a centre of political and literary activity.

of the offensive launched by the 'triumvirate' of Barras, Reubell and La Révellière, the 'bishop' replaced Delacroix at the Ministry of Foreign Affairs. In his Memoirs Barras relates: 'When the appointment had been decided I informed Benjamin Constant so that he could pass on the news.' Talleyrand was at the theatre, where he had been trying to pass away the anxious moments of waiting; he had with him M. de Castellane, his colleague in the Constituent Assembly, whom he subsequently made a peer of France. When Constant announced the news Talleyrand hugged him and M. de Castellane did likewise. The three men left the theatre immediately and Talleyrand said to his friends: 'Let us go to thank Barras at once.' All the way to the Luxembourg Talleyrand talked of the 'vast fortune' he was going to make now that he was in office. The moral standards of the old aristocracy were not really so very different from those of the new bourgeoisie.

THE GOVERNMENT OF ENLIGHTENMENT

The Thermidoreans were not interested solely in money and pleasure. Politically they were obsessed with two powerful passions: hatred of the nobility and hatred of the clergy. They had opposed the royalists with cannons, even though this had meant contravening the Constitution they had themselves drawn up. They believed in education, which was to be their chief weapon against the priests: if the common people were still the prisoners of ancient prejudices, this was because they were ignorant and dependent on priests and their superstitions. Education was therefore to be 'republicanised': in other words, the state intended to instruct the nation in the values of Enlightenment.

Crowning the new structure of education was the Institute, created by the great law of 3 Brumaire Year IV (25 October 1795) during the final session of the Convention. This learned body, which, like the Directory and the two Councils, owed its existence to the Constitution,

Firmin Didot (1764–1836) made his contribution to science and literature by discovering stereotypography. This new method of printing was both cheap and efficient.

was to all intents and purposes a third spiritual power. Many of its members, co-opted by the forty-eight original members appointed by the Directory, were deputies or eminent figures in the government – men like Daunou, Marie-Joseph Chénier and La Révellière.

The Institute was divided into three departments: physical and mathematical sciences, literature and fine arts, and – the great novelty – moral and political sciences. It consequently played an important part in both the cultural and the political life of France, and its influence made itself felt in the events leading up to Bonaparte's seizure of power on 18 Brumaire. Long before this, during the few months which Bonaparte spent in Paris between his Italian and Egyptian campaigns, various people had expressed their surprise at finding him 'timid, inactive and secretive, going to the Institute every day and apparently completely absorbed with his wife, geographical maps and the poems of Ossian'. But Bonaparte's visits to the Institute were to bring their reward. When he was elected as a member in place of Carnot in 1797 he acquired the stature of a hero of antiquity: he was now not only a general, but a man of intellect. He was even heard to say on one occasion: 'My religion is the Institute.' The Institute, representing the intellectual élite of the times, took over the functions of the academies of the eighteenth century, crystallising the tradition of Enlightenment in a common vision of the world, the vision of the 'ideologues'. The physicians, philosophers and *littérateurs* who belonged to it were rarely men of genius, but the most eminent of them – Cabanis, Destutt de Tracy, Volney, Garat, Ginguené – formed a pleiad of distinguished minds with a zest for new ideas. The disciples of Condillac, they rejected the 'innate ideas' of Descartes; they were determined to avoid all metaphysical explanations of human knowledge and to put in their place a system based on the principle that all ideas are derived from physical sensation – hence the name 'Sensationalism' given to their philosophy. They developed their experimental rationalism into a theory of human behaviour which extended even to aesthetics: for men like Fauriel or Ginguené the study of the beautiful had to take into account the relativity of space and time.

These precursors of Positivism looked for inspiration to the progress being made in the sciences, which were now stripped of all metaphysical presuppositions. To those who in 1796 accused Laplace of trying to explain the 'system of the world' without taking Providence into account, he replied that he had not found such an hypothesis necessary. The great scientists of this period – the mathematicians Lagrange and Monge, the chemists Berthollet, Chaptal, Fourcroy and

Berthollet, collaborator of the great Lavoisier, played his part in the creation of modern chemistry. He was devoted to Bonaparte and followed him to Italy and Egypt.

Darcet, the naturalists Lamarck, Cuvier and Geoffroy Saint-Hilaire and the physicians Pinel and Bichat – were not all materialists; but their discoveries and their writings helped to build up and popularise a view of the universe that was new and therefore to be regarded with suspicion by the champions of religion and tradition.

Among the opponents of Sensationalism were Bernadin de Saint-Pierre, an adherent of Rousseau's deism, and Chateaubriand, in London. But the most celebrated writers of the royalist reaction were La Harpe, who had returned to religion with all the passion he had previously devoted to Voltaire and Jacobinism, and Fontanes, who, during the Directory, embarked on the career which he was to pursue imperturbably right up to the Restoration.

The idea of a system of public education that would deliver the people from superstition dates from the Convention of the Montagnards, the plans drawn up by Condorcet and Le Peletier and a law of 30 Frimaire Year II (20 December 1793) concerning primary schools. But the most important measures were not approved until after the fall of Robespierre and were put into effect under the Directory; the new educational policy was really the work of the Thermidoreans.

The principles underlying the new policy were simple. Education was to be both public and secular; in other words, the Church was to be deprived of its old monopoly of schools, and instruction was to be stripped of its religious bias. The Church was still free to run its own establishments, but the new schools, which were open to all and neutral in matters of religion, enjoyed the invaluable financial support of the state. The legislation passed by the Montagnards of the Convention had been concerned chiefly with primary education, but Thermidorean policy was directed more at the bourgeoisie and the sons of property-owners than at the illiterate peasantry. The Thermidoreans were also influenced by financial considerations: they could not afford to do everything at once, and so they decided to give priority to the education of the élite.

The law which laid down the new structure of education was that of 3 Brumaire Year IV which had brought the Institute into existence. In shaping this law the Convention had abandoned some of its original proposals, which it considered too democratic and too costly. Under the terms of the new law one primary school was to be shared by two or more communes; most important of all, the teachers in these schools were no longer to be paid a salary, but would have to depend on fees paid by pupils and the possibility of compensation from the local commune. No mention was made of compulsory education, to which great importance had been attached in 1793. On the other hand, the law of 3 Brumaire Year IV made careful provisions for secondary and higher education, laying down a programme divided into three successive academic courses: first, from twelve to fourteen years, art, natural history and languages ancient and modern; then, from fourteen to sixteen years, the sciences (mathematics, physics and chemistry); finally, from sixteen years upwards, what the text of the law described as 'general grammar', based on a theory of language and a system of logic permeated with the 'Sensationalist' philosophy of the ideologues, and also literature, history (including geography) and law. Courses were optional and in theory were financed by the department; teachers were appointed from candidates approved by an educational board. Though it was doubtless too liberal, this system introduced a series of admirable innovations into French education, embodying many eighteenth-century cultural ideals – secularisation, the promotion of the sciences, the supremacy of French over the classical languages, and the study of philosophy.

Laplace, mathematician and astronomer, became professor of mathematics at the École Royale Militaire at the age of 20 years.

Above the secondary schools was a whole network of institutions of higher education which also owed their existence to the Thermidoreans of the Convention, and where specialists were trained and research carried out: the Conservatory of Arts and Crafts; the School of Public Works for the army and navy and the maintenance of roads and bridges, later to be renamed the Polytechnic; three schools of medicine, at Paris, Lyons and Montpellier; the École Normale Supérieure for the training of teachers; the School of Oriental Languages, the Conservatory of Music, the Museum of French Monuments, the Natural History Museum and the Observatory. This educational system, with the Institute as its apex, was undoubtedly too concentrated in Paris, and was at the same time incomplete, since there was no provision for literature and many of the sciences above the 'central schools', which had replaced the colleges run by the Jesuits and Oratorians under the Old Regime. But the subsequent history of so many of the institutions of higher education set up in 1794–5 is proof enough of the achievement of the Thermidoreans.

When the Thermidoreans became the rulers of the Directory they were confronted with the task of putting their own laws into effect. The development of primary education had already been jeopardised by their own reluctance to introduce major reforms at this level. Teachers in primary schools were poorly paid and often of mediocre quality, and there were not enough of them; as education was not compulsory the teachers were at the mercy of parents, since they depended on fees for their remuneration. The peasants preferred to do as they had always done, keeping their children at home to help on the farm. In any case, what was the point in sending children to schools where they would no longer be taught the catechism and be prepared for their first communion? Many of the private schools had managed to survive and were able to offer the traditional kind of education that the peasants wanted. Consequently, the Directory, lacking both money and the courage of its convictions, found the general public largely indifferent to its educational reforms. It was only after 18 Fructidor, when the government started persecuting the private schools, that the reforms showed any sign of producing the desired effect. Even then, attendance at state schools does not appear to have increased greatly. In the department of Sarthe, for instance, many teachers preferred to close their schools rather than take the oath professing hatred of royalty or the oath to the new religion; but they often continued their work secretly, perpetuating the old faith and the monarchist ideal among their pupils.

In each department of France, however, 'central schools' were set up in accordance with the law of 24 February 1795. There were three of these schools in Paris: in the Place du Panthéon, in the buildings of what is now the Lycée Henri-iv, in the Rue Saint-Antoine where the Lycée Charlemagne now stands, and in the former Collège des Quatre-Nations. By the end of the period of the Directory these three schools had a total of about one thousand pupils, which gives an idea of the narrowness of the basis of selection. Many illustrious men taught in the 'central schools': Cuvier, Vauquelin and Fontanes all taught in Paris, for example. But the new system proved to be too liberal and too ambitious; many pupils chose to take only one course and the majority, instead of respecting the intended sequence of three courses, each of two years, opted for either science or arts and in so doing set the pattern for the 'great divide' of modern times. Moreover, the level of instruction was often too high for a student population that was given too much freedom and was of varying academic achievement

and ability. Thus the Councils of the Directory were anxious to make
the 'central schools' into genuinely secondary establishments by setting
up above them five *lycées* and a number of schools of medicine, which
would have the effect of decentralising higher education (originally,
the *école centrale* had been half-way between the modern *école secondaire*
and *école supérieure*). As in many other fields, the Councils were paving
the way for the reforms of the Consulate and the Empire.

A section of bourgeois youth, especially girls, continued to attend
private secondary schools or were instructed by traditionally-minded
tutors. In the upper reaches of society many heads of families who
themselves read Voltaire wanted both their wives and their children
to have the moral support of the old religious certitudes. But the educational achievement of the Thermidoreans was nonetheless revolutionary. The state had broken the Church's monopoly of education,
the way had been opened up for modern methods of research, and the
sciences and the scientific spirit were being cultivated; it mattered
little that the new system of education failed to achieve its immediate
purpose and to save the government of the day, for it had provided
bourgeois France with lasting foundations of a different order.

THE ARTS

The official music of the Directory was represented almost solely by
the *Marseillaise* and the *Chant du départ*; although the inspiration that
had produced them had dried up, these songs still evoked a deep

The ball at the Opéra. During the Directory themes from classical mythology were
popular at the Opéra. Barras, Mme Tallien and Bonaparte were often to be seen
there.

response among the people of France at the great public festivals of the period. Opera was also performed regularly, combining themes of classical mythology and republican patriotism: in 1797 Boieldieu's *l'Heureuse Nouvelle* celebrated the treaty of Campo Formio.

But the musical activity of the Directory was centred in the concerts that were given all over Paris. There was nothing solemn about these occasions. People flocked in their thousands to hear sentimental ballads performed at the Concert Marbeuf, the Concert Prévost, the Concert des Tuileries, the Concert de la République and the Concert de l'Odéon. The most fashionable of all was the Concert Feydeau, described by one of the Goncourt brothers as 'the Field of the Cloth of Gold of the Directory'. This was the great rendezvous for the cream of society, the place where one had to be seen and which provided the talking-point for the following day. Here Garat, the inimitable exponent of *amoroso cantabile*, reigned supreme as the king of Parisian society. One morning in Pluviôse Year III a minor Parisian journal represented this great star as saying:

O my tutelary divinity! All men complain of their lot, but I beg you not to alter mine one whit. I am surrounded by pleasure and favours, everyone wants me and I cannot resist them. They idolise me and I do nothing to discourage them; my clothes, my conversation and my demeanour set the fashion in society. A song from me is an event, a chromatic cadence is the news of the day, and it is a public calamity if my voice is hoarse and I cannot sing. . . .

The cult of the 'star' is not peculiar to the twentieth century.

In the evenings, when the society of the Directory was not dancing or going to concerts, it went to the theatre. Public places were more suitable than the salons for gathering in large numbers, and playgoing proved so popular that the world of the theatre became an industry in its own right with its own class of speculators. Theatres multiplied so rapidly that the Councils grew uneasy; but they had no reason to be afraid, for nothing of importance was taking place on the stages of Paris. The crowds who thronged into the pits, which the aristocracy had once occupied, were mainly interested in seeing famous actors and actresses of the Old Regime, like Contat and Raucourt, or Talma and Mlle Lange, who represented the new France. The public lives of actors and actresses had become part of the social gossip of the times, setting an example to a society that was already obsessed with pleasure-seeking.

The plays that were performed had changed less than the audiences. The tyranny of classical aesthetics, which had been so evident throughout the revolutionary period, was a long-established feature of the Parisian theatre, but it had gathered momentum with the cult which Thermidorean society devoted to the world of antiquity in general.

The Return of Marcus Sextus by Guérin. The lines of the dead woman and the mourning husband form a symbolic cross. This painting, which some interpreted as an allusion to the return of the emigrés, was a great attraction at the 'Salon' (exhibition) of 1799.

Tragedy still reigned supreme, with Corneille and Racine, Voltaire and Crebillon, and a host of third-rate imitators who aped the great dramatists. Legouvé was hailed as another Racine, Arnault as another Corneille, and the young Lemercier as another Aeschylus. The society which had received its classical education from the Jesuits, and which alone could have seen the hollowness of the new writers, was no longer there to form a true comparison.

Like the ladies of the new society, draped in their classical robes, the so-called 'tragedians' of the Directory were desperately trying to resurrect ancient modes in an attempt to conceal their own mediocrity. However, the most popular forms of diversion during the Directory were the vaudeville, the crude farces at the Théâtre Montansier or

353

Above and opposite: Monsieur and Madame Anthony and their children, painted by Prud'hon. By combining the neo-classical elegance of the eighteenth century with the subjectivity of nineteenth-century Romanticism, Prud'hon provided a link between the two movements.

the melodramas of Pixérécourt, which provided three hours of spine-chilling entertainment: behind the barren façade of neo-classicism, which no longer held any real appeal for theatre-goers, the romantic drama of the nineteenth century already existed in embryo.

Although the Revolution is regarded by Frenchmen as the great turning-point in the history of their country, dividing ancient and modern France, it did not disrupt the continuity of artistic life: the neo-classical style, which eventually smothered the baroque and rococo styles and blossomed as the Directory style, dates back to the reigns of Louis xv and Louis xvi. Ledoux, Boullée and Houdon had all undertaken their most important work before 1789, and in 1784 David had

completed in Rome the *Oath of the Horatii*, which was to be the manifesto of the new school of painting.

The novelty of the new school lay not so much in using subjects borrowed from antiquity – baroque art had also frequently treated classical themes – as in its concern with line, dramatic composition and the didactic ideal so dear to the century of Enlightenment. The subjects taken from antiquity were no longer ornamental, but a part of living experience: eighteenth-century France felt a close affinity to Roman virtue and reproduced countless triumphal arches, rotundas, peristyles and curule chairs. This flowering of Latin culture, absorbed in the colleges of France, no doubt marked an attempt to find a substitute for a religion that was being practised by fewer and fewer people; churches were even turned into pagan temples. The events of 1789 were to strengthen these links with the world of antiquity, as is illustrated by the political career of David: revolutionary France

355

imagined itself to be reliving Roman history, from which it borrowed its rhetoric, its festivals, its titles and its décor. The Tennis Court Oath was an echo of the oath of the Horatii as depicted by David, and in the Convention, Girondins, Montagnards and Thermidoreans all in their turn invoked the memory of Brutus, the great advocate of liberty.

The Directory, less heroic than the earlier periods of the Revolution, was at the same time less exclusively Roman in its taste, looking for inspiration to the arts of other ancient cultures, and in particular those of Greece and Egypt. Imitating Greek art, the neo-classical pictorial style sought purity by restricting itself to single lines. It was in this atmosphere of rigid extremism that the young Ingres served his apprenticeship, beginning his long career in 1800. David, the great master, developed along with the younger artists: in contrast with the Roman style of the *Oath of the Horatii* he painted the *Sabine Women* (1796) in his Greek style, still anxious to rid his art of any trace of artifice and virtuosity. But the artists of the neo-classical school extended their horizons beyond the boundaries of the ancient world; the return to calmer times encouraged the kind of intimate subjects dear to Louis Boilly and brought a revival of portrait-painting and the romantic melancholy of Prud'hon. David's *M. and Mme Sériziat* and Prud'hon's *M. and Mme Anthony* were the new heroes of an old *genre*: they were far removed from the old aristocrats who had seemed imprisoned in the consciousness of their own superiority, and whose complacency had been mirrored in their portraits; the subjects painted by David and Prud'hon seemed to be fully aware of the outside world and prepared to assume responsibility for the great upheaval brought about by the Revolution. A barrier had been lifted in human relationships and within individual consciences.

In the field of architecture the Revolution had destroyed more than it had built, despite the efforts of the Committee of Education and its commission towards the preservation of national monuments. Building began again under the Directory, but styles remained dominated by the last generation of the architects of the Old Regime, men like Ledoux, Boullée, Bélanger and Lequeu. In their building projects, which were not always realised, these architects aspired to create the kind of city that had formed the background to David's *Sabine Women*: they showed the same preference for massiveness, bareness and simple geometrical forms; for them the house and city of antiquity represented the ideal of Rousseau's Utopia. But inevitably the architecture of the Directory remained essentially theoretical, since its exponents did not have sufficient opportunity to put their ideals into practice.

During the Directory the interiors of houses underwent a major transformation, as the revival of social life and its refinements led to a

In architecture the grandeur of ancient Rome and Greece was recalled, as is shown in Bélanger's design for the Théâtre des Arts, which was never actually built.

new interest in decoration, furniture and fashion. But, once again, the Directory had not broken its links with the last years of the Old Regime, when David had returned from Rome with his notebooks filled with sketches of ancient chairs, tables and candelabra and had reproduced these objects in Paris so that he could use them as models in painting *Brutus* and *Paris and Helen*. What has come to be known as the 'Directory style' in fact originated in the years between 1785 and 1790 when Bélanger, Dugourc and Jacob produced their little 'Pompeian' bas-reliefs, their delicate geometric inlays and bronze appliqués, and the colonnettes which Percier and Fontaine imitated in profusion in the last years of the century. Throughout the Directory period David was the artist responsible for setting the fashion, in furniture and ornaments, in stage décor and in clothes.

In its artistic life the new bourgeois France, while continuing the traditions of the last years of the Old Regime, developed freely and with less vulgarity than has sometimes been supposed. The old stultifying monopoly of the royal academies was demolished and the creation of the Institute made the plastic arts an integral part of intellectual progress. More important still, the museum was invented at this period, giving the public the opportunity to discover for itself the history of art. Since 1791 the Louvre had been exhibiting pictures

357

which the state had obtained by seizing the collections owned by the king, the nobility and the clergy, and to these were soon to be added the masterpieces pillaged in Italy in 1796–7. In 1795 the painter Alexandre Lenoir, who was head of the commission for the preservation of national monuments, succeeded in having the Museum of French Monuments set up; this was the first museum of medieval and Renaissance sculpture in Europe and was organised on principles of chronological classification that set the pattern for the modern museum system.

THE NEW RELIGION AND THE POPULAR FESTIVALS

In the Thermidorean period the French clergy were torn by dissensions. The schism of 1791 between 'juring' and 'non-juring' priests (i.e. those who agreed to take the oath of loyalty to the new Constitution and those who refused) had far-reaching consequences. Juring priests were themselves divided into several different categories: those who had not accepted any new office, those who had taken the opportunity to advance their careers during the Revolution, those who had retracted and those who had married – in fact a whole new clergy, some of whom had been ordained secretly by non-juring bishops and the others who had been ordained by 'constitutional' bishops. By 1795 the oath of 1791 had little meaning, since Church and State had been separated by the Convention; but the clergy were still confronted with what was basically the same choice, as they were requested to declare their submission to the laws of the Republic.

The relaxation of political tensions that followed the Terror was accompanied by a revival of Catholic worship. The local acts of violence committed by the *sans-culotte* dechristianisers had failed to stifle the traditional forms of religious sentiment so deeply embedded in the past; moreover, as politics and religion were always inextricably bound up with one another during the Revolution, the decline of Jacobinism had resulted in the reopening of many churches. But this did not weaken the position of the juring or constitutional clergy; on the contrary, the latter believed the time was now ripe for the organisation of a new Church of France on a permanent basis.

In Paris the Abbé Émery of Saint-Sulpice was the guiding force behind a movement that broadcast its propaganda through *les Annales religieuses*. At the national level the Bishop Grégoire took the initiative in revivifying the Constitutional Church in March 1795 when he joined a number of his colleagues in signing a pastoral letter which urged the reorganisation of the dioceses. After paying token respect to Rome the text of the letter professed loyalty to the Republic, but at the same time condemned the marriage of priests and divorce; it proposed that all unworthy priests be excluded from the ministry, that new priests be elected to vacant offices and that each diocese be administered democratically by the bishop and his clergy jointly. These ideas were not new, for they bore traces of the two great currents of thought in the Church of eighteenth-century France: Gallicanism, which aimed to reduce Rome to a purely honorary primacy and to transfer real power to the national Churches, and Jansenism with its Richerist overtones, which demanded that a clerical democracy be established by promoting the lower clergy. It was doubtless no mere coincidence that so many constitutional bishops – such as Le Coz, bishop of Rennes – had Jansenist sympathies.

However, the movement appeared to be supported by only a minority. It did not win over enough priests, and its following among the laity was even smaller. The constitutional bishop of Toulouse – who admittedly controlled a diocese where Jacobinism and persecution were especially strong – estimates that sixty out of a hundred Catholics were against the Constitutional Church, and that twenty-five of the remaining forty were apostates who eventually tended to side with the rebels, which left a mere fifteen per cent of the faithful supporting the official clergy. The Pope in Rome, the pretender to the throne and the emigré bishops in London all maintained their attitude of hostility, and in France the rebel clergy were widening the rift between themselves and the constitutional clergy. According to the directives issued by the bishop of Boulogne, the purchase of national property was invalid, tithes were still payable and appointments of juring priests were null and void – in other words, the Republic had put itself outside the law of the Catholic Church. But this intransigent attitude was widespread only in those regions where civil war and the Chouan movement prevailed. In the country as a whole its effect was to bring uncertainty to the individual conscience by casting doubt on the validity of the sacraments of the Constitutional Church. Public opinion was probably more concerned to see the Church reunited than to see one side defeating the other.

But the Thermidoreans who ruled in the Directory had no desire to see the religious issue solved by reconciliation; most of them remained anti-clerical, hostile to both the Papacy and the clergy and firm believers in the emergency laws of the Terror. In the later part of 1796, after the suppression of the Babeuf conspiracy, Carnot used his influence to relax the laws against refractory priests and outlined a plan for a compromise with Rome, thereby giving Grégoire a chance to advance the claims of the Constitutional Church, which held a council in 1797. But the 'triumvirs' reacted against this policy in the *coup d'état* of 18 Fructidor.

The anti-clericalism of the Directory stemmed directly from the philosophy of the Enlightenment: in other words, hostility was directed not only at priests and the temporal organisation of the Church, but against revealed religion itself. This essentially bourgeois anti-clericalism coincided with the current of popular feeling which had inspired the *sans-culotte* dechristianisation movement of 1793. Thus the bourgeoisie found an ally which hardly existed under the Old Regime, except possibly in the form of the popular Jansenism of 1730–60. But it is not known how far popular anti-clericalism extended, or what were its social and geographical boundaries. In the late eighteenth century this movement, which was to have such a profound effect on the large towns and some of the rural areas of modern France, was very much a minority movement, even in the towns. Nevertheless, while a large section of bourgeois opinion returned to the traditional Church, a counter-current of anti-clericalism was beginning to gather momentum among the working classes.

This movement also helps to explain why the French Revolution, which was becoming more and more anti-Catholic, never ceased to be profoundly religious. As the heir to kings who had ruled France by divine right, the Revolution was passionately concerned to found the new order on some form of substitute liturgy and ritual, exemplified by the cults to the goddess of Reason and the Supreme Being. Having secularised society, it wanted to offer the people some other outlet for religious feeling that would provide the foundations for public morality and good citizenship. The hard, efficient world of bourgeois France was born of the collective myth of the 'ideal city', an expression commonly used in European culture since the Renaissance to exorcise the 'fanaticism' and 'superstition' of the past.

Freemasonry, one of the breeding grounds of this cultural myth, began to flourish once again under the Directory. The two great authorities of freemasonry, the Grand Orient and the Grand Lodge, had been suspect during the Terror because of their oligarchic structure, but they were now able to develop more freely and to prepare themselves for the great role they were to play during the Empire. However, the Directory was also somewhat suspicious of freemasonry and its allegedly royalist tendencies, and so preferred to give its support to a new cult whose patron was one of their number, La Révellière. The professed principles of the cult were similar to those of the majority of masonic lodges: the new cult was given the title of 'theophilanthropy'. The opening ceremony took place on 26 Nivôse Year IV (15 January 1797) on the Rue Saint-Denis, in a room decorated with tapestries and flowers, and consisted of edifying speeches and readings intended to open men's hearts to the harmony of nature. The eighteenth-century worship of nature found new expression in

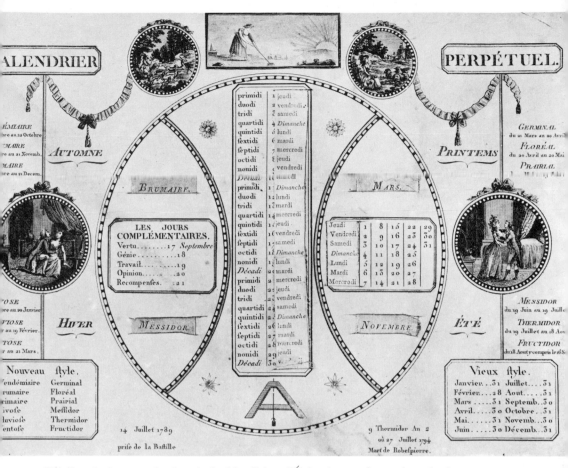

The Revolutionary calendar, devised by Fabre d'Églantine. 22 September, the date of the proclamation of the Republic, marked the first day of the year.

theophilanthropy, which numbered among its adherents Bernardin de Saint-Pierre, Dupont de Nemours, Marie-Joseph Chénier and Servan; but the cult also attracted former dechristianisers of 1793, men like Rossignol and David. La Révellière would have liked to see theophilanthropy become the state religion; but, either because they could not forget Robespierre's cult of the Supreme Being, or because they were afraid of upsetting atheists, both the Directory and the Councils opposed the idea, with the result that the cult attracted only moderate support. Loyalty to the Revolution, to its calendar and festivals, was the regime's chief weapon against Catholicism and its link with popular anti-clericalism.

In Year VII the *décadi* – the new Sunday of the 'decade', the ten-day week of the Republican calendar – became the day on which a new religious service was celebrated: the administrators of the cantons assembled the local population round the Altar of the Fatherland, read out the laws of the Republic and commented on them, and then delivered a sermon on civic virtue to the accompaniment of the organ and patriotic songs. Often this ceremony, with its symbolically pastoral trappings, was held in the middle of the church, the Altar of the Fatherland taking the place of the church's own altar, as if to mark the passing from superstition to enlightenment. On the *décadi* the local priest had to celebrate Mass at dawn and before making way for the priests of the Republic had to remove or veil all external signs of the Catholic faith; he also often had to let the theophilanthropists use his church. Such a state of affairs was hardly likely to favour the cause of the Constitutional Church.

In 1797, at the instigation of the Directory and a number of local authorities, the Republican calendar and its ten-day week were imposed more rigidly than ever. Not only on religious belief but the habits of fifteen centuries were being upset: the dates of local fairs and markets and the dates for hiring labour and for the expiry of leases had to be changed, making the slightest act of peasant life unnecessarily complicated. People had to abstain from work on the *décadi*, and those who did not were guilty of 'incivism', but Sunday was still observed as a day of rest. The regime was interfering with a tradition as old as France itself, and the Republican cult suffered the backlash of popular resentment.

The Directory was more successful with the political festivals it organised to commemorate the great events of the Revolution or the various aspects of nature: 14 July, 22 September, 9 Thermidor (the regime had no wish to deny its own origins) and 10 Messidor (28 June), when the Festival of Agriculture was held.

The revival which took place in the Church during the Consulate is sufficient proof that the Directory failed in its anti-Catholic campaign. Nevertheless, its inevitable failure and the tyrannical methods employed should not be allowed to conceal the importance of this period in the religious history of France. The anti-clericalism of the Directory was to have a more lasting influence on the religious climate of modern France than either the dechristianisation movement of the *sans-culottes* or Robespierre's Republic of Virtue.

12

THE END OF THE REGIME

The key to the drama of the Directory is to be found in the very nature of its origins. The men who had toppled Robespierre and destroyed the Terror were committed to restoring democracy and legality to the government of France; but at the same time they were determined to bring the great revolutionary adventure to completion and, in their challenge to the rest of Europe, to organise a society with neither king nor nobility. These two aspirations were totally irreconcilable, all the more so because the men who had drafted the Constitution of Year III (1795), true to the principles of the Enlightenment, had allowed their democratic ideals to get the better of practical considerations. The new legislature and executive, their powers now separated, tended to act independently of one another and were both subject to annual elections, at which one-third of the Councils and one of the Directors were replaced. This meant in theory that electoral campaigns would become a semi-permanent feature of the political scene, but in fact the Republic, which could no longer resort to the guillotine and had as yet no tradition of its own to fall back on, did not dare offend the bourgeoisie it had chosen as its judge. In 1795 the two-thirds decrees and the repression of the royalist uprising of Vendémiaire had shown clearly that if the new regime was to survive it would have to remain under the control of the men who had brought it into being; in other words, free electoral competition was out of the question. The Republic now depended for its existence not on Virtue and Terror, but on the determination of the politicians of the Revolution to perpetuate their own powers and on military conquest. The advent of a loi générale, one of the great dreams of the century, had necessarily to be postponed until more 'enlightened' times.

The politicians who undertook the defence of the Republic came to be known by the curious names of the revolutionary calendar: the Thermidoreans became the Vendémiaireans, then the Fructidoreans. Barras had proved his inimitable mastery of political manoeuvre in each of the great crises of Thermidor, Vendé-

miaire and Fructidor. But the regime found its burden a heavy one. By constantly denying its origins it was undermining its own authority. The coup *of 18 Fructidor had not made the regime the army's prisoner: after all, Hoche and Bonaparte had merely answered the civil power's call for intervention; Hoche was now dead and Bonaparte was leaving for Egypt. But the new strength that the Directory derived from the intervention of the army tended to reduce the powers of the legislative Councils: in the year following the* coup *the results of the elections were 'corrected' in Floréal and over a hundred allegedly 'Jacobin' deputies were arbitrarily deprived of the office to which they had just been elected. Even the useful reforms that had been introduced in the meantime, such as the reorganisation of the national finances, were discredited along with the regime. The Directory, indifferent to the opinions of the populace, had finally lost that minimum of respect among the ruling classes which is the prerequisite for the survival of any representative regime.*

The Directory could not, however, be accused of failure to act. While it pursued its policy of revolutionary expansionism abroad, at home it vigorously set about uprooting the Anglo-royalist conspiracy, reintroducing the Terror's laws against emigrés, persecuting priests and deporting both to Guiana or to the prison-ships of Oléron. It went further than the Convention of Year II in its anti-Catholicism; and in its concern to give France a substitute religion helped to promote theophilanthropy, instituted more and more commemorative festivals and, above all, systematically organised the decadal cult. But, in professing its mighty ambition to change mankind, the Directory merely strengthened the bonds uniting its two great enemies, royalism and the Church, bonds which already had the advantage of fifteen centuries of history behind them; at the same time it was seen to be representative only of a bourgeois oligarchy that was daily becoming more sectarian and divided in its aims.

The 'triumvirs' had been persuaded to unite in organising the coup d'état *of Fructidor only by the urgency of the royalist threat. After Carnot had fled and Barthélemy had been deported, the two new Directors, François de Neufchâteau (replaced in the spring of 1798 by Treilhard) and Merlin, added nothing to the declining prestige of the executive; Merlin assumed Carnot's role and was content to observe the Jacobins closely, while his colleagues continued to deport royalists. The two pillars of the Directory, Reubell and Barras, grew increasingly jealous of each other. Barras seemed to be at the height of his power after his role in the events of 18 Fructidor, but he was becoming ever more obsessed with money and pleasure. The very consistency of his personal successes in Thermidor, Vendémiaire and Fructidor no doubt encouraged him to think that, despite his laziness and his failure to devote his energies wholeheartedly to politics, he would always be able* in extremis *to put the Republic back on course. As he waited for the next crisis to occur he sat back and enjoyed his power, listening wearily to all those who came to him with ideas for rectifying the Constitution: was not their clamouring in itself proof that he would be indispensable when the moment of danger came? But Barras was now too discredited to be able to lead a regeneration of the*

Republic. His role was taken over by another veteran of the Revolution, Sieyès, the man who helped to set the Revolution in motion and who was now to bring it to its conclusion. This former 'Conventionnel' and regicide had the immense advantage of belonging to the Thermidorean syndicate without having been tainted by the discredit that had fallen on the regime, which he had denounced in advance in 1795. The Council of Elders approved his appointment as a Director and he replaced his enemy Reubell in the spring of 1799. Sieyès' arrival in the Directory put an end to the already weakened tyranny of the executive. The Councils acquired a new authority and confidence, stimulated by the results of the latest annual elections, which had once again seen the overwhelming defeat of pro-government candidates. In the spring of 1799 they insisted on the resignations of Treilhard, Merlin and La Révellière-Lépeaux, who had come to be regarded as the symbols of the corruption and abuse of power of the Fructidoreans. Sieyès had supported the Councils in their action – in fact he may well have put the idea into their heads; in place of the three Directors, who would have proved irksome colleagues, he chose a close friend, Roger Ducos, and two insignificant republicans, Gohier and Moulin. Barras, the only survivor of the old Directory, had sacrificed his colleagues to save himself; this was tantamount to resignation, which meant that Sieyès would have a free hand. In Prairial Sieyès was the central figure in the great swell of anti-government protest which united within its ranks generals, the small Bonapartist faction, the neo-Jacobins and the 'revisionists' of the Councils and the Institute.

The precarious state of the regime was evident throughout the provincial administration, which for years had been suffering the repercussions of instability in Paris. The Directory's commissioners, who were appointed according to their political loyalties rather than for their ability and who were frequently moved around, found their authority declining rapidly; many of them had taken part in the Terror of Year II and after Fructidor revived the Jacobin tradition, more intent on harassing the public than governing it. Catholic and royalist disobedience was turning to anarchy. The Chouans felt that their great opportunity had come and were preparing a general insurrection in the west and the south; the public highways of France were infested with bandits who robbed travellers and terrorised the countryside; villagers lived in fear, more concerned with taking reprisals than trying to maintain civil order.

The Continental war had resumed its course and the defeats of spring 1799 added to the general panic. The Army of Germany was driven back to the Rhine and Italy was evacuated as far as Piedmont. The territory of France was threatened once again, and the fear of foreign invasion led to a resurgence of Jacobinism. In the Council of Five Hundred the deputies of the majority indulged in the alarmist and melodramatic rhetoric that had typified the assemblies of the Convention during the Terror; the reintroduction of conscription, forced loans and the law of hostages revived memories of the dictatorship of the Committee of Public Safety. Once again political crisis in France had been aggravated by war.

Although the final struggle for power under the Directory might appear to have been a three-cornered contest amongst Jacobins, royalists and the men of Brumaire, there were in reality only two opposing camps. When Sieyès and the Bonaparte brothers carried out their successful assault on the Council of Five Hundred, Jacobinism had already been annihilated by the French military victories of September.

The key to the drama of Jacobinism in Year VII lay in its preoccupation with past memories rather than present realities. It was all very well for the deputies to plead the dangers of foreign invasion in justification of repressive measures at home: they lacked the popular support of the suburbs which had been the main-stay of Jacobinism in Year II. Twice the Republic had succeeded in disarming the Parisian sans-culottes *in defence of property-ownership – first in Year III, then against Babeuf. These two defeats had delivered a grave blow to the revolutionary activity of the Jacobin movement. The good harvests of the following years and the lowering of prices that resulted from deflation deprived the movement of what little life it still possessed, and the urban masses were content to watch impassively as the regime of the new wealthy class disintegrated.*

From this moment onwards Jacobinism had sought to establish itself in the positions of power, and had continued to provide inspiration for the left-wing elements in the administration of the Thermidorean Republic; the Jacobins in the Council of Five Hundred reflected the opinions of departmental commissioners and police officials. The pattern was even more marked in the army: the mass mobilisation of Year II, which provided the main strength of French military resources until the Jourdan decree of 1798, had drawn together the flower of patriot youth and had enabled young Jacobins to win their officer's epaulettes in the war against the monarchies of Europe. In 1799 the Jacobins, like Sieyès, were looking for a soldier to lead them. There was certainly no shortage of candidates, for Augereau and Jourdan, who were deputies in the Five Hundred, and Bernadotte, who was Minister of War, were all available and already active in politics. By the end of the Directory no faction was more closely associ-ated with the military than were the Jacobins; between his return from Egypt and the coup d'état *of 18 Brumaire Bonaparte was to enjoy a specially favoured position among them.*

In the end the Jacobins were more concerned to conserve and consolidate than to conquer new ground. Like Barras, Sieyès and Bonaparte himself, they were revolutionaries who had achieved their ambitions, usurping the name of 'Jacobin' with which frightened moderate opinion had branded them. In summer 1799 a ghost emerged from Jacobinism's past when Fouché was put in charge of police. Although Fouché was not taken completely into the confidence of the conspirators of Brumaire he sensed what was coming and made efforts to rally all the old terrorists to the cause. Summoning Bernadotte, he admonished him in these words: 'Imbecile! Where do you think you are going and just what are you trying to do? In '93 we had everything to gain. . . . Now that we have achieved what we wanted and stand only to lose it all, why carry on?' Fouché realised that the image of Jacobinism was feared by the public, that it divided and weakened the revolutionary camp and at the same time provided the counter-revolution with easy propaganda. Indeed, though the Council of Five Hundred seemed preoccupied with the remedies of the past in its constant warnings about 'public safety', its anxiety was based on a true assessment of the situation: never had the danger of a royalist restoration been so great.

All factors seemed to favour a restoration: the nation's longing to see the end of foreign and civil war, the crisis of authority in France and the general contempt into which the government had fallen, the fears aroused by the reintroduction of forced loans and the law of hostages, and the fact that Bonaparte was away in Egypt. Public opinion turned in desperation to monarchy, an institution fashioned by centuries of history, as the only solution to the country's troubles; in wishing to entrust the welfare of the nation to a single person the people of France were not looking for an emperor, but were simply reverting to the old monarchic tradition. A royalist agent, Hyde de Neuville, wrote: 'There were several great moments during the Revolution when there seemed to be every chance of a restoration of legitimate authority in France, but surely circumstances were never more favourable than during the period which preceded the downfall of the Directory and the usurpation of Bonaparte.' While it is true that the political situation was more favourable to royalism than to a Jacobin revival, the great strength of the Republic lay in the extraordinary feebleness of the royalist party, which had been undermined by the fanaticism of its agents, the stupidity of the princes and emigrés and its alliance with a foreign country. But the republicans were unaware of their adversary's weakness, imagining the royalists to be a much more powerful force than they were in reality. With the Chouans threatening Toulouse in August and capturing Le Mans and Nantes in October the royalist movement seemed to be gaining strength. All the more need, then, to act quickly.

Sieyès now made himself the champion of the Revolution, while Barras, his reputation shattered, abdicated responsibility and in his anxiety to save his own skin intrigued with all parties, even with the royalists. Sieyès, the former priest, elected deputy by the Third Estate of Paris, was the perfect symbol of the Revolution: contemptuous of the nobility, he was the theoretician of bourgeois supremacy and the inspiration behind the Estates-General, the Plain and the Fructidoreans. His priest's temperament had led him to indulge in the kind of cryptic political prophecy that had earned him a reputation unique among revolutionary politicians. In Year VII his relentless activity brought its reward, and Sieyès undertook the task of finally establishing the Revolution on rational foundations. It was his intention to widen the limits of the Thermidorean party to include all the bourgeoisie, to gather all the revolutionary elements of the past ten years around a Constitution that would strengthen the executive and at the same time safeguard the liberties of individuals and the sacred rights of property-owners. Was Sieyès perhaps thinking in terms of a constitutional monarchy as a means of uniting the France of the Feuillants and the France of the Thermidoreans? This is not altogether impossible, considering the political situation in Year VII and the discredit into which the Republic had fallen. His enemies accused him of supporting the Duc d'Orléans and also of making approaches to a German prince in Berlin, where he was the Directory's ambassador. Certainly, a constitutional monarch could easily have been substituted for the 'Grand Elector' whom Sieyès proposed to make head of the executive in his new Constitution. But, if in fact Sieyès was thinking on such lines, he was nonetheless bitterly opposed to every aspect of the Old Regime. This becomes clear enough when one considers the names of the early Brumaireans, the men of spring 1799 – Daunou, Marie-Joseph Chénier, Cambacérès, Benjamin Constant, Talleyrand, all protégés of Barras, members of the Institute or former 'Conventionnels': these were the men who had helped to bring about the coup d'état *of 18 Fructidor, repudiating ultra-royalism, aristocracy and clergy, and who wanted either a moderate Republic or a constitutional monarchy.*

However, the republican conspiracy needed the support of the army in order to impose itself on the regime, and it was here that the real drama of Brumaire lay: Sieyès could not count on the Jacobin generals, who were the prisoners of a myth and perversely sectarian in their political views; he also wished to avoid having as partners men of excessive ambition who might well be tempted to reach for too much power. He approached Joubert, who agreed to join him but was killed at Novi in August. After the victories of Vendémiaire had restored order and destroyed the Jacobin menace, he made approaches to Moreau, but on the same day in October 1799 Paris learned of Bonaparte's return. The landing at Fréjus introduced a new factor into the political situation which Sieyès had not anticipated: a popular hero had appeared on the scene. The monarchic principle was thus reincarnated in the person of the minor Corsican noble who surreptitiously assumed the role of saviour formerly assigned to the king of France. The part fitted him perfectly and he acted it magnificently, challenging the factions and establishing himself straight away as the conciliator and judge of the new democratic France, a second Henri IV. Bonaparte dominated his associates right from the beginning, for he represented the people in the world of the notables.

Brumaire was therefore neither a victory of the bourgeoisie over the Jacobins, nor a victory of the army over the Thermidoreans. It was a conspiracy hatched by the protagonists of the Revolution to protect the conquests they had made in the defeat of the Old Regime; but at the very last moment a Caesar had intervened when everyone was looking for a Louis-Philippe.

THE TERROR OF FRUCTIDOR

In the days following the *coup d'état* of 18 Fructidor the immediate task of the Councils was to replace Barthélemy and Carnot, the two Directors who had been 'purged'. The Elders opted for two ministers, Merlin de Douai and François de Neufchâteau, who obtained marginally greater support than Masséna and Augereau, the military candidates backed by the Five Hundred. The Elders' ingratitude upset Augereau in particular, for he had been counting on being made a Director as a reward for having supported the *coup*; instead he was sent to take command of the Army of Germany in place of Hoche, who had just died. The purge of the executive involved a large number of its agents; the decree of 19 Fructidor gave the Directory the power to appoint officials and hundreds of them were replaced, though the new administrators were not always obeyed, particularly in the departments of western France.

The new Directory was especially anxious to put into effect the terrorist decrees of 19 and 22 Fructidor, aimed primarily at emigrés. Those who had returned to France were obliged to leave within fifteen days under pain of death; military commissions set up to hunt down emigrés executed their victims indiscriminately, whether they were royalist conspirators or simply nobles who had come back home. From autumn 1797 to spring 1799 one hundred and sixty emigrés were sentenced to death in Paris, fifty-six in Toulon and twenty-four in Marseille. Relatives of emigrés remained subject to the law of 3 Brumaire Year IV.

At one stage Sieyès, who was already a powerful influence behind the scenes, was urging the government to go even further. In his Memoirs La Révellière states that the former spokesman of the Third Estate, still consumed with hatred for the nobility, proposed that the Directors should expel all nobles from France. When La Révelliére and Reubell objected, Sieyès put his proposal to Boulay, who defended it to the Five Hundred on 25 Vendémiaire (16 October 1797). But the suggestion that the entire nobility (except of course those who had rallied to the Republic, like Barras) should be banished from France angered the centre and Boulay withdrew his motion. In November the Councils passed a less radical motion depriving all nobles of their rights as citizens, though the new law did not apply in the case of a noble who was able to obtain 'naturalisation' in the same way as a foreigner; however, no list of exceptions was ever drawn up and so the law was never to be put into effect.

The second category to be affected by the terrorist laws of Fructidor was the clergy. The decrees of the Montagnard Convention had put many priests on the same footing as emigrés. Those who had returned since 9 Thermidor were subject to the same penalty – i.e. sentence of death unless they left France within fifteen days. About forty such priests were executed. With regard to the rest, the juridical basis of persecution was somewhat vague since the text of the law of 19 Fructidor appeared to restore the laws of 1792-3 against refractory priests, although the Directory never actually admitted this; the death penalty for refractory priests was replaced by deportation to Guiana. The terrible measures of Fructidor affected all those priests already subject to the Montagnard decrees and, at the same time, all priests who, since the passing of those decrees, had refused to take the oath of 'hatred of royalty and anarchy', or who were simply suspected of 'incivism'. As always, the intensity of the persecution varied from one part of the country to another: in the department of Sarthe, between 18 Fructidor and 18 Brumaire, forty-five priests were arrested, one of them was executed, nineteen were deported and the rest were put in prison; in Côte-d'Or, on the other hand, none of the clergy was arrested. For Belgium, the Directory introduced a special decree ordering the deportation of the entire clergy.

Most of the victims of the terrorist laws managed, however, to flee the country or take refuge in the loyal rural areas. Only three ships left the islands of the Charentes for Guiana, and one of these was captured by the British; the other two took away two hundred and sixty-three French and Belgian priests, over half of whom were to die in Guiana. The rest of those sentenced to deportation – over a thousand in all – remained in the hulks at Ré and Oléron, where they lived in atrocious conditions.

The Terror of Fructidor also introduced a whole system of restrictive measures which called to mind the days of 1793: private houses were visited by the police, certain villages were systematically searched by the National Guard, mail was opened and informing was encouraged. The preventive arrest of suspects was common in many departmental administrations. Finally, the laws of 19 and 22 Fructidor gave the Directory complete control of the press. The royalist journals were suppressed and their editors, men like La Harpe and Fontanes, went into hiding. The others had to act very cautiously as they were at the mercy of the executive: on 17 December 1797, for instance, the Directory issued an order suppressing sixteen journals. Even the theatre was closely watched by the authorities.

The Terror of Fructidor, more limited and less bloody than the Terror of Year II, was operated solely by the government: the committees of the people played no part in it; this Terror was the result not so much of popular zeal as of the government's desire to destroy the royalist movement. In fact, the Directory was frustrating its own ends, for the political climate produced by its measures indubitably played an important part in alienating public opinion, and in particular Catholic opinion, from the Directory, thereby paving the way for its inglorious downfall. But in the short term the terrorist decrees of Fructidor certainly did succeed in removing the royalist menace. Royalist feeling remained strong in certain regions of France – in the south-east, for example – but conspiracies were no longer being planned from abroad, as had occurred before 18 Fructidor. Towards the end of 1797 the Chouan chiefs Puisaye, Frotté and Bourmont wrote to the Comte d'Artois telling him that he had been misled into believing that France was monarchist – it was merely discontented. The constitutional monarchists suffered an even more overwhelming defeat than the ultra-royalists. Dandré fled to Switzerland and the Philanthropic Institute was disbanded. Louis xviii (the Comte de Provence), driven out of Germany at the instigation of the government in Paris, sought asylum from the tsar and settled in Courland, where he was to remain for nine years.

POLITICAL INSTABILITY

Although the royalist threat, which was probably not as great as the republicans had imagined, was now demolished, the Terror of Fructidor had not solved France's problems; the survival of the regime had depended on a return to emergency legislation. The Councils had weakened themselves by submitting to the illegal curtailing of their powers. In theory the executive was master of France, though the five Directors were always divided amongst themselves: François de Neufchâteau was no more than an administrator, but Merlin de Douai assumed Carnot's old role and tried to rally the timid La Révellière to the camp of the *honnêtes gens*; Barras had given himself up entirely to pleasure and intrigue, leaving the energetic Reubell as the dominant figure in the Directory. Of the old ministers only Ramel was left, and apart from Talleyrand the new men had little stature. The authority of the executive had not benefited at all from the humiliation of the legislature.

This confused situation had already led to the first stages of a 'revisionist' campaign formed with the purpose of modifying the Constitution of Year III (1795). In his Memoirs Barras relates that various persons came to him suggesting that he should take over sole power; it is quite possible that Mme de Staël and Constant, who were very close to the Director at this time, were in favour of such a proposal, for Constant published a eulogy of Cromwell and Robespierre which stressed the value of a strong and stable executive. Sieyès, for his part, was beginning to make capital out of the hostility he had always shown to the Constitution of 1795, and was now putting himself forward as the indispensable reformer. Furthermore, the feebleness of the regime was very much in the mind of Bonaparte: in a letter to Talleyrand written only two weeks after the *coup d'état* of Frucidor, the conqueror of Italy submitted his own plan for strengthening the executive, asking Talleyrand to put his ideas confidentially to Sieyès. In December, when the Directory gave him a grand reception in Paris to celebrate Campo Formio, Bonaparte declared: 'When the happiness of the French people is established on better organic laws, the whole of Europe will be free.'

However, the immediate concern of politicians was the yearly elections: there were four hundred and thirty-seven seats to be filled, including those of the second half of the 'Conventionnels' re-elected in 1795. The government decided to take precautionary steps, and at the beginning of 1798 the deputies of the Councils voted themselves the right to ratify the election of their future colleagues and to appoint the new Director; in this way they were hoping to prevent the royalists from establishing themselves even more firmly in the Councils. François de Neufchâteau drew the lot of the retiring Director and returned to the Ministry of the Interior; he was replaced in the Directory by the former 'Conventionnel', Treilhard. Meanwhile, the Directory made its own careful administrative preparations for the elections. At the instigation of Merlin, who was particularly afraid of the Jacobins, it advised its supporters, many of them government officials, to engineer as many rival electoral assemblies as possible, so that the government could choose between two alternative deputies.

Merlin's assessment of the electoral situation proved to be the more accurate: the royalists, who had been persecuted constantly since Fructidor, tended to keep away from the electoral assemblies, and the supporters of the Directory found themselves having to contend chiefly with the left. A number of Jacobins managed to get themselves elected – among them the two Lindets and Barère – but the Directory persuaded the docile Councils to invalidate the elections of one hundred and six of them; the decree of 22 Floréal Year VI (11 May 1798) annulled outright the elections in eight departments, which were thereby deprived of parliamentary representation, ratified the elections of deputies chosen by rival assemblies in nineteen divisions, and made other arbitrary modifications to the results. The new intake of deputies had been largely hand-picked by the executive in a breach of legality that was perhaps even more serious than the *coup d'état* of Fructidor – this time the Directory could hardly plead the survival of the Republic in defence of its actions.

The regime certainly gained a precious year's respite by interfering with the elections, and was thus able to pursue its struggle against the royalists and to support the reforms of Ramel and François de Neufchâteau. But it was to find itself facing the electoral campaign of 1799 in much more difficult circumstances, complicated by the resumption of the war. The Jacobin deputies whose election had not been quashed by the decree of Floréal attacked the corruption and irresponsibility of the regime more and more violently. General Bonaparte's younger brother, Lucien, who had been elected deputy for Corsica the previous year, was beginning to make a name for himself. Moreover, these 'neo-Jacobins', who could not claim the support of the suburbs enjoyed by the original Jacobins, often had the support of ambitious army

officers: Augereau, Jourdan, Bernadotte, Joubert, Brune and
Masséna were all on bad terms with the Directory. The government
majority in the Councils was unhappy about its subjection to a dictatorial executive. 'Revisionism' was becoming increasingly fashionable.

The results of the 1799 elections demonstrated a general hostility
towards the Directory: out of the one hundred and forty-three candidates 'recommended' by the executive, only seventy-one were elected.
The Councils, yielding to public opinion, refused to ratify the election
of the deputies chosen by the rival assemblies. On 16 May, before the
new 'third' even took its seats, they had made their 'revisionist' intentions quite clear by electing Sieyès as a Director. The retiring Director,
whose name was decided as usual by drawing lots, was Reubell, one
of the last bastions of the Thermidorean Republic. The Five Hundred
had opted for General Lefebvre, who was supposed to be loyal to the
regime, but the Elders chose Sieyès instead, by one hundred and eighteen votes out of a total of two hundred and five. In electing Sieyès, the
Elders were anticipating their role in the *coup d'état* of 18 Brumaire for
his entry into the Directory marked the beginning of the crisis: the
chief conspirator had now become a member of the government he
was planning to overthrow.

For the Councils the hour of vengeance had come: the Directory's
unpopularity was being aggravated by French military defeats
abroad, for which the government inevitably became the scapegoat.
At the beginning of June, Sieyès returned from Berlin, where he had
been ambassador, and immediately established relations with the
parliamentary opposition, which was composed of Jacobins and moderate 'revisionists'; Lucien Bonaparte now became his constant com-
panion. Sieyès' first task was to expel the Directors that he did not
want as colleagues, so that he could impose his own authority on the
executive. It is not known whether Barras was taken into the conspiracy, but he certainly did not oppose its execution. On 17 June the
Councils annulled the election of Treilhard on the dubious pretext
that a full year had not elapsed between his departure from the Five
Hundred and his entry into the Directory. Treilhard gave way under
pressure from Sieyès and Barras. He was replaced by Gohier, an
honest but limited republican, who had been Minister of Justice under
the Convention. Then came the turn of La Révellière and Merlin;
violently attacked in the Councils and out-manoeuvred by Barras, the
two Directors eventually resigned on 30 Prairial (18 June). From the
lists submitted by the Five Hundred, the Elders chose in their place the
former 'Conventionnel' Roger Ducos and the most obscure of the
generals, Moulin, who was commander of the Army of the West.
Sieyès was sure of Ducos, but it was Barras who had insisted on
Moulin, who was a 'Jacobin'. The two men carried out a similar re-

shuffle in the ministries: Sieyès had Cambacérès appointed to the Interior; Barras chose the 'Jacobin' Bernadotte as Minister of War.

The *coup* of 30 Prairial, a pale reflection of 9 Thermidor, marked the victory of the legislature over the executive. In counteracting the decree of Floréal Year VI it was doubly effective, since it gave the Jacobins their revenge (the three new Directors had all suffered by the decree of Floréal) and at the same time left the Directory discredited and weakened: the survival of the Republic now depended only on Barras, whose influence was non-existent. Sieyès, the 'mole of the Revolution', had made a brilliant beginning in his plan to undermine the regime, but the generals had also gained by the humiliation of the civil authority: the reorganisation of 30 Prairial had finally given them control of the Ministry of War and the army. In fact, the *coup* represented the victory of all discontents, heralding the final collapse of the Directory; it marked the first stage in the battle for power which was to be decided in Brumaire.

In the course of Year VI a series of laws had been enacted in accordance with the programme of religious reform which La Révellière had initiated well before 18 Fructidor, and which, it was hoped, would replace Catholicism with a new religion designed to regenerate France by spreading Enlightenment and uprooting age-old superstitions from the consciences of the nation. Theophilanthropy, launched and encouraged by La Révellière, had found no response among the people. This esoteric, moralising cult bore the unmistakable stamp of its founder, a narrow-minded and somewhat ridiculous figure. The adherents of the cult had also been involved in a number of political skirmishes with the Directory.

During his term as a Director Merlin devoted himself to organising an official cult aimed at a much wider public and based on the Republican calendar: there were to be solemn celebrations on the anniversaries of all the great revolutionary events that had led to Thermidorean domination – the institution of the Republic, 9 Thermidor and 18 Fructidor, for example – and also, every ten days, the more ordinary celebration of the *décadi*, which was to be the new Sunday. In creating the decadal cult, the promoters of the decree of 13 Fructidor Year VI were hoping to replace the Mass with a service at which the citizens of France, led by their local officials, would render homage to the laws of the Republic.

Churches were renamed 'temples' and were now used for three different forms of worship: the traditional rites of the Constitutional Catholic Church, which was being restricted within ever narrower limits, theophilanthropy and the *décadi*, the only form of worship officially recognised by the state. Catholicism and theophilanthropy were tolerated only as private religions, and any attempt to hold pub-

The Directory's
policy of dechristian-
isation led to anti-
religious propaganda.
In this engraving the
priest drinks the
blood of the innocent
Christ and eats His
flesh.

lic services was penalised. In July 1796, for instance, the Parisian
police had the following report to make in connection with the revival
of 'priestly fanaticism':

> In view of the fact that, in defiance of article 13 of the law of 7 Vendémiaire
> Year IV, a number of citizens are known to have made public displays of an
> unauthorised religion by placing crosses, holy-water basins and other ritual
> objects around corpses laid out on the drives or in the gateways of their
> houses, the Central Bureau has advised the forty-eight police commissioners
> to ensure that the law is observed.

FINANCIAL REFORM

During the period from 18 Fructidor 1797 to the spring of 1799 the
Directory, subordinating the Councils to its own will and modifying
election results as it chose, held sole control of domestic affairs; it took
this opportunity to introduce a number of reforms that laid the foundations for the work of reconstruction undertaken during the Consulate.

Immediately after 18 Fructidor, as soon as the royalists' attempts at parliamentary obstruction had been thwarted, the Councils passed the great financial law of 9 Vendémiaire (30 September) 1797, which had been drafted by the minister Ramel. The government was anxious to redeem the public debt, which was a heavy burden on the Treasury, and therefore resorted to the well-tried expedient of selling the lands it had seized from the clergy and the nobility – the Revolution's eternal source of wealth: the bonds given to *rentiers* in repayment of their capital were to be valid for purchasing national lands. Ramel wanted to liquidate the whole of the debt by this method, but eventually it was decided to pay off only two-thirds. The remaining third was to be carried forward. Ramel's liquidating operation came to be known as the 'bankruptcy of the two-thirds' or the 'consolidated third'.

'Bankruptcy' was a not inappropriate description of the manoeuvre: apart from the fact that the Treasury was compelling the *rentier* to convert his capital into real estate, the bonds which were being issued for that purpose had to compete with many other forms of paper-bills, and in particular the warrants with which the government paid contractors. Moreover, when, at the beginning of Year VII, national property transactions became payable solely in currency, the capital represented by the 'two-thirds' bonds was reduced to between two and a half and five francs per hundred francs of their nominal value. The consolidated third, worth eighteen francs in Year VI, had dropped to half this amount by the following year. As interest was also paid in the

The financial crisis led to a reduction in the salaries of civil servants ('les employés'). Here they stand outside the *Bureau des Oppositions*, which has just rejected their petition.

form of bonds, the situation of *rentiers* remained highly precarious right up to the end of the Directory. In 1801 the return to the practice of paying interest in currency was welcomed as a sign that order had been restored to the French economy.

At least Ramel's financial operation helped to offset the government's budgetary expenditure of one hundred and sixty millions. It now remained to increase Treasury receipts, firstly by speeding up the inflow of taxes, which, since the beginning of the Revolution, had been a long and inefficient process. The law of 22 Brumaire Year VI (12 November 1797) set up revenue offices in all the departments of France: the Directory's commissioners supervised the compilation of registers and a tax-inspector was assigned to each *arrondissement* to see that the collectors did their job properly. This represented one step towards the creation of an autonomous fiscal administration. The Directory would have liked to go further, but the Councils objected, for they were afraid that this would make the executive more powerful than ever. The Directory commissioners, overworked and badly paid, often had great difficulty in making any real improvements to the fiscal system, the framework of which was still based on the registers of the Constituent Assembly, which had in turn been inherited from the Old Regime: as a general rule land was overtaxed, personal estate undertaxed and regional inequalities were often quite irrational (in Puy-de-Dôme the poor mountain regions continued to pay relatively higher taxes than the urban cantons). However, although the Directory failed to reform the framework of the fiscal system, it did at least succeed in making tax-collection more efficient, chiefly by sending out its agents to demand payment from recalcitrants and defaulters.

The Directory would have liked to increase indirect taxation, but the Councils put up a long resistance to such a proposal. In the autumn of 1798, confronted with a persistent deficit and the continuing burden of the war, they yielded to the Directory by passing two important laws on stamp-duty and registration; at the same time they modified the *patente* (the tax on commercial and industrial profits) and instituted a 'door and window' tax.

But these measures came too late in the day to prevent the regime from having to resort to emergency action – selling national properties, pillaging conquered countries and issuing loans. The pursuit of the war against Britain after Campio Formio compelled the government to issue a loan of eighty millions at five per cent, in bonds of one thousand francs, half of which was payable in currency. Although the issue met with a fairly heavy response at first, demand soon began to slacken off and the government had to introduce a compulsory tax on contractors. There was a certain harsh justice in this measure, for the chaotic state of public finances during the past two years had enabled the contractors who supplied the government – men like Ouvrard, Hinguerlot, Seguin and Simons – to make scandalously high profits. The resumption of the continental war in Year VIII put the state even more at the mercy of these ruthless speculators, and the government found itself having to resort to all the old expedients of royal absolutism, accepting advance payments on properties that had not yet been nationalised and on taxes that had not yet been collected. Men in high positions set the example of corruption, and in August 1798 the Directory had to dismiss the secretary-general of the Ministry of War, the brother of the minister, General Scherer, though the minister himself remained in office.

The financial problem was aggravated by the scarcity of metallic currency, which in 1797 once more became the sole legal instrument for the exchange of goods. Money was disappearing from circulation and inflation was succeeded by deflation. After the failure of the assignat, savers large and small began hoarding more than ever, or invested their money in real estate. The absence of a banking network, necessary for mobilising capital on a large scale, intensified the deflationary trend: prices dropped and money became increasingly expensive (the minimum rate of interest on loans was ten per cent). The few banks founded at this period by shrewd financiers – such as the Bank of Current Accounts formed by Perrégaux and Récamier – could do little to overcome the misgivings of the public and were able to operate only within a very limited economic field.

In conditions such as these, with the growing insecurity of communications and the ruin of maritime trade, the last years of the Directory were hardly favourable to the spirit of enterprise. Inflation had made the first Directory unpopular with the working classes, and deflation was now alienating the capitalists from the second Directory. Despite the enlightened efforts of François de Neufchâteau, who in 1798 inaugurated France's first National Exhibition and laid the foundations of industrial statistics, the sluggishness of national production contributed its own devastating effects to the fiscal and financial crisis.

The bourgeoisie had never shown any enthusiasm for the Directory, a regime that had been established by the Thermidoreans to advance their own interests. This class might well have been prepared to tolerate the Directory as a lesser evil – the regime had, after all, restored a certain kind of wealth and business activity to the French economy. But the financial reforms of 1797–8 were too drastic and had harmful effects on bourgeois interests. The 'bankruptcy of the two-thirds' had completed the ruin of the *rentiers*, who found themselves holding devalued bonds; at the same time, deflation and the

Deflation and falling prices impoverished the *rentiers*.

return to metallic currency had caused prices to fall and money had become scarcer. Commerce was stagnant and the government refused to encourage the initiatives taken by private banks to raise credit.

The fall in prices was accelerated by the three excellent harvests of '96, '97 and '98. In Paris, for example, a four-pound loaf of bread cost eight *sous* in spring '98: two *sous* a pound was the 'right price' which the poorer classes had been demanding for so long. In a report for the last quarter of Year VI the administration of the department of the Seine made the following observation: 'The inhabitants of Paris have seen their dream come true: bread at eight *sous*, wine at eight *sous* and meat at eight *sous*.' But the good fortune of one sector of society was the misfortune of another: the peasant producer and the urban capitalist were both hit by the fall in prices. The world of commerce was discontented. In January 1799 the executive commissioner for the department of the Seine wrote: 'The low price of grain is exasperating the growers. Nearly all of them claim they have no means of paying their taxes and are offering wheat instead of money.'

The Directory had at least managed to pacify the masses whom it had feared so greatly. But the attitude of the masses was one of contempt rather than sympathy: those who looked back in nostalgia to the days of Robespierre could not forget the Directory's repression of the Babeuf conspiracy, the Jacobins still bore a grudge for the purges of Floréal, and the people as a whole resented a regime founded on illegality. Republican activity was now concentrated in the army. In short, Frenchmen were no longer involved in politics: public affairs had become the preserve of the élite.

Now that the people had been deprived of its political role, discontent turned to brigandage, as the latent forces of royalism and resistance to conscription spread anarchy throughout the Republic. Vagabonds and bandits were a recurring feature of old rural France, but the feeble tyranny of the final year of the Directory had given them a pretext and had encouraged them to show greater daring. The discredited regime was being disobeyed more and more by local authorities, which were subject to annual elections and to the arbitrary interference of the executive. Moreover, the corruption that was rife in Paris

Here brigands attack the inhabitants of an inn, torture the owner, rape the women and take with them everything of value.

gave local officials little inducement to be honest. Although it had a vast civil service the France of 1799 was suffering from a lack of firm administration: the nation realised it was without a government.

Travelling by stage-coach had become a dangerous adventure: at a bend in the road or at the entrance to a forest, passengers were likely to find themselves being stopped by one of the countless bands of brigands which terrorised the countryside. These bands were recruited from all the debris of the old and the new France – smugglers, deserters from the army, survivors of the royalist insurrections, dispossessed nobles and common highwaymen. The danger was especially great for any traveller who happened to be in a position of authority, a local

notable, a purchaser of national property or a constitutional priest – in short, anyone who represented the regime and public order. Such a person was likely to lose his life in a hold-up, while his travelling-companions were usually able to buy their freedom. But the 'royal brigands' did not restrict their acts of violence to the public roads; at night they maintained a reign of terror, attacking republican officials and guards as they slept. Many local disputes were settled by murder or blackmail.

This rural terrorism was common to nearly the whole of France, according to contemporary sources, but it was naturally most intense in the regions where the Chouans and the royalists were active – in a dozen or so departments in the west, between Le Mans and Vannes, in the south where the White Terror raged, in the Rhone valley and the bordering Cévennes.

The collapse of the government's authority at home enhanced the already considerable prestige of the army, which now became the depository of the nation's frustrated hopes. The army was a semi-professional body, strengthened by the Jourdan decree of 19 Fructidor Year VI introducing compulsory military service, but it still owed its allegiance to the Republic; it was an army of social advancement and revolutionary loyalty, the last refuge of the republican principle which had been distorted by the politicians in Paris.

Since 30 Prairial the Councils had shown new confidence. The victory gained by the victims of Floréal Year VI, the appointment of Bernadotte as Minister of War and, most important of all, the return of Robert Lindet as Minister of Finance heralded a fresh wave of Jacobin agitation as the clubs reopened their doors and the press began to criticise and to attack once more. In the Council of Five Hundred, the leaders of the left – Destrem, Grandmaison and Poullain-Grandprey – accused the regime of corruption and demanded that the ex-Directors and the ex-minister Scherer be brought to justice.

The new Jacobinism had not sprung from a movement of the urban populace, but arose almost solely from the catastrophes of the war abroad. Jourdan, defeated at Stokach, had retreated to the Rhine; Moreau and Macdonald were evacuating Italy, and in Switzerland Masséna had withdrawn behind the Limath. For the first time in six years the territory of France lay under threat of invasion. Inside France the militant royalists, who had been waiting for so long, believed that their opportunity had come at last. The Chouans began co-ordinating their efforts and prepared themselves for the assault; the Comte d'Artois even considered landing in France.

The Jacobin deputies retaliated with three important decrees which revived memories of 1793. On 10 Messidor (28 June) mass conscription was decreed: the five categories of conscripts laid down by the

Jourdan decree were called to arms, and all discharges granted since
'93 were cancelled. On 24 Messidor (12 July) the terrible law of
hostages was passed: in all the departments of France specified by the
Councils, at the recommendation of the Directory, the authorities
were empowered to take relatives of emigrés and Chouans as hostages;
every time a public official, a purchaser of national property or a
constitutional priest was assassinated, four of these hostages would be
deported, and the hostages would also have to provide compensation
for any damage to property caused by rebellion. The third decree
concerned finance: a forced loan of one hundred millions from the
rich, proposed by Jourdan but modified by the Elders, was finally
approved on 19 Thermidor (6 August). This measure, based on a
graduated scale, affected those paying at least three hundred francs a
year in land-tax; from four thousand francs upwards the amount of
the loan had to represent three-quarters of annual revenue. In the
case of personal fortunes a panel of non-taxpaying citizens was set up
to assess the amounts to be levied, starting from an annual income of
one hundred francs. Those affected were given little time in which to
pay, and non-payment made it impossible to obtain the certificate of
residence distinguishing citizens from emigrés.

The forced loan created a climate of panic in the world of commerce
and property. More and more money vanished from circulation and
the wealthy were concerned only to find ways of cheating a government that was conducting its affairs so incompetently. But conscription affected all Frenchmen and was all the more unpopular because
the army had suffered the disgrace of defeat. Roughly half of those
called up actually joined the army; many conscripts went into hiding
or swelled the bands of brigands that were terrorising the countryside –
if they had to die, these men were determined to die on French soil.

The Jacobin offensive launched by the Councils disturbed the two
central figures of the Directory, Barras and Sieyès. Barras felt his
position threatened by the deputies' denunciation of corruption and
their indictment of his former colleagues. Sieyès, suspected of wishing
to restore the monarchy by recalling the duc d'Orléans or a German
prince, was attacked by the left-wing press and the Manège Club,
where the Jacobins had begun to meet; he was anxious to take
moderate republican opinion in hand and to persuade it to accept his
programme of revision. In August, supported by Barras, he launched
a counter-offensive: Marbot was deprived of the military command of
Paris and was replaced by the faithful Lefebvre; the ex-terrorist
Fouché, emerging from several years of obscurity and eager to win the
favour of the future rulers of France, became chief of police; and the
Jacobin Club, which had become the terror of the *honnêtes gens*, was
closed at the end of August without any sign of protest from the masses.

The royalist uprising in the south (which for a time threatened Toulouse), the French defeat at Novi (15 August) and the British landing in Holland provoked a fresh surge of Jacobin fever in the Councils: the deputies wanted to decree *la patrie en danger* as the first stage in a revival of the old Committee of Public Safety; but they could not call on the suburbs for support, and so, like Sieyès, they turned to the generals. However, Jourdan and Augereau were now deputies and had resigned their commands; Bernadotte temporised and was dismissed by Sieyès, with the support of Barras. Sieyès was establishing his authority more and more firmly, but what exactly were his intentions?

THE SIEYÈS CONSPIRACY

Since his return from Berlin, Sieyès had been perfectly placed to plan his reorganisation of French political institutions and fulfil his cherished ambition. He had refused to join the original Directory; his enemies suggested that he had refused because he detested Reubell, but Sieyès was a shrewd politician and had been pessimistic about the new regime's chances of success; consequently, he had been reluctant to risk compromising his future. While remaining politically active, he deliberately kept out of the limelight until the Council of Elders called for him again. This time he was consulted almost as an oracle, for he now enjoyed the tremendous authority of one who had foreseen the failure of the regime and had decided to bide his time and avoid compromising himself. The man who had been able to win power in '89 and refuse it in '95, the great theoretician of Constitutions, had acquired an extraordinary reputation among his fellow-politicians. During the first few sessions of the Directory which he attended, he hustled his colleagues without actually telling them what he wanted. 'Enigmatic and deliberately unintelligible, he seemed always to be pondering some great secret concerning the fate of France.' (Vandal)

Sieyès, a man of reputedly abstract temperament, who had displayed such boldness in his political ideas (see Chapter 8, page 259), manoeuvred with consummate tactical skill during the summer of 1799. He sensed that public opinion was weary of instability, war and those revolutionary voices that were warning of fresh misfortunes. He rallied round him those Jacobins who, like Lucien Bonaparte, did not seem to be beyond the pale; at the same time he gathered the moderate republicans together as a rival force, a kind of third party which included Daunou, Boulay, Chénier, Benjamin Constant, Roederer and Talleyrand, who had just left the Ministry of Foreign Affairs and whose influence can be traced throughout the 'revisionist' conspiracy. Sieyès gave the key posts to men he could trust – Roger

Portrait of Sieyès by J.-L. David, 1817.

Ducos, Cambacérès, Fouché, Lefebvre. Barras let him do as he wished and even gave him his support; at the same time Barras involved himself in all kinds of tortuous manoeuvres and took every possible precaution for the future, ingratiating himself with the royal pretender, with the Jacobins and with the revisionists. In theory he was still the head of the executive, with Gohier and Moulin to one side and Sieyès and Ducos to the other, but he spent more time in intrigue than in action. In reality it was Sieyès who was now master of the Directory.

In crushing the Jacobin offensive, the former leader of the Third Estate had never intended to make the pretender king of France. On the contrary, though he despised the common people, his over-riding passion remained his hatred of the nobility; behind the scenes, he had prompted the repression of Fructidor and Boulay's pro-posal for expelling the nobility. His great fear in Year VII was that moderate opinion might throw itself before the legitimate monarch in desperation and thus unwittingly bring about the counter-revolution which Sieyès, both as a political theorist and as a regicide, feared so greatly. His plan was consequently similar to that of the Thermi-doreans of Year III: to halt the Revolution by establishing a strong ruling authority that would consolidate its achievements and protect them from the survivors of the Old Regime. Like his predecessors, Sieyès was seeking to build a defensive wall behind which the new political class produced by the Revolution could enjoy the fruits of victory. He was probably prepared to go further than his predecessors in broadening the composition of the ruling élite in order to build the new France on solid foundations. Was he thinking in terms of a king? In drafting his famous Constitution Sieyès advocated that the execu-tive power be entrusted to a single person, a 'Grand Elector', instead of a group acting collectively, like the Directory. If in fact he was con-templating a restoration of the monarchy at some future date, did he have in mind the duc d'Orléans, to whom he had already been of service, or a German prince, as the Jacobin press was suggesting? One thing at least was certain – only a constitutional monarch would have been acceptable.

However, Sieyès was more concerned to provide for the immediate future of France. With the support of the Council of Elders, where he controlled a majority, he had been drafting his plan for a *coup d'état*. On the pretext of a Jacobin plot the Council of Elders was to vote that both assemblies be moved to Saint-Cloud; as soon as they were settled there they would rally to the plan put forward by Sieyès, which pro-vided for a 'Grand Elector' as head of the executive, three Consuls elected for ten years, a Senate elected for life and a system of universal suffrage modified by reference to 'lists of notabilities'. But the opera-tion would have to be backed by a threat of military intervention. Sieyès had been looking for a general whom he could trust; he had approached Joubert, the young republican general who had inherited Hoche's reputation, but Joubert, put in command of the Army of Italy, had been killed at Novi.

The Jacobins had been making similar plans and made approaches to their own generals in the crisis following the defeat at Novi. How-

'Flight from Egypt', an English caricature of Bonaparte's departure from Egypt. The Army of Egypt was horrified to hear that the general had left, and so was Kléber, whom Bonaparte had appointed to take over.

The 'first flight of the eagle', from Alexandria to France, is symbolised by this engraving showing the general of the Army of Egypt standing in an ancient chariot, being crowned by Fortune and protecting goddesses. Bonaparte's return to France was triumphant.

ever, their schemes came to nought when the threat of invasion was removed by the French victories of Vendémiaire (Brune's victory in Holand and, in particular, Masséna's triumph at Zurich).

Sieyès was considering sounding Moreau when Bonaparte landed at Fréjus. The two frigates which brought Bonaparte and his small escort moored at Fréjus on 9 October, after spending two weeks at Ajaccio. The great news reached Paris on the evening of the 13th. Josephine, who was dining with Gohier, set off to meet her husband; she had not been faithful to him in his absence and was anxious to forestall the Bonapartes, who detested her. But she took the Dijon road, while Bonaparte came through Bourbonnais and was met by his brothers, Joseph, Lucien and Louis, who spared him no details of Josephine's infidelities. He entered Paris on the morning of the 16th; Josephine did not arrive back at their house in the Rue de la Victoire until the 18th, but after several hours of emotional melodrama, in which Hortense and Eugene added their own explanations to their mother's tearful pleading, Napoleon finally opened the door to his wife: he could not allow private scandals to mar the future he was already planning for himself.

The hero's return provoked a vast movement of opinion in France. Among the politicians Sieyès was respected, but Bonaparte was a popular figure. He was the personification both of good fortune and of victory, and in the eyes of Frenchmen victory was the only path to peace. A contemporary commentator had this to say: 'The return of Bonaparte is seen as a happy omen for our armies, a guarantee of quick and brilliant victories if the outcome of the war were ever in doubt.' It mattered little that the military situation had already been righted by Brune and Masséna while Bonaparte was still at sea, for it was his arrival back in France that seemed to symbolise the republican armies' successes. 'The victory that follows Bonaparte everywhere,' wrote *le Moniteur*, 'has preceded him on this occasion, and he has come back to strike the final blows at the dying Coalition. Oh, Mr Pitt, what terrible news for you after the total defeat of the Anglo-Russian forces in Holland! To have lost three more battles would have been better for you than Bonaparte's return!' The eighteen months of exile in Egypt had done as much as the Italian campaign to foster the Napoleonic legend.

In the Council of Five Hundred the news of his return was received with enthusiasm, and the Jacobins joined readily in the grandiloquent speeches of welcome for the man who symbolised victory and peace:

Peoples of Europe and you, the ministers who have contemplated the humiliation and ruin of this country . . . know that France is invincible, that it is she who will give peace to the world. . . . The man who dictated the terms of victory and peace at Campo Formio is still worthy of the confidence of republicans and will soon be leading our armies; soon he will have exhausted all the compliments we can pay him.

Public opinion was so solidly in favour of Bonaparte that the Directory did not dare oppose it openly; but secretly the Directors were displeased at this unexpected turn of events, which had upset all their calculations by bringing a new and powerful figure into the struggle for power. When the news of the landing at Fréjus reached the Luxembourg, Sieyès was waiting for Moreau who had just returned from Italy. There was now nothing for the two men to discuss, for Moreau immediately declared to Sieyès: 'Here is your man; he will carry out your *coup d'état* much better than I can.'

France had been saved from invasion, but still lay under the threat of civil war. The victories of Vendémiaire, in thwarting the Jacobin resurgence, had rekindled the flames of royalism: on 14 October, at a signal from Bourmont, the Chouans attacked the large towns of western France and managed to hold some of them for several hours. At his home in the Rue de la Victoire Bonaparte – already known simply as 'the general', as if his colleagues no longer existed – received visitors in steadily increasing numbers, listening to what they had to say but not committing himself. He had planned his political strategy: to avoid associating himself with any particular faction and to be seen as the conciliator, the man of order and peace. This son of the decadent Corsican nobility felt himself closer to the people than to the bourgeois regicides, but he could not yet see for certain where lay the road to power.

He played the part of a modest and pure republican, flattering the Jacobins and Moulin and Gohier, who visited him frequently. 'The unanimous welcome he received,' Lucien explains in his Memoirs, 'seemed at first to require that he should avoid offending anyone.' His relationship with Barras was of long standing and he maintained the appearances of friendship without going any further for the present, for Barras' discredited reputation could well be compromising. His most important dealings were with Sieyès, through an intermediary. As soon as Bonaparte arrived back in France Lucien informed him in full detail of the proposed *coup d'état* and the constitutional reforms which Sieyès had planned; Napoleon agreed to the plan in principle but would not commit himself, and he refused to meet Sieyès in private: 'I do not want the limelight yet. It does not suit my purpose to adopt the colours of any party. In any case, I need time to study the terrain.' Napoleon was suspicious not only of Sieyès, but also of his brother Lucien, who had been made president of the Council of Five Hundred and had his own ambitions.

Relations between Bonaparte and Sieyès were slow to develop and were fraught with personal friction, stemming from the vanity and

Outside his house in the Rue de la Victoire Bonaparte talks to the generals and colonels, asking them to help him save the Republic.

prejudices of two men who were poles apart. But each was helpless without the other, and they shared the same accomplices – the moderate politicians and the Voltairean intellectuals of the Institute, men like Benjamin Constant, Cambacérès, Boulay, Daunou, Cabanis and Volney. Roederer and the inevitable Talleyrand, who had been bound up with Bonaparte since Campo Formio, were their most trusted intermediaries. Discussing the details of the *coup* first with one, then with the other, Bonaparte continued to hedge; he made regular visits to the Institute, was friendly towards Bernadotte and Jourdan, who maintained a guarded attitude, and sounded Barras, who demanded too much. He finally made his decision on 10 Brumaire when he met Sieyès at Lucien's house: he agreed to the proposal to move the Councils to Saint-Cloud, but insisted on one major modification – the purpose of the *coup d'état* must be not to impose Sieyès' Constitution on France, but to establish a provisional government of three consuls, including himself, which would undertake the drafting of a new Constitution with the assistance of a committee chosen from the

Councils. Bonaparte made it quite clear that, unless the others agreed, they could no longer count on his support. Sieyès had no choice and gave way to Bonaparte, fully aware of the risk he was taking: 'In any great enterprise,' he confided to a friend, 'one is always obliged to leave something to chance.' The plan was to be put into effect on 18 Brumaire. In the meantime, while Bonaparte dined in the city and indulged himself, Sieyès took riding lessons in the Luxembourg Gardens in preparation for the great day.

BRUMAIRE

Everything went smoothly on the 18th. On the following day, however, the conspiracy was nearly foiled.

At dawn on the 18th, two manoeuvres were carried out simultaneously. The Elders were summoned from their beds at seven o'clock in the morning on the pretext that an anarchist plot was brewing. The Place de la Concorde had already been occupied by the 9th Dragoons under the command of Sébastiani. At the same hour, going over the head of the Minister of War, Dubois-Crancé, and anticipating a decree that had not yet been voted, Bonaparte called together all the army chiefs at his house in the Rue de la Victoire; when some of them showed hesitation, he offered bribes and made promises of future appointments. At half past eight the deputation from the Council of Elders arrived with the decree transferring the two Councils to Saint-Cloud and entrusting Bonaparte with the execution of the move. The guise of legality thus given to the conspiracy gave the generals greater confidence: it was now a matter of 'saving the Republic'.

The procession of officers, in their magnificent braided uniforms, made its way on horseback through the centre of Paris, towards the Place de la Concorde. Bonaparte, riding at the head of the procession, was the hero of the day. Behind him rode Murat, Marmont, Berthier, Lefebvre, Lannes and Macdonald, the future marshals of the Empire. From the windows of his house, the financier Ouvrard watched them pass; immediately grasping the situation, he lost no time in informing Bonaparte that his coffers were at the general's disposal.

The streets of Paris were being covered with the posters prepared by Roederer, when the procession arrived at the Tuileries. Bonaparte now made his parliamentary début. He entered the hall where the Elders were sitting, followed by the other generals, but instead of simply swearing an oath, he made a short but carefully weighed speech which ended with these words: 'We want a Republic founded on true liberty, on civil liberty and national representation. We shall have such a Republic, I swear it in my own name and in the name of my companions-at-arms.' 'We swear' echoed the generals in unison. The

The Directory has collapsed: Sieyès and Ducos have resigned voluntarily, and Barras has been forced to resign. This engraving shows Gohier and Moulin refusing to listen to the Elders, who are urging them to resign.

style of the announcement seemed rather too military even for the Elders, but they quietly agreed to adjourn until the following day, when the assemblies would be sitting at Saint-Cloud. The Council of Five Hundred was fiercely opposed to the *coup d'état*, but had to submit.

Sieyès now made his appearance, having ridden on horseback from the Luxembourg and already eclipsed by the greater brilliance of his associate. Bonaparte took him down into the Tuileries Gardens, where they found Barras' secretary, Bottot, who had just heard the news. The unfortunate Bottot, seized by the arm and planted between the generals and the troops like some relic of the past, was made the target of another piece of calculated rhetoric from Bonaparte: 'What was the state of France when I left her and in what a state I now find her! I left you peace, and I come back to find war! I left you conquests, and now the enemy is crossing our frontiers! I left our arsenals fully stocked, and now I find them empty! I left you with all the millions of Italy, and now I find extortionate laws and poverty everywhere!' The troops gave their chief a long ovation.

The ministers, led by Cambacérès and Fouché, joined the Elders and declared their support for the *coup d'état*. With them were the two Directors involved in the conspiracy, Sieyès and Roger Ducos, who had now formally resigned from the executive. During the morning Barras had received two visitors, Admiral Bruix and Talleyrand, who had brought him a letter of resignation drawn up in advance by Roederer. He signed the letter and shortly afterwards set off for his private estate, escorted by a detachment of dragoons. What had happened to this once-powerful but now weary politician, who had displayed energy and determination in earlier crises? Perhaps he had underestimated the little general he had once helped; perhaps he really hoped that the conspirators would not be able to manage without him, that he would have his part to play, but then found it was too late to go over to the Jacobins; or it may have been simply that Talleyrand had brought him a few millions from the funds which the contractor Collot had advanced to the conspirators – after all, Barras and Talleyrand shared the same devotion to money and must have understood each other's character perfectly. There only remained Gohier and Moulin, the Jacobin nonentities of the Directory, who refused to recognise the *coup*; it was decided to detain them in the Luxembourg under Moreau's guard.

While Paris remained calm and the 'consolidated third' began a recovery at the Bourse, the conspirators discussed plans for the following day. Sieyès wanted to have forty Jacobin deputies put in prison under preventive detention, but Bonaparte refused, anxious to avoid any unnecessary breach of legality; he wanted at all costs to abide by 'regular' parliamentary procedure. He had no experience of parliamentary assemblies and did not realise that the methods he had used on 18 Brumaire to establish his supremacy were beginning to disturb even his supporters. On the following day victory was nearly turned into defeat.

At about noon on the 19th, the esplanade of the château of Saint-Cloud became the scene of great agitation. Food-vendors were making a small fortune feeding the politicians and the military of Paris; the workmen who were preparing the two rooms in the palace were behind schedule (the Elders were to occupy the first floor of the palace and the Five Hundred the annex in the orangery) and the deputies in their long toga-like robes had to walk up and down outside. The Jacobins of the Five Hundred were already plying their colleagues of the upper chamber with highly embarrassing questions: why this sudden move to Saint-Cloud on the pretext of a non-existent plot? Why this show of military strength if it was simply a matter of reforming institutions? Was a dictatorship about to be imposed on France? The events of the previous day had given them plenty to worry about, and had disturbed many of Sieyès' friends.

Bonaparte, impatient to open the proceedings, walked up and down with a feverish and savage expression. As soon as the session of the

Saint-Cloud, on the morning of 19 Brumaire. Infantry, cavalry and artillery surround the château. Tension mounts as the members of the Councils become increasingly apprehensive.

Council of Five Hundred opened, at about two o'clock in the afternoon, it became violently critical. Lucien Bonaparte, who was presiding, was helpless against the Jacobins' cries of 'the Constitution or death!'; yielding to this wave of hostility, he agreed to a proposal that the deputies should individually swear an oath of loyalty to the Constitution of Year III and in this way he gained a valuable hour's respite. But the situation was even more serious in the upper chamber, where the conscience-stricken Elders, after much wavering, finally decided that a message should be sent to the Directory demanding explanations. The secretary-general, Lagarde, told them that the Directory no longer existed, as four of its members had resigned (in fact only three had done so); at half past three the session was suspended so that Lagarde's reply could be sent to the Five Hundred. At this stage nothing seemed certain: the majority of deputies seemed to be in favour of a compromise between the two rival factions, the committed Brumaireans and the extreme Jacobins. As the Directors had resigned, why not elect more energetic men in their place and in this way strengthen the executive without infringing the Constitution? All Sieyès' fears had been justified: the lawyers and the Brumairean intellectuals who dominated the Council of Elders had been shaken by the reaction of the Jacobins and were being drawn by the irresistible logic of parliamentary compromise. 'The Institute was on the point of thwarting its own *coup d'état*,' writes Albert Vandal. Talleyrand, who had been waiting nearby, was becoming impatient – an ominous sign.

Bonaparte, waiting with Sieyès in a room next to the assembly

394

chamber, decided to intervene personally: 'the wine is drawn, it must be drunk,' he replied when Augereau and Bernadotte came to consult him. He still had a chance of winning over the deputies, if only he could address them effectively. But as an orator he was capable of little but monologue, and was nervous about addressing a parliamentary assembly. Entering the chamber, where the Elders had been debating among themselves during the adjournment, Bonaparte launched into a violent and incoherent harangue which dismayed his colleagues. To give him time to recover himself they had the assembly pass a motion that the session be resumed, but Bonaparte allowed himself to be carried away by his military, pseudo-Roman rhetoric. When he was interrupted and questioned he could not find an effective reply and ended by uttering a threat he had previously hurled at the Muslims in Cairo: 'Remember that I march accompanied by the god of victory and the god of war.' Everything he had said to the assembly had been to his own discredit.

Why did he then go straight to the Council of Five Hundred, which he had just insulted in his speech to the Elders? He was simply employing the tactics he had used at the battle of Arcola, where he had

Lucien, Napoleon's brother, was the hero of 19 Brumaire: he was mainly responsible for the success of the *coup d'état*.

charged at the enemy with a handful of trusted grenadiers. He intended to denounce the Jacobins for their hypocritical invocation of the 'Constitution' and to tell the assembly of his conversations with Jourdan and Augereau. But he was not given a chance to speak. Greeted with shouts of 'outlaw!', pushed and struck by Jacobin deputies, he found himself caught up in a brawl at the foot of the rostrum. With the help of Lefebvre and Murat his soldiers managed to free him and led him away, choking and on the point of fainting: his face was white and marked with spots of blood.

Sieyès, the 'priest', now took the initiative, suggesting that the order be given for the troops to march on the Councils. But Bonaparte had been shaken by his failure to execute his 'legal' *coup d'état* and was uncertain of the loyalty of his men, who were stationed in front of the palace with arms ordered. Would the grenadiers of the Legislative Corps agree to march against the Five Hundred, or had they already been won over by the deputies? While Bonaparte hesitated, his brother Lucien was still attempting to quell the Jacobins, who were indulging in violent abuse of Napoleon and had eventually proposed that he be declared an 'outlaw', a terrible indictment echoing Robespierre's fate on 9 Thermidor. Laying down his robe and cap in a theatrical gesture, Lucien left his chair and was escorted out of the hall by a squad of grenadiers who had been sent to him. He joined his brother, who by now had recovered his composure, and they both took up their positions in front of the troops, ready to act out the final scene of this great drama in the November twilight. In his Memoirs Lucien says that he was the first to speak; his harangue to the grenadiers was decisive in its effect: the president of the Council of Five Hundred was ordering them to drive out the seditious deputies, the 'representatives of the dagger'. The troops, who were devoted to Napoleon and believed that the deputies had tried to murder him, did not need to hear their general speak to give him an ovation. Now that the situation lay in their hands it was quickly brought to a conclusion. Leclerc, who was Napoleon's brother-in-law, and Murat, who was soon to become his brother-in-law, completed this family operation. When Murat reached the entrance to the assembly room, where the Five Hundred were protesting vociferously, he curtly ordered his soldiers: 'Get these people out'. In five minutes the room was empty.

The expulsion of the Five Hundred marked the final victory of the conspiracy and ended the hesitations of the Elders, who approved a decree replacing the Directory with a provisional executive committee of three members. But the events of 19 Brumaire, which had followed the course feared by Sieyès, had ended with a conspicuous intervention by the military. Both Sieyès and Lucien Bonaparte wanted to bring the whole affair to a more 'legal' conclusion. An order was

Napoleon, master of France at the age of 30.

therefore given to search the restaurants and eating-places of Saint-Cloud and round up those deputies from the Council of Five Hundred who would agree to come back to the palace for a final session. A hundred or so willing deputies were found. In the hall of the orangery annexe, lit by candles, the silence was dramatic by contrast with the noisy scenes that had taken place earlier. Lucien persuaded the deputies to draw up a text professing gratitude to the generals and providing for the creation of a 'consular executive committee composed of citizens Sieyès and Roger Ducos, formerly Directors, and General Bonaparte, who will all bear the title of Consuls of the Republic'. The Councils were to be replaced with two committees of twenty-five members which would be invited to discussions with the three Consuls. For the benefit of the press, parliamentary procedures were scrupulously observed by this rump-assembly: a 'study commission' was appointed to examine the proposals put forward, then Boulay reported on the commission's findings, and finally a 'discussion' was held, at which nobody dared to speak against the proposals. The farce ended in the early hours with a passionate speech by the indefatigable Lucien, who, at twenty-four years of age, had just lived through the greatest day of his life. The Elders, who had been kept waiting until four o'clock in the morning, ratified the proposals and left.

Bonaparte returned to Paris in a silent mood, not particularly pleased with the way things had gone; that same evening he dictated his own version of the events of 18–19 Brumaire, which became the 'official' version and in which he tried to rally all *honnêtes gens* against Jacobinism.

Yet the Parisian populace had not stirred; admittedly Fouché's police had a firm grip on the city, but the people were quite indifferent to the *coup d'état* – what reason had the suburbs to come to the defence of the Thermidorean regime? The alleged resurgence of Jacobinism in the historic suburbs of Paris was a myth fostered by the bourgeoisie. Throughout 19 Brumaire Mme de Staël, who had gathered her fortune together from her Parisian business friends, was ready to leave the capital: 'Every quarter of an hour I received news from Saint-Cloud; one moment I was preparing to leave, the next moment I was postponing my departure, according to the nature of the news.' For most of her contemporaries, 18 Brumaire had been just another of the Revolution's upheavals. Few men realised the true significance of Brumaire, concealed beneath the allegations of a Jacobin conspiracy: the Revolution was over at last.

CHRONOLOGICAL TABLE

1787

22 *February*   Meeting of the Assembly of Notables

8 *April*   Dismissal of Calonne
Ministry of Loménie de Brienne

25 *May*   Brienne has the Assembly of Notables dissolved

19 *November*   Royal session for the registration of Brienne's loan
Edict granting toleration to Protestants

1788

3 *May*   The Parlement of Paris publishes a 'Declaration of the fundamental laws of the kingdom'

5 *May*   Arrest of Duval d'Éprémesnil and Goislard de Montsabert

8 *May*   Lamoignon's judicial reforms reorganising the courts and legal procedures to the detriment of the parlements

7 *June*   Revolt in Grenoble: the mob demands the reinstatement of the local parlement

21 *July*   Vizille Assembly

8 *August*   The Estates-General are convoked for 1 May 1789

16 *August*   Government payments are suspended

24 *August*   Brienne is dismissed

26 *August*   The king turns to Necker

27 *December*   With the consent of the king Necker agrees to the doubling of the Third Estate's representation at the forthcoming meeting of the Estates-General: the Third Estate will now have as many deputies as the other two orders put together

1789

5 *May*   Opening session of the Estates-General
Necker's speech

17 *June*   The Third Estate constitutes itself as the National Assembly

20 *June*   Tennis Court Oath

23 *June*   Royal session: Louis XVI's programme of reform is made public

11 *July*   Dismissal of Necker

12 *July*   Riots in Paris

13 *July*   The electors of Paris form a standing committee and a citizens' militia

14 *July*   Fall of the Bastille

16 *July*   Recall of Necker

17 *July*   Louis XVI is received at the Hôtel de Ville by Bailly. The Prince de Condé and the Comte d'Artois emigrate

End of July   Municipalities and citizens' guards are formed throughout the provinces

End of July/ beginning of August   The Great Fear and peasant insurrections

4 *August*   Abolition of feudalism and of certain seigneurial rights

26 August	Declaration of the Rights of Man and the Citizen		17 July	Champ-de-Mars massacre
5 October	The women of Paris march on Versailles		5 August	'The French nation undertakes not to enter into any war for the purpose of conquest'
6 October	The king is brought back to Paris		27 August	Declaration of Pilnitz
2 November	The Church's lands are nationalised		12 September	Annexation after a plebiscite of the county of Avignon
19 December	Introduction of assignats: first issue of four hundred millions		13 September	Louis XVI approves the revised Constitution
			28 September	The Rural Code authorizes the enclosure of commons
	1790		30 September	The Constituent Assembly is dissolved
13 February	Prohibition of monastic vows and suppression of religious orders except for teaching and charitable orders		1 October	First session of the Legislative Assembly
17 April	Assignats are made paper-currency		29 November	Priests refusing to take the 'civic oath' are declared suspect
14 May	Decree dividing national lands into lots for auction. Payment in twelve annual instalments			**1792**
21 May	Paris is divided into forty-eight Sections		End of January	A hundred *livres*-assignats worth only sixty-three *livres*
19 June	Decree abolishing the nobility's hereditary titles and coats of arms		1 March	Death in Vienna of the emperor Leopold II. His son Francis II succeeds him
12 July	The Civil Constitution of the Clergy finally approved		20 April	France declares war on the king of Hungary and Bohemia
14 July	Federation ceremony		27 May	The Assembly decrees that all refractory priests are liable to be banished from France
31 August	Bouillé crushes a mutiny of patriot soldiers at Nancy			
29 September	Sale of national lands for a new issue of eight hundred million *livres*		29 May	Decree dissolving the king's personal guard
27 November	'Civic oath' imposed on the clergy		8 June	The Assembly decrees the constitution of a camp of *fédérés* outside Paris
			11 June	The king vetoes the decrees of 27 May and 8 June
	1791		12 June	The king dismisses the Girondin ministers
3 January	Priests refusing to take the oath are barred from exercising their ministry in public		15 June	The king appoints Feuillant ministers
2 March	The 'Allarde law' suppressing the corporations		20 June	The people invade the Tuileries
10 March	Papal brief 'Quot Aliquantum' condemning the Civil Constitution of the Clergy and revolutionary principles		11 July	Proclamation of 'la Patrie en danger'
			25 July	The Duke of Brunswick's manifesto
2 April	Death of Mirabeau		27 July	Properties of emigrés confiscated
14 June	The 'Le Chapelier law' prohibiting all workmen's associations and *combinations* (strikes)		10 August	Constitution of the revolutionary Commune of Paris. Capture of the Tuileries
20 June	Flight of the king and his family		14 August	Distribution of communal land except for forestland. Sale of emigrés' properties
21 June	The king is arrested at Varennes		17 August	Creation of a criminal court
			18 August	Abolition of the last religious orders

Chronological Table

23 August	Longwy surrenders to the Prussians
2/5 September	Massacres in the prisons of Paris
20 September	French victory at Valmy. Civil registry established. Law on divorce. End of the Legislative Assembly
21 September	First session of the National Convention. Abolition of the monarchy
22 September	Year 1 of the Republic
6 November	French victory at Jemappes
19 November	Decree granting 'fraternity and succour' to the nations of Europe wishing to be freed of imperial domination
27 November	Annexation of Savoy
10 December	Opening of Louis XVI's trial by the Convention
15 December	Decree instituting the dictatorship of the revolutionary minorities in occupied Europe

1793

21 January	Louis XVI is guillotined
1 February	The Convention declares war on Great Britain and Holland
23 February	The Convention decrees a mass conscription of three hundred thousand men
7 March	The Convention declares war on Spain
11 March	Beginning of the Vendéan war: massacre of republicans at Machecoul
16 March	Defeat at Neerwinden
1 April	Treachery of Dumouriez
6 April	Creation of the Committee of Public Safety
4 May	Maximum prices fixed for grain and flour
5 May	Quétineau surrenders to the Vendéans at Thouars
10 May	The Convention moves from the Manège to the old theatre in the Tuileries
31 May	Uprising against the Girondins
2 June	A second demonstration against the Convention. Arrest of Girondin deputies
Early June	'Federalist' uprisings in the west, south-west and south-east
9 June	The Vendéans take Saumur
24 June	The Constitution is adopted by the Convention
10 July	Reorganisation of the

	Committee of Public Safety: Danton resigns
13 July	Assassination of Marat
17 July	Abolition without indemnity of remaining seigneurial rights
26 July	Emigrés' properties divided up for sale
27 July	Robespierre is elected to the Committee of Public Safety
28 July	Fall of Valenciennes
1 August	The Convention orders the systematic destruction of Vendée
4 August	The Constitution is ratified by 1,880,000 votes to 17,000
14 August	Carnot and Prieur of the Côte-d'Or enter the Committee of Public Safety
23 August	Mass conscription decreed
24 August	The Great Book of the Public Debt is introduced
27 August	Toulon surrenders to the British
5 September	Demonstration of sans-culottes. Arrest of Jacques Roux
6 September	Collot d'Herbois and Billaud-Varenne enter the Committee of Public Safety
9 September	Creation of the Revolutionary Army
11 September	'Maximum' on grain
17 September	Law of suspects
29 September	'General maximum' on food and wages
5 October	Adoption of the Republican calendar
9 October	Lyon recaptured by the Republicans

Year II

19 Vendémiaire	10 October France declared under revolutionary government for the duration of the war
25 Vendémiaire	16 October Execution of Marie-Antoinette. French victory at Wattignies
26 Vendémiaire	17 October The Vendéans are defeated at Cholet
20 Brumaire	10 November Ceremony of Liberty and Reason in Notre-Dame
24 Brumaire	14 November Arrest of Chabot, Basire, Delaunay and Julien
2 Frimaire	22 November National lands divided up for sale
14 Frimaire	4 December Decree on the

401

	organisation of the revolutionary government
15 Frimaire	*5 December* First number of the *Vieux Cordelier*
29 Frimaire	*19 December* Recapture of Toulon
November and December	The first churches are closed in and around Paris
December	One hundred *livres*-assignats worth forty-eight *livres* in metal currency
3 Nivôse	*23 December* Victory against the Vendéans at Savenay

1794

23 Nivôse	*12 January* Arrest of Fabre d'Églantine
16 Pluviôse	*4 February* The Convention decrees the abolition of slavery in the colonies
8–13 Ventôse	*26 February–3 March* Saint-Just has the Convention approve two decrees redistributing properties taken from suspects
1 Germinal	*21 March* Opening of the trial of the Hébertists
4 Germinal	*24 March* Execution of the Hébertists
13 Germinal	*2 April* Trial of the Dantonists
16 Germinal	*5 April* Execution of the Dantonists
March and April	Waves of dechristianization
18 Floréal	*7 May* Decree of the Convention recognising the Supreme Being
20 Prairial	*8 June* Festival of the Supreme Being
22 Prairial	*10 June* Law of suspects
8 Messidor	*26 June* Jourdan's victory at Fleurus
9 Thermidor	*27 July* Debate in the Convention. Robespierre fails to obtain a hearing and is arrested along with several of his supporters
10 Thermidor	*28 July* Execution of Robespierre, Saint-Just, Couthon and nineteen other Robespierrists
13 Thermidor	*31 July* Reorganization of the committees
14 Thermidor	*1 August* The law of Prairial is revoked and Fouquier-Tinville is indicted
18 Thermidor	*5 August* Release of large numbers of prisoners
7 Fructidor	*24 August* The government is reorganised into sixteen committees

Year III

19 Vendémiaire	*10 October* Foundation of the École normale supérieure
	In October '94 one hundred *livres*-assignats are worth twenty *livres* in metal currency
22 Brumaire	*12 November* Closing of the Jacobin Club
18 Frimaire	*8 December* The seventy-three Girondin deputies removed on 2 June 1793 return to the Convention
26 Frimaire	*16 December* Execution of Carrier
4 Nivôse	*24 December* Abolition of the 'maximum'

1795

30 Nivôse	*19 January* The *Réveil du peuple* is sung for the first time
3 Pluviôse	*22 January* Capture of the Dutch fleet at Helder
19 Pluviôse	*4 February* Arrest of Babeuf
20 Pluviôse	*5 February* The Convention decides that the remains of the Revolution's heroes shall be removed from the Panthéon
29 Pluviôse	*17 February* Signing at La Jaunaye of the agreements between the Republic and the Chouan leaders (Charette, Sapinaud and Cormatin)
3 Ventôse	*21 February* Decree granting freedom of worship and separating Church and State
12 Ventôse	*2 March* Arrest and indictment of Barère, Collot d'Herbois and Billaud-Varenne
2 Germinal	*21 March* Their trial by the Convention begins
12 Germinal	*1 April* Uprising against the Convention
13 Germinal	*2 April* Pichegru suppresses the uprising
16 Germinal	*5 April* Peace of Basle between France and Prussia
15 Floréal	*4 May* Massacre of Jacobins imprisoned at Lyon
18 Floréal	*7 May* Fouquier-Tinville is guillotined
27 Floréal	*16 May* Treaty of The Hague between France and Holland

1–4 Prairial	*20–23 May* Uprisings
12 Prairial	*31 May* Suppression of the Revolutionary Tribunal
20 Prairial	*8 June* Death of Louis XVII in the Temple
5 Messidor	*23 June* First landings of emigrés at Quiberon
6 Messidor	*24 June* Manifesto of Verona
16 Messidor	*4 July* First reading of the projected Constitution
July	One hundred *livres*-assignats worth eight *livres* in metal currency
26 Messidor	*14 July* The *Marseillaise* is sung for the first time for a year
3 Thermidor	*21 July* Hoche's victory at Quiberon Bay
4 Thermidor	*22 July* Peace of Basle with Spain
19 Thermidor	*8 August* Ten Montagnard deputies, including Fouché, are indicted
5 Fructidor	*22 August* The Convention adopts the new Constitution
20 Fructidor	*6 September* First day of the referendum on the Constituion

Year IV

1 Vendémiaire	*23 September* Proclamation of the Constitution of Year III
9 Vendémiaire	*1 October* Annexation of Belgium
October 1795	One hundred *livres*-assignats worth only 1.4 *livres* in metal currency
13 Vendémiaire	*5 October* The royalist insurrection in Paris is crushed by Barras and Bonaparte
24 Vendémiaire	*16 October* Bonaparte appointed major-general
29 Vendémiaire	*21 October* Elections to the Councils
3 Brumaire	*25 October* A law is passed excluding relatives of emigrés from public office. Reintroduction of terrorist laws against priests
4 Brumaire	*26 October* The Convention is dissolved. Bonaparte made commander-in-chief of the army of the interior. The Place de la Révolution is renamed the Place de la Concorde
9 Brumaire	*31 October* Election of the Directory

1796

30 Pluviôse	*18 February* Ceremonial destruction of plates used for printing assignats
12 Ventôse	*2 March* Bonaparte appointed general-in-chief of the Army of Italy
28 Ventôse	*18 March* Issue of the *mandat territorial*
10 Germinal	*30 March* Babeuf forms the 'Secret Directory of Public Safety'
23 Germinal	*12 April* Victory of Montenotte
24 Germinal	*13 April* Victory of Millesimo
26 Germinal	*15 April* Victory of Dego
2 Floréal	*21 April* Victory of Mondovi
21 Floréal	*10 May* Lodi. Arrest of Babeuf and his friends
26 Floréal	*15 May* Bonaparte enters Milan
Early Prairial	Revolt of Pavia against the French troops
July	End of the experiment with the *mandat territorial*. Return to metal currency
18 Thermidor	*5 August* Castiglione
22 Fructidor	*8 September* Bassano
25 Vendémiaire	*16 October* Proclamation of the Cispadane Republic at Bologna
27 Brumaire	*17 November* Arcola

1797

January	The theophilanthropy cult is founded
25 Nivôse	*14 January* Rivoli
14 Pluviôse	*2 February* Surrender of Mantua
16 Pluviôse	*4 February* All payments henceforth to be made in metal currency
1 Ventôse	*19 February* Treaty of Tolentino with the Holy See
Germinal	Elections for new 'third' in the Councils
29 Germinal	*18 April* Peace preliminaries at Leoben
1 Prairial	*20 May* Barthélemy replaces Letourneur in the Directory
8 Prairial	*27 May* Babeuf and Darthé are guillotined
21 Prairial	*14 June* The Treasury is given complete control of public finances
13 Messidor	*1 July* Hoche orders his troops to march on Paris
21 Messidor	*9 July* Foundation of the Cisalpine Republic

26 Messidor	*14 July* Hoche and Talleyrand enter the government		*7 Pluviôse*	*26 January* Proclamation of the Republic of Naples
18 Fructidor	*4 September* The Directory's *coup d'état* against the Councils		*7 Ventôse*	*25 February* Bonaparte enters Gaza
19 Fructidor	*5 September* Return to the emergency laws of the Terror		*14 Ventôse*	*4 March* Siege of Jaffa
22 Fructidor	*8 September* Law against the press		*29 Ventôse*	*19 March* Siege of Acre
			5 Germinal	*25 March* Jourdan is defeated at Stokach

Year VI

9 Vendémiaire	*30 September* 'Bankruptcy of the two-thirds'
26 Vendémiaire	*17 October* Treaty of Campo Formio

21 Germinal	*10 April* The Pope is moved to France
Germinal	Elections for the Councils
8 Floréal	*27 April* Moreau is defeated at Cassano
9 Floréal	*28 April* Assassination of the French plenipotentiaries at Rastatt
27 Floréal	*16 May* Election of Sieyès to the Directory
28 Floréal	*17 May* Bonaparte raises the siege of Acre

1798

Floréal	Elections for the Councils
22 Floréal	*11 May* Coup d'état by the Directory and the Councils against the left
27 Floréal	*16 May* François de Neufchâteau is replaced in the Directory by Treilhard
30 Floréal	*19 May* Bonaparte embarks for Egypt
Floréal– Thermidor	*May–August* Three boats containing French and Belgian priests leave Oléron for French Guiana
29 Prairial	*17 June* François de Neufchâteau appointed Minister of the Interior
3 Thermidor	*21 July* Battle of the Pyramids
14 Thermidor	*1 August* Naval battle off Aboukir
17 Thermidor	*4 August* Institution of the *décadi* as the official day of rest
23 Fructidor	*9 September* Organisation of the decadal cult and its festivals

1 Prairial	*20 May* The British re-embark at Ostend
30 Prairial	*18 June* The victory of the Councils over the Directory
1 Messidor	*19 June* Macdonald defeated by Suvorov on the Trebbia
7 Thermidor	*25 July* Victory over the Turks at Aboukir
28 Thermidor	*15 August* Joubert killed at Novi
6 Fructidor	*23 August* Bonaparte leaves Egypt
10 Fructidor	*27 August* The Anglo-Russian forces at Helder
19 September	Brune's victory at Bergen

Year VII

24 Vendémiaire	*15 October* National exhibition
4 Frimaire	*24 November* Door and window tax

Year VIII

5 Vendémiaire	*27 September* Masséna wins the battle of Zurich
17 Vendémiaire	*9 October* Bonaparte arrives back in France
1 Brumaire	*23 October* Lucien Bonaparte is elected President of the Five Hundred
18 Brumaire	*9 November* Decree transferring the Councils to Saint-Cloud Sieyès, Ducos and Barras resign. Bonaparte appointed commander of the army in Paris
19 Brumaire	*10 November* After a chaotic session the remaining deputies elect Bonaparte, Sieyès and Roger Ducos as consuls

1799

4 Pluviôse	*23 January* Championnet enters Naples

BIBLIOGRAPHY

A complete bibliography of the history of the French Revolution would far exceed the scope of this book – in fact, it would require at least twice as many pages as the present volume. Readers who would like to obtain more detailed information on various aspects of the Revolution could consult *les Révolutions, 1770–1790* by Jacques Godechot (1963), and the quarterly issues of *les Annales historiques de la Révolution française*. Only the great landmarks in the historiography of the Revolution and the more recent studies that have opened up new lines of approach are listed here. The authors hope they will be excused for omitting to mention the often invaluable articles and lecture-courses of Georges Lefebvre and Marcel Reinhard, which have been duplicated by the *Centre de documentation universitaire* and which, though frequently used, rarely receive the formal acknowledgement to which the printed volume is entitled.

If the works of historians antipathetic to the Revolution were to be compared in volume with those of historians loyal to the tradition of 1789 and 1793, it would be difficult to say which would prove the more bulky. Yet, despite moments of blindness and partiality, the historians who have approached the Revolution with sympathy have shown greater insight than those opposed to the French revolutionary tradition. Let us not include in this latter category the nostalgic, but nevertheless lucid, accounts written by historians absorbed by the possibility of what the eighteenth century might have been, if the Revolution had not taken place: from Alexis de Tocqueville (whose *l'Ancien Régime et la Révolution*, which appeared in 1856, should be read in the critical edition published in 1952) and Hippolyte Taine (*les Origines de la France contemporaine*, 1876–93) to Pierre Gaxotte (*la Révolution française*, 1928, new edition 1962), fine minds have attempted to resist the dominant trend of historiography, without lapsing into the kind of trivial writing which is concerned chiefly with the martyrs and saints of history. Admittedly, revolutionary piety has also inspired many mediocre historians. But let us ignore them and consider only the best: first of all, Michelet, whose history (published from 1847 to 1852) displays such a brilliantly intuitive understanding both of individual men and of mass-movements that it makes the work of Louis Blanc (1847–62) seem dull in comparison. Fifty years later, the *Histoire politique de la Révolution française* by Aulard (1901) and the *Histoire socialiste* by Jean Jaurès (1901–04), though of unequal value, mark an important stage in the historiography of the Revolution. With Aulard, the history of the Revolution entered the syllabus of the universities of the Third Republic: his work, nowadays held in unjustified disdain, no doubt betrays signs of narrow-minded conformism, which was partly influenced by the mounting tide of radicalism of those years; but it is nonetheless a seriously documented study and represents a coherent and sustained appreciation of French parliamentary history. However, while Aulard was gathering disciples round him at the Sorbonne, the socialist Jaurès was stirring the passions of French Jacobinism. His vision of the continuity of the revolutionary tradition and his evocation of a happiness born of wealth and intelligence have lost neither their value nor their freshness. Albert Mathiez – both a university historian (though hostile to Aulard's theses) and a socialist (though briefly influenced by Bolshevism) – aroused a passionate response among our own generation with the three small volumes (*la Révolution française*) which were published between 1922 and 1927 and have been constantly re-issued. His prejudices, now self-evident, were reviewed in a spirit of detachment, and with the scrupulousness of a historian imbued with the moral obligations of his craft, by Georges Lefebvre, whose great synthesis *la Révolution française*, written in 1930, was brought completely up to date shortly before his death in 1951. The dazzling pages contributed by Ernest Labrousse to the *Histoire générale des civilisations* (1959) offer the most recent general study of the Revolution.

Over the past thirty years a great many theses, review articles and even a number of popular works have helped to elucidate certain problems, or simply to pose them. Only those works which, rightly or wrongly, have seemed essential to the authors of the present volume are mentioned below.

★Aristocratic revolution or liberal revolution? The problems of the 'pre-revolution' (1787–8) and the leading role played in it by the nobility and the parlements have been astutely examined by J.Egret (in *la prérévolution française*, 1962). There are too few studies of the French nobility in the eighteenth century. Three are essential: F.Bluche, *les Magistrats du Parlement de Paris au XVIIIe siècle*, 1960; R.Forster, *The Nobility of Toulouse in the 18th Century*, 1960; and F.Ford, *Robe and Sword, the Regrouping of the French Aristocracy after Louis XIV*, 1953. The important book by J.Meyer, *la Noblesse bretonne au XVIIIe siècle*, appeared in 1966.

★French revolution or Atlantic revolution? The problem posed by Jacques Godechot (in the work cited above) following the important contribution of R.P.Palmer (*The Age of Democratic Revolution*, 1959) seems to us to have been treated without the special character of the events in France being taken into account. The study by E.J.Hobsbawn (*The Age of Revolution*, 1962) will enable readers to obtain a more balanced view.

★Revolution born of poverty or prosperity? The theories of Ernest Labrousse, his *Esquisse du mouvement des prix et des revenus en France au XVIIIe siècle* (1933) and his *Crise de l'économie française à la fin de l'Ancien Régime et au début de la Révolution* (1944), have provided the guidelines of pre-revolutionary historiography for the past thirty years.

★Revolution of the intellect or of accumulated frustrations? Challenging the old theories based on a fundamental conflict between the ideologies of aristocracy and bourgeoisie, the lectures of Alphonse Dupront (*Art, Littérature et Société au XVIIIe siècle*, Centre de documentation universitaire, 1963–5) have put forward a new interpretation.

★Revolution conceived as a single entity, or a conjunction of heterogeneous movements? The thesis proposed by Georges Lefebvre in *les Paysans du Nord* (1924) and in his articles (and which he took up once again in *Études sur la Revolution française*, 1954) has inspired a number of recent works (particularly Paul Blois in *les Paysans de l'Ouest*, 1960) which have thrown light on the independent character of the peasant movement. Daniel Guérin (*la Lutte de classes sous la première république. Bourgeois et bras-nus*, 1946) paved the way for studies of the Parisian crowds: this particular subject has now been well covered by Albert Soboul (*Sans-Culottes parisiens en l'an II*, 1958), Georges Rudé (*The Crowd in the French Revolution*, 1959), Kare D.Tönnesson (*la Défaite des sans-culottes: mouvement révolutionnaire et réaction bourgeoise en l'an III*, 1959) and Richard Cobb (*l'Armée révolutionnaire*, 1963). It is all the more regrettable that there are no good studies of the social group most closely connected with the Revolution – the bourgeoisie. Certainly, a number of good biographies have been written, including *le Grand Carnot* (1950–2) by Marcel Reinhard, *Robespierre* (1935) by James Thompson, *Saint-Just ou la force des choses* (1954) by Albert Ollivier, and *Barère* (1961) by Leo Gershoy. After *The Jacobins* (1930), by C. Brinton, the American historian M.J. Sydenham attempted to reassess the place of the Girondins in the successive revolutionary governments (*The Girondins*, 1961). But on the whole, and especially in France, little effort has been made to grapple with the very complex question of the bourgeoisies of the late eighteenth-century. Even Marxist historians differ on this point: without going back to Kautzky (*la Lutte des classes en France en 1789*, translated into French in 1901), one only needs to compare the account by the Soviet historian Manfred (*The Great French Revolution*, Moscow, foreign languages editions, 1961) with that of Albert Soboul (*la Révolution française*, 1964) to realize the difficulties of this problem.

The problem is all the more important

Bibliography

because it lies at the heart of a debate about the French Revolution which is now in progress between French, American and English historians. The historiographical tradition in France – faithful, on the whole, to the Jacobin-Marxist tradition and to a social interpretation of events conceived in terms of class-struggle – has been attacked by A. Cobban (*The Myth of the French Revolution*, 1955, and *The Social Interpretation of the French Revolution*, 1964). The same line of argument has been directed against the Marxist concept of 'bourgeois revolution' by George V. Taylor in an important article in the *American Historical Review* (January 1967) which appeared after the publication of the original French text of the present book.

More briefly, there are important aspects of the Revolution which the reader will find discussed in various works the significance of which has not been greatly diminished by recent research. For the religious history of the period, André Latreille's *l'Église catholique et la Révolution française* (1946–50) is recommended. The history of the relationship between the French Revolution and monarchic Europe has been brought up to date and summarized by A. Fugier in the fourth volume of the *Histoire des relations internationales*, under the general editorship of Pierre Renouvin. In his book *Contre-Révolution* (1961) Jacques Godechot collated the results of researches into the ideologies, conspiracies and individual protagonists of the royalist movement. Various books published in Great Britain and the United States in the past few years have modified our view of the Vendéan wars.

The first of our two original volumes entitled *la Révolution*, of which this is an abridged translation, was completed in 1963, and the second in October 1965. The continual progress of historical research has already caused the two French volumes to become outdated in certain respects. We make no apology for this: the knowledge of History is always relative, and even a single sentence can be invalidated almost as soon as it is written. But we should like to stress the fact that the two original volumes of *la Révolution*

were completed several years ago, for we are anxious to avoid appearing to make claims for the present work which it has never been our intention to make. This book is merely a cautious and loving reappraisal – made at a particular moment in history and in a particular set of circumstances which will be clearly intelligible only to future historians – of a past without which there would be no present. These ten years in our national history stirred such intense passions among earlier generations of Frenchmen that they eventually acquired too great a familiarity, when they should still, on the contrary, provoke wonder. By having been born into the present age the authors have been given the chance, together with their contemporaries, to witness the death agony of the ideologies of the nineteenth century. They accept the challenge, with all its promises and limitations – the opportunity to look back on a past which is undoubtedly less obscure than it once was, but which will be revealed in even greater clarity to the historians of the future.

THE AUTHORS

While the authors have worked together in complete harmony of views and have consulted one another constantly, they have each had to assume responsibility for drawing up the final text of the various parts of this book.

François Furet has written the following chapters:
The France of Louis XVI – The Revolt of the Nobles – The Three Revolutions of Summer '89 – The Bourgeois Republic – The New France – The End of a Regime – In the chapter 'A Year of Peace' he also wrote the text concerning the work of the Constituent Assembly.

Denis Richet has written the following chapters:
A Year of Peace (except for the text concerning the Constituent Assembly) – The Revolution Blown off Course – The Gironde and Revolutionary Romanticism – A Time of Anguish – Thermidor Year III – Bonaparte's Campaigns.

407

INDEX